Martin

Thanks for
a great
debate and
inspiring talks
on Philosophy, &
arvelle.

Best

[signature]

MANAGING KNOWLEDGE INTEGRATION ACROSS BOUNDARIES

Managing Knowledge Integration across Boundaries

Edited by
FREDRIK TELL, CHRISTIAN
BERGGREN, STEFANO BRUSONI,
AND ANDREW VAN DE VEN

OXFORD
UNIVERSITY PRESS

OXFORD
UNIVERSITY PRESS

Great Clarendon Street, Oxford, OX2 6DP,
United Kingdom

Oxford University Press is a department of the University of Oxford.
It furthers the University's objective of excellence in research, scholarship,
and education by publishing worldwide. Oxford is a registered trade mark of
Oxford University Press in the UK and in certain other countries

Published in the United States of America by Oxford University Press
198 Madison Avenue, New York, NY 10016, United States of America

British Library Cataloguing in Publication Data

Data available

Library of Congress Control Number: 2016939416

ISBN 978-0-19-878597-2

Printed in Great Britain by
Clays Ltd, St Ives plc

Preface

Managing the integration of advanced and specialized knowledge across boundaries constitutes a key challenge for solving complex corporate, social, and technical problems in an increasingly pluralistic world. In this volume, researchers from Australia, Canada, Singapore, Germany, Italy, Sweden, Switzerland, the United Kingdom, and the United States have joined forces to explore how engineers and scientists, corporate managers, and professional communities devise mechanisms, mediators, processes, and systems for boundary-crossing knowledge creation and knowledge integration in a range of social and organizational contexts.

The book contributes to a lively international discussion on these topics and also constitutes a new milestone in the KITE research programme, Knowledge Integration and Innovation in Transnational Enterprise, supported by Riksbankens Jubileumsfond (The Bank of Sweden Tercentenary Foundation), 2007–2015. Oxford University Press published the main findings from the programme's first four years in *Knowledge Integration and Innovation: Critical Challenges Facing International Technology-based Firms* (Berggren et al., 2011).

The present volume builds on and goes beyond this publication, both in terms of geographic coverage and thematic scope, theoretically as well as empirically. Together distinguished international scholars and KITE researchers apply, examine, and develop the concept of knowledge integration in new settings, revisit existing conjectures, and suggest new approaches and theoretical endeavours.

The project of writing the book commenced in 2014 when authors around the globe where invited to submit proposals for chapters. We, as KITE programme leaders, were overwhelmed by the positive response. A virtual workshop conducted in November 2014 proved the full commitment of chapter authors. We want to take the opportunity to express our gratitude to our co-editors and all the invited authors for their dedication, passion, and persistence to make this project come into fruition. The making of the book would not have been possible without the unwavering support from commissioning editor David Musson, editorial assistance by Karin Sjöberg Forssberg, and language advice from Cynthia Little. Our sincere thank you also to all our KITE colleagues and KITE Advisory Board members over the programme's duration, and of course our principal research funder, Riksbankens Jubileumsfond!

Christian Berggren and Fredrik Tell
Directors of the KITE research programme

Linköping and Uppsala,
June 2016

Foreword

Robert Grant

The topics discussed in this book—integration and boundaries—are central themes in the design of organizations. By addressing these issues from a knowledge perspective, this collection of studies provides real evidence of the willingness and ability of today's management researchers to integrate knowledge across disciplinary and functional boundaries.

It is well known that some types of boundaries have created barriers to innovation by business enterprises—and this is explored by several of the chapters in this book. At the same time, boundary spanning has been achieved by management scholars whose role has been central to the development of organizational theory over the past two decades. This is especially evident in the case of organizational design theory, where scholars working in the fields of strategic management, technology management, and information systems have played a vital role in reinvigorating the analysis of organizational structure and design.

I am encouraged by the developments taking place in the analysis of organizational structure and design. When I look back to my own student days, it is apparent to me that the glorious five-year period between the release in 1965 of Dylan's *Highway 61 Revisited* and the Woodstock Festival of 1969 was also a golden era for research into organizational theory and exciting contributions from Joan Woodward (1965), Jay Lawrence and Paul Lorsch (1967), James Thompson (1967), and the Aston group (Pugh et al., 1968). However, this momentum was not sustained. While the break-up of the Beatles signalled regression in popular music, organizational theory during the 1970s and 1980s experienced similar loss of impetus. By the early 1990s leading organizational scholars Richard Daft and Arie Lewin (1993: i) were warning that 'organization theory is in danger of becoming isolated and irrelevant'.

At the heart of organizational theory's failure to make substantive advances during the 1970s and 1980s was an unwillingness to build on the foundations laid by Herbert Simon, Thompson, and Lawrence and Lorsch in developments related to the analysis of coordination within organizations. The emphasis on cooperation problems as opposed to coordination problems extended to organizational economics, whose theoretical core was transaction cost theory and principal–agent relations.

However, from the mid-1990s, there was a resurgence of interest, and several theoretical advances occurred—especially in the analysis of coordination within and between organizations. Much of the drive came from outside the traditional organizational theory field, from scholars working in strategic management, systems theory, computer science, and information systems. Among some important contributions from outside traditional organizational theory, the knowledge-based view of the firm has been especially influential in directing attention back to the core issues of organization. As well as providing a rationale for the existence of the firm and other economic organizations, which was distinct from the prevailing transaction costs, and nexus-of-contracts approaches, the knowledge-based view offered a new perspective on the central organizational problem of reconciling the efficiency advantages of division of labour with the need to integrate the efforts of multiple specialists in order to achieve a common purpose. The knowledge-based view emphasizes the need to reconcile the specialized forms in which knowledge is created and acquired, with the diversity of the knowledge that is required for the production and supply of goods and services.

The resulting insights specifically acknowledged the constraints inherent in organizational learning, the need to ensure that the processes of knowledge integration does not compromise the efficiencies of specialization, and the nature and architecture of organizational capability. Emphasizing knowledge as the primary factor of production in the modern economy has enabled analysis of coordination that goes beyond conventional notions of integrating tasks to encompass both human and non-human repositories of knowledge, and includes the potential for self-adaptive organizational systems. The concept of knowledge integration allows a perspective on coordination within economic organizations that is grounded in the core purpose of economic organizations: production, that is, creating value through the transformation of inputs into outputs.

An important outcome of this new perspective on the crucial organizational tasks of specialization and integration was recognition of the importance of modularity to the study of organizational design. The notion of modularity has been integral to the development of analyses of organizational boundaries and their interfaces. One aspect of these developments is the acknowledgement of hierarchy as a coordination mechanism rather than a mechanism for the exercise of authority. The modular structure of knowledge and its relationship to other types of boundary—intraorganizational, interorganizational, locational, and temporal—are central themes in several of the contributions to this volume.

In addition to renewed research on organizational theory, knowledge-based approaches and other organizational structure and design methods have stimulated interest and sometimes confusion over what firms are, what they do, and how they operate. Different theories of the firm and different approaches to economic organization offer different perspectives on these issues, perspectives that are associated with differing notions about what constitutes the basic elements and units of analysis of economic organizations.

Organizational theory is concerned with investigating and analysing the organizational functions of specialization, cooperation, and coordination, using the actions of organizational members—'tasks' or 'activities'—as the unit of analysis. Economics and strategic management approaches take a different view. Economic organizations (firms) are considered primarily as decision-making units where the focus of analysis is managerial choice. In an economic model of the firm, decision-making is oriented to optimization. Other theoretical approaches, including several deployed in strategic management such as Nelson and Winter's evolutionary theory, March and Simon's behavioural theory, and complexity-based models, also emphasize decision-making as the primary activity of economic organizations. However, these latter tend to be more cognizant of the constraining influences of uncertainty and/or bounded rationality, and view *search* as the most important decision-making activity. Despite this common emphasis on decision-making, these various approaches conceive the basic analytical components of organizations differently. In organizational economics, it is the *transaction* that is important; for evolutionary theorists it is *organizational routines;* in the resource-based view resources and capabilities are crucial; and in complexity models the most important components are the *elements of the system* (whose combinations and performance outcomes form a *fitness landscape*).

In the knowledge-based view, it is knowledge rather than tasks, activities, routines, transactions, or resources that is the basic unit of analysis. A major advantage of the knowledge-based approach is that it allows analysis of both the decision-making (e.g. Nickerson and Zenger, 2004) and coordination-of-action (e.g. Brusoni and Prencipe, 2006) roles of organizations. The knowledge-based view also offers a broader based approach to coordination/integration within organizations, which encompasses coordination of actions (action being the exercise of tacit knowledge), coordination of cognition, and coordination of information.

Future research should focus on building a more general theory of coordination/integration within and between organizations, which integrates the promising knowledge-based view developments, complementarity theory, activity-based approaches, and complexity models with more traditional organizational theory. Rather than adding to the archipelago of separate theories, we need to link new theories to existing bodies of organization theory—and, hopefully, to integrate the whole into what Peter Blau describes as 'systematic theory', where: 'The theoretical generalizations that explain the empirical findings are in turn explained by subsuming them under still more general hypotheses' (Blau, 1970: 202). A prerequisite for such developments is likely greater precision in the definitions of constructs and specifications of the relationships between them. In relation to the organizational challenge of integration, there are several promising lines of research. These include the work of Puranam (Puranam et al., 2012) on the nature of interdependence and the knowledge requirements for effective integration, and his call for a rigorous and systematic organizational theory that pays closer attention to the microfoundations of organizing—what he refers to as the 'micro-structural approach'.

The chapters in this volume make a valuable contribution to this quest to build the microfoundations of organizing—especially in relation to the central dilemma in organizational design: reconciling specialization with integration. Different contributions offer different solutions to this dilemma: Postrel (Chapter 3) and Ceci and Prencipe (Chapter 7) examine the extent to which knowledge integration requires knowledge sharing; Subramanian et al. (Chapter 12), Bredin et al. (Chapter 13) and Van de Ven and Zahra (Chapter 15) address the role of boundary-spanning individuals; while other contributions explore the role of collective knowledge embodied either in artefacts (Kravcenko and Swan, Chapter 11) or in 'boundary organizations' (Perkmann, Chapter 10). However, resolving the specialization–integration dilemma requires that we understand these concepts. Tell's deep dive into how knowledge is organized (Chapter 2) identifies five types of knowledge boundaries and fifteen types of integration mechanism. He points the way to a more complex, nuanced, and, hopefully, practically applicable formulation of the knowledge-based approach to the theory and management of organizations.

Contents

List of Figures   xiii
List of Tables   xv
List of Abbreviations   xvii
List of Contributors   xix

1. Introduction: Managing Knowledge Integration across Boundaries   1
   *Fredrik Tell, Christian Berggren, Stefano Brusoni, and Andrew
   Van de Ven*

PART I. CONCEPTUAL UNDERPINNINGS

2. Managing across Knowledge Boundaries   19
   Fredrik Tell

3. Effective Management of Collective Design Processes:
   Knowledge Profiles and the Sequential Ordering of Tasks   39
   Steven Postrel

4. Relating Knowledge Integration and Absorptive
   Capacity: Knowledge Boundaries and Reflective Agency
   in Path-Dependent Processes   57
   Christian Berggren, Jörg Sydow, and Fredrik Tell

5. Bridging the Individual-to-Organization Divide:
   A Knowledge Creation Approach   72
   Lars Lindkvist and Marie Bengtsson

PART II. BOUNDARY-CROSSING KNOWLEDGE
INTEGRATION IN CONTEXT

6. Open Innovation: Managing Knowledge Integration across
   Multiple Boundaries   87
   *Lars Bengtsson, Nicolette Lakemond, Keld Laursen, and
   Fredrik Tell*

7. Division of Labour, Supplier Relationships, and Knowledge
   Integration   106
   Federica Ceci and Andrea Prencipe

8. Knowledge, Uncertainty, and the Boundaries of the Firm:
   Evidence from a Study of Formula One Racing
   Constructors, 1950–2000   123
   Fabrizio Castellucci and Gianluca Carnabuci

9. Struggling with Knowledge Boundaries and Stickiness: Case Studies of Innovating Firms in an Emerging Economy   139
Solmaz Filiz Karabag and Christian Berggren

10. How Boundary Organizations Facilitate Collaboration across Diverse Communities   155
Markus Perkmann

11. Talking through Objects: The Sociopolitical Dynamics embodied in Boundary Objects in Architectural Work   171
Dmitrijs Kravcenko and Jacky Swan

12. Bridging Scientists and Informal R&D Collaborations: Implications for Firm-Level Knowledge Integration and Patent Performance   191
Annapoornima M. Subramanian, Kwanghui Lim, and Pek-hooi Soh

13. Knowledge Integration at Work: Individual Project Competence in Agile Projects   206
Karin Bredin, Cecilia Enberg, Camilla Niss, and Jonas Söderlund

14. Retrieval of Knowledge across Team Boundaries: Role of Transactive Memory Systems in a Restructuring Global Organization   227
Sirkka L. Jarvenpaa and Yongsuk Kim

15. Boundary Spanning, Boundary Objects, and Innovation   241
Andrew Van de Ven and Shaker A. Zahra

References   255
Index   295

List of Figures

3.1. Proposing unit design space and receiving unit performance   50

4.1. Knowledge dimensions affecting the capacity to cross knowledge boundaries over time   61

4.2. Agency options and knowledge boundaries   67

5.1. A dual-route model of organizational knowledge creation   81

6.1. The relationships analysed   97

10.1. Coding structure   160

10.2. Key mechanisms enacted by boundary organizations   168

11.1. Example of a CAD drawing with comments by the architect   178

11.2. An example of a 'closed off' drawing   183

11.3. Examples of assertive communication   184

11.4. Example of communication without an obviously dominant group involved   186

13.1. A trend from traditional project methods towards agile project methods   213

13.2. T-shaped disciplinary knowledge for traditional projects   222

13.3. M-shaped disciplinary knowledge for agile projects   223

14.1. Framework of effects of organizational restructuring on organizational transactive memory system   230

15.1. Proposed curvilinear relationship between boundary complexity and innovation   245

List of Tables

2.1. Boundary-bridging mechanisms in learning activities   37

6.1. Analysis of how boundary crossing and knowledge integration practices explain innovation   98

6.A1. Factor analysis of knowledge boundaries and knowledge integration practices   104

6.A2. Factor analysis for performance and industry character   105

7.1. Population and sample characteristics   114

7.2. Principal component analysis   117

7.3. One-way Anova   117

7.4. Correlation matrix   118

7.5. Ordered Logit Model 1 and Logit Model 2   119

8.1. Variables descriptive statistics and first order correlation coefficients   134

8.2. Random effect logit estimates of vertical integration   135

9.1. Descriptive information of interviewees and overview of interviews   146

11.1. Empirical data collected   177

12.1. Formal and informal R&D collaborations in the biotechnology industry   197

12.2. Pasteur bridging scientists, informal collaborations on forward citations of patents and patent originality   203

13.1. Individual project competence matrix   225

14.1. Coping mechanisms dealing with unreliable organizations transactive memory systems   235

15.1. Boundary objects or mechanisms for communicating across knowledge boundaries   246

List of Abbreviations

ANOVA	Analysis of Variance
CAD	Computer Aided Design
CEO	Chief Executive Officer
CMV	Common Method Variance
ERP	Enterprise Resource Planning
FIA	Fédération Internationale de l'Automobile
FTSE	Financial Times Stock Exchange
GDP	Gross Domestic Product
GSK	GlaxoSmithKline
IJV	International Joint Ventures
IPR	Intellectual Property Rights
JV	Joint Venture
KI	Knowledge Integration
MNC	Multinational Corporation(s)
OEM	Original Equipment Manufacturer/ing
PCA	Principal Component Analysis
R&D	Research and Development
SECI	Socialization, Externalization, Combination, Internalization
SGC	Structural Genomics Consortium
TCE	Transaction Cost Economics
TMS	Transactive Memory Systems
TSU	Trans-Specialist Understanding

List of Contributors

EDITORS

Fredrik Tell, Professor, Department of Business Studies, Uppsala University; and Visiting Professor, Department of Management and Engineering, Linköping University, Sweden, Co-Director of the KITE Research Group

Christian Berggren, Professor, Department of Management and Engineering, Linköping University, Sweden, Co-Director of the KITE Research Group

Stefano Brusoni, Professor, Department of Management, Technology and Economics, ETH Zürich, Switzerland

Andrew Van de Ven, Professor, Vernon H. Heath Chair of Organizational Innovation and Change, Strategic Management and Entrepreneurship, Carlson School of Management, University of Minnesota, USA

OTHER CONTRIBUTORS

Lars Bengtsson, Professor, Faculty of Engineering and Sustainable Development, University of Gävle, Sweden, Member of the KITE Research Group

Marie Bengtsson, Senior Lecturer, Department of Management and Engineering, Linköping University, Sweden, Member of the KITE Research Group

Karin Bredin, Senior Lecturer, Department of Management and Engineering, Linköping University, Sweden, Member of the KITE Research Group

Gianluca Carnabuci, Associate Professor, Institute of Management, University of Lugano, Switzerland

Fabrizio Castellucci, Associate Professor, Department of Management and Technology, Bocconi University, Milan, Italy

Federica Ceci, Associate Professor, Department of Business Administration, G. D'Annunzio University, Pescara, Italy

Cecilia Enberg, Senior Lecturer, Department of Management and Engineering, Linköping University, Sweden, Member of the KITE Research Group

Solmaz Filiz Karabag, Associate Professor, Department of Management and Engineering, Linköping University, Sweden

Robert Grant, Professor, ENI Chair of Strategic Management in the Energy Sector, Department of Management and Technology, Bocconi University, Milan, Italy

Sirkka L. Jarvenpaa, Professor, Bayless/Refsnes Chair in Business Administration, Center for Business, Technology, and Law, McCombs School of Business, University of Texas at Austin, USA

Yongsuk Kim, Assistant Professor, HKUST Business School, Department of Information Systems, Business Statistics and Operations Management, Hong Kong University of Science and Technology, China

Dmitrijs Kravcenko, Researcher, Warwick Business School, IKON, University of Warwick, United Kingdom

Nicolette Lakemond, Associate Professor, Department of Management and Engineering, Linköping University, Sweden, Member of the KITE Research Group

Keld Laursen, Professor, Department of Innovation and Organizational Economics, Copenhagen Business School, Denmark

Kwanghui Lim, Associate Professor, Melbourne Business School, Co-Director, Intellectual Property Research Institute of Australia, Australia

Lars Lindkvist, Professor Emeritus, Department of Management and Engineering, Linköping University, Sweden, Member of the KITE Research Group

Camilla Niss, Senior Lecturer, Faculty of Engineering and Sustainable Development, University of Gävle, Sweden, Member of the KITE Research Group

Markus Perkmann, Associate Professor, Imperial College Business School, Imperial College London, United Kingdom

Steven Postrel, Lecturer, Paul Merage School of Management, University of California at Irvine, USA

Andrea Prencipe, Professor, Department of Business and Management, LUISS University, Rome, Italy

Pek-hooi Soh, Associate Professor, Beedie School of Business, Technology and Operations Management, Simon Fraser University, Vancouver, Canada

Annapoornima M. Subramanian, Assistant Professor, Division of Engineering and Technology Management, National University of Singapore, Singapore

Jacky Swan, Professor, Warwick Business School, IKON, University of Warwick, United Kingdom

Jörg Sydow, Professor, Department of Management, Pfadkolleg Research Centre, Freie Universität Berlin, Germany

Jonas Söderlund, Professor, BI Norwegian Business School. Member of the KITE Research Group, Linköping University

Shaker A. Zahra, Professor, Robert E. Buuck Chair of Entrepreneurship, Carlson School of Management, University of Minnesota, USA

1

Introduction

Managing Knowledge Integration across Boundaries

Fredrik Tell, Christian Berggren, Stefano Brusoni,
and Andrew Van de Ven

1.1 THE IMPORTANCE OF MANAGING KNOWLEDGE INTEGRATION ACROSS BOUNDARIES

Economic theory and policy rhetoric, and business operations and strategy, often consider knowledge specialization to be necessary to achieve economic efficiency, competitive advantage, and growth. However, knowledge specialization leads to the emergence of boundaries instantiated in, for instance, individual training and specialist experience, cumulative efforts in scientific and technological domains, formal organizations, informal groups and communities, geographical location, and sequencing in time. The chapters in this book draw on the growing literature on knowledge specialization and on its complement, knowledge integration. Knowledge integration refers to the coordination and recombination of knowledge from different individuals, disciplines, and functions (see, e.g., Becker and Murphy, 1992; Grant, 1996; Brusoni et al., 2001; Carlile, 2002; Postrel, 2002; Van de Ven, 2007; Carnabuci and Bruggerman, 2009; Berggren et al., 2011). Knowledge integration is required to create new knowledge, to develop advanced products and systems that can transform the bases of competition and corporate success, and to deliver advanced social services, from urban planning to integrated infrastructures.

Integration is a classic theme in socio-economic and organizational analyses of specialization and division of labour. For instance, Lawrence and Lorsch (1967), in their famous study, point out that differentiated adaptation of firms' core departments—research and development (R&D), manufacturing, marketing—to their various environments creates a need for organizational integration mechanisms to maintain the individual firm's unity of purpose and direction.

Their study draws attention to departmental specialization and the organizational boundaries it creates within the firm. This edited volume is inspired by their work, but applies a broader focus to the specialization and integration of knowledge across boundaries—between individuals within departments, between departments and firms, between firms, and between communities and countries. The chapters in this book discuss the mechanisms used to manage and bridge these boundaries. Knowledge boundaries make organizational integration more complex and difficult, but also highly interesting and significant. We suggest three intertwined aspects highlighting the importance of and need for knowledge integration across boundaries.

1.1.1 Knowledge is Increasingly Specialized and Differentiated

First, the perpetual process of growth in knowledge results in the establishment of new knowledge fields each with its own internal dynamics and processes. Historically, knowledge *specialization* has been the fundamental mechanism of knowledge growth. However, knowledge specialization requires coordination of specialized and differentiated knowledge communities and experts. In classical economic analysis, building upon Adam Smith's invisible hand metaphor, the costs of economic coordination are often overlooked. In more realistic settings, characterized by imperfect information, difficulties related to communicating across boundaries, and the absence of shared knowledge and understanding among actors, the costs of specialization can be substantial, creating the need for appropriate integration efforts (Grant, 1996; Carlile, 2002; Postrel, 2002). The complementarity of specialized knowledge can increase the potential benefits of well-managed knowledge integration and lead to co-specialization and economies of scope (Teece, 1982; Chandler, 1990; Becker and Murphy, 1992). Building on these insights, knowledge-based theories of the firm suggest that organizational capabilities to integrate specialized knowledge are crucial for competitive advantage (Kogut and Zander, 1992; Grant, 1996).

1.1.2 Knowledge is Increasingly Widely Distributed

Second, as knowledge develops, it is *distributed* across various boundaries. Scientific and engineering communities are growing in size and diversity, and are spanning geographic and organizational boundaries. While these growth processes might result in new, specialized communities of scientists and engineers, the production of increasingly complex products requires the integration of inputs from various specialized fields into coherent technological and organizational systems. Knowledge integration across boundaries is fundamental for innovation and competitiveness. According to Schumpeter (1934) and Hayek (1945), for example, the distributed process of knowledge generation and application induced by capitalist markets promotes the creation of novel solutions.

However, these classic works do not explain how this integration of distributed knowledge is accomplished, or how different levels of distribution and different distances affect the process and its associated costs. Cyert and March (1963) suggest that firms tend first to conduct 'problemistic search' in the vicinity of previous solutions, in an effort to maximize reuse of familiar knowledge. From a knowledge integration perspective, refinement or exploitative search is relatively straightforward (Levinthal and March, 1981; March, 1991). However, when existing knowledge and solutions are inadequate to deal with new problems, more distant search is required to obtain the knowledge needed to construct novel solutions and approaches (Laursen, 2012; Bergek et al., 2013). Complex problems involving multiple interdependent subsystems and components tend to involve more difficult search and integration efforts in increasingly rugged knowledge landscapes (Levinthal, 1997). The organization of distant search processes can be a difficult organizational design problem. While expanding the area of search may be critical to find the needed, but unfamiliar knowledge (Lopez-Vega et al., 2016), the integration of this knowledge by the focal organization may be hampered by lack of absorptive capacity (Cohen and Levinthal, 1990; Zahra and George, 2002). In this dynamic, the apparent trade off between local and distant search highlights the importance for firms to develop multiple mechanisms for knowledge integration across different boundaries.

1.1.3 Organizational Knowledge is Incomplete, Uncertain, and Ambiguous

Third, organizations continuously face environmental and technological uncertainties, which challenge their capabilities to adapt and respond. Human knowledge increases constantly, but in firms and other organizations exposed to myriad different trends and changes—in the natural environment, in technologies, in social systems, in political institutions, and in demographic conditions—the available knowledge remains incomplete, uncertain, and ambiguous (Tsoukas and Vladimirou, 2001; Tell, 2004). To survive and prosper, firms need to absorb, assess, and integrate new knowledge continuously, which can result in incremental or radical changes to their practices, structures, and control systems. The traditional way to cope with uncertainty and ambiguity is departmentalization and creation of subunits (Galbraith, 1973; Levinthal and March, 1993). The 'fencing in' of people, interests, and expertise simplifies organizational behaviour by decreasing local uncertainties and information processing requirements, and may be an appropriate temporary solution (Lindkvist et al., 1998). However, over the long run, organizational partitioning reduces the capacity for boundary crossing, information processing, and knowledge integration, which constrains the firm's potential for achieving an overall effective strategic response (Teece and Pisano, 1994). In a competitive landscape characterized by rapid knowledge development and technological change, mechanisms and structures for the integration of knowledge across boundaries, rather than efforts to increase decoupling, may be crucial for successful adaptation and long-term survival.

The notion of boundaries and their relation to knowledge integration have been discussed in several social science fields including psychology, cognitive science, informatics, sociology, economics, organization and innovation, and strategic management studies. New theories and new knowledge of phenomena are typically created by recombining ideas from different communities and disciplines in novel ways. This is achieved when people from different disciplines and perspectives work jointly to understand a complex problem or issue (Van de Ven, 2007). While there is rich literature on boundaries and their implications generally, more detailed studies are required of the challenges and mechanisms involved in the integration of specific types of knowledge across different types of boundaries.

1.2 AIM AND SCOPE OF THE BOOK

During recent decades, the concept of knowledge integration has developed in work on organizations, strategy, and innovation. However, there is no comprehensive account of knowledge boundaries and the management practices adopted to cross these boundaries. The book addresses this gap in order to advance the research both conceptually and empirically. Against a background of increasing specialization, higher coordination costs, and greater need for integration, the chapters in this book investigate the management of knowledge across multiple boundaries: between specialized individuals, between professional communities, and between organizations, social sectors, and countries at different levels of development. The overall problem guiding the research presented in the book is summarized in the question 'How can relevant actors and researchers understand and manage the integration of specialized, distributed, and incomplete knowledge across boundaries?'

The responses to this question include conceptual analysis of the preconditions for boundary-crossing knowledge integration, empirical studies of the contingencies affecting knowledge integration across different types of boundaries, the appropriateness of different knowledge integration mechanisms, and the role of individuals, groups, and organizational designs.

1.3 KNOWLEDGE INTEGRATION ACROSS BOUNDARIES: FIVE THEMES

Knowledge integration has been defined as the purposeful combination of specialized and complementary knowledge to achieve specific tasks (Berggren et al., 2011). Knowledge integration across boundaries succeeds—or fails—at different organizational and social levels. Knowledge integration across boundaries involves stocks as well as flows of knowledge, static and dynamic efficiencies, and the purposeful activities of organizational actors. This book offers a spectrum of approaches, theoretical lenses, and methodologies to examine knowledge integration in various contexts and at different organizational levels. This variety can be seen in the research methods applied in the individual chapters of the book: conceptual analyses and formal modelling, survey studies, patent analyses, and single and comparative case studies. The approaches differ, and the book does not propose a unified theory of knowledge integration across boundaries. Rather, we hope that this variety will stimulate discussion and complementary research in many different directions and disciplines. Below, we discuss five recurrent themes in the chapters, and provide brief chapter outlines.

1.3.1 Learning about Others' Capabilities—the Role of Interactional Expertise

The integration of truly specialized knowledge implies the bridging of a cognitive gap between two parties. The acquisition of trans-specialist understanding requires learning by one specialized party about what the other party knows, which breaks down the knowledge boundary dividing them. In Chapter 3, Postrel describes how boundaries cause glitches. This notion clarifies the basic proposition made in Grant (1996) regarding the trade off between shared and specialized knowledge in the knowledge integration process. Postrel (Section 3.2) describes glitches as involving: 'technical uncertainty, not knowing what the other party can do'. Thus, knowledge integration across cognitive boundaries implies knowing not only what the other party knows but also what the other party can do with that knowledge. This 'can do' knowledge may be difficult to transmit; it may be sticky in relation to the context of application. Postrel suggests that developing trans-specialist understanding (i.e. becoming less specialized through a better understanding of the other speciality) is enabled by education, or by codification of knowledge constraints. Essentially, to overcome boundaries requires learning about others, although it may be sufficient for this learning to be interactional rather than contributory (Collins and Evans, 2007). While contributory expertise requires an ability to contribute to the execution and development of a particular field of knowledge, interactional expertise denotes the ability to discuss a specific knowledge domain.

Interactional and contributory knowledge in the context of managing knowledge across boundaries is examined further by Bredin et al. in Chapter 13, and by Van de Ven and Zahra in Chapter 15. Bredin et al. discuss the development of individual competence in product development projects and teams, contexts that require both interactional and contributory expertise. Van de Ven and Zahra focus on the interactional expertise of boundary spanning entrepreneurs and innovators when innovative recombinations require depth of knowledge in a particular domain, without the ability necessarily to exercise that knowledge. Similarly, Jarvenpaa and Kim in Chapter 14 analyse organizational transactive memory systems in a large multinational corporation. Transactive memories are akin to interactional expertise in that, rather than specifying exactly what needs to be known to execute a task, they provide directories, developed through previous interactions, of 'who knows what'. Focusing on interactions between organizations, in Chapter 7, Ceci and Prencipe analyse the division of labour and knowledge between outsourcing firms and their suppliers. They find that despite product modularity and process standardization, which reduce knowledge overlaps, there is still considerable need for organizational and knowledge interaction among the firms and suppliers involved.

1.3.2 Using or Creating Collective but Individually Distinctive Knowledge

As discussed above, the integration of specialized knowledge requires some level of shared or common knowledge, which potentially reduces the difference (distinctiveness) of the specialized knowledge. Common knowledge can be collective knowledge developed among the involved parties. Several authors in this book discuss different aspects of this collective knowledge and its role in knowledge integration across boundaries. In Chapter 5, Lindkvist and Bengtsson propose an interactionist perspective for understanding the relations between collective and individual knowledge arguing that, in addition to bridging the specialist–specialist divide discussed above, knowledge integration is associated also with bridging the individual–organization divide. Lindkvist and Bengtsson suggest that collective knowledge can be created through interactive processes, resulting in what they describe as objectification and elicitation. Another example of the creation and utilization of collective knowledge—this time between organizations—is in Perkmann's study of a boundary organization, in Chapter 10. Perkmann analyses how this intermediate organization facilitates knowledge integration across diverse communities, and identifies structural and cognitive interventions. In the context of cognitive interventions, he shows that the boundary organization needs to develop an interpretive scheme with major overlaps with each of the boundary organization's constituent member organizations and communities.

Collective knowledge that enables integration across professional communities also can be manifested in boundary objects or artefacts, which embody the knowledge shared by highly specialized communities. Kravcenko and Swan in Chapter 11, which studies the use of drawings in architectural practice, explore some implications of the use of such boundary objects. The authors show that such objects can be shared cognitively, but also embody significant power asymmetries among the involved parties. Hence, while collective knowledge is embedded in such design artefacts, the distribution of authority regarding how to make use of this knowledge may be skewed. Kravcenko and Swan's analysis demonstrates that boundary objects can facilitate knowledge sharing and the preservation of differential power resources, and, implicitly, can sustain the role of agency.

1.3.3 Combining and Absorbing Knowledge for Innovation

Shared knowledge is an important dimension of knowledge integration. However, knowledge integration as the combination of specialized knowledge cannot be reduced to shared knowledge; it involves both static and dynamic efficiencies. The static efficiency of combining knowledge integration with continuous specialization is emphasized by Grant (1996) and Postrel (2002). However, studies of the dynamics involved in combining specialized knowledge to generate innovations are more recent and show that integrating knowledge across boundaries for innovation is a key concern (Berggren et al., 2011).

Combining new specialized knowledge with what is already known requires a certain level of absorptive capacity (Cohen and Levinthal, 1990). Relating absorptive capacity and knowledge integration theories is core to the analysis presented by Berggren et al. in Chapter 4. They suggest that while knowledge integration theories are concerned primarily with the scope of differentiated knowledge, the literature on absorptive capacity focuses on the depth of knowledge development, and the tendency for knowledge to become path-dependent. Making use of notions of organizational path-dependence, the authors propose a new framework that integrates these two dimensions.

Corporate innovation processes present problems related to the absorption and integration of knowledge. In Chapter 6, Bengtsson et al. discuss how firms involved in open innovation need to cross multiple boundaries. Their study highlights the importance of managerial practices related to the capability to absorb knowledge across multiple new boundaries to generate innovation. Absorbing and integrating external knowledge is also crucial for firms in emerging economies keen to enhance their innovation capabilities. Karabag and Berggren in Chapter 9 show how two Turkish firms were able to cross semantic, syntactic, and pragmatic boundaries (Carlile, 2002) by exploiting international windows of opportunity and building internal absorptive capabilities, and how this facilitated the development of new ranges of products and patents.

1.3.4 Organizational Design for the Management of Differentiated Knowledge

A central assumption in this book and in the literature on knowledge integration is that the specialization of knowledge creates opportunities for both efficiency gains and novelty creation, but also erects boundaries, which require appropriate management. Managing the integration of knowledge involves various types of decisions, ranging from high-level positioning strategies to micro-level processes of task allocation in teams. A central aspect of these processes and decisions is organizational design, a topic discussed by several contributors to this book. They show how organizations devise more or less formal mechanisms to coordinate behaviour and achieve their objectives when operating under varying and uncertain contingencies. For instance, Tell, in Chapter 2, discusses a range of knowledge integration mechanisms and how these mechanisms relate to the basic premises of knowledge articulability and learning activities in the context of qualitatively different types of knowledge boundaries.

Examples of organizational designs that cope with knowledge differentiation are provided by Bengtsson et al. in Chapter 6, which analyses to what extent two knowledge integration practices—project management and knowledge matching—are used to bridge different boundaries, and the effects of these practices on innovation. Organizational design can also affect the interorganizational relationships required to cross boundaries. In their study of outsourcing in Chapter 7, Ceci and Prencipe investigate use of a more tightly coupled versus a more disconnected approach to manage the relationship between outsourcing firms and their suppliers. Interorganizational designs, such as joint ventures, can be compared with internally integrated ways of organizing knowledge integration, as Karabag and Berggren discuss in their study of innovative firms in Turkey (Chapter 9). It is clear that the design solution chosen to address the knowledge integration problem will be affected by various contingencies. In Chapter 8, Castellucci and Carnabuci discuss how different types of uncertainty (field-level vs firm-specific) affect the organizational choice between internalizing and acquiring a core subsystem (in their case, an engine for a Formula One racing car). On a conceptual level, Postrel (Chapter 3) demonstrates that the stickiness of specialist knowledge affects design choices with regard to which of the parties involved should take the lead. This knowledge dimension of various arrangements is often neglected in both private sector and public sector decisions.

1.3.5 Boundary-Spanning Individuals

Structural design is one mechanism enabling the integration of knowledge across boundaries. However, individuals inside and outside the organization may be performing similar tasks. In the boundary-crossing contexts discussed in this book, the individuals performing boundary-spanning activities are identified as collectors, brokers, or diffusers of knowledge (Allen, 1977; Tushman and Scanlan, 1981; Hargadon and Sutton, 1997). In Chapter 12, Subramanian et al. examine the role of a particular type of boundary-spanning individual: the biotechnologist who spans boundaries in university–firm and firm–firm collaborations, and the boundaries between basic research (scientific publications) and knowledge applications (patents). They show that informal collaboration between scientists in firms and universities has a significant positive effect on patent performance. They show also that the existence of 'Pasteur scientists', who span scientific and technological domains, is particularly conducive to integrating the knowledge needed to generate successful patents. In the context of individual organizations, Bredin et al. (Chapter 13) discuss boundary-spanning individuals, showing the importance of individual members of interdisciplinary product development teams who need expertise in particular knowledge domains, and the ability to interact and span boundaries between adjacent knowledge domains. This boundary-spanning ability combined with persistent particular disciplinary competence is important for project managers as well as research on product development teams. The general functions of boundary spanning activity are examined by Van de Ven and Zahra (Chapter 15). They analyse different types of boundary spanners and boundary objects, and point to the greater effort needed to span increasingly complex boundaries. They argue that this complexity may ultimately reduce the ability of sophisticated boundary spanners to induce more novelty.

1.4 CONTENT OVERVIEW

This introductory chapter is followed by four conceptual chapters. Core issues and dilemmas related to managing knowledge integration across boundaries are identified using several different theoretical lenses. These four chapters provide clarifications and conceptual understanding of different types of boundary-crossing problems and the theoretical relations between the notion of knowledge integration and other core concepts related to the dynamics of knowledge and organizations, including the relation between knowledge creation and organizational integration.

1.4.1 Conceptual Underpinnings

In Chapter 2, Tell discusses the implications of knowledge specialization for different kinds of boundaries and suggests mechanisms for bridging these boundaries. Since knowledge can be differentiated along several dimensions, the boundaries between knowledge can also differ. Tell proposes five categories of knowledge boundaries: 1) individual boundaries; 2) domain-specific boundaries; 3) task-oriented boundaries; 4) spatial boundaries; and 5) temporal boundaries. He conjectures that managing knowledge integration involves bridging knowledge boundaries across five types of learning activities relating to 1) search; 2) acquisition; 3) assimilation; 4) accumulation; 5) transformation. Combining the learning activities with knowledge articulability (tacit, articulated, and codified knowledge), the chapter classifies fifteen boundary-bridging mechanisms.

In Chapter 3, Postrel demonstrates how organizational design settings with glitches due to uncertainty regarding the knowledge constraints of the other party give rise to two problems. First, how much one party should learn about the other (i.e. thinning the boundary). Second, which party should take the lead in integrating knowledge across boundaries, that is, what should be the sequential ordering. The boundaries he analyses are disciplinary boundaries between parties—boundaries caused by individual and unit specialization and a lack of trans-specialist understanding. Postrel adopts a formal analytical approach to these problems and derives three principles. 1) *Black box principle*: it is efficient to invest in trans-specialist understanding only if performance requirements put pressure on specialist knowledge (i.e. thinning the boundaries); 2) *sticky information principle*: the party with the most difficult, complex knowledge should lead the knowledge integration activity; and 3) *powerboat–sailboat principle*: given the same trans-specialist understanding, the less capable party should lead the knowledge integration effort. Given the propensity for managers in many organizational situations to favour solutions that involve the party with the strongest and most easily codifiable capabilities leading the cross-boundary knowledge integration efforts, these principles have important pragmatic implications.

In Chapter 4, Berggren et al. review work on absorptive capacity and knowledge integration, two key concepts in knowledge-based analyses of firms. They note that the separation between research on knowledge integration and research on absorptive capacity tends to overlook the dynamics of knowledge integration and the problem of boundary crossing. They note also the scarcity of agency studies in relation to path dependency and knowledge integration processes across boundaries. They discuss two particular boundaries: disciplinary boundaries and the problem of knowledge scope, which are the key problems in the literature on knowledge integration, and boundaries related to the depth and dynamics of knowledge over time, which is the focus of analyses of absorptive capacity. The authors identify three types of knowledge boundary paths: 1) boundary reproduction (path-dependency); 2) boundary crossing (path extension); and 3) boundary reconfiguration (path creation). These boundary paths provide a temporal appreciation of how the dynamic capabilities associated with knowledge integration and absorptive capacity change, as boundaries are socially reconstructed. Based on this combination and elaboration of two key concepts in the knowledge-based theories of the firm, Chapter 4 ends with a multilevel perspective on agency and organizational dynamics and renewal.

In Chapter 5, Lindkvist and Bengtsson explore the integration and creation of knowledge in interactive processes, emphasizing that the creation of new knowledge is often required to integrate individual specialist knowledge. They argue that previous approaches—for example Nonaka's SECI (Socialization, Externalization, Combination, Internalization) model (Nonaka and Takeuchi, 1995)—fail to account for the creative and interactive aspects of organizational knowledge generation. Based on conceptual developments, they propose a framework that complements previous models of combination and internalization through the inclusion of two interactive-based routes for creating 'unfathomable' knowledge. *Objectification* involves extending the knowledge horizon by creating symbols and representations whose implications go beyond the context of origin and the intention of their originators. *Elicitation* involves establishing an interaction context that explicates seemingly unfathomable knowledge. Through conceptual critique and development of one of the most widely diffused models of organizational knowledge creation, the chapter provides important insights into how collective knowledge can be created from individual interactions.

1.4.2 Boundary-Crossing Knowledge Integration in Context

The ten chapters following these four conceptual pieces report empirical studies of knowledge integration across different boundaries: between organizations, between firms in countries at different levels of development, between industry and academia, between professional communities, and between individuals and groups in organizations. These chapters investigate the appropriateness of different concepts and theories to explain knowledge integration across these different boundaries and the relevance of various enabling mechanisms.

In Chapter 6, Bengtsson et al. relate open innovation to knowledge integration, and emphasize that this mode of innovation requires the management of several different boundary-crossing knowledge flows. The chapter analyses the interplay between organizational boundaries (in terms of partner types), knowledge boundaries (knowledge depth), and geographical boundaries (international partners), and how these boundaries can be bridged by different integration practices. Data from an open innovation survey of manufacturing firms in Finland, Italy, and Sweden are used to show econometrically how innovation performance relates to the boundaries crossed, and how the bridging of these boundaries is contingent upon specific knowledge integration practices. Project management is identified as one such practice involving organizational structures, roles and responsibilities, control systems, auditing and reporting, and lines of communication. Knowledge matching is another practice, which involves the identification of complementary knowledge assets and technologies. The findings of Bengtsson et al. suggest that project management is relatively more effective than knowledge matching for bridging knowledge boundaries, while knowledge matching is relatively more effective than project management for bridging organizational boundaries. Their chapter demonstrates how managerial practices aimed at integrating knowledge integration across boundaries affect firms' abilities to innovate.

In Chapter 7, Ceci and Prencipe study the implications of outsourcing or the choice to change organizational and knowledge boundaries. Relying on a survey of firms in the European information technology sector, the authors investigate how strategy-related and technology-related factors influence outsourcing in the organization. They also examine how these factors influence the specialization and integration of knowledge. They propose two outsourcing configurations: 'far away', which is characterized by little knowledge overlap among outsourcers and suppliers, market-based relationships, and a clear separation of activities; and 'so close', characterized by knowledge overlaps, interactive relationships, and blurred boundaries between activities. The results of their econometric analysis show that, contrary to expectations, product modularity and process standardization lead to 'so close' relationships. The findings from the analysis in Chapter 7 shed light on circumstances where knowledge integration-related contingencies may prevail over strategic factors in the choice of interorganizational boundary crossing configurations.

In Chapter 8, Castellucci and Carnabuci investigate the relationship between sources of uncertainty and internalized knowledge integration within the focal firm's organizational boundaries. They relate boundary problems to organizational design by investigating how different sources of uncertainty (firm-specific versus field-level) affect the firm's decision to develop critical technology in-house or not. Their interest is in organizational boundaries in terms of vertical integration decisions, and knowledge boundaries across areas of technological activity. The empirical analysis is based on a study of several hundred engine design-related decisions made by Formula One racing car constructors and the cars' eventual performances in various championships. The results indicate that integrating the source of uncertainty is an effective strategy only if the locus of uncertainty is unknown and the candidates for internal knowledge integration are difficult to identify. The authors argue that these two conditions are not met in the case of field-level uncertainty and, in such situations, organizations opt for more flexible solutions. The chapter draws attention to the influence of fallibility and incompleteness of knowledge on crucial organizational design choices.

In Chapter 9, Karabag and Berggren investigate knowledge acquisition and integration in asymmetric contexts by analysing the efforts of firms in emerging economies to upgrade from low cost manufacturing to advanced product development. They look at how emerging economy firms can acquire the knowledge required to develop R&D-based products for global markets. They report a comparative study of two Turkish firms (Arçelik and Fiat Tofaş) in two industries (white goods and commercial vehicles), which adopted different approaches to building international competitiveness in R&D from an initial laggard position. Both firms started by accumulating basic product knowledge through licensing from established multinational firms. The white goods firm, Arçelik, then tried to develop independent innovation capabilities, but encountered a host of difficulties and boundaries. The automotive firm, Fiat Tofaş, started out as a manufacturing joint venture with a multinational company. It then made efforts to build its own innovation capabilities, which went against the strategy of the multinational partner. The analysis considers organizational and geographical boundaries, building primarily on Carlile's (2002) syntactic, interpretive, and pragmatic knowledge boundaries. The analysis shows how firms can develop coping strategies— ranging from recruitment of internationally trained research engineers to overcome syntactic boundaries, joint university–industry projects to manage interpretive boundaries, and mobilization of external resources—to overcome interest-related boundaries. Chapter 9 provides novel insights into the challenges faced by aspiring emerging economy firms involved in the integration of knowledge across geographical and technological context, particularly important in a globalized world economy.

In Chapter 10, Perkmann offers another perspective on boundary-crossing knowledge integration. He investigates how specially designed boundary organizations can facilitate cooperation across social boundaries and thereby support knowledge integration. Social boundaries separate communities oriented towards different institutional logics involved in knowledge generation. Perkmann argues that crossing social boundaries is hampered by cooperation and coordination problems, by tensions and conflicts arising from diverging interests, and by lack of sufficient common ground to attract participants and support their communication. Boundary organizations serve as boundary objects for integrating knowledge in such difficult situations. The chapter reports a case study of the Structural Genome Consortium, a not-for-profit organization created in 2003 as a joint initiative between pharmaceutical firms (GlaxoSmithKline, Merck, and Novartis) and universities (Karolinska Institutet, Oxford University, and the University of Toronto). The findings from this case suggest that the successful integration of knowledge across social boundaries was enabled by reduced frictions from the diversity of interests, structural separation, and a cosmopolitan interpretive scheme, which established sociopolitical legitimacy and facilitated knowledge coordination. This highlights the value of separation between organizations to handle difficult collaboration issues, combined with strong bridging elements to support necessary knowledge transactions, and appropriate intermediaries to accomplish this ambiguous role.

In Chapter 11, Kravcenko and Swan explore the role of specific boundary objects to support knowledge integration across specialist groups embedded in different professional communities. Rather than studying social interaction around boundary objects, as in previous research, they focus on the sociopolitical role of boundary objects as the embodiment of discursive practices across professional boundaries. The chapter reports on a micro-level study of architectural work practices in a large construction project involving over one hundred professionals with different disciplinary knowledge. The study focuses on the use of design drawings in collaborative design development and shows that boundary objects serve as material mediators for communication across professional boundaries, which maintains power relationships. This is enabled by: 1) the sharing of design drawings only between sender-recipient; 2) an implicit hierarchy governing the engagement in the drawings of professionals from different domains; and 3) communicative practice in the form of expert comments imposed on the drawings. The knowledge–power relationship has received relatively scant attention in the knowledge integration literature. Chapter 11 provides a thought-provoking description of the practice of knowledge integration using blueprints to communicate among professionals with different perspectives and power bases.

Chapter 12 by Subramanian et al. shifts the focus from organizational mechanisms to the role of informal individual scientific networks for knowledge integration and innovation, with a particular focus on the boundaries between firms and universities, and between scientific and technological domains. They present an analysis of the role of formal alliances and informal networks in patenting and publishing among scientists in biotechnology firms. Here, informal collaborations refers to published research authored jointly by the focal firm's scientists and external scientists not employed by the organizations with which the focal firm formally collaborates on R&D. Subramanian et al. show that informal collaborations between academic and industry researchers have a significant positive effect on patent performance. However, informal collaborations involving other firms are detrimental to patent performance, perhaps because of conflicts over protecting or sharing knowledge. The chapter also highlights the role of firms' boundary-spanning 'Pasteur scientists' who are able to write both papers and patents, and emphasizes their importance for crossing the boundaries between scientific and technological domains. The authors show that these boundary-spanning researchers enhance the patent-related benefits from informal collaborations with universities and, moreover, diminish the negative effect on patent performance of informal collaborations with other firms. This chapter contributes to a deeper understanding of both the power of informal networks for knowledge integration and innovation performance, and the role of a particular type of boundary-spanning individual in science-based industries.

In Chapter 13, Bredin et al. discuss individuals and their role in enabling knowledge integration across boundaries within temporary organizations such as teams and projects. While previous research mostly investigates the relational skills of project participants for bridging boundaries, they examine individual project competences in terms of disciplinary knowledge and supportive knowledge. The chapter identifies two boundary dilemmas in interdisciplinary projects: how to maintain depth and flexibility simultaneously, and how to balance short-term and long-term interests. These dilemmas are illustrated in a comparative case study of three high-tech, project-based firms that introduced agile project methodologies. The authors suggest that the requirements for supportive and disciplinary knowledge differ between traditional and agile projects, and depict this in an individual project competence matrix. Their findings show that, to deal with the dilemma related to depth and flexibility, individuals in agile project organizations need M-shaped rather than T-shaped disciplinary knowledge, or both contributory and interactional expertise. In relation to the second dilemma of balancing short- and long-term knowledge interests, they find that agile projects require flexible, interpersonal competence rather than the strict planning and more short-term interpersonal competence required for traditional projects. Chapter 13 points to some important implications for the knowledge of individual experts as a consequence of organizational designs aiming to integrate knowledge across disciplinary boundaries.

In Chapter 14, Jarvenpaa and Kim present a study of a different boundary-crossing mechanism: an organizational transactive memory system. Previous research suggests that transactive memory systems are effective for knowledge integration across boundaries within organizations. Jarvenpaa and Kim investigate how knowledge integration is affected by upheaval and change, and how organizational members and teams cope with incomplete and unreliable transactive memory systems during turbulent times. These questions are explored in a case study of team-based organization during the global restructuring of a large US-based, high-tech, multinational corporation. The authors investigate individual boundaries between team members, unit boundaries between teams, and geographical (country) boundaries in a global organization. They suggest that, in normal times, team-level transactive memory systems embed encoding, storage, and retrieval processes, which support their reliability, accuracy, and completeness. However, the authors show that in times of change, organizational members devise coping mechanisms such as patching, knowledge redundancy, social networking, and hierarchy to deal with the sudden incompleteness and unreliability of their memory systems. Jarvenpaa and Kim point to the potential fragility of interactive mechanisms for knowledge integration across boundaries in a dynamic world, but also suggest strategies for how robustness and resilience might be achieved.

In the final chapter of the book—Chapter 15—Van de Ven and Zahra propose a framework comprising the distance or complexity between knowledge boundaries and the objects or mechanisms used to span these boundaries. They build on the findings in the previous chapters and argue that knowledge boundaries vary in their degree (low–medium–high) and type (knowledge transfer, translation, transformation) of complexity. They emphasize the importance of understanding complexities when crossing knowledge boundaries, and highlight the numerous boundary objects that can be used to stimulate technological, product, and administrative innovations. This concluding chapter examines two propositions related to how knowledge-boundary complexity influences the likelihood of innovation. First, the authors propose a curvilinear relationship between the complexity of spanning knowledge boundaries and innovation novelty. Second, they suggest that boundary objects moderate this relationship. To achieve boundary spanning across knowledge boundaries of different complexity requires a range of appropriate boundary objects which fit each different complexity contingency. The chapter provides an integrated perspective on knowledge integration across boundaries, including many dilemmas faced, using the theoretical lens of boundary objects.

The chapters in this edited collection highlight the crucial importance for organizations of integrating knowledge across boundaries to develop the absorptive capacity (Cohen and Levinthal, 1990) and dynamic capabilities (Teece and Pisano, 1994) suggested in previous research. The rich theoretical and empirical variety of the contributions points to crucial challenges pertaining to the management as well as the study of knowledge integration across boundaries.

We are confident that these contributions will advance knowledge on the key mechanisms involved in the sharing, translating, and transforming of knowledge at the boundaries. We envisage that they will inspire new imaginative ideas and empirical studies, and will result in broader research agendas. We hope they will be an incentive for further investigation and elaboration of the claims, concepts, and empirical evidence provided in the chapters of this book in relation to crossing knowledge boundaries.

Part I

Conceptual Underpinnings

Part I

Geological Understanding

2

Managing across Knowledge Boundaries

Fredrik Tell

2.1 KNOWLEDGE BOUNDARIES: A CHALLENGE FOR KNOWLEDGE INTEGRATION

Knowledge integration—the purposeful combination of specialized and complementary knowledge—is becoming increasingly important for an expanding array of organizations facing rapidly changing institutional environments, globalized markets, and fast-paced technological development. Managing knowledge integration has emerged as a key issue for the success of new organizational forms and ideals, and the survival of contemporary organizations. At the same time, managing knowledge integration is far from an easy task.

Successful knowledge integration involves management across various knowledge boundaries. Knowledge boundaries arise as the result of knowledge specialization that leads to collectively shared frames in epistemic communities (Holzner, 1968; Holzner and Marx, 1979; Lindkvist, 2008; Håkanson, 2010). The literature acknowledges the problems involved in managing across knowledge boundaries in the context of, for instance, interdisciplinary research (Rafols and Meyer, 2010), large research programmes (Bulathsinhala, 2012; Tuertscher et al., 2014), development of new hybrid technologies in firms (Berggren et al., 2015), implementation of new IT systems (Wahlstedt, 2014), weather forecasting (Barley, 2015), online communities (Hwang et al., 2015), medical technologies (Edmondson et al., 2001), managing product development teams (Dougherty, 1992; Hoopes and Postrel, 1999; Enberg et al., 2006), and development of firm strategies (Kaplan, 2008). The empirical research reported in these and other studies provides a wealth of evidence that knowledge boundaries emerge in social and organizational settings among groups of people who need to interact to generate and apply knowledge.

This chapter tries to extend and clarify previous findings by providing an overview and typology of knowledge boundaries and the various means suggested to manage knowledge integration across these boundaries. The main questions addressed in the chapter revolve around: What constitutes a know-ledge boundary? Are there different types of knowledge boundaries? What are the mechanisms that can be used to bridge knowledge boundaries?

The chapter is organized as follows. Section 2.2 introduces the notion of knowledge boundaries and the association with the concept of epistemic communities. Section 2.3 discusses a typology of five knowledge boundaries, and Section 2.4 classifies fifteen boundary-bridging mechanisms. Section 2.5 concludes by discussing the contribution of this chapter, and some implications for future research.

2.2 EPISTEMIC COMMUNITIES AND KNOWLEDGE BOUNDARIES

The key to understanding knowledge integration is the positive efficiency and learning properties of knowledge specialization and the requirements it imposes for integrating diverse knowledge (Grant, 1996; Postrel, 2002; Tell, 2011). While individual knowledge specialization, based on refinements made during learning, is a fundamental dimension, also important is the differentiation of knowledge specialization into various socially defined domains. The social organization of work and division of labour provide a means of orientation for organizational members and workers (Holzner, 1968). The cognitive actions of individuals are tested against and justified within a particular social context, and the interaction with others provides legitimacy (Holzner and Marx, 1979; Berger and Luckmann, 1991; Tell, 2004; Tuertscher et al., 2014). Holzner (1968: 58) characterizes the social aspect of knowledge application into work domains:

> The most important consideration is, however, that cognitive action is socially structured. It is shaped, of course, by the available symbolic systems, but also by the specific dynamics of the individual's participation in his social world. Work, and structured work roles emerged as one critical focus for the study of the social organization of cognitive actions ...

These role orientations give rise to what Holzner terms epistemic communities. Epistemic communities are defined by shared role orientation and can be found in scientific fields of enquiry, engineering disciplines, professions, and occupations. They rely generally on common frames of reference and knowledge application and, more specifically, on a shared understanding among community members about the validation of knowledge claims (Holzner and Marx, 1979). While there are some general properties that apply to society as a community, epistemic communities can be defined as socially differentiated knowledge-related groups within society:

The meshing of highly similar role orientations is essential for the establishment of epistemic communities. We are dealing here with those at least partially interlinked roles which are unified by a common epistemology and frame of reference, such as the scientific community, religious communities, work communities, some ideological movements and the like. All members of such a community, in their capacity as members agree on 'the' proper perspective for the construction of reality. In these communities the conditions of reliability and validity of reality constructs are known and the applicable standards are shared. Within such epistemic communities we may thus speak of truly shared modes of construction of reality; rarely is such sharing established on a society-wide basis. (Holzner, 1968: 69)

Applications of the notion of epistemic communities can be found in the international policy literature and, more rarely, in research on the management of organizations (Lindkvist, 2008). In the former literature, Haas (1989) introduced the concept of epistemic communities in an analysis of successful and unsuccessful implementation of the Mediterranean Action Plan to prevent further pollution. Haas (1992) summarizes the defining characteristics of an epistemic community as: 1) a shared set of normative and principled beliefs; 2) shared causal beliefs; 3) shared notions of validity; and 4) a common policy enterprise.

In work on organizational and firm theories, the notion of epistemic communities is not generally employed (see Lindkvist, 2008, for a review). One exception is Håkanson (2010), who draws on the idea of epistemic community in his conceptual elaboration of the knowledge-based theory of the firm. Rather than investigating their role in relation to knowledge boundaries per se, Håkanson discusses the implications of epistemic communities for how knowledge is governed in firms. Håkanson (2010: 1811–12) argues that firms essentially are involved in two activities: the creation of new capabilities, and the exploitation of existing capabilities. These activities typically take place either *within* an epistemic community or *across* epistemic communities. Håkanson proposes a typology of four knowledge processes encompassing these two dimensions, and is interested in particular in the degree of codification involved in the transmission and exchange of knowledge within and between epistemic communities. In the context of Håkanson's argument, the purpose of this exposition is more limited and specific. Rather than exploring all the implications of epistemic community for knowledge-based theories of the firm, the discussion in this chapter is confined to the implications of differentiating epistemic communities along various dimensions, for the management of knowledge across knowledge boundaries. In line with previous research (Tell, 2011), this suggests a focus on the processes of knowledge *combination* (creation of new capabilities across epistemic boundaries), and knowledge *integration* (exploitation of existing capabilities across epistemic boundaries) suggested by Håkanson (2010).

Specialization into epistemic communities creates knowledge boundaries, which, in turn, creates the need for knowledge integration. These knowledge boundaries arise from the knowledge frames shared by epistemic community members. These frames, which are applied by individuals, imply the existence of shared cognitions and social processes involved in justification and legitimacy (Holzner, 1968; Tell, 2004; Håkanson, 2010; Berends et al., 2011).

The literature tends to analyse epistemic communities and the associated knowledge boundaries in a rather uniform way, by comparing specialties using the same justifications, such as occupational communities or scientific disciplines. However, it could be argued that the very basis for distinguishing knowledge boundaries can vary, depending on the constituents in the frames used for the generation and application of knowledge. Similar to Boschma's (2005) discussion of the plurality of proximity concepts in economic geography, knowledge boundaries can take different forms. Boschma (2005) suggests a typology consisting of five forms of proximity: cognitive, organizational, social, institutional, and geographical. In the context of knowledge boundaries, we need a typology that acknowledges their diversity.

2.3 TOWARDS A TYPOLOGY OF KNOWLEDGE BOUNDARIES

The chapters in this book provide empirical evidence and theoretical conjectures related to how knowledge is integrated across knowledge boundaries. The initial assumption is that integrating knowledge within the confines (the knowledge boundaries) of a specific set of knowledge is easier than integrating it across those boundaries, involving different knowledge domains. Sections 2.3.1 to 2.3.5 discuss five knowledge boundaries related to knowledge specialization. This discussion does not offer a pure classification of knowledge boundaries and their defining characteristics; rather, I provide examples showing the variety of knowledge boundaries. I discuss *individual, domain-specific, task-oriented, temporal*, and *spatial* knowledge boundaries. This list is indicative of the complexities but also the commonalities among boundary-specific characteristics, which can have important implications for understanding (the management of) knowledge integration.

2.3.1 Individual Knowledge Boundaries

When Robert Grant (1996) drew attention to the role of knowledge integration in his knowledge-based theory of the firm, his main concern was integration of the knowledge held by specialized individuals. He (Grant, 1996: 112) states that: 'efficiency in knowledge production...requires that individuals specialize in particular areas of knowledge. This implies that experts are (almost) invariable specialists, while jacks-of-all-trades are masters-of-none....production requires the coordinated efforts of individual specialists who possess many different types of knowledge.' An important implication for Grant's analysis is related to the problem of transferability of specialized knowledge between individuals, owing to the tacit element of much practically applicable individual knowledge (Kogut and Zander, 1992). Thus, increased specialization of individual knowledge amplifies the boundaries involved in trans-specialist knowledge integration (Postrel, 2002).

Human beings understand and make sense of the world they live in by developing knowledge that allows them to take actions aimed at their survival in their immediate environment. Throughout their upbringing, and their development as adults, humans learn by being confronted by situations which force them to act and from which they receive feedback. In this evolutionary sense, the human mind develops through consciousness and awareness, guided by interpretive schemes and cognitive maps. At the same time, the individual framing of situations involves subconscious activity (Damasio, 1999). The development of skills required to execute tasks, and expertise in recognizing patterns and situations, contribute to the differentiation of individual knowledge boundaries (Polanyi, 1966). While cognition certainly is an individual ability, supported by developments in science studies (Dunbar, 1997), experimental economics (Tversky and Kahneman, 1974) and neuroexperiments on decision-making (Laureiro Martinez et al., 2015), individual competence also constitutes a social category that can be used to distinguish different role orientations. In addition, empirical studies of individual knowledge boundaries can be found in the literature on the role of innovative individuals in different types of social networks (Cattani and Ferriani, 2008; Andersson and Berggren, 2011; Dahlander and Frederiksen, 2012; Cattani et al., 2013). Particular attention has been devoted to understanding both dispositional as well as relational knowledge characteristics pertaining to knowledge boundaries, since a general finding is that relational attributes help explain the ability to cross knowledge boundaries determined by individual specialization.

2.3.2 Domain-Specific Knowledge Boundaries

Despite the unique features of the individual knowledge that results from experiential learning, knowledge is also a social phenomenon involving the drawing of boundaries among the interactions between individuals and groups. From an interactionist perspective, individual knowledge is formed in the interactions with other individuals, but the process of knowing something is an inherently social process (Mead, 1934; Blumer, 1969). For instance, the framing of a specific problem and how to solve it is affected not only by cognitive dispositions but also by collective assumptions, wisdoms, and 'recipes'. In addition, what constitutes a legitimate approach to the search for knowledge, or even the knowledge itself, involves a process of justification in a social community. Examples of these communities are scientific disciplines and subdisciplines (or rival approaches within disciplines) and other communal practices such as crafts, guilds, and professions. Domain-specific knowledge is the 'knowing-what' of many knowledge-based communities, which define the knowledge domain and knowledge boundaries in specific knowledge bases, for example, scientific disciplines, technological and engineering areas, professions, communities, common interests, and so on. In this sense, domain-specific knowledge, at least to some extent, consists of declarative knowledge (Cohen, 1991). Domain-specific knowledge often includes a set of canonical principles on which the community adhering to the domain draws. The implications are manifold since declarative knowledge may not be sufficient to use the knowledge in practice. In an engineering context, domain-specific knowledge is acquired through the studies and experiences of engineers in a specific domain (Granstrand and Oskarsson, 1994; Lim, 2009; Ullman, 2010).

Work on knowledge integration often takes as its starting point differentiation with regard to domain-specific knowledge. For instance, in their studies of cross-functional product development teams, Dougherty (1992), Iansiti (1995), Hoopes and Postrel (1999), Enberg et al. (2006), and Majchrzak et al. (2012) use differentiation of domain-specific knowledge as a key variable to address the problems of knowledge integration. At an organizational level, Nesta and Saviotti (2006), DiBiaggio (2007), and Brusoni et al. (2001) use measures of domain-specific knowledge (such as patents) to analyse the effects of knowledge specialization and integration, while Takeishi (2002) and Zirpoli and Camuffo (2009) account for domain-specific knowledge in their studies of inter-organizational knowledge integration, in a similar way.

2.3.3 Task-Oriented Knowledge Boundaries

Developing and applying knowledge is often geared towards an end or an objective, which can be defined as the task at hand. The task refers to the assigned piece of work, as in a problem waiting to be solved. Task characteristics are a central concern in organizational analysis, since many organization studies focus on the instrumental nature of organizations. Both Perrow's (1970) seminal studies of task contingencies, such as complexity and uncertainty, and the Carnegie School of organizational analysis (March and Simon,

1958; Cyert and March, 1963), focus on organizations as devices to complete and decompose tasks and problems. Likewise, both the interdependency approach of Thompson (1967) and the institutional analysis of Meyer and Rowan (1977) discuss the technical core (i.e. the task) as a key variable in the analysis of organizational action and organizational boundaries. Nelson and Winter (1982) and others recognized that organizations complete tasks by executing distinguishable routines, involving boundaries between routines and their application. However, Simon (1969) also shows that the knowledge about how to complete a task and/or solve a problem can be abstracted, creating 'artificial' or informational boundaries (Baldwin and Clark, 2000).

While domain-specific knowledge is concerned with knowing what, task-oriented procedural knowledge refers to knowing how (see Cohen, 1991; Kogut and Zander, 1992). Procedural knowledge involves task organization and task execution capabilities, and has been conceived as organizational routines involving the storing and exploitation of organizational know-how (Nelson and Winter, 1982; Becker, 2004). As discussed in Dionysiou and Tsoukas (2013), routines cut across levels, functions, and units, and, in this way, integrate domain-specific knowledge (although they also create new procedural knowledge boundaries).

Empirical studies have looked at interruptions to procedural knowledge and how they interfere with knowledge integration (e.g. Weick, 1993; Feldman, 2000; Edmondson et al., 2001). However, studies of knowledge integration across procedural knowledge domains involving clashing routines or the integration of different communities of practice to accomplish a specific task are scant. This is likely because the meaning often invoked by procedural knowledge is that it assists organizations (by knowing how) to integrate domain-specific knowledge (i.e. knowing what). However, the bridging of procedural knowledge boundaries could also facilitate organizational action, effectiveness, and innovativeness.

2.3.4 Spatial Knowledge Boundaries

Human beings are dispersed across the world in very different physical and cultural environments. Hence, the knowledge focus might vary significantly across geographical locations. As emphasized in anthropology, language, culture, and traditions—all important elements in the development of knowledge— emerge in the local context. Knowledge is developed to enable survival in local conditions and is reinforced by idiosyncratic linguistic expressions and collective norms. Thus, the way problems are framed and potential solutions are envisaged will vary across locations. Relatedly, spatial perception is intimately related also to representation and cognitive development, and research in

economic geography explores the economic implications of spatially constrained learning and the effects of local knowledge spillovers. Knowledge
boundaries emerge in relation to different sites and call for an examination
of the types of proximity that lead to diffusion across space (Capello, 1999;
Boschma, 2005). Although we may be living in an era of globalization,
knowledge is not evenly distributed geographically. Different locations are
endowed with different specialized knowledge, making knowledge integration
a constant challenge. How do location and geographical distance affect
knowledge boundaries? Boschma and Frenken (2010: 4) discuss geographical
proximity as the physical distance between actors in absolute (e.g. miles) or
relative (e.g. travel time) terms, and argue that 'geographical proximity is
beneficial for innovation as effective learning requires face-to-face interaction.
Such interaction is easier (and cheaper) to organise when agents are co-located.'
This quote sums up the view in economic geography that spatial proximity
facilitates collaboration and, thus, positively influences knowledge combination
and innovation (Crescenzi et al., 1997; Morgan, 2004). In other words, greater
spatial distance between people and organizations creates knowledge boundaries that need to be bridged to enable the integration of knowledge.

This line of reasoning has been used in economic geography to explain
agglomeration economies such as regional clusters (Porter, 1990; Cooke,
2001). Several studies investigate the relationship between geographical distance and knowledge networks and knowledge linkages (e.g. Coenen et al.,
2004; Giuliani, 2007; Laursen et al., 2012). Others refer to 'local buzz' versus
'global pipelines' (Bathelt et al., 2004) to indicate the problems in this relationship and the important interrelationships between spatial and other types
of knowledge boundaries. Scholars of international business have also studied
the spatial aspects of knowledge integration. Multinational Enterprises
(MNEs) want to draw on specific locational knowledge and other resources
to achieve the global coordination advantages from operating in different local
environments (Andersson et al., 2014). However, research on the contribution
made by MNEs to subsidiaries' knowledge shows that this is not straightforward. For instance, Blomkvist et al. (2010) examine research and development
(R&D) measured by patents and show that rather than being evenly distributed across MNEs, a few superstar subsidiaries account for most of the
production of this knowledge, which questions the importance of global
coordination advantages for MNEs. The increasing spatial specialization and
coordination is also recognized by the literature on global value chains, which
argues that, rather than being vertically integrated in a single MNE, production
is increasingly developed and produced in a network of value chain organizations that provide inputs (Dedrick et al., 2010). However, empirical data from
UNCTAD (2013) seems to suggest that knowledge specialization is maintained
spatially, for instance while production activities are being offshored to emerging economies, R&D investments are being maintained in mature markets,

raising concerns about the governance of such global value chains (Humphrey and Schmitz, 2001) and the role of spatial knowledge boundaries.

2.3.5 Temporal Knowledge Boundaries

While spatial understanding of a phenomenon is a major ingredient in knowledge development, equally important is temporal conception. For instance, it is difficult to understand a causal statement (i.e. an if-then proposition) in the absence of an assumption about time. Temporal ordering seems a necessary condition for the development of knowledge. The sequencing of events in time creates boundaries between 'slots' in time. This is apparent in many organizations, whether organized according to Fordist principles (where work is determined by the speed and allocation of tasks via conveyor belts) or organized as projects (with work allocated according to milestones and stages). In this sense, temporal knowledge domains may emerge based on the sequence in which the knowledge is applied. Temporal boundaries also emerge in another context. For instance, it can be argued that much knowledge is history-dependent, that is, it is dependent on events that took place in the past. This endows knowledge with a cumulative quality, in which boundaries emerge between different knowledge trajectories or paths in time (see Chapter 4 in this book).

Furthermore, knowledge is contingent, framed, and confined by temporal boundaries. Just as it can be argued that some knowledge is context-specific with regard to place, it can also be context-specific in relation to time. Knowledge is not time invariant; what is considered to be knowledge at one time may not be considered as such in another temporal instance (Lachmann, 1977). In a subjective sense, temporality shapes the being of things and, thereby, influences knowledge boundaries. From an evolutionary perspective, Popper (1963) argues about the conjectural nature of knowledge as 'mere' hypotheses, susceptible always to new trials as time passes. This line of reasoning presents one—linear—time conception: *past* (e.g. historical instances), *present* (e.g. experience), and *future* (e.g. predictions) tenses, which influence how we define knowledge domains and, accordingly, influence knowledge boundaries (cf. Hernes et al., 2013). This is confirmed by studies in psychology which show how individuals experience and devote attention to past, present, and future (Shipp et al., 2009). The bridging and transition between these three tenses constitute an important dynamic in the generation of knowledge (Garud and Nayyar, 1994). Another important temporal dimension in organizational practice is the 'chunky' nature of time. Time is not necessarily continuous; it can be occasional, intermittent, sequenced, parallel, and/or paced. This breaking down of time can help to focus effort and learning, but also creates knowledge boundaries and problems related to synchronization of time.

The importance of varieties of temporal knowledge boundaries has been demonstrated empirically. On the one hand temporal contingencies have been shown to affect the structuring of organizations. For instance, Brusoni and Prencipe (2001) discuss diachronic and synchronic systems integration and their influence on the modularization of knowledge, and Söderlund (2002) examines the impact of global and local time on knowledge integration for projects and project-based organizations (see also Gersick, 1994). On the other hand, subjective time orientations influence organizational behaviour. Griesbach and Grand (2013) study a family firm and analyse how creating sustainable business for future generations (times) requires reconstructive and innovative actions in the present (time). Similarly, subjective time orientations are important for chief executive officers (CEOs) and project teams (Dahlgren and Söderlund, 2001; Mohammed and Nadkarni, 2011; Nadkarni and Chen, 2014). Cumulatively, time influences knowledge boundaries through path-dependence of organizational knowledge development (Levinthal and March, 1993; Sydow et al., 2009; Sydow et al., 2012).

2.4 MANAGING INTEGRATION ACROSS KNOWLEDGE BOUNDARIES

Knowledge specialization is a precondition for knowledge integration. While the division of labour and knowledge is contingent on managerial discretion, knowledge integration is high on the agendas of managers. Managing knowledge integration involves bridging knowledge boundaries to get access to, combine, and assimilate specialized knowledge. This view acknowledges that managing knowledge integration involves crossing knowledge boundaries through various learning activities. From an epistemic perspective, that is, by distinguishing among the types of knowledge involved—tacit, articulated, codified—I suggest a composite approach to boundary-bridging mechanisms that manage knowledge integration across knowledge boundaries within a range of learning activities. I propose the use of boundary-bridging mechanisms that combine two variables—knowledge articulability and learning activity.

2.4.1 Knowledge Articulability

Tacit knowledge is crucial for human knowledge (see also Chapter 5 in this book). In other words, much important learning is implicit, tacit, subconscious, or unconscious. Thus, most analyses of knowledge articulation start from the assumption of tacit knowledge which needs to be articulated. However, whether all tacit knowledge is articulable is debated in work on codification in research into the economics of innovation (cf. Ancori et al., 2000; Cohendet and Steinmueller, 2000; Cowan et al., 2000; Nightingale, 2003; Balconi et al., 2007). Three types of knowledge: tacit, articulated, and codified (Zollo and Winter, 2002), are delineated to provide a classification of the mechanisms that can be used to bridge various knowledge boundaries.

Tacit Knowledge

Evolutionary neurologists, such as Antonio Damasio and Gerald Edelman, and philosophers, such as Michael Polanyi and John Searle, have argued for the important role of subsidiary awareness and tacit assent in the evolution of human knowledge. In perceiving and knowing our world, we are not engaged in passive learning about it, but are drawing constantly on subconscious processes and predispositions, which lead humans to hypothesize about the states of the world they are encountering (see, e.g., Nightingale, 2003). The general argument regarding tacit knowledge recognizes that an important function of subsidiary awareness (or 'indwelling' as Polanyi puts it) is that it allows the executor of a specific task to direct his/her attention to something focal (which, consequently, is not subsumed). The arguments posed by Polanyi (1958, 1966) related to the primacy of the tacit dimension of knowledge compared to explicit knowledge (captured in language) can be summarized as: a) reality is too complex to be captured fully in formalized (incomplete) language (Tsoukas and Vladimirou, 2001; Tsoukas, 2009); b) language is an important resource for knowledge creation, but is never fully utilized by the individual since no single individual has complete language competence; c) the social rules of language ultimately constrain creativity in knowledge generation, since they impose conformity to what is considered socially legitimate; d) explicit knowledge relies ultimately on some implicit knowledge since the ability to use language does not reside only in the language and its grammar.

Articulated Knowledge

Epistemologists, including Polanyi, do not contend that the articulation of knowledge is unimportant. On the contrary, most see it as indispensable to knowledge creation, for example, in science. Polanyi (1958) discusses knowledge articulation as an asymmetric process in which tacit knowledge is primordial (particularly in relation to the symbolic representation of knowledge). In so doing, he does not deny the power of articulation. However, while articulation refers to the reversible logical operation of known symbols,

Polanyi is more interested in the articulation of knowledge associated with discovery, with the irreversible creation of concepts that enhance our understanding or provide a solution to a problem. Such knowledge articulation, Polanyi argues, is grounded essentially in ineffable knowledge, that is, tacit subsidiary awareness (see Chapter 5 in this book). Nonaka (1991) and Hedlund (1994) describe the process of converting tacit knowledge to explicit knowledge as articulation (see Tell, 2014).

Codified Knowledge

In some sense, knowledge codification is an extension of knowledge articulation. The ability to codify knowledge depends on externalized knowledge in the form of linguistic and symbolic representations. The process of codification involves great effort and high costs (Zollo and Winter, 2002). Among individuals in organizations who codify articulated knowledge into 'codebooks' (Cowan et al., 2000), the aim is often to reveal stronger links between actions and outcomes. Ancori et al. (2000) suggest that the cognitive and organizational mechanisms mobilized by codification are particularly important. In line with the discussion in Foray and Steinmueller (2003), we can distinguish two functions of codified knowledge. The first is to allow for storage and transfer of knowledge across time and space; the second is to allow humans to rearrange, manipulate, and examine symbols and symbolic relationships in order to transform the underlying knowledge represented.

2.4.2 Bridging Knowledge Boundaries in Learning Activities

Achieving knowledge integration involves a number of learning activities. I draw on work on knowledge integration (Carlile and Rebentisch, 2003; Carlile, 2004), organizational learning (Huber, 1991), and absorptive and transformative capacities (Garud and Nayyar, 1994; Zahra and George, 2002) to identify learning activities that require boundary-bridging mechanisms to achieve knowledge integration. This section discusses the five learning activities of search, acquisition, assimilation, accumulation, and transformation. These learning activities are juxtaposed with knowledge articulability, as discussed above, to provide a matrix presenting fifteen boundary-bridging mechanisms (see Table 2.1 for a summary) that are briefly outlined.

Boundary-bridging Search

The identification of search as a key activity in behavioural theories of organizations and firms was developed by the Carnegie School (see March and Simon, 1958; Cyert and March, 1963) and is a cornerstone of evolutionary economics (see Dosi, 1982; Nelson and Winter, 1982). Further refinements of the implications of knowledge search have been proposed in the context of complexity theory (e.g., Kauffman, 1993; Levinthal, 1997). By considering problem-solving as the main objective of organizations for forming and sustaining their capabilities, knowledge search refers to the activities of economic agents searching the environment to find the knowledge required to solve the organization's immediate and long-term problems. This involves both local and distant search (see Laursen, 2012, for a review). For economic and cognitive reasons, most search tends to be local, that is, agents search for new knowledge in the vicinity of previous solutions, that is, for knowledge similar to knowledge already in their possession. This similarity facilitates understanding and subsequent assimilation of that knowledge. However, local search will exacerbate path-dependence and lock-in to inferior solutions, while more distant search will be more likely to generate new solutions if the knowledge obtained can be integrated into the firm's existing knowledge. March (1991) makes a distinction between exploitation of what is known (local search) and exploration of new knowledge (distant search).

Spanning is one approach to the problem of knowledge integration across boundaries. Chapter 15 in this book shows that boundary spanning involves the activities of sensing, identifying, learning about, and gathering information on developments outside the organizational actors' knowledge domains. Boundary spanning is accomplished by boundary spanners, which are individuals or groups that utilize their tacit knowledge to connect with other actors across knowledge boundaries. In search activities, boundary spanners act as 'gatekeepers', 'brokers', or 'liaisons' between individuals with differentiated knowledge, who may also be geographically separate (Allen, 1977; Hargadon and Sutton, 1997; Cattani and Ferriani, 2008; Lissoni, 2010; Andersson and Tell, 2016; Chapter 12 in this book). In an empirical study of patenting activity in optical disk technology, Rosenkopf and Nerkar (2001) show how boundary spanning in organizational search takes place across both task-oriented organizational boundaries and domain-specific technological boundaries.

Analogy is another mechanism used to bridge boundaries during organizational search (Gavetti et al., 2005; Gary et al., 2012; Lopez-Vega et al., 2016). In this case, search is enabled through use of analogical reasoning (Gentner, 2002) and involves structural comparison between the base and the target domain (whose knowledge content is more or less unrelated). Searching for structurally similar knowledge across boundaries can provide insights into the problems faced by the focal organization. The ability to identify structural similarity requires some form of knowledge articulation by the organizational actors (Tell, 2014). Drawing on an experimental study, Franke et al. (2013) demonstrate that solutions derived from problem-solvers in analogous markets are more novel although less immediately useful. Wagenstetter et al. (2013), in a study based on interviews with logistics services providers, show how inventive analogies can be used to find solutions to current problems. These studies demonstrate how analogy can be used to bridge domain-specific and task-oriented boundaries. Lopez-Vega et al. (2016) discuss the potential for analogies to cross spatially defined boundaries (see also Chapter 6 in this book).

Hypothesis acts as a boundary-bridging mechanism through formal conjecture about the causal relationships among variables. Formal hypotheses require the knowledge to be codified in documents or software. Its codification allows it to be scrutinized by a wide range of actors across knowledge boundaries. Since the actors involved are able to understand the code applied to the hypotheses, their knowledge and suggestions can be understood and applied across boundaries. In a case study of an R&D organization, Lindkvist (2004) exemplifies how establishing a formal new project organization served as a hypothesis that triggered more mindful attention and responsiveness to customer needs and cross-disciplinary collaboration. Lopez-Vega et al. (2016) demonstrate how established theories in one knowledge domain enabled sophisticated search in another knowledge domain in different open innovation projects.

Boundary-bridging Acquisition

Knowledge search implies that knowledge found to be appropriate is acquired by the searcher. Grant (1996) suggests that efficient knowledge integration does not presuppose complete knowledge transfer, since this would imply inefficiencies. However, the integration of specialized and complementary knowledge involves sharing and/or transfer of knowledge in the sense that the right to use this knowledge is conferred on another actor by the actor currently in possession of that knowledge. There is a large body of literature on knowledge transfer and knowledge sharing, and the review in Tell (2011) shows that many studies of knowledge integration use knowledge sharing to proxy for knowledge integration. However, Oukhysen and Eisenhardt (2002) point out that knowledge sharing and knowledge transfer are not sufficient conditions for knowledge integration. The growing literature on external knowledge acquisition (see, e.g., Cassiman and Veugelers, 2006; Berchicci, 2013; Monteiro, 2015; Lakemond et al., 2016) suggests that the activity of acquisition helps to focus on precisely what knowledge is shared or transferred, and how it is embodied.

Enrolment is a boundary-bridging mechanism that recognizes the specialized tacit knowledge of individuals or collectives, and allows for the acquisition of knowledge in the absence of much *ex ante* common knowledge. Hiring, recruiting, and buying allow the acquisition of unfamiliar knowledge from different knowledge domains. Recruitment or temporary employment can facilitate the integration of knowledge by bridging individual, domain-specific, task-oriented, spatial, and temporal boundaries (Rao and Drazin, 2002; Söderlund and Bredin, 2011; Borg and Söderlund, 2014). Domain-specific, task-oriented, and spatial knowledge boundaries can be bridged via mergers, acquisitions, and joint ventures (Bresman et al., 1999; Zollo and Sing, 2004; and see Chapter 9 in this book).

Objects can serve as a boundary-bridging mechanism for knowledge acquisition. This mechanism is based on the attractiveness of tacit and codified elements of artefacts as boundary objects, which may be 'weakly structured in common use, and become strongly structured in individual-site use' (Star and Griesemer, 1989: 393; see also Carlile, 2002). Objects can serve as the articulation of an idea or product, without prescription of a formal theoretical conjecture (see also Chapters 11 and 15 in this book). Much empirical research on boundary objects and knowledge integration emphasizes how objects, such as prototypes, drawings, and so on, facilitate, but also hamper, the bridging of domain-specific knowledge boundaries such as those between occupational communities or task-oriented boundaries (e.g. Carlile, 2002; Bechky, 2003a; Majzhrak et al., 2012; Nicolini et al., 2012; see Chapter 11 in this book). Moreover, Yakura (2002) presents a case study of an information and communication technology consulting firm to explore how Gantt charts and other visualization methods using timelines enable the bridging of temporal boundaries.

Intellectual property consists of codified knowledge in the form of legal documents, such as patents, copyrights, or trademarks (Teece, 2007; Granstrand, 1999; Somaya, 2012), whose ownership can be shared or transferred via licences, or sale in markets for technologies (Arora and Gambardella, 2010). Thus, intellectual property becomes a boundary-bridging mechanism since it can be acquired across knowledge boundaries. For instance, research in economic history has shown patent transfer rates of around 30 per cent in the US and the UK (Sokoloff and Lamoreaux, 1999; Bottomley, 2014), with lower figures reported for Germany (8.1 per cent, Burhop, 2010) and Japan (14.4 per cent, Nicholas and Shimizu, 2013).

Boundary-bridging Assimilation

Cohen and Levinthal (1990) made a seminal contribution to the literature on organizational capabilities and innovation, and proposed that organizations invest in absorptive capacity by conducting R&D in order to obtain learning benefits from the acquisition and integration of new knowledge. They argue that investing in the search for a specific type of knowledge through R&D activity is only one element in the development of technological capabilities, which also draws on more generic knowledge developed in the course of continuous R&D activity that facilitates the absorption of more specific types of knowledge. This suggests that the successful integration of foreign knowledge might be contingent on the preconditions for knowledge assimilation and learning more generally. The absorptive capacity literature is extensive, and is at the base of our understanding of knowledge integration across boundaries (see Murtic, 2016; and Chapter 4 in this book).

Socialization is considered by Nonaka (1991, 1994) to describe the conversion of some tacit knowledge into some other tacit knowledge. Knowledge can cross boundaries in social interactions via mimicking behaviours. Its tacit character is maintained while it is used in new contexts. An example of the transfer of tacit knowledge across boundaries can be seen in the activities of a community of practice (Brown and Duguid, 1991; Lave and Wenger, 1991), where more peripheral members of the community gain legitimacy through socialization with more experienced members. Thus, knowledge is transferred across individual, domain-specific, spatial, and temporal boundaries as newcomers are assimilated. Examples of communities of practice where socialization is used as a boundary-bridging mechanism include midwives (Lave and Wenger, 1991), repair technicians (Orr, 1996), and product development teams (Wenger and Snyder, 2000).

Concept formation serves as a boundary-bridging mechanism in assimilation when concepts are developed to facilitate denotation of and provision of the attributes of a particular phenomenon. In the social sciences, Gerring (1999) proposes eight criteria for judging the quality of concepts: familiarity, resonance, parsimony, coherence, differentiation, depth, theoretical utility, and field utility. Although it may not be possible to meet all of these criteria in practical situations of concept formation, they are indicative of some important aspects of knowledge articulation in concept formation and their potential role as boundary-bridging mechanisms. Chapter 5 in this book refers to the discussion in Nonaka and Takeuchi (1995) of how adoption of the 'Tall Boy' metaphor facilitated a shared coherent direction, and the bridging of domain specific boundaries, in the design of a new car at Toyota.

Exact replication of knowledge takes place when an exact copy of an identifiable piece of template knowledge is transferred across a knowledge boundary, and the subsequent acknowledgement of knowledge transfer as a replicating unit (such as a franchisee) executes this knowledge (Winter and Szulanski, 2001; Bengtsson and Lindkvist, 2013). In such cases, knowledge transfer may be taken to mean that knowledge (or its outcome, such as a capability) can be codified, otherwise it is difficult to demonstrate that knowledge transfer has taken place exactly. In addition to bridging knowledge across task-oriented boundaries such as routines, replication also involves the crossing of spatial and temporal boundaries (Winter, 2010). For instance, replication as knowledge integration has been studied in contexts of best practices across task-oriented, temporal, and spatial boundaries at Banc

One (Szulanski, 1996), in quick printing (Knott, 2003), an Israeli franchising firm (Szulanski and Jensen, 2006), and Rank Xerox in Europe (Jensen and Szulanski, 2007).

Boundary-bridging Accumulation

The accumulation of knowledge to form capabilities is an important learning activity and enables future knowledge integration through knowledge recombination. Accumulation refers to the storing of knowledge gained from previous activities in a knowledge repository, which differentiates the organization. The knowledge accumulated must be retrievable for integration with new knowledge. This requires the ability to retrieve knowledge and implement it to integrate new knowledge.

Skills and routines enable smooth, trouble-free coordination among specialized activities (Nelson and Winter, 1982). Skills describe individual capacities to perform particular activities (such as fixing a broken engine) (Polanyi, 1966); routines describe their organizational equivalent and enable coordinated actions across knowledge boundaries (Dionysiou and Tsoukas, 2013). Although empirical studies of organizational routines are scarce (Parmigiani and Howard-Grenville, 2011), Birnholtz et al. (2007) in a study of a summer camp show not only how routines enable bridging of domain-specific knowledge boundaries but also how temporal boundaries are bridged as the camp regenerates after the winter closure.

Dialogue refers to the Socratic element of knowledge articulation as expressed, for instance, in Plato's dialogues. Drawing upon different literatures, several authors have argued about the importance of communication among practitioners in order to bridge knowledge boundaries (Boland and Tenkasi, 1995; Nonaka et al., 2000; Göranzon et al., 2006; Håkanson, 2007; Nonaka and von Krogh, 2009; Tsoukas, 2009; Lindkvist et al., 2011). Majchrzak et al. (2012: 3) describe this boundary-bridging mechanism as 'traversing' across knowledge boundaries when it is applied in cross-functional product development teams. Sieg et al. (2010) study the use of a specific innovation intermediary in seven chemical firms and find that to bridge domain-specific, spatial, and task-oriented boundaries, a key contribution of the intermediary was to formulate the problem in a dialogue with the client to enable a novel solution. Faraj and Xiao (2006) report on the coordination of distributed expertise in a medical trauma team and suggest that time-critical responses to novel events through dialogic coordination practices help to ensure error-free operations.

Rules can be emerging or imposed. By adherence to rules about specific sequences of interactions, that is, 'the rules of the game', specialized knowledge can be coordinated across boundaries. Thus, rules can be seen as similar to routines, but formalized and codified as standards or directives, and are identified by Grant (1996)—drawing on Galbraith (1973)—as the primordial form of knowledge integration mechanism, since rules enable coordination without the need for costly communication. Moving beyond the confines of single organizations, Kogut (2000) suggests that the emergence of rules explains network structures and coordination across boundaries. In a longitudinal analysis of the rules that governed Stanford University over a period of 100 years, March et al. (2000) show the emergence of organizational rules and how rules facilitate coordination among domain-specific disciplines and idiosyncratic individual knowledge, as response and adaptation to environmental dynamism. Moreover, rules, as they are diffused, can transcend task-oriented boundaries, leading to standardization among ecologies of organizations such as universities.

Boundary-bridging Transformation

An important ingredient in knowledge integration is the transformation of specialized knowledge and the activities involved. Kogut and Zander (1992) suggest that combinative capabilities are key to the establishment and renewal of firms and influence decisions about firm boundaries and firm strategy. The economist Joseph Schumpeter (1934) suggested that innovations are essentially the product of new combinations of knowledge, rather than the invention of new knowledge. This is the basis of the recent interest in technology brokering and fusion (Hargadon, 2002), knowledge combination (Gruber et al., 2012), recombinative capabilities (Carnabuci and Operti, 2013), knowledge arbitrage (Perkmann, 2007), and knowledge transformation (Teece, 2007) for the creation of dynamic capabilities.

Bricolage refers to tinkering with what is already known and the knowledge emerging from improvisation, as important sources of renewal and transformation through 'making do' by exploiting new combinations of existing resources and applying them to new problems and opportunities (Levi-Strauss, 1962; Weick, 2001; Salunke et al., 2013; Senyard et al., 2014). Similar to the concept of ingenuity, bricolage emphasizes how intimate, tacit knowledge of resources, serendipity, and improvisation can result in transformations based on recombination and minimum use of resources. Recent research on frugal or Jugaad innovation (Athreye and Kapur, 2009; Govindarajan et al., 2012; Radjou et al., 2012), shows how less resourceful organizations in emerging economies are bridging domain-specific, task-oriented, and spatial boundaries (see also Chapter 9 in this book).

The term *bisociation* was coined by Koestler (1964) to describe the act of creation through clashes and bridging of knowledge boundaries. The idea of bisociation is that creative acts are the result of perceptions of ideas or situations where two habitually incompatible frames meet. Each frame can be thought of as governed by a matrix encapsulating hidden assumptions and logics. Bisociation occurs as the intersection—at the boundary—between these

Table 2.1. Boundary-bridging mechanisms in learning activities

	Search	Acquisition	Assimilation	Accumulation	Transformation
Tacit knowledge	Spanning	Enrolment	Socialization	Skills and routines	Bricolage
Articulated knowledge	Analogy	Objects	Concept formation	Dialogue	Bisociation
Codified knowledge	Hypothesis	Intellectual property	Exact replication	Rules	Combination

frames, which reveals hidden matrices which enable the achievement of a transformative creative act. As discussed by Majchrzak et al. (2012) in an analysis of a product development team, juxtaposition of knowledge domains not only demarcates knowledge boundaries but also enables the ability to transcend knowledge domains by recognizing and coupling common assumptions.

Combination involves the restructuring of explicit knowledge (Nonaka, 1994; and see Chapter 5 in this book). Knowledge combination requires two important preconditions: a) some decomposability (Simon, 1969) of knowledge into knowledge elements that can be combined; and b) some degree of architectural knowledge (Henderson, 1994) constituting an understanding of the interrelationships to facilitate experimentation and reconfiguration of these elements. In the context of innovation, it is useful here to consider the distinction introduced by Henderson and Clark (1990) between modular innovations, which are the fruits of experimentation with elements within a given knowledge architecture, and architectural innovations, which imply a reconfiguration of the relationships between elements to achieve a new architecture.

Table 2.1 provides a schematic summary of the fifteen boundary-bridging mechanisms discussed above. While by no means exhaustive, the classification of boundary-bridging mechanisms has been made with regard to the two dimensions of knowledge articulability and learning activities. As indicated above, I suggest that it should be helpful in furthering our understanding of how different knowledge boundaries may be bridged to achieve knowledge integration.

2.5 CONCLUSIONS AND IMPLICATIONS FOR FUTURE RESEARCH

The review and analysis of management across knowledge boundaries in this chapter contributes by exploring and delineating different kinds of knowledge boundaries and elaborating a framework that comprises a range of boundary-bridging mechanisms. I have shown how knowledge boundaries arise according to different dimensions. Combining the dimensions of knowledge articulability and learning activities provides a matrix for defining and positioning different knowledge-based mechanisms, which are both theoretically grounded and relate to findings in the empirical literature.

In addition to providing a classification of knowledge boundaries and boundary-bridging mechanisms, the analysis in this chapter raises questions about the nature of knowledge boundaries and the possibility of bridging them. At an epistemological level, the sociological arguments in this chapter push knowledge integration beyond the methodological individualism under-lying, for example, the seminal work of Grant (1996). At the same time the proposed categorization of knowledge boundaries is not specific about the relationship between individual and collective knowledge (see Chapter 5 in this book), and future conceptual and empirical work could elaborate on this relationship.

By implication, at least, the suggested framing of the problem of integration across knowledge boundaries seeks to address the complexity, uncertainty, fallibility, and incompleteness of knowledge. Future studies could examine how these properties of knowledge affect the use and effectiveness of different types of boundary-bridging mechanisms. The analysis in this chapter provides a framework for understanding knowledge integration across boundaries of the same type, although, in reality, it is likely that several different knowledge boundaries will be involved concomitantly (see, e.g., Chapter 6 in this book). Future research could explore the implications of multiple knowledge bound-aries for knowledge integration of different types of knowledge. This leads to another limitation of the present analysis, namely, that the application of boundary-bridging mechanisms might promote the emergence of new know-ledge boundaries grounded in these mechanisms. Despite this potential infin-ite regress problem, the overview and classification provided here should stimulate more discussion on a problem that is of both empirical and theor-etical significance.

3

Effective Management of Collective Design Processes

Knowledge Profiles and the Sequential Ordering of Tasks

Steven Postrel

3.1 INTRODUCTION

Many kinds of boundaries divide people who are engaged in joint problem-solving activities. For example, individuals developing a new product might be separated by firm boundaries, unit boundaries within a firm, professional boundaries, industry boundaries, generational boundaries, and so on. Each of these institutional or demographic boundaries consists of a complex stack of behavioural, cognitive, and affective layers: There are layers of loyalty, identity, common interest, social interaction, factual knowledge, interpretation, and so on, and each of these enforces a specific kind of separation between the people and groups on either side of the particular boundary.

Differences in loyalty, identity, or interest may cause people to consciously act at cross purposes. Differences in social interaction, knowledge, or interpretation may cause them to accidentally interfere with one another; so individuals and groups on either side of these barriers may find that their respective actions fail to align. Alignment failures can be very costly, causing unnecessary expense, delays, or underachievement, which can compromise entire projects. The purpose of integration between units is to avoid such misalignments.

This chapter focuses on how to manage the knowledge layer of boundaries. One key question is how 'thick' such a layer should be, that is, how differentiated should the knowledge be that is held by people on either side of the boundary. Operationally, this amounts to a decision about how much time and effort units should dedicate to teaching and learning across unit boundaries, at the expense of accumulating disciplinary depth and solving specialized problems. 'Common sense' might suggest that avoiding misalignments requires 'thinner' barriers between units, making them less specialized, but careful analysis shows that this intuition would only sometimes be correct.

Another important issue for managers is how best to structure interactions across boundaries. For example, which unit should offer the first proposed solution to a joint problem? Again, common sense might suggest that the more capable unit or the one that is better at explaining its point of view should take the lead in problem-solving. It turns out, however, that systematic analysis leads to a different conclusion.

3.2 GLITCHES AND DISCIPLINARY BOUNDARIES

This chapter focuses on how to minimize a single important class of potential alignment failures, called 'glitches' (Hoopes and Postrel, 1999), in which one unit violates the technical constraints facing another unit across the knowledge layer of a disciplinary boundary. Therefore, conflicts of interest among agents are beyond the scope of this discussion. In addition, our focus on knowledge specialization boundaries means that we do not explore problems of knowledge transfer between similarly specialized units, as discussed in the literature on replicating best practices (Winter and Szulanski, 2001). We also ignore the presence or absence of firm boundaries, since differences in specialized knowledge occur both within and between firms. The barriers we are concerned with are those that separate one kind of specialist from another on the basis of their knowledge (defined at whatever degree of granularity is most appropriate) These barriers exist, for example, between design engineers and manufacturing experts, editors and libel lawyers, avionics designers and aerodynamicists, architects and building contractors, medical scientists and statisticians, military operations and logistics officers, and scientific theorists and empiricists.

Some examples of glitches include:

- the Mars Climate Observer spacecraft navigation group's loss of the probe, partly because it lacked sufficient understanding about how the spacecraft would respond to thrust commands, solar light pressure, and other dynamic factors, although the probe's designers did understand these matters (Postrel, 2002);
- marketing/user-domain experts specified features of a piece of software that could not be coded even with greatly expanded time and money constraints, although the team's software experts readily recognized

this impossibility. Meanwhile, the software experts produced versions of requested features that failed to meet basic customer requirements, although these requirements were obvious to the marketing/user-domain experts (Hoopes and Postrel, 1999). All of this work was useless and had to be discarded;

- product designers created designs that could not be manufactured within cost and quality constraints, although their infeasibility was clear to the firm's manufacturing experts once they saw the designs. Extensive redesign was required. Much of the improvement in automobile product development since the 1980s has addressed failures to 'design for manufacturability,' such as blueprints arriving at manufacturing which called for techniques that had been discontinued the year before, or water leaks owing to sunroof designs that could not be manufactured to the necessary tolerances (Clark and Fujimoto, 1991: 208–10);

- in 2007, financial managers misunderstood the meaning of quantitative risk models, leading to unintended portfolio risk-taking despite the creators and operators of these models ('quants') being well aware of what the models actually indicated (and what they were able to indicate).[1] The result was widespread financial stress and a liquidity crisis (Shreve, 2008);

- a new government insurance-purchasing portal on the Internet mandated by the US Patient Protection and Affordable Care Act failed to meet functionality and launch date requirements even though experts in creating such information systems knew in advance that the schedule and scope were too ambitious, and that the system specifications had been released too late for the developers to complete the required tasks. The result was a delayed and incomplete launch, and repeated crashes when large numbers of users tried to access the system (Pear et al., 2013).

The *proximate* cause of each of these mismatches is a knowledge gap across specialty boundaries. If the members of one specialty had fully understood the

---

[1] 'During the boom years, everybody could reel off reasons why the Gaussian copula function wasn't perfect. Li's approach made no allowance for unpredictability: It assumed that correlation was a constant rather than something mercurial. Investment banks would regularly phone Stanford's Duffie and ask him to come in and talk to them about exactly what Li's copula was. Every time, he would warn them that it was not suitable for use in risk management or valuation. In hindsight, ignoring those warnings looks foolhardy. But at the time, it was easy. Banks dismissed them, partly because the managers empowered to apply the brakes didn't understand the arguments between various arms of the quant universe.... One reason was that the outputs came from "black box" computer models and were hard to subject to a commonsense smell test. Another was that the quants, who should have been more aware of the copula's weaknesses, weren't the ones making the big asset-allocation decisions. Their managers, who made the actual calls, lacked the math skills to understand what the models were doing or how they worked. They could, however, understand something as simple as a single correlation number. That was the problem' (Salmon, 2009).

knowledge domain of the other, then they would not have engaged in costly activities that had zero or negative pay-off for both themselves and the project as a whole. (Any given proximate cause of a misalignment may be the terminus of a chain of distal events and conditions, a chain that is highly context specific and path dependent. Such a distal chain can involve conflicts of interest or other factors besides knowledge conditions, but, in a glitch, this causal chain creates alignment failure by generating a technical knowledge gap at a critical decision point.)

That precise proximate causation—ignorance of technical constraints across a knowledge specialization layer—is what marks out the glitch as a phenomenon distinct from other potential sources of mismatched actions. In contrast, conflicts of interest across boundaries can generate *cooperation failures*, which occur when the mismatch is due to a unit's calculation that the mismatched outcome, net of effort levels and rewards, is better for that unit than the properly aligned one. For example, LG's purchase of WebOS achieved poor results in adapting this superior interface to its 'smart TV' line because LG managers were incentivized to cram their own departments' features on to the phone at the expense of overall systems integration.[2] Achieving integration across the self-interest layers of a boundary requires different tools (e.g. monitoring or incentives) from those needed to integrate across disciplinary knowledge layers.

It is particularly important to distinguish glitches from coordination failures, which involve mutual ignorance across a boundary about the choices that each party has made, rather than about the technical constraints that each faces. In a coordination failure, one party 'zigs' while the other party 'zags' because a) the two actions are chosen simultaneously and b) either 'both parties zig' or 'both parties zag' would be suitable outcomes. In game-theoretic terms, simultaneity is an informational rather than a purely temporal property. If A places its choice in a sealed envelope on Monday, and B makes its choice on Wednesday without the first envelope being opened, then, effectively, A's and B's moves are simultaneous. Of course, temporal simultaneity itself may be the reason for informational simultaneity, and, in fact, the effect of simultaneity is formally described as causing a game to have imperfect information.

Coordination failures are about strategic uncertainty (Van Huyck et al., 1990), that is, not knowing what another player has done when there are multiple equilibria. Glitches are about technical uncertainty, not knowing

---

[2] 'On the engineering side, the webOS team also struggled with a culture clash of sorts that pitted company politics against its attempt to simplify the company's smart TV platform. Sources told me that LG had a policy in place to reward managers with bonuses or even promotions if their features were part of the final product. The result was a constant feature bloat, as everyone tried to add on one more thing' (Roettgers, 2014).

what the other party can do. Coordination failures can be dispelled by better communication, by preplanning the desired match, or by sequentializing the choices of the parties. None of these measures, however, is sufficient to dispel glitches, because the mismatch there results from unknowingly violating a pre-existing technical constraint on another party, not from conflicting with that party's contingent project-specific choice. In a coordination failure, if each party is required to guess about the other's action, then one might bring Phillips-head screws and the other a straight screwdriver, or one party might bring straight screws and the other a Phillips-head screwdriver. In a glitch, one party might bring Phillips-head screws and the other a hammer, because the former does not understand that only nails are appropriate for the job. Coordination failures represent the incompatibility of parties' choices from commonly understood, feasible action repertoires. Glitches represent mismatches caused by erroneous understandings of another party's repertoire.

Thus, coordination failures and glitches involve different kinds of knowledge gaps across boundaries. In the former case, the parties fail to share the kind of information which can be readily codified and whose implications are understood once it is attended to, given the initial common knowledge possessed by the two parties; for example, 'I'm going to finish my part of the job by Friday', 'We're using a 100 volt standard on our component', or 'I'm going to design the "customer" object class so it inherits the properties of the "region" to which it belongs'. In a coordination failure, the implications of these statements would have been immediately intelligible to the other party had they been transmitted and attended to; the information could be described as 'mobile' between the agents. In a glitch, by contrast, the gap between the parties consists of 'sticky' information (von Hippel, 1994), which cannot be readily transmitted and comprehended because of a lack of underlying specialized knowledge to provide context.[3] This type of knowledge gap can be overcome only by costly teaching and learning efforts. Glitches occur when these knowledge gaps go unrecognized by the parties on both sides of the barrier until they receive a bad surprise.

Puranam et al. (2012: 425) partly reinvent game theory ideas with their concept of 'epistemic uncertainty', which they define as a state where 'the optimal action of each agent depends on a prediction of what the other agent will do'. They use this notion to explain coordination failures as being caused by a lack of 'predictive knowledge' about what other agents will do. While this approach blurs a number of distinct game-theoretic issues—imperfect

---

[3] In economics, much (though not all) of the study of information assumes that information is mobile, and the problem is how to keep it secret or reveal it strategically. (This might be called the 'Hollywood' model of valuable information, where stealing the secret formula or blueprint is sufficient to make a fortune or change the balance of international power.) But in the study of education and human capital, knowledge transfer is generally assumed to be costly and laborious, and the strategy and technology management literatures usually focus on this 'sticky' case.

information, multiple equilibria, and equilibrium refinement—it is clear that it has no bearing on glitches because the theory assumes that agents are equally and perfectly capable of accomplishing any assigned task. Therefore, Puranam et al. (2012) has no scope for knowledge specialization or for one agent to pass another an intermediate output (e.g. a blueprint passed to a manufacturing engineer) that is outside the competence of the receiver to process. It rules out glitches by assumption.[4]

3.3 KNOWLEDGE INTEGRATION

The term 'knowledge integration' fills a number of different roles in the literature on capabilities. At the most basic level, it is sometimes used to describe a *process* of integration, and sometimes an *attribute*, an achieved level of integration. In this chapter I use the term 'integration' to describe processes and 'level of integration' to describe the corresponding attribute.

Beyond semantics, the context of application matters. This chapter focuses entirely on problems of design rather than invention, so there is no discussion of cross-disciplinary creativity; that is, the recombining of different pieces of specialized knowledge to create an entirely new category of artefact to serve either old or new purposes. Instead, this chapter focuses on the design and development of solutions after that general category has been invented or discovered—including the first model ever introduced in the category. So we will not be analysing questions such as how the concept of a ballistic-missile-launching, nuclear-powered submarine—combining missile technology, submarine technology, reactor technology, nuclear explosives technology, and game theory—was discovered as the solution to certain problems of nuclear deterrence. However, we will be analysing problems relevant to designing a specific example of such an artefact, problems that come from having to make all those domains work together. Our target of explanation, therefore, is not how the combination of any particular roster of specialty knowledge domains is discovered to be productive. Instead, we will study how, given this roster, the various specialists can work together to produce specific designed solutions.

---

[4] The paper is also equivocal about why all tasks would not always be accomplished; its initial definitions and distinctions rely on cooperation problems (agent incentives) to create a gap between task assignment and task accomplishment, but its later theory development assumes cooperation problems away without providing an alternative explanation for the gap. Hence, it is not clear why agents would not have perfect 'predictive knowledge' simply by relying on other agents to complete their assigned tasks. Its examples do not contain situations where there is more than one way for a task to be accomplished, which would give scope for coordination problems, but focus entirely on one-way tasks that are either finished or not.

Even within this restricted design context, differing concepts of knowledge integration are rife in the literature (Tell, 2011). The view taken here is that:

1. integration, in general, is the process of avoiding mismatches between the actions of collaborating differentiated individuals or subunits;

2. one of the boundary layers that often differentiates subunits is a disciplinary knowledge layer (A and B are trained and have experience in different specialties, such as marketing and engineering, or product design and manufacturing), rather than merely a task assignment layer (A and B share the same background and specialist knowledge, but each works on a different task), or a circumstantial information layer (A and B share the same background and specialist knowledge, but come upon different pieces of contingent environmental information such as different suppliers' queue lengths);

3. when such disciplinary knowledge boundary layers exist in a team then there is the possibility for one agent's actions to ignorantly violate the technical constraints of another agent across the boundary;

4. one method for reducing the incidence of such mistakes is to engage in 'knowledge integration' processes, which increase the level of shared knowledge between the units in question. Here, I take the view of 'knowledge integration' that Tell (2011: 24, original emphasis) characterizes as 'sharing or transferring knowledge', in contrast to two alternatives: as 'use of similar/related knowledge' or as 'the *combination* of *specialized, differentiated,* but *complementary* knowledge'. Here, knowledge integration is the sharing of complementary knowledge; other methods of combining knowledge besides sharing are forms of integration, but are not forms of knowledge integration;

5. there are two primary techniques for accomplishing this partial sharing of knowledge:
   a) education, where one specialty teaches the other about its domain. While the end result of such a process is a degree of despecialization of the learner, it need not be total; that is, the learner need not become the equal of the teacher in its expertise about the teacher's domain;
   b) codification of constraints, where one specialty invests in developing explicit menus or descriptions of the contours of what it can actually do. Again, these descriptions may fall far short of communicating the full description of what can and cannot be done by the codifying specialty, but they do increase the level of knowledge integration on the team;

6. knowledge integration is just one method of integrating differentially knowledge-specialized people or units. But, in certain circumstances (which are specified in Section 3.6 in the description of the black box principle), it may be the only practical option.

3.4 KNOWLEDGE SPECIALIZATION

As in Postrel (2002), I distinguish between knowledge specialization and task specialization. An individual's learning process is heavily affected by the context of what he has assimilated already, with prior items of knowledge forming the contextual 'docking points' for subsequent items to be learned. Some items of knowledge are learned together more cheaply than others because they share content-based affinities, such as common sets of under-lying concepts, joint definition in terms of a particular setting, relations of hierarchical subsumption, and so on. Other sets of knowledge items do not bear economies of joint learning. Learning about integration in calculus is much cheaper when learned in combination with differentiation, but there is no joint economy between learning integrals and learning the Napoleonic Code. Mastering a particular set of knowledge items because of their low joint cost of learning makes an individual knowledge specialized. By contrast, task specialization might be undertaken by an individual who is not very know-ledge specialized. The chief executive of a firm is doing one job, but calling on knowledge from multiple business disciplines as well as general knowledge about people, and so on. A private detective might specialize in matrimonial cases, but call on knowledge about psychology, surveillance, photography, accounting, and law.

With teams and units that are composed of individuals, this distinction easily generalizes. A group of polymer chemists will tend to share common conceptual maps and be able to share information about polymer chemistry at low cost while working jointly on a problem, but a polymer chemist, a mechanical engineer, and a salesman will occupy different 'thought worlds' and will have difficulty in communicating items from their particular domains while working together. Nevertheless, individuals or groups of similar special-ists can invest in learning outside their disciplines, and counterparts from different disciplines can invest in teaching them. Ventures in learning and teaching across disciplinary boundaries tend to be very costly, which is why knowledge specialties develop in the first place, and so these cross-disciplinary exercises usually end well short of both units knowing the same amount about a given domain. Instead, the learning specialist acquires a *partial* understand-ing of the other discipline.[5] As that understanding increases, the learner is becoming *less* knowledge specialized; a generalist would have equal under-standing of the two domains. Holding constant individual cognitive ability, there is a trade off between these two kinds of learning and teaching, because

---

[5] Collins and Evans (2007: 35, original emphasis) distinguish between *interactional* and *contributory* specialist expertise, where one possessing the former 'may be able to *understand* scientific things, and to *discuss* scientific things but is still not able to *do* scientific things' The kind of learning across specialties discussed here is likely interactional in this sense.

the more time and effort expended outside one's specialty the less there is available to strengthen one's specialist know-how, and vice versa.

A key point is that the same task may be addressed by problem-solvers with varying degrees of knowledge specialization. Two economists, who are each equally good at theory and econometrics, could write a paper testing a particular hypothesis with a set of data, but so could a team comprising a theory specialist and an econometrics specialist. The former team would be less 'deep' in each specialized area, but would find it easier to understand one another; the latter would be better at solving problems in each individual domain, but would have more trouble communicating information about their separate pieces of the job.

Thus, an individual (or group of similarly knowledge-specialized individuals) has a level of ability to solve problems presented to it in its domain. The more (and more difficult) problems it can solve, the higher is its *specialist capability*. At the same time, that knowledge-specialized individual or group has some knowledge of the problem-solving capabilities of differently specialized units, based on what it knows about those other domains. We call A's ability to predict whether B can successfully solve a given problem A's *trans-specialist understanding* of B. Specialist capability and trans-specialist understanding are two different kinds of knowledge, one directed toward solving problems in one's own domain, and the other useful for estimating whether a differently specialized unit can handle specific problems passed to it.

3.5 A FORMAL MODEL OF INTER-SPECIALIST PROBLEM-SOLVING

The model here is a variation of the approach in Postrel (2002). Suppose there are two specialized units both of whose contributions are needed to accomplish a given set of project objectives. These units can be thought of as individuals or specialized departments, as previously outlined, and are assumed to be knowledge specialized in distinct domains. For concreteness, it might help to think of a product development project in which one of the units is a product technology/marketing group and the other a manufacturing group, but the analysis would apply equally well to a user domain expert and a software designer, or a film screenwriter and director. The project requires problem-solving in each domain, with a unit receiving a task in its domain as part of the design process. Importantly, we assume that there are no conflicts of interest between the units so that each acts to maximize the pay-off of the entire team.

We first modify Postrel (2002) by making explicit the relationship between problem difficulty and specialist capability. Define y as the minimum performance level asked of a unit in solving its task x chosen from a design space X. For any x sent to it, the unit can perform at a level z(x). It succeeds if z(x) $\geq$ y. The higher is y, the harder it is for the unit to succeed at any given task. Now p(y) is the probability that the unit can succeed on any random task x, which is a decreasing function of the required performance level y. Different units will have different p(y) functions, and each has a range between zero and 1.

Each unit also has a degree of trans-specialist understanding of the other unit. Let h_{ij} be unit i's ability to predict whether unit j can succeed at its task; h_{ij} is the probability that i is correct when it says that j can or cannot accomplish a task, and $1-h_{ij}$ is the probability that i is wrong in its assessment.[6] One can think of i receiving a zero-one 'signal' about whether j can perform a task x and h_{ij} = Pr(j can do x | i's signal is one) = Pr(j can't do x | i's signal is zero). h_{ij} ranges from ½ to 1, with ½ being no TSU and 1 being perfect TSU. (h cannot go below ½ because equal probabilities of being right or wrong is the least-informative signal possible; a value below ½ would allow the unit to invert the signal and make better-than-random predictions.) For simplicity, we assume also that each unit is a perfect judge of its own ability to accomplish a given task x.

The main postulate we are trying to capture in our idealized model is that sticky specialized knowledge is hard to transmit across disciplinary boundaries. This is where we get the imperfect nature of trans-specialist understanding with h < 1 in general. If we allowed the two units to go back and forth during the project and somehow overcome this limitation, we would be violating this core, empirically compelling, assumption. In fact, empirical study of extended back-and-forth exchanges between different specialties finds that breaking the process into multiple steps of proposal, evaluation, counterproposal, evaluation, and so on, does not suffice to overcome the knowledge barriers and prevent glitches (Hoopes and Postrel, 1999). One reason for this is that, in many cases, messages from one specialty to another are not interpretable or even comprehensible by the recipients, and the message senders are highly imperfect at detecting and correcting misapprehensions.

The model captures this dynamic in a very simple manner: all communication occurs in one step, with a single design proposal from one unit to another that is either accepted or rejected by the receiving unit. This proposal includes a task x for the receiving unit to accomplish. (For example, a proposed product design requires a manufacturing unit to be able to produce that specific configuration x at acceptable cost and quality.) If the proposal is accepted by the receiving unit, then the project goes forward; if it is rejected the project is killed (the window is closed). A launched project earns a positive pay-off of 1 if, and only if, it meets the constraints of both units (which means

---

[6] For simplicity, h is assumed to be independent of y, so that a unit can guess equally well about tasks at all difficulty levels, and it is assumed that the rate of false positives is the same as the rate of false negatives so that a single parameter h can capture both.

the receiver must be able to accomplish the task x embedded in the proposal); otherwise it incurs negative pay-offs. A killed project earns a pay-off of 0.

It follows from these assumptions that the proposal receiver should launch the project if, and only if, it knows that it can accomplish the task x embedded in the proposal. If it cannot accomplish x, then it should kill the project. From the proposer's point of view, it wants to pick a design that meets its own constraint and also is feasible for the other specialty to handle. Since any specialist can always tell whether its own constraint is satisfied by a proposed design, the proposer will never make a mistake about that. (We will assume that the project constraints are not so rigorous that it is impossible for either specialty to meet them; the alternative is an uninteresting trivial case.) Thus, the only way the team can fail to achieve a positive pay-off from project launch is if the proposer mistakenly sends over a proposal that the receiver cannot handle. Making such a mistake is the kind of misalignment—a glitch—that was discussed at the start of the chapter. The expected value π of the process is therefore $1-\text{Pr}$ (proposer sends a project that the receiver cannot handle).

Without loss of generality, suppose unit 1 is the proposer and unit 2 is the receiver. Unit 1 submits a particular proposal x if and only if it knows that it can accomplish task x at performance level y_1 and it believes that unit 2 can accomplish task x at performance level y_2. The possible events that can happen are: a) 1 is correct in its assessment of 2's ability to handle x and the product is launched with pay-off 1; or b) 1 is incorrectly optimistic about 2's ability to handle x and 2 kills the project with pay-off 0. Event a) occurs with probability $p(y_2)^*h_{12}$ and event b) occurs with probability $[1-p(y_2)]^*[1-h_{12}]$. It follows that

$$\pi = p(y_2)^*h_{12} / \{p(y_2)^*h_{12} + [1 - p(y_2)]^*[1 - h_{12}]\} \qquad (3.1)$$

where π is the fraction of good proposals out of all proposals.

3.6 THE BLACK BOX PRINCIPLE

So far we have largely followed Postrel (2002), and a key implication of the model as described there is the 'black-box principle', which says that 2's specialist capability, $p(y_2)$, and 1's TSU of 2, h_{12}, are largely *substitutes* for one another in producing expected pay-offs at all but very stringent performance requirements, which means they are highly substitutable at all but very low prior probabilities of project success.[7] For example, to maintain an expected value of ½ for the project, the marginal rate of substitution between

---

[7] To be clear, I am referring to substitutes here in the sense of the theory of neoclassical production functions (e.g., Varian, 1978: 44–5) and not in the sense of the supermodularity in organizations literature (Milgrom and Roberts, 1992: 108).

Steven Postrel

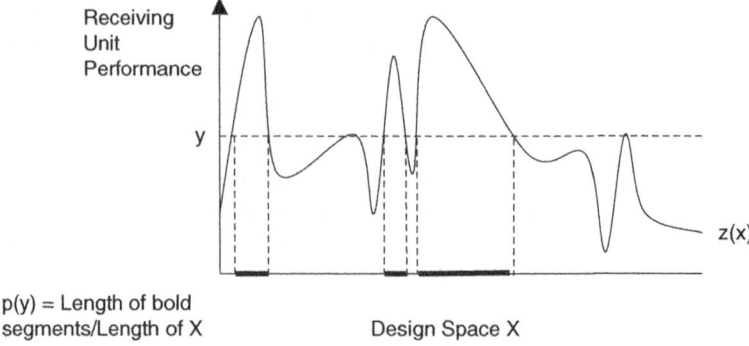

Figure 3.1. Proposing unit design space and receiving unit performance

the two kinds of knowledge is a constant –1, with p = 1 – h for all h between ½ and 1, so they are perfect substitutes. At higher expected values, the trade off between p and h actually becomes 'hyper-substitutable' as the two forms of knowledge interfere with one another's marginal benefit.

A heuristic understanding of the black box principle can be gathered from Figure 3.1.

The horizontal axis displays the design space X for a proposing unit. Each point on the axis is a different potential design. The vertical axis measures the level of performance of the receiving unit for each possible design, as shown by the curve z(x). Given a minimum performance target y, only those designs x for which z(x) exceeds y, depicted by the bold segments on the design axis, are good for the team. Any proposal outside the bold regions results in project failure. Thus, the specialist's capability at handling any random design, p(y), is the ratio of the bold segment lengths to the length of the entire design space X.

If we were to shift the z(x) function upward at some or all points, then the receiving specialist would have more specialist capability and p(y) would increase. We could achieve a similar effect by lowering y, the required performance. The proposer's trans-specialist understanding h is its probability of correctly guessing that any given x that is thought about is either in or not in one of the bold segments. As these bold segments grow to occupy more of the horizontal axis, even a bad guesser is likely to be successful in sending something that works to the receiver. Similarly, a very good guesser can achieve a high success rate even if the bold segments are small.

We could imagine h developing from the proposer learning something of the receiver's domain, along the lines of Collins and Evans's (2007) 'interactional expertise'. This process would involve a partial immersion of the proposer in the discourse of the receiver's domain. Alternatively, we could imagine the receiver developing some kinds of navigation tools or menus that *codify* and *structure* the design space for the proposer, creating orderings or distance metrics that group together designs with higher performance z(x). If there were some way to index designs x and say 'all x between 0 and .45 are viable for target y', then as long as the proposer can find an x in that range that also satisfies its own specialized problem the project will succeed. Both of these processes for generating trans-specialist understanding—immersion and codification—are likely to be costly.

The importance of the black box principle is that it helps answer, in a precise but somewhat counterintuitive way, the first managerial question raised in this chapter: How thick should the knowledge boundary be between two units in the face of potential misalignments; that is, how differentially specialized ought they to be given the risk that poor trans-specialist understanding may give rise to glitches? What the principle shows is that reducing the incidence of glitches need not require eschewing knowledge specialization by investing in costly learning across disciplinary boundaries. Rather, the substitutability of specialist capability and trans-specialist understanding implies that, with enough specialist capability—enough ability to handle random tasks thrown into a receiving unit's 'in-basket'—a team can avoid glitches with low or even zero levels of trans-specialist understanding. Since, by definition, knowledge specialization is easier than trans-specialist learning, this approach should be taken wherever possible.

Note, however, that the level of specialist capability p is a negative function of the performance requirement y. This implies that a specialist's ability to handle random tasks is a relative thing, dependent not only on intrinsic knowledge but also on just what one means by 'handle'. At low enough target performance levels, not much specialist know-how may be needed to have a high probability of successfully accomplishing random problem-solving tasks, and at high enough target performance levels, even a very skilled specialist unit may have a low probability of accomplishment on random tasks. This relationship implies that the need for trans-specialist understanding at a given level of specialist know-how is likely to increase as performance requirements increase. Conversely, if a specialty advances rapidly against static or slower-growing performance requirements, then the need for trans-specialist understanding may decline.

The implications of these ideas are pursued in much greater depth in Postrel (2002), but one broad conclusion is that the vast majority of interactions in the economy function quite well at near-zero levels of trans-specialist understanding. It is only when specialist knowledge is pushed hard by demanding performance requirements that it pays to invest in costly learning across specialty domains. For example, dinner menus are usually planned without worrying about the details of laundering technology, since any spills or stains can be taken care of adequately. But, in the case of large parties, hosts who have white furniture often refuse to serve red wine because they understand that there is a good chance that a stain will be created that cannot be easily 'handled' by available cleaning technology. Less picturesquely, application programmers can get away with knowing little about the workings of the underlying operating system software and the hardware on which their code runs so long as their programs are not expected to run too fast or handle large amounts of data. But if performance requirements are raised, then they may well have to tailor their code to work around the slowest or most overload-prone functions of the system's infrastructure. Similarly, a product designer may not have to know much about manufacturing issues if the manufacturing unit has strong know-how relative to cost and quality targets. But if the manufacturer has less know-how, or the product must be produced at very low cost and/or very high quality, then it may be necessary for the designer to try to choose a design that it believes will be easier to make. For that belief to be accurate, trans-specialist understanding is required. Management scholars tend to over-sample situations where trans-specialist understanding matters, since these are the situations in which adroit management of interactions is more likely to matter.

3.7 THE STICKY INFORMATION PRINCIPLE

Having addressed the first managerial question posed at the beginning of the chapter on boundary thickness, we turn to the second question about which unit of a pair of specialized joint problem-solvers ought to take the lead. Recall that our model abstracts from multi-stage communication dynamics between the specialties and summarizes the outcome of such a process with a one-shot proposal from 1 to 2 or 2 to 1, with the receiver accepting or rejecting and no further opportunities for communication. Given this abstraction, an agent 'going first' or 'sending a proposal' should be interpreted as that agent's specialty concerns being prioritized or taken as given by its partner in the course of their give and take, and not necessarily as a literal first move (although allowing an agent to 'set the agenda' or place fundamental con-straints on a design at the outset is a natural way to implement letting that agent 'go first' in the sense of the formal model).

We can apply our formal model to answer this question directly. Let π_{ij} be the expected pay-off where unit i proposes a solution to the receiver unit j and we have

$$\pi_{12} - \pi_{21} = \{p(y_2)^*h_{12}/\{p(y_2)^*h_{12} + [1 - p(y_2)]^*[1 - h_{12}]\}\} \\ - \{p(y_1)^*h_{21}/\{p(y_1)^*h_{21} + [1 - p(y_1)]^*[1 - h_{21}]\}\} \tag{3.2}$$

In order to clarify our analysis we will consider separately the two different ways in which units' knowledge varies. First, suppose the two units had the same specialist capability $p(y_1) = p(y_2) = p$. Then the sign of (3.2) reduces to the sign of

$$p(1 - p)(h_{12} - h_{21}) \tag{3.3}$$

and since p lies in the [0,1] interval, by definition, this reduces to the sign of $h_{12}-h_{21}$. What this means is that 1 should be the proposer if and only if 1's ability to guess whether 2 can handle a given task is better than 2's ability to guess whether 1 can handle a given task.

I call this the 'sticky information principle' after von Hippel's (1994) hypothesis (backed by a case study) that problem-solving should move to the locus of sticky information, meaning that it should move into the hands of people who know about the part of the problem that is hardest to communicate outside its specialized domain. This is exactly what (3.3) implies, since 1's information being 'stickier' than 2's is identical to $h_{12} > h_{21}$ so that 2 finds it harder to guess about 1 than vice versa. One difference with von Hippel's analysis is that the model does not specify *why* h_{12} and h_{21} might differ; one interpretation is intrinsic stickiness a la von Hippel, but another might be an inappropriately low level of effort devoted to generating one of the h values even though the underlying knowledge would not be especially hard to learn. In addition, variation in human learning ability might cause variation in relative h levels across teams; if the manufacturing group at firm A is especially quick to grasp product performance issues, for example, then they might have higher trans-specialist understanding of design than the designers at A have of manufacturing, while at a competing firm B the opposite might be true.

In this model, the logic of the sticky information principle is clear. If there is an equal need to steer around the limitations of each specialty (as we have assumed with a common p), then the specialty that is less abstruse to its counterpart is the one that should receive the proposal. This policy minimizes the chance of getting an infeasible proposal and a zero pay-off since the proposer has the higher trans-specialist understanding.

The advice given by the sticky information principle may not be naturally followed in real-life design problems since the more articulate and better-understood specialty may be expected by all to set the agenda and structure the problem-solving process. That would be a plausible mistake. In fact, the less-understood unit ought to take the lead, picking designs that get around its intrinsic weaknesses and being more likely to guess correctly how to avoid stumping its partner. On the other hand, it is possible that the process 'naturally' migrates problem-solving to the stickier of the two knowledge domains even if the initial assignment is incorrect, as the premium for trans-specialist understanding becomes more visible when the process snags.

3.8 THE POWERBOAT–SAILBOAT RULE

Now we consider the opposite kind of knowledge difference across units, namely difference in specialist capabilities. To isolate this effect, we assume that trans-specialist understanding is the same across the two units, that is, that $h_{12} = h_{21} = h$. Now the sign of (3.2) reduces to the sign of

$$h(1 - h)[p(y_2) - p(y_1)] \qquad (3.4)$$

which means that 1 should propose to 2 if and only if 1 has a *lower* specialist capability than 2. I call this the 'powerboat–sailboat rule' by analogy with the nautical law that a less manoeuvrable sailing craft has right of way over a more manoeuvrable powerboat if the two are on converging paths.

The model logic for this finding is straightforward. As long as trans-specialist understanding is imperfect, with $h < 1$, then the way to minimize the odds of an infeasible proposal being made is to let the unit with the highest chance of *not* being able to handle a *random* task steer around its own limitations by non-randomly choosing a task it knows it can accomplish. Having a design that satisfies its own more-stringent limitations for feasibility, it can then propose that design and its embedded task x to the other specialist, who will have a better shot at success by dint of its superior capability. For a hypothetical example, consider a restaurant that varies its menu daily and sources fresh ingredients from a nearby market, with one chef who sets the menu and one who goes out to procure ingredients. Suppose both understand the other's capabilities equally. If the procurement chef is very good at hunting down a wide range of inputs at affordable prices (and/or the local ingredient market is well provisioned), then the menu ought to be set first and then the ingredients found to satisfy it; if the procurement chef's ability to find ingredients is lower, then the purchases should be made first and the menu adapted to fit the limitations of what has been acquired.

Once again, the advice generated by the model is not necessarily what real world organizations would naturally do without understanding the analysis. In many organizations, the most capable and high-reputation units accumulate power and credibility and are asked to take the lead in joint problem-solving. The false intuition involved is that since they know more, their judgements are more likely to be correct. But since the weaker specialties' involvement cannot be avoided, giving the more capable units more freedom to structure the joint solution does not really give those units more power; their ideas must still pass through the 'bottleneck' represented by the less capable units. Instead, the more capable units' superior know-how should be exploited by having them *adapt* to the solutions that their more constrained partners are able to propose.[8]

---

[8] Goldratt and Cox (1992), in their popular book *The Goal*, present a fictional narrative in which the importance of eliminating successive bottlenecks eventually drives a plant manager to adopt ideas similar to the powerboat–sailboat rule.

3.9 SEQUENTIAL ORDERING OF TASKS

The basic model and analysis of (3.2) generates two useful heuristics—the sticky information rule and the powerboat–sailboat rule—for deciding which units should propose designs and which should receive them, bearing in mind that every proposal contains within it an embedded specialty task for the receiver to accomplish. Since each of these rules was developed by assuming away one possible difference in the units' knowledge profiles, it is natural to ask what the model says about cases where both specialist capability and trans-specialist understanding differ between specialties.

If one specialty has both lower specialist capability and higher trans-specialist understanding, then both rules point in the same direction: that unit ought to propose designs to its partner. But if one unit has both higher specialist capability and higher trans-specialist understanding then the two rules point in opposite directions and it becomes a quantitative question that can be calculated using (3.2) within the idealized model. If the sticky information effect is bigger than the powerboat–sailboat effect, then the more knowledgeable unit ought to propose designs, while if the powerboat–sailboat effect is bigger then the less-knowledgeable unit should be the proposer.

In the restaurant example, if the menu-setter is a) less capable at solving her demand/competition problem than the ingredient-procurer is at solving his sourcing problems, and b) the ingredient-procurer finds it more difficult to understand the demand/competition conditions set by culinary trends and rivals' menus than it is for the menu-setter to understand probable ingredient availabilities and prices, then both rules point in the direction of the menu-setter proposing ingredient purchasing lists to the procurer. If a) and b) were reversed, then both rules say that the ingredient-procurer should tell the menu-setter what he has to work with. If only one of a) or b) were reversed, however, then the rules point in opposite directions and a quantitative assessment of equation (3.2) is needed to determine which rule is more important in that particular situation.

From an empirical point of view, merely observing who takes the lead and what happens on particular projects is insufficient to 'confirm' or 'refute' these recommendations. The inference problem occurs because 1) we do not observe what would have happened if the proposer role had been given to the opposite party, and 2) the effects of either protocol are stochastic. Furthermore, since this is a normative theory, if we did observe firms deviating from their prescriptions we would not be able to tell whether this was a fault in the theory or in the firms' management, and, if the latter, we could not be sure (without a powerful research design) whether the problem was a mis-estimate of the parameters ($p(y)$ and h) or a misunderstanding of the theory.

3.10 CONCLUSION

When diversely specialized units separated by knowledge boundaries must jointly solve challenging design problems, their success is limited by the possibility that they will generate glitches. Mutual incomprehension of one another's technical constraints is a natural by-product of efficient learning, that is, of the economies of knowledge specialization that create disciplines in the first place. 'Managing' them by wiping them out through despecialization is unlikely to be a practical solution.

Instead, managers should bear in mind the basic principles of interaction among knowledge specialists. First, the black box principle implies that investing in trans-specialist understanding pays only when specialist capability cannot be improved enough to overpower the needed level of performance. Second, the sticky information rule tells us that groups whose specialties are the most opaque to the other members of the team ought to have a leading role in the design process. Third, the powerboat–sailboat rule tells us that groups with the lowest ability to solve random problems assigned to them also ought to be given more up-front design authority. None of these prescriptions is patently obvious without an analysis along the lines of the model presented here.

Finally, it should be remembered that glitches are only one boundary problem that teams face and that managers need many other tools in order to fend off cooperation and coordination problems, as well as to make sure that all units share the same interpretation of what their common goal weights and priorities should be. Dealing with so many factors generally is a difficult task, but for narrow contexts it may be possible to formally model all of these issues (e.g. Postrel, 2009).

4

Relating Knowledge Integration and Absorptive Capacity

Knowledge Boundaries and Reflective Agency in Path-Dependent Processes

Christian Berggren, Jörg Sydow, and Fredrik Tell

4.1 INTRODUCTION

Absorptive capacity is a key concept in the literature on organizations and innovation (Cohen and Levinthal, 1990) and, according to the Web of Science, in September 2015, was referred to in more than 3,100 articles in social science. Absorptive capacity is generally understood as the organizational ability to absorb and utilize new external knowledge and apply it in novel processes and products. This perception implies a dynamic view of boundary crossing and capacity to acquire and transform knowledge originating outside the organization. Knowledge integration, another key concept in knowledge-based theories of the firm, was introduced by strategic management scholars in the 1990s as a more generic notion to analyse the integration of specialized knowledge. In the classical formulation proposed by Grant (1996), knowledge integration refers to the means, routines, systems, and standards used by individuals in organizations to coordinate their activities with minimum knowledge overlap in order to execute the firm's value-adding processes efficiently. This idea has produced a rich stream of research on knowledge absorption and transformation (Tell, 2011).

Absorptive capacity emphasizes the role played by prior knowledge in the search for, assessment and absorption of new knowledge external to the focal firm. Absorptive capacity helps to explain issues related to how 'knowledge paths' evolve, that is, how the accumulation of domain-specific knowledge progresses. However, this idea needs to be contrasted and compared with other knowledge-based concepts to enable an understanding of the development of solutions to complex problems involving an extended scope of specialist knowledge.

This chapter analyses and compares absorptive capacity, knowledge integration, and related notions. The purpose is both to contribute to clarity and rigour in their use, and to suggest a synthesis, implying a dynamic understanding of knowledge integration processes that acknowledges the roles of both structure and agency (Giddens, 1984). Specifically, we address the following questions:

- How are knowledge integration and absorptive capacity related to each other, and how do they inform each other?
- How can the concepts of knowledge integration and absorptive capacity be applied to develop a theory of 'knowledge boundaries' and organizational change, which could inform work on path-dependence and dynamic capabilities?
- What are the implications of agency in such a dynamic conceptualization; that is, who initiates and conducts change along or beyond established organizational and knowledge-based paths, and how do various types of agency enable and constrain the acquisition and integration of new knowledge?

The chapter is structured as follows. Section 4.2 examines the literatures on knowledge integration and absorptive capacity and enquires particularly into how they are related. Section 4.3 discusses two related concepts—organizational path-dependence and dynamic capabilities—which, in different ways, address the tension between stability and change in innovation processes and their knowledge bases. Section 4.4 contributes to this discussion of change by analysing the role of agency at different levels in the organization, and in their environment. Section 4.5 concludes the chapter by suggesting a preliminary synthesis. Here, the evolutionary dimension of absorptive capacity is used to inject a dynamic view into the scope dimension of knowledge integration, and to discuss the role of actors and the focal organization in knowledge development processes that go beyond the firm's established knowledge boundaries.

4.2 ABSORPTIVE CAPACITY AND KNOWLEDGE INTEGRATION—BOUNDARY IMPLICATIONS

4.2.1 Knowledge Integration and the Role of Scope

According to knowledge-based theories of the firm, the coordination of specialized and distributed knowledge is a central problem in modern economies

(Demsetz, 1991; Kogut and Zander, 1992; Grant, 1996; Nickerson and Zenger, 2004). This means that firms need to integrate increasingly specialized individuals and domains of knowledge in order to produce goods and services in an efficient way (Winter, 1991). While the specialization of knowledge facilitates deep learning and opportunities for efficiency gains, increasing specialization creates boundaries and potential barriers to trans-specialist learning and, by implication, obstacles to its efficient integration (Hoopes and Postrel, 1999; Postrel, 2002). Thus, it is crucial for firms to manage this knowledge scope and to understand how scope affects the efficiency/effectiveness of knowledge integration.

Work on knowledge integration identifies a number of mechanisms related to the integration of specialized knowledge and the contingencies affecting the choice of these mechanisms. Tell's (2011) overview of the literature identifies three types of contingencies: task characteristics, knowledge characteristics, and relational characteristics. Regarding task characteristics, Grant (1996) discusses how interdependencies affect the use of specific integration mechanisms such as rules and directives, sequencing, routines, and group problem-solving. In a more elaborate scheme, Grandori (2001) outlines how knowledge complexity, knowledge differentiation, and conflicts of interest may affect the choice of governance mechanisms such as hierarchy, rules, property rights sharing, communication networks, knowledge integrators, teams, and communities (see also Postrel, 2002; Carlile, 2004; Enberg et al., 2006).

So far most of the research in this field tends to focus on knowledge integration as a static problem, that is, a problem of scope or the differentiation and integration of existing specialist knowledge necessary to deliver products, services, and solutions in a cost efficient way. Berggren et al. (2011) suggest the need for dynamic analysis to understand and explain the rates and directions of innovation based on the creation and accumulation of new knowledge over time. Successful innovation requires a combination of differentiated and novel knowledge, which emphasizes the need to combine scope and time (evolution) perspectives in knowledge integration.

4.2.2 Absorptive Capacity and the Role of Prior Knowledge

The crossing of knowledge-related boundaries is a main focus of the absorptive capacity literature. However, in contrast to knowledge integration theories, most research inspired by the concept of absorptive capacity is devoted to knowledge development over time, and how prior knowledge and knowledge processes affect and direct the absorption of new and external knowledge.

According to the classical article by Cohen and Levinthal (1990: 128), absorptive capacity refers to 'the ability of a firm to recognize the value of new, external information, assimilate it, and apply it to commercial ends'. Cohen and Levinthal focus on technical and scientific knowledge and suggest that firms' investments in research and development (R&D) lead to both greater capacity for generating new products and processes, and capabilities that help the future integration of external knowledge. Based on theories of learning, Cohen and Levinthal (1990: 128) emphasize that 'the ability to evaluate and utilize outside knowledge is largely a function of the level of prior related knowledge'. The emphasis on prior knowledge informs an understanding of firm development as generative and dynamic, but simultaneously confining and narrowing: 'These two features of absorptive capacity— cumulativeness and its effect on expectation formation—imply that its development is domain-specific and is path- or history-dependent' (Cohen and Levinthal, 1990: 136). Moreover, 'the cumulative quality of absorptive capacity and its role in conditioning the updating of expectations are forces that tend to confine firms to operating in a particular technological domain' (Cohen and Levinthal, 1990: 137), a self-reinforcing behaviour that can result in lockout from non-related areas: 'lack of investment in an area of expertise early on may foreclose the future development of a technical capability in that area... when new opportunities subsequently emerge, the firm may not appreciate them' (Cohen and Levinthal, 1990: 136).

Cohen and Levinthal (1990: 150) conclude by highlighting an unresolved agency problem:

> When, however, a firm wishes to acquire and use knowledge that is unrelated to its ongoing activity, then the firm must dedicate effort exclusively to creating absorptive capacity (i.e., absorptive capacity is not a by-product). In this case, absorptive capacity may not even occur to the firm as an investment alternative.

The notion of absorptive capacity has inspired research in several areas (for reviews, see Lane et al., 2006; Volberda et al., 2010). A frequently cited contribution is Lane and Lubatkin's (1998: 462) paper on relative absorptive capacity, which presents a study of partner learning in interorganizational alliances. In their study the unit of analysis shifts 'from the firm to the "student-teacher" pairing (the learning dyad)'. In their study, 'absolute absorptive capacity', measured by R&D intensity, is less important for explaining alliance-related learning than the organizational similarities of the partners involved, which is a relative attribute. Lane and Lubatkin (1998: 473) state that:

> Cohen and Levinthal view the role of prior relevant technological knowledge as paramount and discuss the role of knowledge-processing systems only in terms of internal communication for sharing knowledge. Absent from their theory, but central to ours, is the argument that valuable knowledge tends to be embedded in specific knowledge-processing systems.

This emphasis on the organizational embeddedness of knowledge reinforces our understanding of absorptive capacity as a path-dependent phenomenon. Not only are firms restricted to cognitive domains that are related to their own but also—if they need to acquire knowledge from outside partners—they are confined to learning from partners with similar organizational systems.

According to a more open-ended interpretation suggested by Zahra and George (2002: 198), absorptive capacity can be perceived as consisting of four capabilities or activities: acquisition, assimilation, transformation, and exploitation of knowledge. Instead of viewing absorptive capacity as a 'unidirectional and patterned developmental path' dependent on prior knowledge, Zahra and George propose that it should be interpreted as a 'multidirectional and nonpatterned (fluid) developmental path (locus of search is continually redefined)'. This is somewhat removed from the original concept. In addition to Cohen and Levinthal's interest in industry conditions external to the organization, Zara and George's reconceptualization underlines the importance of endogenous contingencies, especially the importance of 'broader managerial roles in influencing knowledge search patterns' (Zahra and George, 2002: 198). This emphasis on management activity highlights the unresolved agency problem in Cohen and Levinthal (1990), which is related to the potential effects of scope on knowledge absorption.

4.2.3 Relating Knowledge Integration and Absorptive Capacity

Figure 4.1 provides a simple depiction of the concepts of knowledge integration and absorptive capacity in relation to the requirements for boundary-crossing capacity over time. One such requirement is knowledge scope, that is, the differentiated and complex knowledge that must be integrated. The other

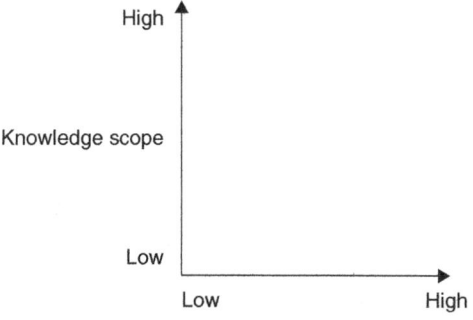

Figure 4.1. Knowledge dimensions affecting the capacity to cross knowledge boundaries over time

dimension refers to knowledge absorption and the relative distance of the new knowledge from the existing knowledge. These two dimensions describe a field characterized by, at least partly, opposing forces, which create tensions and contradictions in organizations.

The absorptive capacity approach builds on learning theories to explain how firms keep abreast of new knowledge in specific domains. Drawing upon Cyert and March (1963) and subsequent literature (e.g. Levitt and March, 1988; Levinthal and March, 1993), this approach recognizes that when organizations try to learn and to solve problems they tend to look for solutions and knowledge closely related to what they already know. This path-dependent search for related knowledge is justified by the fact that only a few or no boundaries exist between their current knowledge and the required knowledge, which increases the ease with which organizations can absorb and integrate the new knowledge. In the case of more distant search, thicker boundaries create difficulties for firms to understand and assimilate the needed knowledge. A generalized prediction based on absorptive capacity is that firms will tend to develop the capacity to accumulate deep knowledge in relatively close knowledge domains over time.

The knowledge integration approach, which complements the absorptive capacity perspective, focuses on the implications of knowledge specialization. This approach is concerned mainly with knowledge scope and the processes and mechanisms used by firms to integrate differentiated and complex knowledge at a specific point in time (Grant, 1996; Grandori, 2001; Postrel, 2002; Nickerson and Zenger, 2004). The knowledge integration approach suggests that similar and simple (in terms of interdependencies) knowledge creates few boundary problems and can be integrated using low-cost and standardized mechanisms. In contrast, differentiated and complex knowledge requires task-specific and communication-intensive mechanisms to bridge the related knowledge boundaries (Carlile, 2002; Bechky, 2003b). Complementing the absorptive capacity perspective, the knowledge integration approach predicts that firms will develop mechanisms to facilitate the integration of various types of distinct knowledge predicated on their organizational needs. However, the literature on knowledge integration largely neglects the dynamics involved when capabilities change over time (Berggren et al., 2011).

The contrast between these two concepts in the knowledge-based theory of the firm calls for a differentiated discussion of organizational change and inertia, how new knowledge is integrated and absorbed across boundaries, and the possible role of agency in such knowledge-based change processes. In Section 4.3 we discuss organizational path-dependence and dynamic capability as two ways of understanding change; the first emphasizes the increasing constraints on change over time, the second is focused on building the capacities to overcome these constraints.

4.3 THE PROBLEM OF CHANGE: PATH-DEPENDENCE AND DYNAMIC CAPABILITIES

4.3.1 Path-Dependence and the Accumulation of Change Constraints

Studies of organizational path-dependence complement traditional research on path-dependence in relation to technologies (David, 1985; Arthur, 1994) and institutions (North, 1990; Pierson, 2000), and provide insights into the cumulative process of knowledge development in and among organizations (Sydow et al., 2009; Burger and Sydow, 2014). Three different phases in this process have been identified (Sydow et al., 2009). Phase I, the pre-formation phase, is characterized by a largely unrestricted scope for action, in which organizational choices cannot be predicted based on prior events or initial conditions. However, this phase is influenced by the past: all choices are framed historically and, therefore, in some way, they are imprinted. In Phase II, the range of organizational options narrows increasingly, which makes it progressively more difficult to reverse the initial choice. In this path formation phase, a new regime takes over, and the dynamics of self-reinforcing processes set in. Arthur (1994) has elaborated on these driving forces as increasing returns. This notion highlights positive feedback processes in which an increase in one particular variable leads to further increases in this variable. The economic and institutional studies mentioned earlier identify several types of self-reinforcing dynamics—coordination effects, complementarities, learning effects, and adaptive expectations—which are considered to govern path-dependent processes within and among organizations. The notions of increasing returns or positive feedback point to the benefits of these self-reinforcing processes when a specific pattern of action, knowledge, or routine is used. Eventually, a dominant organizational solution emerges, rendering the whole process ever more difficult to reverse. In this phase, decision processes and action patterns are still contingent, although choices, albeit constrained, are possible. In Phase III the effectiveness of one or several of these self-reinforcing mechanisms implies that the organization or inter-organizational network has become locked in, and there are no longer available alternatives (Schreyögg et al., 2011; Burger and Sydow, 2014).

So far, only a few authors, for example Nooteboom (1997), Eriksson et al. (2000), and Coombs and Hull (1998), explicitly discuss the path-dependent development of organizational or organizationally embedded *knowledge*. Debates on the evolution of knowledge commonly refer—as do the first two papers cited above—to path-dependence in the metaphorical sense that history matters. However, Coombs and Hull (1998) point to the prominent and possibly self-reinforcing role of organization-specific routines, when a firm's knowledge base develops in a path-dependent manner. While none of these authors mentions the concepts of absorptive capacity or knowledge integration, Coombs and Hall adopt a practice perspective, which, because of the agency implied, allows for the intentional shaping of the knowledge base, despite path dependencies.

Organizational path-dependence theory emphasizes the power of cumulativeness, from the initial conditions in the first phase, through self-reinforcement in the second phase, to final lock-in (see also Garud et al., 2010). In the context of this chapter, it should be noted that potentially every knowledge integration activity, including transfer or sharing, combining, recombining, or adapting knowledge, *can* be a source of organizational path-dependence and, as such, shapes the development of a particular knowledge path within or among organizations. These activities are more likely to be sources of path-dependence the more often they recur and extend across time and space, that is, they appear as more or less institutionalized social practices, enabled and restrained by structures of the organization, its subsystems, or the network or field in which the organization is embedded (Giddens, 1984).

According to classical path-dependence theory, only one path is available for an organization in the lock-in phase. However, building on Giddens's (1984) argument that 'knowledgeable agents' have to reproduce the organizational path, recent contributions also allow organizational agency in this phase of a path-dependent process. Similar to the case of organizational routines (Feldman and Pentland, 2003), agents may devise idiosyncratic ways to deviate from this path when 'performing' it. In addition, organizational agents may strategically extend or modify this path and, under exceptional circumstances, even create a new one (cf. Garud et al., 2010; Sydow et al., 2012). This injection of agency into path-dependence, including in the lock-in phase, is related to the issue with which Cohen and Levinthal (1990: 150) conclude their paper: 'When, however, a firm wishes to acquire and use knowledge that is unrelated to its ongoing activity, then the firm must dedicate effort exclusively to creating absorptive capacity.'

The paradoxical possibility for operational and strategic agency in path-dependent processes has important implications for understanding how knowledgeable agents and institutional reflexive environments can initiate extended search and integration activities beyond the present, including the creation of new 'knowledge paths' (see Section 4.4).

4.3.2 Dynamic Capability and Path-Dependence

The concept of dynamic capability proposed by David Teece and colleagues (Helfat et al., 2007) allows a move beyond the concepts of organizational path-dependence and 'core rigidity' (Leonard-Barton, 1992), and opens the way to studies of organizational change and innovation. The dynamic capabilities literature developed from strategic management studies and focuses on how firms create and sustain competitive advantage in turbulent environments. In its initial formulation (Teece and Pisano, 1994; Teece et al., 1997), dynamic capabilities took account of organizational processes, such as coordination and learning, and the reduced opportunities for innovation imposed by the prevailing path dependencies. Later work focuses on how the recombination and reconfiguration of knowledge should be understood as core elements of the dynamic capabilities required by firms to move beyond these constraints (Eisenhardt and Martin, 2000; Zollo and Winter, 2002; Helfat et al., 2007).

Dynamic capability is a higher order ability to identify and to address the need for strategic changes to the organization's competence and resource bases, the capability to manage 'continuous renewal of organizational capabilities, thereby matching the demands of (rapidly) changing environments' (Schreyögg and Kliesch-Eberl, 2007: 914). Teece (2007) operationalizes this higher order ability as managerial capability to sense/shape market developments, seize opportunities, and transform firm assets. Conceived in this way, dynamic capabilities address the problem of both technical fitness, that is, operational effectiveness through the execution of functions (static efficiency), and evolutionary fitness (dynamic efficiency), which enables survival and growth in a changed selection environment. Sensing/shaping refers to the ability to filter and recognize opportunities through internal R&D, partner collaboration, scanning of developments in science, and identification of new markets and market segments. Seizing refers to the design of organizational structures and processes to allow the firm to appropriate rents from new opportunities. Finally, transformation of assets refers to combination and recombination, including the ability to manage learning and new knowledge.

Although the concept of dynamic capabilities is not based on a deeper analysis of path dependencies, Teece et al. (1997) and many of their followers (e.g. Helfat and Peteraf, 2003; Katkalo et al., 2010) acknowledge the role of path-dependent processes in the development of organizational and even dynamic capabilities. Routines or meta-routines are at the heart of organizational capabilities and, in an incisive analysis, Vergne and Durand (2011: 366–7, emphasis added) point to their paradoxical role in dynamic capabilities: organizational path-dependence builds on routines and 'seems to confer an advantage to dynamic capabilities, *and* to concurrently represent a threat to the sustainability of that advantage'. Work on dynamic capabilities emphasizes the importance of both path-extending and path-breaking activities. However, Vergne and Durand (2011: 375, emphasis added) observe that path-breaking activity 'is likely to be limited to application to lower-order organizational processes. A path-dependent dynamic capability cannot monitor itself reflexively to avoid lock-in—*a higher-order process is then required.*' This formulation rather begs the question of where to locate the source of this 'higher order' reflexive potential and where to find the agents that might drive transformation of the firm's knowledge base. Is it the top management team that is associated with such decisive organizational action? If so, what is the role of the R&D or engineering departments, or other knowledge agents, in path reproducing, path transforming, and/or path creating? The literature on dynamic capabilities suggests that it is the responsibility of senior management to initiate and sustain dynamism, but it is not clear what renders executives and top management teams less imprinted by previous formative experiences than other organizational actors. The empirical evidence in the literature on managerial cognition (Porac et al., 1999) suggests that top management's cognitive schema remain relatively stable over time. For instance, a study by Hellgren and Melin (1992) shows that a top manager's 'managerial recipe' stayed basically intact despite moving around and acting as chief executive officer in firms in industries with very different composition and dynamics. Thus, an enquiry into the dynamics that might overcome the rigidities of path dependencies seems to require a broader framework and more open search.

4.3.3 Interim Conclusions

We have argued that work on knowledge integration tends to focus on the efficiency problems involved in managing knowledge scope (the integration of diverse and differentiated expertise), while research on absorptive capacity investigates the acquisition and accumulation of new knowledge within domains constrained by prior knowledge. Cumulative capacity is key to the development of organizational expertise, but can create dangerous path dependencies leading to knowledge lock-ins at times when profound changes to the firm's knowledge base and capabilities are required. In addition, work on organizational path-dependence emphasizes the path-dependent character of organizational knowledge development. Studies in the strategic management literature seek to formulate and identify more dynamic approaches that also address the capability issue. However, it is not clear how the higher order processes of redefinition/renewal are initiated and maintained in organizations. This makes it important to explore the possible roles of knowledge-based agents at several levels, and the interaction of these agents with more or less institutionalized reflexivity in wider social and inter-organizational contexts.

4.4 REFLECTIVE AGENCY IN PATH-DEPENDENT PROCESSES

The literatures on dynamic capability and organizational path-dependence propose different solutions to the problem of the capabilities required for change.

The dynamic capability argument tends to view the deliberate though not unconstrained strategic management actions as the locus of agency. Organizational path-dependency research implies that organizational practices and institutionalized reflexivity are crucial for understanding unfolding events. We draw on theories of knowledge integration across boundaries and practice-oriented approaches to account for the general role of reflective agency, and specific knowledge-integrating, boundary-spanning agents. Inspired by Giddens's (1984) theory of structuration, we conceive knowledge boundaries as social structures that are continuously created and reproduced. This view considers knowledge boundaries as parts of paths or paradigms, and agency as the activities undertaken by agents to reproduce or change these paths. Figure 4.2 suggests a synthesis of the two boundary dimensions proposed in the absorptive capacity and knowledge integration literatures, and three agency options related to the maintaining or crossing of these boundaries.

1. Boundary reproduction (path-dependence)

   Existing knowledge boundaries are maintained and reproduced; the focal organization searches for new knowledge to solve problems in domains close to the organization's current knowledge, which will be easy to absorb (Cohen and Levinthal, 1990). The existing knowledge scope is maintained, allowing for knowledge integration through established routines, directives, sequencing, and standardization (Grant, 1996). The result is a path-dependent process (path 1 in Figure 4.2), in which distinctive capabilities are established and amplified by self-reinforcing mechanisms, implying rigidity over time.

2. Boundary crossing (path extension)

   Knowledge boundaries are crossed; this can be done in two ways. Path 2a in Figure 4.2 indicates the crossing of multiple boundaries as the firm expands its knowledge scope by acquiring increasingly complex and interdependent knowledge from an array of diverse sources (the

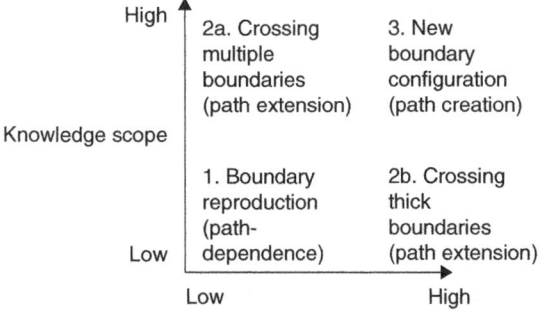

Figure 4.2. Agency options and knowledge boundaries

knowledge integration dimension). Path 2b illustrates situations when the firms builds on and deepens its current knowledge base by searching and absorbing new knowledge domains (absorptive capacity dimension). Path extension may thus involve different types of actions to expand current paths through the spanning of various types of knowledge boundaries. Work on absorptive capacity, dynamic capabilities, and knowledge integration suggests that boundary crossing efforts are costly and require investment in boundary objects, boundary spanning, and knowledge brokering (Rosenkopf and Nerkar, 2001; Carlile, 2002; Hargadon, 2002), as well as articulation and appropriation of new knowledge through inter-personal communication (Zollo and Winter, 2002).

3. New boundary configuration (path creation)

New opportunities emerge for knowledge convergence and recombination, involving the spanning of boundaries across technologies and industries, and the creation of new paths (3 in Figure 4.2), such as new platforms and architectures (Henderson and Clark, 1990). Rather than extending existing trajectories, these types of boundary crossing imply that the extent of absorptive capacity and knowledge integration needs to change within a paradigmatic shift (Dosi, 1982; Garud et al., 2010; Sydow et al., 2012). Such transformations are difficult to manage and influence directly from an absorption or integration perspective. Agency on several different levels is required, and may involve intrapreneurial actions as well as strategic reorientation based on creative knowledge accumulation initiated by specialist groups, new or old partners, and innovative individuals (Andersson and Berggren, 2011; Bergek et al., 2013).

The type of agency required to realize these options can evolve in several different contexts and organizational arenas. Here we discuss four stylized contexts, within and outside the focal organization (see Lewin et al., 2011). Within the organization there are two levels, the executive (top management) and the non-executive (e.g. engineers, customer representatives, middle managers). In the organizational environment two other 'levels' can be identified: communities of practitioners and the organizational field. Both may also provide access to the knowledge of other organizational actors through collaboration. We discuss these four types of agency here:

(1) Within organizations, the first arena of agency concerns the *executive level*, that is, the agency conducted by individuals or groups with formal authority to make decisions on behalf of the organization's principal. This type of agency is implicit or explicit in most organization and strategic

management theories. The literature on managerial cognition suggests that top management's cognitive schema remain stable over time, which does not support dynamic capability per se. However, several studies (e.g. Burgelman, 2002) show that path-breaking change can be initiated by the actions of the principal in introducing new leadership or articulating knowledge already existing in the organization. Changes initiated by the principal or executive are likely to result in significant repositioning of organizational perspectives and procedures. These changes may be domain-specific, that is, they may imply recognition and valuing of new knowledge-domains, and/or procedural, involving new ways of working that facilitate the organization's acquisition and absorption of new process knowledge.

(2) The second arena of agency inside organizations is the *non-executive level*, which includes managers and experts, and is where new technological and market knowledge tend to be developed. Organizations can foster a strong inward-looking culture that confines perceptions and actions to a previously selected path. However, the interaction of managers and experts with actors in other organizations can lead to path-extending or path-breaking activities in the search for solutions to new or 'wicked' problems. Groups at this level can function as *collectivities* (Lindkvist, 2005), based on a common interest in solving a particular problem, and distinguished by the inter-disciplinary composition of their members. Based on a strong motivation to solve difficult problems, these diverse groups will be more likely to find less conventional and, possibly, path-breaking solutions to problems, and to experiment with new approaches.

(3) Outside the focal organization there is a third arena—the *communities of practitioners* involved in utilizing and developing the knowledge embodied in the focal firm's products and services. These communities can include academics, engineers, medical doctors, other professionals, students, activists, and others, and their activities can include corporate or public R&D, industry fairs, open-source software development, and advanced use and maintenance of machinery. Studies of communities of practice show how social and cognitive forces affect the rate and direction of members' efforts towards the reception and further development of new knowledge (Brown and Duguid, 1991; Wenger, 1998). Such creative activities require heterogeneous knowledge, while knowledge overlaps facilitate sharing and transfer among participants (Lindkvist, 2005). The strength of the ties, bonds, and power among community members affects the distribution and potential for the impact of agency within the community (Dahlander and O'Mahony, 2011). Common disciplinary background and education, professional loyalty, guilds, and social pressure all drive a cohesive community and the development of a common framing of the solutions to problems. This can result in a path which maintains the existing scope of knowledge integration. However, communities are seldom loyal to specific firms, and are not narrowly defined by organizational

membership, which gives their members agency—in line or out of line with formal organizational aspirations and directives.

(4) The final arena of agency refers to the *organizational field* (DiMaggio and Powell, 1983), which is the collection of actors, regulations, stakeholders, and practices influencing the focal organization. Agency theory in economics usually refers to the principal–agent relationship between the owner and executives as pivotal. Stakeholder theory (Freeman, 1984) suggests that the range of actors that can influence organizational processes and decisions also includes customers, unions, suppliers, politicians, and public administrations. This system notion of agency is supported by other approaches to organizational action such as resource-dependence theory (Pfeffer and Salancik, 1978), neo-institutional theory (Scott, 2008), and social network theory (Burt, 1980). Empirical studies from a systems perspective show the pervasive influence on organizational action of extra-organizational actors. At this level, one end of the stability continuum is represented by large socio-technical systems (e.g. energy and communications), where initial investments in one technology erect barriers to the use of other technologies owing to network externalities, increasing returns to adoption, and political and economic interests (Hughes, 1983; David, 1985; Arthur, 1994). Research on so-called sustainability transition suggests a multi-level framework. Here, incumbent firms are portrayed as the defenders of existing technologies and development paths at 'regime level' (Geels, 2005; Geels and Schot, 2007; Schot and Geels, 2008), and path-breaking agency is located at the level of strategic niches, involving new firms (actors) commercializing technologies in interaction with local communities, and policymakers. However, recent studies suggest that established firms may operate on several levels and may design integrated strategies, which leverage niche activities to the regime level, and create new development paths (Berggren et. al., 2015). Firm agency, beyond established paths, can also be instigated by active stakeholder interventions, such as the introduction of new laws, standards, or specific political initiatives. In addition, the impact of competent and demanding customers (see, e.g., Fridlund, 1999) or suppliers (Baldwin and Clark, 2000), can force firms to focus on the generation and integration of new knowledge. Whatever the type or level of agency, the knowledgeability of individual actors is influenced by the reflexivity and interactive capacity of their context, that is, their communities or their organizational environment.

4.5 CONCLUDING DISCUSSION

We began by comparing two key concepts in knowledge-based theories of the firm—absorptive capacity and knowledge integration, summarized in

Figure 4.2. One dimension represents knowledge integration and knowledge scope, that is, the different types of knowledge that need to be integrated; the other dimension is knowledge accumulation, which is related to absorptive capacity. Knowledge integration emphasizes action (agency), while knowledge accumulation focuses on the path-dependent development of knowledge.

The ensuing discussion of organizational path-dependence and dynamic capabilities highlighted the importance of the change perspective. The discussion indicated a persistent problem regarding agency and reflexivity in established notions related to change, and the need for a new conceptualization. This led us to propose a synthesis of the knowledge integration and knowledge absorption perspectives, which elaborates the duality of structure and agency, and recombines the dimensions of knowledge scope and knowledge evolution.

This synthesis implies an extension of the knowledge integration research agenda, from the mechanisms, routines, and rules involved in the integration of existing specialist knowledge, to the inclusion of the agents and activities involved in the integration of qualitatively new and different types of knowledge. In turn, this might lead to a redefinition of knowledge boundaries, boundary crossing, and other unanticipated changes.

Our analysis of organizational path-dependence and dynamic capability suggests that studies of knowledge integration as a potentially path-breaking or path-creating activity requires an interest in and understanding of change, agency, and reflexivity. This, in turn, implies an open-ended search for sources of agency and knowledgeable agents, at various levels and in various organizational and extra-organizational contexts. Such multi-level research would benefit from a longitudinal research design, to allow for the interplay between structure and agency. Studies using such a design would enable further elaboration of absorptive capacity and knowledge integration as a dynamically integrated conceptual pair.

5

Bridging the Individual-to-Organization Divide

A Knowledge Creation Approach

Lars Lindkvist and Marie Bengtsson

5.1 INTRODUCTION

A predominant theme in the knowledge integration literature is how differently skilled employees communicate and collaborate efficiently. This has led some to focus on knowledge transfer attempts as a means of bridging the differentiated knowledge bases involved and others to investigate the integration mechanisms which require only a limited base of common knowledge in order to function (see, e.g., Grant, 1996; Carlile, 2004; Tell, 2011; Nicolini et al., 2012). However, specialist collaborations tend to involve not only the combined use and exploitation of different knowledge bases but also the creation of new knowledge (see Lindkvist et al., 2011; Lindkvist, 2012). Although many empirical studies reported in the knowledge integration literature concern the development of new products or services (see Berggren et al., 2011), the issue of how new knowledge emerges and what firms can do to promote the growth of knowledge has received scant attention. In this chapter, we set aside the issue of how to bridge specialized knowledge bases and focus instead on the type of bridging required for new knowledge to emerge from knowledge integration endeavours.

One of the main challenges involved in an examination of knowledge growth is how to understand and conceptualize the relation between individual and organizational knowledge creation. The importance of considering the individual level is signalled clearly by Simon (1991: 125), who states that all learning 'takes place within human individual heads', and by Grant (1996: 112), who claims that 'knowledge creation is an individual activity'. At the same time, we know that, left to themselves, individuals will experience many difficulties. For example, as observed by Dunbar (1997: 483), 'individuals have great difficulty generating alternative inductions from data and also have great difficulty limiting and expanding inductions'. Moreover, individuals may be more interested in verifying their theories than in falsifying them (Popper, 1972), and may favour interpretations that confirm their own prior understandings (March, 1995). Thus, as Ward et al. (1997: 1) conclude, 'The human mind is an enormously creative instrument. Our ability to go beyond concrete experiences and produce novel ideas is one of our most salient characteristics.' Nevertheless, it can be difficult for organizations to use and leverage this creative input, to become a well-aligned part of the organizational knowledge base. We can think of knowledge integration as a field of enquiry that involves two boundary-spanning challenges: overcoming the specialist-to-specialist divide, and overcoming the individual-to-organization divide. In this chapter we address the latter.

Bridging between individual and organizational knowledge raises both fundamental epistemological questions and more practice-related questions about what kind of organizational processes might be used to promote the growth of knowledge. One of the most prominent, at least in terms of Google citations (in excess of 47,000), approaches was proposed by Nonaka (1994) and Nonaka and Takeuchi (1995). Nonaka's theory of organizational knowledge creation is intimately linked to Polanyi's (1966) concept of tacit knowledge (or knowing) and acknowledgement of the individual's formidable power subconsciously to shape and integrate knowledge; 'the great and indispensable power by which all knowledge is discovered, and once discovered, is held to be true' (Polanyi, 1966: 6). Nonaka's SECI (Socialization, Externalization, Combination, Internalization) model depicts how a sequence of four conversion modes serves to transform individual tacit knowledge into collective tacit knowledge, into explicit knowledge, into combinations of explicit knowledge, and finally into internalized tacit knowledge. The logic of the model is, thus, to suggest how the organization can take advantage of, or exploit, inputs of individual knowledge and, through four successive stages, make the knowledge increasingly more organizational. However, while it is assumed that all four stages have the potential to create new knowledge, it is only in the first two modes that such an outcome is conceptually substantiated and clearly associated with Polanyi's epistemology. We would suggest that the latter two modes, that is, combination and internalization, are more closely related to implementation than creation. A careful reading reveals that neither of the latter two modes is entrusted with much creational power—even by Nonaka (1991).

Gourlay (2006) and Jakubik (2011) point out that, while parts of the framework initially suggested by Nonaka et al. have been modified, the SECI model remains a central element. This model has several attractive properties. A major advantage is that it departs from a clearly specified epistemology. Hence, as Gueldenberg and Helting (2007: 118) state, a major strength of the SECI model 'resides in the fact that it is aimed at a *comprehensive* and *deep* concept of knowledge' (original emphasis). This allows a fairly deep discussion of the alternative or complementary epistemologies which might be adhered to. Another advantage is that the SECI model is accompanied by several practice-related examples of the activities that managers can engage in, in the various stages of the organizational knowledge creation process.

However, what the SECI model does not acknowledge is the generative potential and bridging power of interactive knowledge creation. The importance of interactive knowledge processes in project and product development processes is frequently highlighted in the literature (see Sydow et al., 2004; DeFillippi et al., 2006). At the same time, the need to develop new ways of conceptualizing such knowledge processes has also been highlighted. For example, Cross and Sproull (2004: 447) recognize that 'we know little regarding how actionable knowledge is created through interaction with others', and Hargadon and Bechky (2006: 484) would prefer approaches that focus on how insights 'emerge in the *interactions* between individuals'. In addition, Tsoukas (2009: 941) concludes, based on his comprehensive overview of the literature, that 'despite the proliferation of empirical studies and the important insights gained, more theoretical work is needed to further expand on the processes through which new organizational knowledge emerges'.

In order to develop the SECI model in this direction, we need an epistemologically informed conception of how knowledge can grow within an interactive knowledge process. In this chapter we propose a conceptualization that recognizes the 'unfathomable' nature of knowledge (Bartley, 1987, 1990), and views knowledge creation as contingent on the interaction between individuals' subjective idea generation and objectified knowledge (Popper, 1994). Hence, while interaction is generally considered as occurring between people, a distinctive mark of this Popperian view is its explicit recognition of knowledge as an additional participant.

In what follows, we start by scrutinizing how Nonaka et al. utilize Polanyi's epistemological framework to develop their SECI model. We introduce the concept of 'unfathomable knowledge' and identify two additional modes, Objectification and Elicitation, which together form an additional route to the original SECI model. This extends Nonaka's view of organizational knowledge creation to become an epistemologically informed dual route model which includes the importance of individual-to-organization bridging as part of the knowledge integration processes.

5.2 THE FIRST ROUTE: CONVERSION-BASED BRIDGING

Like Polanyi, Nonaka recognized that much or most of what people know is known only tacitly. This tacit knowledge is seen as deeply rooted in action and commitment, involving both body and mind, which makes it 'highly personal and hard to formalise' (Nonaka et al., 2000: 7). Making this kind of individual knowledge organizational is not a minor issue. To address this problem, Nonaka proposed the SECI model and its four knowledge conversion modes of Socialization (from tacit to tacit), Externalization (from tacit to explicit), Combination (from explicit to explicit), and Internalization (from explicit to tacit). While it is assumed that each of these four modes has the capacity to create knowledge independently (Nonaka, 1994: 21), two do not rely on any interaction between tacit and explicit knowledge. In fact, Nonaka (1994: 20) points out that both socialization and combination have demerits.

In the Socialization mode, shared experience is seen as a key way to generate a common (but still tacit) perspective. Nonaka and von Krogh (2009: 9) recognize that 'tacit knowledge can be acquired only through shared experience, such as spending time together or living in the same environment'. As Nonaka (1994: 19) points out, such tacit knowledge sharing processes may proceed silently: 'One important point to note is that an individual can acquire tacit knowledge without language'. This idea closely parallels the 'communities of practice' idea (Wenger, 1998), and its reliance on socialization to bring about tacit knowledge transfer and 'knowledge-base-similarity' among community members (see Lindkvist, 2005). These views basically reiterate enculturation practices, which enable the transfer of tacit knowledge and bring about homogeneity of knowledge, but say little about the creation of new knowledge. Pure socialization is also impaired, as the 'silence' makes it difficult to apply the knowledge in fields beyond the specific context in which it was created. Hence, on its own, Nonaka (1991: 99) admits that 'Socialization is a rather limited form of knowledge creation'.

On the other hand, pure combination refers merely to putting well-known things together, exemplified by how a 'comptroller of a company collects information from throughout the organization and puts it together in a financial report' and by the Matsushita team's efforts to standardize their articulated knowledge into a manual or workbook (Nonaka, 1991:99). Such processes do not involve tacit knowing or personal knowledge and do 'not really extend the company's knowledge base either' (Nonaka, 1991: 99). Furthermore, scant attention is paid to the creational qualities of the internalization mode, which is exemplified by the use of training programmes that teach trainees how to understand the organization, and the use of virtual learning techniques such as simulation and experimentation (Nonaka et al., 2000: 10). As a result, if we want to create new knowledge, we must place our faith first in the capacity of the externalization mode, since, as Nonaka and Takeuchi (1995: 66) state, 'Among the four modes of knowledge conversion, externalization holds the key to knowledge creation, because it creates new, explicit concepts from tacit knowledge.'

While the socialization mode serves to homogenize the individuals' tacit knowledge into shared tacit knowledge, the resulting knowledge should then be articulated in the externalization phase, that is, it should become explicit knowledge. This view of the possibility of making tacit knowledge explicit is in line with Polanyi's (1958/1998; 1966) recognition that the tacit particulars may sometimes be explicitly identified and integrated. For example, in the example of machine operation, Polanyi explains how an engineer's understanding of the machine's construction and operation can provide insights far beyond those provided by tacit integration. So, while we can 'know more than we can tell', our tacit knowledge is not immune to analysis, and we may sometimes be able to say something about what we know tacitly.

Here, Nonaka et al. advocate the use of metaphor as a way to trigger the development of team members' tacit knowledge into novel higher order concepts: the world is full of contradictions, and dialogue allows us to go beyond such dualities and create new knowledge (Nonaka and Toyama, 2005). The metaphor idea is also central in conceptualizing what comes out of the externalization phase. In Nonaka and Takeuchi (1995: 66) this view is substantiated by a quote from Nisbet (1969: 5): 'much of what Michael Polanyi has called tacit knowledge is expressible—in so far as it is expressible at all—in metaphor'. So, for Nonaka et al., knowledge creation is not just a metaphor-driven process, it is also the case that the knowledge created has the nature of metaphor, and such a 'new metaphor' constitutes new knowledge. A novel metaphor formulation, such as the car project 'tall boy' (see Nonaka, 1991), may well be a powerful way of bringing about a coherent and communal sense of direction, for example, in product development work. Thus, externalization efforts can be worthwhile and can generate insights that are useful in the pragmatic context of firms. For example, as shown in the case of Nonaka and Takeuchi's (1995: 106 ff) much discussed bread-baking machine study, the 'twisting stretch' notion mirrored a significant enough portion of bakers' tacit knowledge for it to be of use in the further development of the machine.

However, while recognition of the significance of tacit knowing processes has attracted little opposition, many are fiercely opposed to the possibility of knowledge conversion being focused in the socialization and externalization modes of the SECI model, and have argued that tacit knowledge is essentially ineffable (see Tsoukas, 2003; D'Eridita and Barreto, 2006). Tsoukas (2003: 426) states clearly that: 'Tacit knowledge cannot be "captured", "translated" or "converted", but only displayed and manifested, in what we do.' In this chapter, we set aside this controversy and focus on an additional way of achieving individual-to-organization bridging.

5.3 A SECOND ROUTE: INTERACTION-BASED BRIDGING

Polanyi's epistemology is often summarized by the maxim 'we can know more than we can tell'. However, there are also instances when 'we tell more than we can know'. As teachers soon realize, what they have said in the lecture hall is not always what the students have heard. Sometimes the difference is to be regretted, but it may also lead to new and interesting ideas that are far beyond the imagination of the teacher. More generally, this example can serve to illustrate the view of knowledge as 'unfathomable', as discussed by Popper (1972) and Bartley (1987, 1990). The concept of unfathomable knowledge is rooted in the epistemology of Popper and the concept of 'objective knowledge'. Objective knowledge, said Popper (1994: 10, original emphasis), 'consists of guesses, hypotheses, or theories—usually published in books, journals and lectures. It also consists of unsolved *problems* and *arguments* for and against the various competing theories.' As individuals' subjectively held knowledge is objectified, it is 'freed' from its maker and turned into a non-personal knowledge item. Then, as this knowledge item loses its 'slave-like' relationship to specific knowing subjects, it may enter its own unfathomable developmental trajectory (Bartley, 1990: 32): 'Bodies of knowledge, while created and explored by men, do not bend and yield like slaves to those who would create and master them.... After their birth, bodies of knowledge remain forever unfathomed and unfathomable. They remain forever pregnant with consequences that are unintended and cannot be anticipated.'

As Bartley (1990) explains, this view takes us beyond ordinary (Popperian) fallibilism which asserts that we can never know anything with certainty. The idea of unfathomable knowledge implies also that we cannot fully know or understand our existing theories. Even the creators of theories and hypotheses do not and cannot understand them completely, which, taken to the limit, means that '*we do not know what we are saying or* (since of course we act partly in terms of what we know) *what we are doing*' (Bartley, 1990: 33, original emphasis).

Instead of thinking of knowledge as an individual possession or something that is personal in a strong sense, this view of knowledge as non-personal implies that the idea content of knowledge is 'rendered strange' (Bartley, 1987: 439) and, thereby, able to be reflected on and developed further. Using a pencil and a piece of paper may then be a very simple way to bring about a process of interaction which can serve as a bridge between the subjective knowledge of an individual and the world of objective knowledge, even in the context of Big Science, as Popper (1994: 31) suggests.

[...] Einstein once said, 'My pencil is cleverer than I am'. What he meant, of course was that by putting things down in writing and by calculating them on paper, he could often get results beyond what he had anticipated. We may say that by using paper and pencil he plugged himself into the third world of objective knowledge. He thus made his subjective ideas objective. And once these ideas were made objective, he could link them with other objective ideas, and thus reach remote and unintended consequences far transcending this starting point.

Thus, unfathomable knowledge provides a concept of a dynamic and creativity-promoting force in interactive knowledge generation. Once the knowledge discovered by individuals has been separated from its authors and been suitably objectified, it is ready to enter into further interactive processes. However, it should be recognized that a new knowledge item's potential to promote further knowledge growth is not necessarily realized: 'What is crucial about an item of objective knowledge […] is its *potential* for being understood or utilized (by an entrepreneur in the market or an abstract thinker in the "marketplace of ideas") in some ways that has not yet been imagined, a potential that may exist without ever being realized' (Bartley, 1990: 435, original emphasis).

Therefore, there is a need also for processes of interaction that contribute to the realization of this growth potential. As the above quote shows, Bartley is suggesting 'the marketplace of ideas' as a fitting image to underline the similarities between ideational and economic activities. In referring to Hayek (1945), he points to how markets are not only efficient means of utilizing existing, dispersed knowledge in the best interest of the society, but also that the interaction and communication among market participants constitute 'discovery processes' which elicit implicit and not-yet-fathomed knowledge. However, we should point out that such a view of the market-like-ness of interactive knowledge creation processes does not imply that these are seen as open-ended and unregulated. Just as the processes Hayek discusses serve the welfare goals of society, organizational and individual level processes should be looked upon as subordinated to higher-level goals or restrictions.

In order to illustrate how such interactive processes can operate to elicit so far unfathomed features of knowledge in a product development context, we draw on Hargadon and Bechky's (2006) study of Reebok's development of a new form-fitting shoe. In this case, an idea emerged first in a brainstorming session, when one designer suggested that an inflatable splint might prevent injuries. Another participant, who had worked with hospital equipment, recognized the possibility that a certain medical bag could be modified to provide the oddly shaped bladders needed. In a subsequent meeting with designers who had worked with diagnostic instruments, a functioning solution emerged for how to inflate and deflate the shoe easily. Finally, the project resulted in a new shoe which was well received in the market and also prized for its creativity.

What we want to show by this example is how the participants, by express-ing their subjective ideas in explicit form, provided the opportunity for others to develop these ideas further or complement them with objective knowledge from other fields. Metaphorically, we can consider the different conjectures as containing a seed, which can start to grow as a result of the nutrition supplied through the interaction with other fields of objective knowledge. The interaction between subjective and objective knowledge may, thus, result in the realization of the potential for knowledge growth that is inherent in the various conjectures suggested. However, as noted by Hargadon and Bechky (2006: 487), this is not guaranteed: 'One designer's suggestion of a shoe-as-a-splint might easily be dismissed as crazy, and ultimately forgotten. Or, the same crazy suggestion is considered and built on by others, becoming more realistic and, ultimately leading to a creative solution.'

We can think also of industrial settings where a multitude of interacting specialists benefit from material and clearly visible knowledge objects as a means to 'plug into' the world of objective knowledge. The literature recog-nizes that prototypes and semi-finished products can function as mediating objects that allow those involved to connect to a variety of specific knowledge areas (Star and Griesemer, 1989; Bechky, 2003b; Carlile, 2004). Hence, when such a material object is also expressive of a specific idea or conjecture, it becomes possible for those involved to connect to a variety of specialist knowledge areas and, in so doing, to enhance their abilities to identify new problems or imagine new solutions.

A study of product development within the telecom company Ericsson (Lindkvist et al., 1998; Lindkvist, 2012) is a good illustration of how almost complete product prototypes can work as mediating knowledge objects. The aim of the project was to develop a new mobile phone system for the Japanese market. At a late stage in the development process it was decided to build a complete radio base station, which, in principle, would be ready for shipment to Japan. It was demonstrated at a meeting in which all involved participated, and which Ericsson top managers attended. One of the project leaders described how this led to those involved identifying many new problems:

> We ordered a radio base station from the warehouse. Everybody thought that it was destined for shipment to Japan. However, we arranged a quality demonstra-tion in Stockholm and invited top management, quality managers, designers, etc. When we did this demonstration, it turned out that the product did not work. There were all kinds of problems, such as mechanical problems, packaging problems, things were missing, and that created enormous attention. (Lindkvist et al., 1998: 939)

Hence, the product represented a conjecture of what would be a well-functioning radio base station, and its material and visible form facilitated the process of connecting the different problems to a number of interrelated fields of knowledge. The product, while not able to speak or 'know what it knew', 'unknowingly' was able to inform those who were exposed to it what was not yet good enough, and to trigger their imaginations.

Finally, management's role is to arrange a context that is conducive to eliciting the inherent, unfathomable potential for knowledge growth of new conjectures. Interactive knowledge creation is not a matter only of spontaneous collaboration; it can benefit from various kinds of managerial support (see von Krogh et al., 2012). A study by Rittiner and Brusoni (2013) of the introduction of lean management in four automotive companies is illustrative here, and demonstrates how the use of specifically appointed facilitators can help those at lower levels to benefit from more distant knowledge bases. In their study, Rittiner and Brusoni show how Continuous Improvement Facilitators arranged meetings and prototype workshops, which supported local processes of 'problem identification' in the socialization and externalization phases. In addition, based on their extensive knowledge of generally available solutions or knowledge of improvements, these facilitators were able to act as knowledge brokers in the combination and internalization phases. As a result, they were able to help people connect to and interact with fields of enquiry beyond the confines of their current knowledge or, to put it differently, with the 'world of objective knowledge'.

In sum, the introduction of unfathomable knowledge suggests, first, that new knowledge, if suitably *objectified*, has the power continuously to extend the conceivable knowledge horizon. In fact, as Popper (1975: 75) states, we can think of such knowledge as constituting an additional sense organ: 'the tentative adoption of a new conjecture [...] invariably opens up many *new* problems, for a new revolutionary theory is exactly like a new and powerful sense organ'. Second, in order to benefit from this potential it is necessary to establish an interaction context which enables the *elicitation* of not yet fathomed and 'implicit' possibilities of such objectified knowledge. In Section 5.4, we discuss how objectification and elicitation processes operationalize the 'unfathomable knowledge' view and allow us to generate a revised model of organizational knowledge creation.

5.4 REMODELLING KNOWLEDGE CREATION

We are suggesting that the original SECI model could be developed into a dual route model, including a bridging route based on interactive knowledge creation. It should be underlined that the SECI model we hope to extend has a distinct focus on *organizational* knowledge creation. Nonaka (1994: 14) explains 'that while new knowledge is developed by individuals, organizations play a critical role in articulating and amplifying that knowledge'. Thus, individual tacit knowing is not an endogenous part of this model, which starts by identifying socialization and externalization as organizational processes that contribute to converting the tacit knowledge of individuals into explicit knowledge. It is assumed that this bridging route will result in the creation of new knowledge, for example, in the form of new metaphors.

As discussed in Section 5.3, conceptualization of the succeeding combination and internalization modes leaves little room for knowledge creation. Both combination and internalization refer mainly to implementation efforts aimed at aligning the knowledge generated and externalized in the first two phases, with the organization's knowledge base. Indeed, it is somewhat strange that the 'combination' mode as a source of new knowledge is largely neglected—connected neither to ideas about collective creativity nor to synergistic knowledge growth. However, the reason for this neglect could be that its formulation as an explicit–explicit knowledge combination lacks any association to the tacit dimension. As a result, it would in no way be 'Polanyian'. This mode focuses on 'the reconfiguration of existing information' (Nonaka, 1994: 19) rather than on new knowledge creation. Nevertheless, these modes qualify as important means to make knowledge more generally available and 'more organizational'. New knowledge will be of little use if it is not successfully implemented and integrated into the firm's practices and products.

In a sense, our efforts to remodel and extend the original SECI model by adding yet another route represents a possible logical continuation when knowledge creation essentially comes to a halt as tacit knowledge is converted in the first two modes of this model. We would suggest that the promotion of interactive processes entails further possibilities for knowledge creation. The model in Figure 5.1 shows that we think of what the organization can do to promote such interactive knowledge creation processes in a two-step manner. First, the subjective knowledge of individuals has to be constituted as an objectified and stand-alone conjecture. Second, we need some kind of (subjective-objective knowledge) interaction to elicit its inherent possibilities and realize its inspirational power.

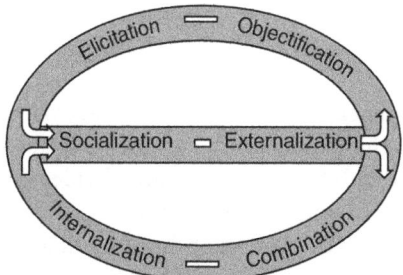

Figure 5.1 A dual-route model of organizational knowledge creation

As a first move in this remodelling effort, we suggest the insertion of *Objectification* as the first step in the additional route. In principle, any type of material or conceptual item of new knowledge which is set free from its author into a form that allows inspection and critical reflection may qualify as an item of objectified knowledge. However, some degree of ambiguity is desirable to make it work well as an unfathomable knowledge object. A too simple idea or conjecture would not support much 'pregnancy' and would trigger only limited degrees of imagination among those involved. Furthermore, as suggested by the Ericsson example, some level of materiality and visibility would be beneficial for such objects to gain the simultaneous attention of the participants in interactive settings. As pointed out by Ewenstein and Whyte (2009), visual representations can be a particularly useful means of facilitating interdisciplinary collaboration within architectural design projects. Finally, it is essential that such objects enjoy a significant level of 'autonomy'. The importance of this characteristic is illustrated in Henderson's (1991) study of the introduction of a CAD/CAM system, which shows that objects that are too closely interconnected with higher level regulations can hamper the desired creativity and flexibility. In sum, the objectification of new knowledge should be sensitive to the level of ambiguity, materiality, and autonomy that is crafted into such objects.

For the second move in our remodelling effort, we suggest the inclusion of *Elicitation* as the next step. As the Reebok shoe, Ericsson, and automotive examples show, there is a need also to bring about a context that enables connection and interaction between individual ideas and the world of objective knowledge. However, while the outcome of these interactive processes is unpredictable, we should not regard them as unconstrained. For example, we should conceive of these processes in product development projects as constrained by a variety of established rules and goals, and think of market-like processes within firms more generally, as subordinate to hierarchical strategies, policies, and regulations (Lindkvist, 2004).

5.5 CONCLUSIONS

Knowledge integration can be thought of as associated with two different boundary spanning challenges; bridging the specialist-to-specialist divide, and bridging the individual-to-organization divide. Our study focused on the second of these two, and how it is related to organizational knowledge creation. We began with a discussion of the SECI model proposed by Nonaka et al., and showed how it could be extended into a two route model. We contribute by suggesting an interaction-based route which would allow organizations to benefit from and develop the knowledge of their individual members. This route complements the conversion-based path suggested by Nonaka et al.

The interaction-based route includes objectification and elicitation as closely related process steps. In relation to objectification, we also suggested a set of knowledge object characteristics, such as ambiguity, visibility, and autonomy, which would increase the potential of these knowledge objects to elicit new ideas. These characteristics describe the proper form or nature of the knowledge objects. The literature mainly discusses the *roles* played by various kinds of material and conceptual objects (see, e.g., the overview in Nicolini et al., 2012). As Ewenstein and Whyte (2009: 8) conclude, 'In the existing literature, the emphasis has been placed on the role that the objects play rather than on the nature of the objects themselves.' The second step, elicitation, focuses on the kind of organizational arrangements or processes that are conducive to realizing the growth potential of new knowledge. The 'marketplace of ideas' is here suggested as a guiding image, mirroring the discussion in Hayek (1978) and Bartley (1990) of the nature of markets as discovery processes. We also use the sports shoe, telecom, and automotive examples to show a number of close-to-practice ways that facilitate for those involved to plug into and interact creatively with existing fields of objectified knowledge.

With regard to implications for practice, the notions of objectification and elicitation in the revised model should help managers to visualize what they might do to promote a process of continuing knowledge growth. The original SECI model is useful for managers since it is accompanied by a substantial amount of advice about the possible actions related to the different steps in the model. However, its identification of combination and internalization as the logical next steps after the externalization phase risks managers focusing too soon on implementation issues that involve aligning the new knowledge with existing reporting systems, manuals, and training programmes. Confining managerial efforts in strict accordance to this model limits the possibilities to develop the new knowledge, which may be needed to accomplish the goals involved in the entire knowledge integration effort. The revised model provides a remedy by pointing to additional ways in which managers can promote knowledge. In embarking on the interactive knowledge creation route, the objectification notion serves to sensitize managers to the need to carefully consider what level of ambiguity, visibility, and autonomy should be crafted into knowledge objects in order for them to function well in that context. The notion of elicitation reminds managers of the need to establish a context that encourages the realization of the unfathomable growth potential of new knowledge.

We suggest that knowledge integration should become a field of enquiry that inhabits a double bridging problematic. Future studies, which pay attention to the specialist-to-specialist as well as the individual-to-organization divide, would provide an interesting option for developing the knowledge integration literature. This chapter rather one-sidedly focused on the individual-to-organization divide. Our suggestions with regard to this side should be useful for developing the conceptual underpinnings for similar future studies.

Part II

Boundary-Crossing Knowledge Integration in Context

6

Open Innovation

Managing Knowledge Integration
across Multiple Boundaries

Lars Bengtsson, Nicolette Lakemond,
Keld Laursen, and Fredrik Tell

6.1 INTRODUCTION

Few firms are able to develop globally competitive products and services on their own, and product development projects increasingly involve collaboration with different kinds of partners to enable low cost access to new knowledge and technologies. This shift from almost total reliance on internal innovation capabilities, to an approach where firms are increasingly keen to benefit from mutual exchanges of knowledge and technologies has been described as a change from closed to open innovation (Chesbrough, 2003). Although research into and the practice of interorganizational product development is fairly well established (see, e.g., Trott and Hartmann, 2009), the growing attention to open innovation models makes it relevant to analyse how firms can manage knowledge flows effectively in more open innovation processes.

One approach is to analyse openness in terms of knowledge flows across boundaries. These knowledge flows are necessary to integrate external knowledge with the firm's internal knowledge in order to achieve competitive advantage (Lawson et al., 2009). Knowledge is considered to be the most valuable resource in the context of innovation, competitive advantage, and firm survival (Grant, 1996). In the open innovation literature, openness tends to signify permeability of the boundaries in the innovation funnel (Dittrich and Duysters, 2007) or refer to the crossing of organizational borders (Elmquist et al., 2009). Chesbrough and Bogers (2014: 17) propose a definition of open innovation as 'a distributed innovation process based on purposively managed knowledge flows across organizational boundaries, using pecuniary and non-pecuniary mechanisms in line with the organization's business model'. This definition stresses boundary crossing and that firms engaging in open innovation need to manage the bridging of those boundaries in order to integrate external with internal knowledge.

However, firms are faced with several kinds of boundaries when they open their innovation processes. This chapter focuses on three types of boundaries: organizational, knowledge, and geographical. The most obvious and most extensively studied boundary is the organizational boundary. Many works focus on analysing the effects of involving different partners in the innovation process (e.g. Laursen and Salter, 2006). These partners include various organizational entities, such as universities, consultants, customers, suppliers, and competitors, all of which require a specific type of collaboration for innovation.

Opening the innovation process to include external partners and resources also involves knowledge exchange across knowledge boundaries. Previous research shows that organizational and knowledge boundaries do not always overlap (Brusoni et al., 2001). Knowledge boundaries are related to the different types of knowledge resources that need to be combined in an open innovation process. Research shows that firms with dissimilar knowledge resources find it more difficult to cross knowledge boundaries, and that a certain level of common knowledge facilitates the integration of knowledge from different actors and areas (Grant, 1996; Postrel, 2002).

The third type of boundary refers to geographical distance, an issue discussed in the literature on research and development (R&D) offshoring. Collaboration that involves geographical distance and the crossing of geographical boundaries poses considerable problems related to the integration of knowledge (Bertrand and Mol, 2013). The significance of geographical boundaries has been stressed in research on how different kinds of proximity affect the prerequisites for the integration of knowledge in interorganizational collaboration (Knoben and Oerlemans, 2006).

In highlighting these different types of boundaries, we show that managing open innovation involves the problem of managing knowledge integration across multiple boundaries. Previous work has studied these boundaries mostly in isolation, and there are few insights into how these various boundaries jointly affect knowledge flows (Laursen and Salter, 2014). To study this aspect requires an analysis of how knowledge flows are affected by the organizational boundaries between different partners, by the geographical boundaries created by partner location, and by the boundaries imposed by the specific types of knowledge that partners bring to a collaboration. A deeper investigation of these aspects would contribute to a better understanding of how firms manage knowledge integration across boundaries in open innovation settings. Greater openness does not mean that boundaries disappear or that a boundaryless organization will emerge (Hirschhorn and Gilmore, 1992). Rather, increased openness implies that new boundaries emerge, and these need to be bridged in order for the knowledge flows across boundaries to be effective.

The main topic addressed in this chapter concerns the managerial challenges resulting from the crossing of multiple boundaries and, specifically, the knowledge integration practices that may be effective for bridging these boundaries. Previous research on interorganizational product development (e.g. Lakemond et al., 2006; Lawson et al., 2009) and work in the outsourcing literature (e.g. McIvor, 2009) points out that how firms manage their relationships is important for the outcomes of collaboration. We analyse knowledge flows by applying a knowledge integration perspective (see, e.g., Berggren et al., 2011). A basic assumption in this perspective is that the outcome of open innovation depends on how well firms manage knowledge integration and the bridging of multiple boundaries. However, there are several issues that need further investigation; for example, which knowledge integration practices are effective for particular boundaries, and what the combined effects of these management practices are. Is there a risk of suboptimization, that is, that a practice used to manage one kind of boundary conflicts with efforts to bridge another type of boundary?

The chapter provides a general discussion on how different knowledge integration practices can be used to bridge multiple boundaries. Our empirical analysis is confined to examining how two kinds of knowledge integration practices are applied, and how effective they are for bridging multiple boundaries in the open innovation process. These knowledge integration practices cover a practice that allows managers to steer projects to a degree (project management) and a practice that allows for synergies between different bodies of knowledge (knowledge matching). Our approach draws on research which suggests that successful integration of external knowledge requires internal and overlapping knowledge and capabilities (Brusoni et al., 2001; Takeishi, 2002; Hillebrand and Biemans, 2004; Koufteros et al., 2010). At the same time, these knowledge integration practices are aimed at allowing organizations to make use of specialized knowledge without unnecessary knowledge transfer (Grant, 1996; Postrel, 2002; Berggren et al., 2011).

The purpose of this chapter is accordingly to analyse how firms manage knowledge integration (e.g. through project management and knowledge matching) across multiple boundaries (organizational, knowledge, and geographical boundaries) in open innovation, and how this affects their innovation performance. Data from an international survey of 415 firms that asks about open innovation is used to illustrate the significance of knowledge integration practices for bridging multiple boundaries.

In Section 6.2, we conceptualize the boundaries in open innovation and discuss different knowledge integration practices that might be effective for bridging those boundaries. Section 6.3 uses data from the survey to analyse and discuss two questions: (1) the innovation effects of crossing multiple boundaries in open innovation; and (2) the moderating effects of knowledge integration practices. Details of the methods used are presented in the Appendix. The chapter concludes with a summary of our findings and contributions regarding the management of knowledge integration across multiple boundaries in open innovation.

6.2 CONCEPTUALIZING BOUNDARIES AND KNOWLEDGE INTEGRATION IN OPEN INNOVATION

6.2.1 Boundaries in Open Innovation

The approach to investigating knowledge flows in open innovation in terms of crossing and bridging different kinds of boundaries is not unique. In addition to Chesbrough and Bogers's (2014: 17) definition of open innovation, which focuses on 'knowledge flows across organizational boundaries...', there is a quite long tradition of innovation studies that use this type of approach. There are also several analyses of interorganizational innovation processes that focus on boundary crossing (e.g. Brusoni et al., 2001; Grandori, 2001; Elmquist et al., 2009). For instance, Brusoni et al. (2001) distinguish between organizational boundaries and knowledge boundaries, stressing that both need to be taken into account when analysing and managing innovation processes. Rosenkopf and Nerkar (2001) discriminate between spanning organizational boundaries and spanning technological boundaries. Laursen and Salter (2006) capture organizational boundaries by investigating the breadth and depth of partner collaboration. In addition, the open innovation process has been conceptualized in relation to the permeability of the boundaries to the 'innovation funnel' (Chesbrough, 2003; Vanhaverbeke et al., 2008; Grönlund et al., 2010; Lind et al., 2012). In similar vein, Lazzarotti et al. (2011) analyse how firms open their boundaries in the different phases of innovation—from idea generation to commercialization. One of the main reasons for embarking on open innovation is to access complementary knowledge from actors outside the firm (Grant and Baden-Fuller, 2004), which requires both organizational and knowledge boundaries to be crossed. Open innovation may require actors with specialized knowledge to integrate that knowledge. However, firms' knowledge boundaries and organizational boundaries may not always overlap and, sometimes, a considerable overlap is required to integrate the knowledge (Takeishi, 2002). Further, the decomposability of the firm's knowledge base structure may affect the flows of knowledge in open innovation (Yayavaram and Ahuja, 2008).

Another way to analyse boundaries is to apply the notion of proximity, in which the distinction between closed and open can be seen as analogous to proximate and distant. Previous studies in this field identify different kinds of proximity and investigate how organizational, cognitive, and geographical proximity affect learning and innovation (see, e.g., Boschma, 2005). Knoben and Oerlemans (2006) discriminate between organizational, technological, and geographical proximity. Our focus on organizational, knowledge, and geographical boundaries is inspired by this literature.

We want to emphasize that increased openness does not mean that boundaries disappear. On the contrary, increased openness in terms of deeper involvement of diverse partners, in different locations, and with different knowledge assets makes the management and bridging of boundaries more complex. This insight suggests that a boundary perspective will add to our knowledge about how to manage knowledge integration in open innovation.

The investigation of organizational boundaries is motivated by the fact that formal organizational boundaries affect both access to and governance of the knowledge flows in open innovation. Governance of knowledge flows refers to deployment of mechanisms and structures to maximize the benefits to be derived from open innovation (Foss and Mahoney, 2010). For example, firms own intellectual property rights (IPR) in the form of patents and copyrights. These can both signal ownership of and protect valuable and codified knowledge to potential collaboration partners (Roberts, 2001).

The effect of organizational boundaries on knowledge flows depends on the type of partner the focal firm is collaborating with in open innovation. The statement that 'not all the smart people work for us' (Chesbrough, 2003: xxvi) suggests that a variety of different partners could be involved in an open innovation process and also that these organizations may differ with respect to objectives, organizational arrangements, and ways of working. A distinction can be made between partners who collaborate for pecuniary reasons, such as suppliers, and those who collaborate for non-pecuniary reasons, such as universities (Dahlander and Gann, 2010). The former generally consider the economic outcomes while the latter are more likely to focus on knowledge creation and exchange. It is reasonable also to expect that aspects such as power and dependency, for example between the firm and its customers, and competitive position will affect knowledge flows. These arguments suggest an analysis of the impact of organizational boundaries on knowledge flows via an investigation of the effect of the involvement of different partner types in open innovation. In the survey study presented in the appendix, we follow the approach in Laursen and Salter (2006) to analyse organizational boundary crossing by capturing the number of partner types involved in open innovation collaborations.

The analysis should be not limited to formal organizational boundaries when trying to understand the challenges of boundary crossing in open innovation. For example, in the context of IPR and as a consequence of the increased openness, co-patenting has become more relevant (Belderbos et al.,

2014). This development would suggest that formal organization is insufficient for governing knowledge since knowledge boundaries are extending beyond the organizational boundaries, captured in the phrase 'firms know more than they make' (Brusoni et al., 2001). The firm's collective knowledge assets go beyond what is currently exploited within its organizational boundaries, which calls for a more in-depth examination of knowledge boundaries.

Opening the innovation processes reveals new knowledge boundaries which must be managed. These boundaries are characterized by the kind of knowledge that is at the centre of the open innovation process. We can distinguish between disciplinary and generic knowledge, which is usually held by and nurtured by universities and research institutes, and more product- and technology-specific knowledge associated with customers and suppliers in particular value chains and by competitors in the same industry. These distinctions indicate that knowledge boundaries are associated with specific partners. It is reasonable also to suggest that knowledge boundaries become more explicit and exposed, and are more difficult to bridge the more intense the collaboration. Drawing on this, in the empirical analysis we capture the existence of knowledge boundaries by measuring the intensity (depth) of partner collaboration.

As discussed by Schumpeter (e.g. 1911/1934: 66), the combination and recombination of knowledge is an essential characteristic of the innovation process. In developing and producing increasingly advanced products and services, firms combine knowledge and technologies from many different domains (Granstrand et al., 1997). These knowledge domains may reside in different organizations, but the relevant knowledge may be partly overlapping (Takeishi, 2002). In open innovation, the focal 'open' firm sources knowledge from different types of partners, with distinct knowledge. We acknowledge that distinctly different knowledge might be captured from the same type of partner, suggesting that competitive priorities and core competencies vary among firms (Prahalad and Hamel, 1990). However, in our empirical analysis we disregard this fact and assume that one type of partner provides a distinct type of knowledge, which needs to be managed and combined with the focal firm's corresponding internal assets. In other words, we assume that the variation among different partner types is larger than the variation between similar partners.

To elaborate, one of the rationales for involving different types of partners is that they provide unique knowledge and technologies that are valuable for the innovation process. Previous studies (e.g. Faems et al., 2005; Bengtsson et al., 2015) show that collaboration with universities and research institutes is oriented to produce more explorative knowledge. In contrast, collaboration with customers and suppliers is more exploitative and provides knowledge valuable for incremental product innovations that are more easily and quickly commercialized. Collaboration on product development with competitors, or 'co-opetition', is more common than might be supposed (Lechner and

Dowling, 2003). Co-opetition networks and horizontal relationships occur in mature industries and in high tech areas in the form of standardization of technological platforms, interfaces, protocols, and so on, which are important prerequisites for and drivers of innovation.

In the context of geographical boundaries, the importance of partners' location in collaboration for innovation has been well studied (Laursen et al., 2011). It is clear that industry value chains are becoming global (Dedrick et al., 2010) and there is increasing involvement of international partners in innovative activities (Narula and Martinez-Noya, 2014). Previous studies show that global sourcing and collaboration can provide access to new knowledge and technologies (see, e.g., Kotabe et al., 2008). However, these efforts present some substantial managerial challenges. Innovation and knowledge integration processes are characterized by fuzzy interfaces between different technologies and competencies. This complexity requires proximity and the integration of key activities (see, e.g., Huang and Rice, 2013). Thus, co-location and local networks are critical for innovation (see, e.g., Liu et al., 2013; Podmetina and Smirnova, 2013).

6.2.2 Managing Knowledge Integration across Boundaries

The open innovation literature has started to pay attention to management aspects that are related to how external knowledge is combined with internal knowledge (Paruchuri, 2010; Foss et al., 2011). It is assumed that effective management practices are key to the integration of knowledge across boundaries. These practices involve governance mechanisms which create opportunities for knowledge recombination, and allow firms to mitigate the costs of creating and sharing knowledge and combining external knowledge with internal knowledge to achieve innovative outcomes (Foss et al., 2010). Thus, knowledge integration is closely related to the governance of knowledge flows (Lakemond et al., 2016). In this chapter, we argue that the governance of knowledge flows, through the application of various knowledge integration practices, produces different innovation outcomes (Felin and Zenger, 2014).

We also argue that the management of knowledge integration across organizational, knowledge, geographical, and other boundaries is a crucial issue in open innovation. There are several management practices that can be used to manage knowledge flows across boundaries (Grandori, 2001). The empirical analysis in this chapter considers two types of knowledge integration practices—project management and knowledge matching—which, arguably, are central to the management and coordination of knowledge flows in collaborative projects. Project management and knowledge matching are both externally and internally oriented, which is in line with previous studies showing that the effectiveness of integrating external knowledge depends on the internal integration process (Takeishi, 2002; Droge et al., 2004; Hillebrand and Biemans, 2004; Koufteros et al., 2005; Bengtsson et al., 2013), and that both internal and external integration are important for the effective development of new products (Tessarolo, 2007). It is in line also with the idea of relative absorptive capacity. Lane and Lubatkin (1998) suggest that fruitful learning processes require some knowledge similarities between the partners and the organizational mechanisms to successfully capture, assimilate, and exploit external knowledge.

In more detail, *project management* includes formal mechanisms such as organizational structures, roles and responsibilities, control systems, auditing and reporting, and lines of communication (Pitsis et al., 2014). *Knowledge matching* can be defined from a knowledge integration perspective (Berggren et al., 2011) and is about actively identifying complementary knowledge assets and technologies (see, e.g., Grant and Baden-Fuller, 2004; Lin and Chen, 2006; Parmigiani and Rivera-Santos, 2011). We use Hagedoorn's (1993) definition of technological complementarity, which, among other things, includes cross-fertilization among scientific disciplines and technological fields. Hagedoorn (1993: 372) claims that close collaboration between companies is required to create 'the necessary complementary technology inputs enabling these companies to capitalize on economies of scope through joint efforts'. In addition, several researchers have stressed the need for common knowledge (e.g. Grant, 1996) for knowledge integration, that is, the existence of sufficient common ground to allow specialists to communicate with and understand each other, and assess each other's domain-specific knowledge and solve problems (Bechky, 2003b; Enberg et al., 2006; Nicolini et al., 2012).

It is reasonable to enquire how the knowledge integration practices implemented bridge across different knowledge boundaries and leverage innovation performance. This acknowledges that firms apply several kinds of management practices, which, hopefully, will act as bridges in open innovation. However, in line with the distinction between potential and realized absorptive capacity (Zahra and George, 2002), we can expect that some practices are effective and realized as intended, while others might have no or even a counterproductive effect. The ultimate indicator of which of the management practices applied is effective for bridging boundaries is performance outcome.

6.2.3 Performance Effects of Boundary Crossing and Knowledge Integration

One of the driving forces of open innovation is the expectation that it will provide innovative products and services at reduced costs and with less risk

(Chesbrough, 2003). Most research in this area takes the claimed benefits for granted, despite some ambiguity related to the realized performance effects (Gassmann et al., 2010). Some empirical studies show that increased openness is followed by better performance, justifying the benefits of involving external partners in the open innovation process (e.g. Leiponen and Helfat, 2011; Garriga et al., 2013; Plewa et al., 2013; Wu et al., 2013).

However, the seminal study by Laursen and Salter (2006) shows that increased openness, in terms of involving more partner types, exhibits an inverted U-shaped relationship with performance; that is, having too few or too many partners has a negative effect on performance. Knudsen and Bøtker Mortensen (2011) show that the involvement of numerous partners in new product development projects can bring unexpected cost effects. However, most studies in this field assume that openness is beneficial, but do not articulate the pros and cons despite a call from Dahlander and Gann (2010) for more research on this aspect.

In this chapter, we analyse open innovation from a knowledge integration perspective to try to reduce this ambiguity. This means that we explore the different types of boundaries and knowledge integration practices in relation to innovation performance, and in relation to the ultimate goal of increased openness. To our knowledge, there are no studies that systematically investigate the benefits and costs of different kinds of knowledge integration practices to bridge multiple boundaries.

Investigating the crossing of multiple boundaries and efforts to integrate knowledge across those boundaries in relation to innovation performance is not straightforward. Such investigation acknowledges the complexity of the open innovation process which involves changes to several boundary dimensions and multiple knowledge flows. Although the opening and boundary-crossing processes are intentional and positively motivated, predicting outcomes is not easy.

On the one hand, opening organizational boundaries through collaboration with specialized partners with distinct knowledge, and outsourcing activities where the firm is at a relative disadvantage, means that the firm can expect improved innovation performance (Chesbrough, 2003). Since innovation is often based on new combinations, the variety implicit in openness to different knowledge domains will benefit innovation performance. Despite the cognitive challenge related to combining knowledge from many different domains, we would expect the gains from new combinations of heterogeneous knowledge resources to be high. There are similar benefits from crossing geographical boundaries. The search for cutting-edge knowledge and technologies is increasingly international (Narula and Martinez-Noya, 2014). Expanding the search environment increases the available external knowledge and, thus, the opportunities to capture and integrate valuable knowledge to create innovations.

On the other hand, the costs involved in crossing boundaries and cooperating with many different kinds of partners cannot be neglected (Laursen and Salter, 2006; Knudsen and Bøtker Mortensen, 2011). The costs of bridging geographical boundaries have been thoroughly explored in studies of offshoring (e.g. Mol et al., 2009).

The crucial question, then, is when are the gains from crossing boundaries eaten up by the costs of the efforts required to integrate the external knowledge. Although increased boundary openness has positive effects on innovation, there are associated challenges that need to be overcome. Another question is concerned with whether the applied knowledge integration practices are effective for managing knowledge flows across multiple boundaries. We assume that innovative firms adapt and apply management practices that are appropriate and effective to manage the boundaries that are opened and need to be bridged. This requires a positive link between each boundary, and a certain knowledge integration practice.

A problem for empirical analysis is that the different kinds of boundaries are likely to overlap (Rosenkopf and Nerkar, 2001). Different partners may involve organizational, knowledge, and geographical boundaries. Conceptually, we argue that it is important to distinguish among these three types of boundaries in order to understand how they can be bridged to facilitate knowledge integration.

6.3 EMPIRICAL ANALYSIS AND DISCUSSION OF FINDINGS

6.3.1 Research Questions and Empirical Analysis

The foregoing suggests an empirical investigation of the issues surrounding knowledge integration across the different types of boundaries and the effects on innovation performance. In this section we present a statistical analysis of three types of boundaries and two types of knowledge integration practices. The analysis and subsequent discussion of the findings are structured around two research questions (see also Figure 6.1).

RQ1: How does open innovation in terms of crossing boundaries (organizational, knowledge, and geographical) relate to innovation performance?

RQ2: What knowledge integration practices (project management and knowledge matching) are effective for bridging the boundaries in open innovation?

The data used are from an online survey on open innovation which received responses from R&D managers in 415 firms in Italy, Sweden, and Finland.

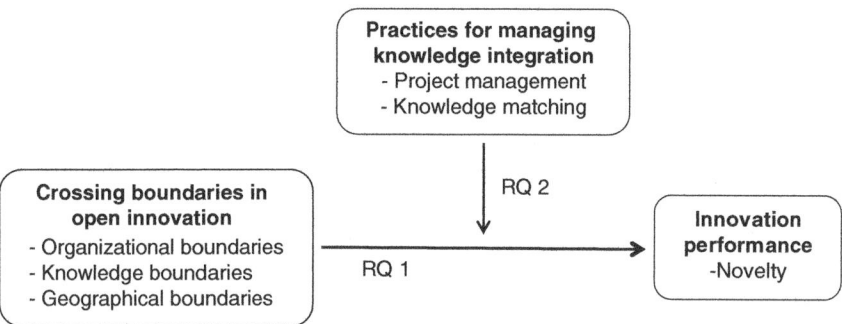

Figure 6.1. The relationships analysed

The organizational boundaries are represented by the number of different partner types that the focal firms involve in their innovation projects. The study included eight possible partner types grouped under academic partners, supply chain partners, and competitors. The knowledge boundaries are represented by the intensity (depth) of the firm's collaboration with these different partners. The geographical boundaries are measured by the extent to which the partners are located abroad. Each knowledge integration practice—project management and knowledge matching—are captured by three items. Innovation performance is measured in terms of new or significantly improved products/services and/or processes, and new market shares. The methodology is described in the Appendix.

The results of the empirical investigation provide new insights into how firms manage knowledge integration across multiple boundaries, and how this affects their innovation performance.

6.3.2 Innovation Outcomes from Crossing Three Boundaries

We are interested in how open innovation (crossing boundaries) relates to innovation performance by enabling knowledge flows across boundaries (Chesbrough and Bogers, 2014). While open innovation involves many kinds of boundaries, we would expect that the benefits as well as the costs might differ among these boundary types. Our empirical analysis of organizational, knowledge, and geographical boundaries, which identifies the type of collaboration partner and the intensity of the collaboration, provides some support for this prediction. The innovation performance linked to crossing different kinds of boundaries is presented in Table 6.1 column 2 (all firms). There are three main findings from our analysis.

First, the results show that crossing many organizational boundaries (measured as numbers of partner types) in the innovation process is negatively

Table 6.1. Analysis of how boundary crossing and knowledge integration practices explain innovation (Linear regression models. Unstandardized coefficients)

Dependent variable = Innovation novelty	All firms		Project management (knowledge integration practice 1)				Knowledge matching (knowledge integration practice 2)			
			High		Low		High		Low	
	Coefficient	S.E.	Coefficient	S.E.	Coefficient	S.E.	Coefficient	S.E.	Coefficient	S.E.
Boundaries										
Organizational boundaries (no of partner types)	−.096*	(.038)	−.080	(.053)	−.094	(.055)	−.051	(.051)	−.119*	(.057)
Knowledge boundaries related to:										
– Academic partners	.267***	(.062)	.237**	(.075)	.198	(.110)	.199*	(.078)	.323**	(.103)
– Value chain partners	.167**	(.053)	.151*	(.069)	.146	(.082)	.152*	(.068)	.158	(.088)
– Competitors	.133*	(.054)	.147*	(.071)	.076	(.083)	.075	(.067)	.187	(.097)
Geographical boundaries	.086**	(.033)	.110*	(.044)	.070	(.049)	.108**	(.040)	.003	(.060)
Controls										
Size (ln)	−.073**	(.026)	−.078*	(.032)	−.114	(.042)	−.086*	(.034)	−.066	(.041)
Innovative industry	.351***	(.046)	.367***	(.065)	.288***	(.068)	.303***	(.061)	.363***	(.074)
Adjusted R sq	.245		.282		.098		.204		.203	
F	19.390***		11.508***		4.213***		9.333***		7.098***	
N	396		187		208		227		168	

*p<0.05; **p<0.01; ***p<0.001

related to innovation performance. This relates to the findings in Laursen and Salter (2006, 2014), which show that the involvement of too many different types of partners and too many sources of knowledge is detrimental to innovation performance (i.e. shows a curvilinear relationship) because it is cumbersome to manage too many relationships with other organizations. Our empirical findings partly support this claim, although we found an overall negative performance effect regardless of the number of partners involved in the open innovation project. This might be because our survey was addressed only to firms that engage in open innovation, that is, they have all passed a certain threshold to external collaboration.

Second, crossing knowledge boundaries seems to provide benefits for innovation, that is, intense collaboration with partners is positively related to performance regardless of the kind of partner. In other words, getting access to new knowledge through close collaboration with universities and consultants, but also customers and suppliers along the value chain, and competitors, seems to be successful.

These findings support Granstrand et al.'s (1997) observation that innovative firms combine knowledge from different domains, and provide further support for Schumpeterian claims that access to new knowledge provides increased combinatory opportunities, which result in increased innovation novelty. The positive outcomes from accessing knowledge from different partners likely follow from the assumption that different knowledge domains reside within different organizations. In studies of co-patenting, Belderbos et al. (2014) show that collaboration with different partners provides different outcomes. It is often assumed that the knowledge and technologies held by universities and consultants are generic, and that more product-specific technologies occur among value chain partners and competitors in certain industries (Un et al., 2010). In many cases this is an oversimplification since the different knowledge boundaries and resources may be overlapping (Takeishi, 2002), indicated in the empirical analysis in this chapter by correlation between partner types.

Third, our results also suggest that crossing geographical boundaries is beneficial for innovation. This suggests that the search for specialized knowledge is more successful if the search is not restricted to local partners and includes international collaborators. A few studies in the open innovation literature explore innovation outcomes in detail. For instance, Schmiele and Sofka (2007) show that firms prefer to collaborate with international rather than local partners. However, there are some studies that argue in favour of local partners to increase innovation (e.g. Simard and West, 2006), and others highlight the costs involved in integrating knowledge from distant actors (Knudsen and Bøtker Mortensen, 2011). The insights in these works have led to some researchers (e.g. Patel et al., 2014) suggesting that a balanced approach (inclusion of both local and foreign partners) is likely to be the most successful. However, while this would produce a curvilinear effect, our results show a positive correlation throughout. This would seem to indicate that the studied firms have found effective ways to bridge geographical boundaries to international partners, an explanation that is consistent with the data set including only firms that use open innovation.

The reasoning is in line with purchasing strategies that assume that global purchasing has positive effects on cost and innovation (Kotabe et al., 2008), but also involve increased risk and higher transaction costs (Mol et al., 2009; Holweg et al., 2011). The results of studies of global purchasing are ambiguous (Schiele et al., 2011; Chiang et al., 2012), leading Steinle and Schiele (2008: 3) to conclude that a 'high global sourcing quota does not necessarily improve a firm's competitiveness'.

The somewhat mixed findings on the innovation outcomes of boundary crossing call for an examination of how the opportunities provided by increased access to knowledge in open innovation are exploited using a firm's recombinative capabilities (Carnabuci and Operti, 2013).

6.3.3 The Moderating Effects of Knowledge Integration

It is difficult, both theoretically and practically, to identify the optimum knowledge integration practices for various boundaries, and to distinguish them from practices that are neutral and incur higher costs or are counter-productive. Our results do not provide a clear answer, but our analysis of two knowledge integration practices sheds some light on this issue. This leads us to the second research question concerning how different knowledge integration practices are able to bridge boundaries and, thus, leverage innovation performance in the open innovation process.

Table 6.1 columns 3–6 show the moderating effect of project management and knowledge matching on innovation novelty by separating firms into two groups based on the extent of their use of knowledge integration practices. The overall pattern indicates that the performance effects of crossing multiple boundaries are mostly positively moderated by the two types of knowledge integration practices; that is, that exploitation of the studied knowledge integration practices enables a positive outcome from boundary crossing.

In more detail, it can be seen that the negative effect on innovation of crossing many organizational boundaries is mitigated in firms that use knowledge matching to a higher extent. The use of project management does not exhibit this moderating effect. In contrast, crossing knowledge boundaries to academic partners has a positive effect on novelty only if there is good project management. It is evident also that the positive effect of drawing knowledge from value chain partners is positively moderated by both project management and knowledge matching. Our results also reveal that working with competitors is beneficial for innovation in firms with good project management. Finally, we observe that the effects of crossing geographical boundaries on novelty are positively moderated by both of the analysed knowledge integration practices.

The finding that the knowledge integration practices have partly differing moderating effects suggests that they might be complementary, that is, they bridge different boundaries. More generally, this implies that, as long as the costs of the knowledge integration practices do not exceed their benefits, firms that implement and use several (appropriate) knowledge integration practices are likely to be more effective than other firms in exploiting the knowledge flows resulting from crossing multiple boundaries in open innovation.

How can these moderating effects be explained? In general, knowledge integration practices are used to facilitate knowledge flows across boundaries. One way to explain how they function is to apply the definition of 'knowledge integration as the bringing together and combining different types of knowledge required for developing new products, systems and solutions and generating the requisite complementary knowledge' (Berggren et al., (2011: 7). In open innovation, knowledge integration practices can be seen as organizational means that combine complementary internal and external knowledge assets (Hagedoorn 1993; Lin and Chen, 2006).

This is in line with studies of absorptive capacity (see, e.g., Zahra and George, 2002) which suggest that successful acquisition, assimilation, and exploitation of external knowledge requires both internal knowledge assets and organizational mechanisms to help firms combine existing internal knowledge with external knowledge. We would suggest that knowledge integration practices are likely to be effective for different kinds of knowledge and different phases of the innovation process, from the search for knowledge to the integration and exploitation of that knowledge. We can apply this reasoning to our analysis of two knowledge integration practices. So why is project management more effective for bridging knowledge boundaries compared to organizational boundaries, and why is knowledge matching more effective for bridging organizational boundaries than project management? One explanation might be that the project management construct applies to the knowledge integration process and captures how the firm manages and promotes knowledge flows among selected partners through the use of project management techniques, formal assessment, and incentive systems. Thus, this practice is directed primarily to managing existing projects and partners and, therefore, is not effective for managing and bridging multiple organizational boundaries.

Knowledge matching focuses on the search and selection process. The construct captures how firms match partners' technological competences, provide access to partners' knowledge resources, and search for synergies through combination. Knowledge matching focuses on the early phases of innovation, that is, on what Zahra and George (2002) call acquisition, directed to improving the knowledge selection process and the management of organizational boundaries. This explains why in firms that apply knowledge to a high extent, the negative impacts of crossing multitude organizational boundaries are mitigated. It would seem that successful firms are those able to adapt knowledge integration practices to the boundaries that need to be crossed in an open innovation process. We suggest that the ability to take a selective approach to the implementation of complementary knowledge integration practices allows a good balance between the benefits and costs of knowledge integration practices.

We find also that the control variables firm size and innovative industry contribute significantly to innovation performance. Being a smaller firm and belonging to an industry characterized by rapid renewal and advanced technologies helps to explain innovativeness.

6.4 CONCLUSIONS

In this chapter we analysed how firms manage knowledge integration across multiple boundaries, necessitated by the inclusion of various external partners in the innovation processes, and the resulting performance effects. Our empirical analysis suggests three conclusions.

First, the crossing of multiple boundaries represents both opportunities and challenges related to managing knowledge flows across these boundaries. Our empirical analysis showed that the effects on innovation performance of crossing organizational, knowledge, and geographical boundaries are mixed. On the one hand, the involvement of many partner types, which requires the crossing of many different kinds of organizational boundaries, has a negative effect on innovation. This supports the view that the benefits to be derived from accessing and combining new knowledge are associated with the costs of managing the resulting knowledge flows. However, it would seem that crossing multiple boundaries may be beneficial for innovation. Specifically, we showed that intensive collaboration with different kinds of partners, involving both knowledge and geographical boundaries, is positively related to innovation.

Second, the application of knowledge integration practices moderates the innovation outcomes in the context of crossing multiple boundaries. The analysis showed that knowledge integration practices can mitigate and/or leverage innovation outcomes. For instance, the negative effects of having to cross numerous organization boundaries can be mitigated by knowledge matching, which focuses on the knowledge and partner selection process rather than management of the knowledge integration process. Knowledge matching is also effective for bridging geographical boundaries. On the other hand, the application of project management techniques and methods was shown to be an effective knowledge integration practice mainly for bridging knowledge and geographical boundaries, but not for managing a variety of organizational boundaries.

Third, we observed a complementarity effect. Analysis of the interplay between boundaries and knowledge integration practices suggests that there is no single best knowledge integration practice; different practices are effective for different kinds of boundaries. This highlights the need to identify the productive link between boundaries and knowledge integration practices. Our findings suggest that the application of a combination of complementary knowledge integration practices is the optimum, based on two main effects. The use of knowledge integration practices allows firms to be open to different kinds of boundaries and, by applying a combination of selective knowledge integration practices, the firm can exploit the benefits of knowledge integration and keep the costs of integration at a reasonable level.

The main contribution of this chapter is that we show, through an analysis of the innovation performance effects of crossing of multiple boundaries, how knowledge flows across boundaries that can be bridged using a combination of complementary knowledge integration practices.

APPENDIX

The results are based on a firm level survey of open innovation in Italy, Finland, and Sweden. The population consists of manufacturing firms (codes 10–32 and 98 in NACE Rev.2) with more than ten employees. Data collection in each country was based on a randomized stratified sample (strata defined by number of employees) of 1,000 manufacturing firms representing the targeted population. The survey design and data collection process used common guidelines in order to ensure comparability of the results across the countries (Forza, 2002). In order to improve the quality of the instrument, pilot tests were conducted with knowledgeable academic colleagues and target respondents in selected firms.

The questionnaires were administered by email to respondents knowledgeable about open innovation in their firm. Respondents were mainly R&D managers. After three reminders we obtained 415 completed questionnaires from firms declaring that they had engaged in open innovation during the previous five years, corresponding to a response rate of about 13 per cent. The 415 completed questionnaires include 152 from firms in Italy, 176 from firms in Sweden, and 87 from firms in Finland. The number of employees varies between 10 and 56,000, with a mean value of 867 employees (standard deviation 4,239 and median 50 employees). A seven-point Likert scale (1 = not at all to 7 = to a great extent) was applied to most of the questions in the survey.

The core independent variables in the analysis are the three types of boundaries. *Organizational boundaries* are represented by the number of different partner types engaged in the open innovation process with the focal firm. Respondents were asked to rate the intensity of collaboration in open innovation with eight suggested partners: universities and R&D centres, innovation intermediaries, government agencies, customers, suppliers, consumers, competitors, and companies in other industries. The partners that collaborated 'to some extent' (more than 1 on the scale) were counted as real partners. The results show that firms engaged in open innovation have between one and eight partners, with a median of 5, mean value of 5.26, and standard deviation 1.95. This means that the number of organizational boundaries that firms need to span differs quite widely.

Knowledge boundaries are based on the knowledge possessed by the different partner types, manifested by the intensity of partner collaboration. Factor analysis (see Table 6.A1) reveals that the eight partner types can be reduced to three main types

Table 6.A1. Factor analysis of knowledge boundaries and knowledge integration practices

	Knowledge boundaries defined by knowledge of			Knowledge integration practices	
	Academic partners	Value chain partners	Competitors	Project management	Knowledge matching
Partners					
Universities	0.798				
Innovation Intermediaries	0.641				
Government agencies	0.789				
Customers		0.798			
Suppliers		0.788			
Consumers		0.556			
Competitors			0.940		
Knowledge integration practices					
Use of project management techniques to manage collaboration				0.736	
Formal assessment of performance and results of collaborative projects				0.872	
Incentive system to recognize the benefits of collaborative innovation				0.728	
Interaction between functions					
Partners' technological competences match up					0.856
Access to partners' knowledge resources					0.852
Synergy created by combining knowledge among participating firms					0.861
Variance explained	24.9%	24.2%	15.3%	61.1%	73.2%
Cronbach's alpha	0.628	0.613	n/a	0.675	0.817
N	415	415	415	415	415

Table 6.A2. Factor analysis for performance and industry character

	Innovation novelty	Innovative industry
Performance		
New or significantly improved products/services	0.816	
New or significantly improved processes	0.841	
New markets	0.751	
Industry character		
Products based on technological breakthroughs		0.740
Technology changes fast		0.751
Important to follow technology development		0.805
Technological complexity increases		0.826
High mix of scientific disciplines and technologies		0.819
Surveillance of many technologies important		0.837
Variance explained	64.6%	63.6%
Cronbach's alpha	0.719	0.885
N	415	415

of partners: academic, value chain, and competitors (firms in other industries were omitted due to equal loading) all of which represent different kinds of knowledge. This means that firms engaging in open innovation encounter different types of knowledge boundaries depending on the intensity of their involvement with the three types of partners.

Geographical boundaries apply to international partners and are measured by a single item capturing to what extent (scale 1–7) R&D activities are performed by external partners located abroad (minimum = 1, maximum = 7, median = 5, mean = 2.23, standard deviation = 1.42).

The moderating variables categorized as management practices for *knowledge integration* were measured by three items in Table 6.A1. The resulting factors represent the practices of project management and knowledge matching. The moderating effects were tested by dividing the sample of firms into two groups for each management practice (high and low; high means above the mean value and low means below the mean value for the analysed practice).

The dependent variable innovation performance was measured by the question: 'Please indicate how well collaboration with external partners in innovation activities has performed against the following objectives over the last three years.' The items used to build the construct in this analysis are displayed in Table 6.A2. Factor analysis resulted in a factor that we call *innovation novelty*.

We used two control variables for the regression analysis: firm size measured as number of employees (natural logarithmic value) and industry type (see Table 6.A2), which reflects the perceived innovativeness of the industry (see, e.g., Gassmann, 2006; Huizingh, 2011).

7

Division of Labour, Supplier Relationships, and Knowledge Integration

Federica Ceci and Andrea Prencipe

7.1 INTRODUCTION

The increasing complexity of products and services, customers' demands for the latest technologies, and high competitive pressure have increased the use of outsourcing as a strategy to reduce costs and access specialized knowledge located outside firms' boundaries. Although we have a relatively thorough understanding of the advantages and disadvantages of outsourcing, we know very little about how firms manage knowledge integration (Bounfour, 1999; Gilley and Rasheed, 2000; Rothaermel et al., 2006; Holcomb and Hitt, 2007; Maskell et al., 2007; McIvor, 2008; Wüllenweber et al., 2008; Bengtsson et al., 2011; Dabhilkar and Bengtsson, 2011; Miozzo and Grimshaw, 2011). Whenever firms decide to make use of outsourcing, they are required to make decisions regarding the definition of their boundaries, their closeness to suppliers in terms of knowledge, capabilities, and which sensitive information to share (Gulati, 1998; Parmigiani, 2007; Parmigiani and Mitchell, 2009; Kapoor and Adner, 2012).

In this chapter, we focus on the knowledge integration requirements related to the implementation of an outsourcing strategy, that is, the mix of decisions that defines whether to outsource or not, the amount of knowledge to retain in house, and the types of relationships with suppliers. The locus of competitive advantage lies in the ability to acquire and retain specialized knowledge and to integrate knowledge bases across different organizational boundaries (Grant, 1996; Henderson and Cockburn, 1996; Patel and Pavitt, 1997; Dibiaggio and Nasiriyar, 2009). According to the literature on transaction cost economics and the resource based view, firms' implementation of outsourcing is influenced by: i) strategic factors which affect resources and capabilities; and ii) technological factors related to the technical characteristics of the production process. Boundaries are shaped in various ways, ranging from close interaction with suppliers, which involves high levels of knowledge sharing, to rigid divisions of labour involving clearly identified tasks, rules, and roles. The range of outsourcing decisions occurs along a continuum between the two extreme points of low integration among firms and a rigid division of labour in which firms are distant from both a cognitive and organizational perspective, and high integration among firms and a blurred division of labour in which cognitive and organizational boundaries are imprecise. In this chapter, we address the following research questions. How do technological and strategic factors affect the implementation of outsourcing in a client–supplier relationship? And, more specifically, how do these factors influence knowledge specialization and integration?

Our analysis is based on a fast-evolving industry: information technology solutions (Oliva and Kallenberg, 2003; Davies, 2004), whose offerings comprise customized bundles of products and services. The offer of solutions drove the elimination of the traditional division between service and manufacturing, allowing firms to provide bundles of products and services in unique packages. More specifically, enterprise resource planning systems, comprising hardware, software, and technical support, are offered as solutions. Clients do not buy individual components from different firms; they purchase a complete enterprise resource planning system from a single supplier, which provides the software and the hardware along with consultancy services, post sales assistance, system customization, and hardware maintenance (Foote et al., 2001; Galbraith, 2002). The offer of solutions poses a number of challenges for firms that need to integrate different activities often performed by diverse firms. The activities involved in solutions are often developed in collaboration with external suppliers, and the solutions provider is responsible for integration and final delivery (Windahl and Lakemond, 2006). Our study focuses on a sample of solutions providers, taking the firm as our unit of analysis.

7.2 THEORETICAL BACKGROUND

7.2.1 The Boundaries of Organizations

When Coase (1937) first proposed the notion of transaction cost economics, this constituted a major departure from the dominant neoclassical economic orthodoxy. As Joskow (1988) pointed out, one of the most important contributions of transaction cost economics is its comparative perspective, that is, its recognition that there is a wide range of arrangements which can be used to govern transactions. Markets and hierarchies roughly define the two extremes of a variety of resource allocation arrangements. However, there is no rigid separation between markets and hierarchies in either practice or the literature.

The decision process is more complex and, once the production process is moved outside the firm's boundaries, firms are required to define the types of relationships with their suppliers. Firms are supposed to define their closeness with suppliers and, more importantly, how much knowledge and sensitive information to share.

Strategy and innovation scholars have begun to explore the structure of the relationships among agents in an industry. Empirical research on a variety of empirical contexts, for example, computers (Baldwin and Clark, 2000), text books (Schilling, 2000), and mortgage banking (Jacobides, 2005), suggests that industries are moving towards increasing disintegration and specialization. The structure of the industries so defined both influences and is influenced by how firms develop, share, and integrate labour and knowledge (Dalziel, 2007; Pisano and Teece, 2007; Fixson and Park, 2008). New dynamics, such as the transition from vertical integration to vertical disintegration, accelerate and alter consolidated boundary divisions. This shift poses new challenges for the integration of heterogeneous knowledge bases and the effectiveness of established knowledge integration mechanisms (e.g. systems integration) (Brusoni et al., 2009; Ferraro and Gurses, 2009).

7.2.2 The Boundaries of Knowledge and its Integration

Management scholars have long acknowledged the value and challenges of knowledge integration. Design, production, and commercialization of products and services require the ability to acquire and integrate different knowledge bases (Henderson and Clark, 1990; Rumelt, 1991; Iansiti and Clark, 1994). Integration could be seen as among an organization's primary objectives; according to the knowledge-based view, selecting appropriate knowledge bases and facilitating their integration are the ultimate reasons for a firm's existence (Kogut and Zander, 1992; Grant, 1996). In fact, the evolution of new products derives from the interaction among a variety of knowledge bases, and coordination of a network of suppliers (Prencipe, 1997). Several scholars have studied how 'firms identify and create means of sharing, shaping, and reorganizing knowledge' (Brusoni et al., 2009: 211), and the role of specialized knowledge bases as sources of competitive advantage, combined with the importance of developing dedicated mechanisms to integrate this knowledge. Thus, the ability to integrate heterogeneous knowledge bases is a prerequisite for the achievement of long-term competitive advantage (Prencipe et al., 2003).

Integration has been defined as 'the quality of the state of collaboration that exists among departments that are required to achieve unity of effort by the demand of the environment' (Lawrence and Lorsch, 1967: 11). In the context of information technology solutions, knowledge integration includes all the activities, processes, and routines a firm deploys to facilitate collaboration among different partners contributing to the various components of its offering, with the objective of developing product–service bundles in a more efficient manner. This coordination effort is de facto a knowledge integration process 'that facilitates a common understanding of project objectives and the means to reach those objectives' (Mitchell, 2006: 924). Mitchell (2006) identifies two different kinds of knowledge integration approaches: boundary spanning and integrative. In an initial phase, knowledge integration should fulfil a boundary spanning role allowing firms to import external knowledge (i.e. knowledge about the functioning of a specific component developed by an external supplier). In a second phase, this externally acquired knowledge needs to be blended so that different stand-alone elements can be recombined into a single bundle (Dawson et al., 2010).

Outsourcing poses important questions about how to coordinate and integrate the outsourced knowledge and, in conceptualizing the possible solutions, we identify two configurations that represent the poles of a continuum of configurations decisions that firms might adopt. The two configurations represent two different challenges for firms called on to integrate different knowledge bases.

In the first configuration (faraway), firms opt for market-based relationships, with little overlap of knowledge and capabilities, and with a rigid separation of activities. In this configuration, it is vital that outsourcers retain close control over externalized activities, because higher control and rigid division of labour limits supplier opportunism (Demsetz, 1968; Conner and Prahalad, 1996; Takeishi, 2002). This configuration is appropriate for simple and well-structured problems (Farjoun, 1994; Macher, 2006). The knowledge that is outsourced overlaps very little with the knowledge that is kept in house, and coordination and integration occur via an arm's length relationship.

In the second configuration (so close), firms opt for close integration with suppliers with cognitive and administrative overlap (Petersen et al., 2003; Das et al., 2006). A close relationship with suppliers facilitates the development of similar capabilities (Borys and Jemison, 1989), lowers the risks of technological uncertainty (Kapoor and Adner, 2012), and facilitates knowledge sharing (Bonaccorsi and Lipparini, 1994; Parmigiani, 2007). This solution is appropriate for ill-structured and complex problems (Macher, 2006). In this case, there is important knowledge overlap among the collaborating firms, and knowledge integration is based on continuous and informal exchanges of knowledge and information.

7.3 HYPOTHESES DEVELOPMENT

In order to explore the knowledge integration requirements for these two configurations, we identified two sets of factors which, according to transaction cost economics and resource-based view literatures, influence outsourcing implementation and, therefore, knowledge integration. The first set of requirements is technology related and influenced by the technology underlying the activities outsourced. Firms have less freedom to modify them. There are two factors affecting this category: i) degree of product modularity; and ii) level of process standardization. The degree of modularity depends on the possibility of developing common product interfaces, and is influenced largely by the characteristics of the activity being outsourced; the level of process standardization depends on the technical characteristics of the activity.

The second set of factors is strategy related: they do not depend on the technical characteristics of the outsourced tasks, but are influenced by the firm's decisions. These strategic factors are: i) the core-ness of the task; and ii) the frequency of the activity's inclusion in the solution. These factors influence the firm's strategic positioning, and depend on the firm's characteristics and decisions.

These four factors are identified based on the specificities of the information technology solution. Drawing on previous studies, we selected a set of factors influencing the firm's outsourcing decision (Davies, 2001, 2004; Galbraith, 2002; Windahl et al., 2004; Davies et al., 2006; Ceci, 2009; Ceci and Masini, 2011). We know how these factors impact on the decision whether or not to outsource, but we do not know the extent to which they impact on the other aspects of outsourcing. A review of the literature leads to the development of our hypotheses.

7.3.1 Modularity of Products

In modular architectures, module interfaces are standardized and must remain unchanged for a specified period of time (Schilling, 2000). Each module performs a specific function and can be designed and improved independently. Products designed according to modularity principles can be easily interconnected and bundled (Ulrich, 1995). Modularity offers several advantages: it enables the benefits of customization to be captured without incurring its full costs and, therefore, allows greater specialization; it helps firms achieve flexibility and respond quickly to the market through the introduction of new products, the extension of existing product lines, and rapid product upgrades (Sanchez and Mahoney, 1996; Schilling and Steensma, 2001). Tiwana (2008b) highlights that technological modularity can substitute for more formal control mechanisms, such as alliances, because it facilitates the decoupling of inter-operating subsystems. Modularity is an interesting approach to knowledge integration, because firms' learning processes are enacted at both the component and architecture levels (Sanchez and Mahoney, 1996). In order to coordinate and manage modular products, firms must act as system integrators

(Brusoni and Prencipe, 2001), which means they face different knowledge integration requirements: thus, modularity can act as a knowledge integration mechanism. For these reasons, modularity facilitates extensive use of outsourcing, which allows the firm to concentrate on downstream activities to provide more lucrative services and solutions to customers, and mitigate the risk of technology appropriation by alliance partners, which decreases the need for intensive inter-firm interactions (Prencipe et al., 2003).

Hypothesis 1: A 'faraway' outsourcing strategy is preferred in the case of modular products.

7.3.2 Standardization of Processes

Process standardization facilitates control over the production process, making the decision to outsource more viable. However, it is not clear how high processes standardization affects relationships with the supplier. The systems integration literature suggests that a strong relationship with the supplier, and high integration, are preferred in the case of non-standardized processes (Prencipe et al., 2003; Hobday et al., 2005). On the other hand, in the case of a decision to implement a standardized process, lower integration with suppliers is required. In fact, once common protocols are developed, the integration of different subcomponents is straightforward: a standardized production process facilitates the production of components that work together easily, facilitating division of labour and integration of different bodies of knowledge (Beimborn et al., 2009). Absence of standardization makes it difficult to integrate knowledge, since it requires integration of knowledge bases that are not entirely under the focal firm's control, because they originate from both the firm and its suppliers (Sanchez-Gonzalez et al., 2009).

Hypothesis 2: A 'faraway' outsourcing strategy is preferred in the case of highly standardized processes.

7.3.3 Frequency

Another factor that influences the outsourcing strategy decision is the frequency of transactions. Transaction cost economics points out that 'specialized governance structures are more sensitively attuned to the governance needs of non-standard transactions than are unspecialized structures, *ceteris paribus*' (Williamson, 1985: 60). The cost of a specialized governance structure is higher than the costs of an unspecialized structure, so the number of transactions is central in the decision about whether to adopt an ad hoc governance structure or not. In our empirical context, in the case of a one-off transaction there is no need for ad hoc transaction meetings or dedicated agreements: the market is preferred because it is less expensive.

Hypothesis 3: A 'so close' outsourcing strategy is preferred in the case of frequent activities.

7.3.4 Core

Firms tend to specialize in activities in which they have comparative advantage (Kogut and Zander, 1992; Teece et al., 1997; Jacobides and Winter, 2005). As pointed out by Hamel and Prahalad (1994), successful growth requires the development of adequate core capabilities. By core capabilities we mean all the capabilities essential for the firm's achievement of competitive advantage (Barney, 1991; Leonard-Barton, 1992; Patel and Pavitt, 1997). Firms' core capabilities allow access to a number of markets, contribute significantly and positively to the client's perception of the product, and make its imitation difficult. Thus, core capabilities provide the firm with strategic differentiation (Leonard-Barton, 1995). Outsourcing strategies are influenced by the firm's configuration capabilities because firms tend to retain in house those activities that are core to their business.

Hypothesis 4: A 'so close' outsourcing strategy is preferred in the case of outsourcing core activities.

7.4 THE EMPIRICAL CONTEXT: THE INFORMATION TECHNOLOGY SOLUTIONS BUSINESS

In an increasing number of industry sectors, firms are moving toward the provision of bundled services and products, or integrated solutions (Galbraith, 2002; Oliva and Kallenberg, 2003; Windahl et al., 2004; Kapletia and Probert, 2010; Miozzo and Grimshaw, 2011). Solutions or integrated solutions, initially adopted by the information technology sector, are now widely diffused (Windahl and Lakemond, 2006; Kapletia and Probert, 2010). The provision of solutions consists of offering a bundle of activities. These activities (e.g. financing contracts, after-sales support, maintenance, user training, software, hardware) differ among customers and require unique, highly heterogeneous knowledge bases, which makes their integration requirements stringent, possibly undermining the effectiveness of previously developed mechanisms (Windahl and Lakemond, 2006; Ceci and Prencipe, 2008). The emergence of these new offers is forcing firms to change their approach to the definition of boundaries: they are required to incorporate new knowledge bases that span the entire value chain and beyond. Manufacturers need to include service elements; service firms need manufacturing elements; both need to include consulting and post-sales activities. In addition, the scope of knowledge reservoirs can shift dynamically: knowledge hitherto considered critical may become unnecessary, and new knowledge bases not previously considered may become a *condicio sine qua non* for remaining competitive.

7.5 METHODS

7.5.1 Data Collection: Sampling and Questionnaire Administration

The data for this study were obtained via a survey of a sample of solutions providers operating in the information technology sector. In the first phase of data collection, we drew on the literature and empirical evidence to generate valid items to measure the constructs in our theoretical model. The literature review focused on four topics: solutions, systems integration, project-based organization, and firm boundaries (Oliva and Kallenberg, 2003; Prencipe et al., 2003; Brady and Davies, 2004; Cerasale and Stone, 2004; Davies et al., 2006). This was supplemented by a multiple case study analysis (Ceci and Prencipe, 2008; Ceci, 2009).

In the second phase of data collection, we administered a questionnaire to a sample of information technology solutions providers in Europe. Our unit of analysis is the solution provider; thus, we analyse strategic decisions from a firm point of view. Sample selection was based on an ad hoc sampling procedure. In the absence of a database of solutions providers, we developed a procedure to estimate this population, from which we extracted a sampling frame. We used the Amadeus database of European companies to construct the population of generic information technology firms. Since firms that provide solutions are former software houses, hardware producers, and consultancy firms, we considered the following NACE codes: 3001 and 3002 (manufacture of office machinery and computers), and 7210, 7221, 7222, 7230, 7240, 7250, and 7260 (computer and related activities). We then randomly selected a sample of 200 firms from this population and examined their websites to ascertain whether they provided solutions. This resulted in a group of generic information technology firms that had moved into the solutions business, stratified by number of employees, and computed on the population of information technology solutions providers. Finally, to ensure sample homogeneity, we restricted our survey population to four countries—Italy, Spain, the UK, and Sweden, which are representative of the overall population of information technology solution providers in Europe, and which offered favourable

Table 7.1. Population and sample characteristics

		No. of employees			
	Location	20 to 99	100 to 499	500+	Total
Firms operating in the	Italy	895	293	65	1,253
information technology	United Kingdom	1,791	792	202	2,785
sector					
(source: Amadeus database)	Sweden	610	131	29	770
	Spain	813	301	56	1,170
	Total	**4,109 *(69%)***	**1,517 *(25%)***	**352 *(6%)***	**5,978**
Firms offering solutions	Italy	421	147	65	632
	United Kingdom	842	396	202	1,440
	Sweden	287	65	29	381
	Spain	382	150	56	588
	Total	**1,932 *(63%)***	**758 *(25%)***	**352 *(12%)***	**3,042**
Sample	Italy	20	6	4	30
	United Kingdom	16	4	7	30
	Sweden	12	7	4	23
	Spain	11	5	3	19
	Total	**62 *(61%)***	**23 *(22%)***	**17 *(17%)***	**102**

opportunities for data collection. To select the sampling frame from this population of 3,042 firms (Table 7.1), we randomly chose forty firms from each country, yielding a final sampling frame of 160 firms. We obtained contacts for these firms from information technology professional associations, alumni databases from business schools and universities, and distribution lists from specialist newspapers and chambers of commerce.

Because our survey required respondents to have direct and personal involvement in a solution project, the ideal respondent was identified as a project manager who had completed at least one project with the firm. In order to guarantee that project level data was a reliable proxy for all of the firm's (our unit of analysis) activities, project managers were asked to refer to a project that was highly representative of the company's activities (i.e. in the class of projects that generated the largest proportion of revenue for the organization) (Subramaniam and Venkatraman, 2001). To increase the response rate, we guaranteed that all data would remain confidential and would be used only for academic purposes; we also promised to provide personalized feedback, benchmarking the respondent's firm against a representative sample.

Telephone interviews were chosen as the preferred mode of data collection because they allowed the researcher to complement the data derived from the questionnaire with qualitative information that could be used to better characterize the firms. This method yielded a 64 per cent response rate, which is higher than in similar studies (Miller and Roth, 1988; Bensaou and Venkatraman, 1995). The final sample included 102 firms.

7.5.2 Data Analysis: Operationalization of Variables

Previous studies (Ceci and Prencipe, 2008; Ceci, 2009) identify seven types of activities offered by solutions providers: post-sales (hardware maintenance, software assistance, software problem-solving, hotline service, software upgrading, user training); consulting (business consulting, network and technology consulting, engineering consulting); systems integration (all the activities that contribute to a high level of integration among different components); software development (software design, building, and testing); financial (leasing, flexible payment structure, competitive interest rate, buyout options); hardware and infrastructure manufacturing (hardware manufacturing and assembling, building works, cable and network creation); and delivery activities (software customization and installation, hardware delivery). For each solution project, we considered only the outsourced activities and, to test our hypotheses, we measured: i) outsourcing strategies (dependent variables); ii) the four factors influencing outsourcing strategies (independent variables); and iii) the characteristics of firms and projects (control variables). Since all the firms in the sample operate in the same industry, we do not need to control for sector specificities.

To investigate outsourcing strategies, we use two dependent variables that capture two distinct but complementary aspects: use of concurrent sourcing, and type of relationship with suppliers.

Firms adopt a concurrent sourcing approach if there is an overlap of activities and knowledge with those of suppliers: the term 'concurrent sourcing' is used by Parmigiani (2007) to describe the phenomenon of a firm that simultaneously buys and makes the same good or service (Harrigan, 1986; Bradach and Eccles, 1989; Parmigiani, 2007; Gulati and Puranam, 2009). Concurrent sourcing has specific characteristics: it is not a mix of make and buy, and represents the firm's discrete choice. Concurrent internal and external sourcing provides a wider range of knowledge sources, enabling the firm to exploit its cumulative knowledge and explore a broader set of technologies from suppliers (Bradach, 1997; Cassiman and Veugelers, 2006; He and Nickerson, 2006; Rothaermel et al., 2006; Parmigiani, 2007). The variable concurrent sourcing is a dummy variable based on a Likert scale. The questionnaire asked for the percentage of work done internally, with responses coded as follows: 0 = none; 1 = up to 20 per cent; 2 = 21 per cent to 40 per cent; 3 = 41 per cent to 60 per cent; 4 = 61 per cent to 80 per cent; 5 = 81 per cent to 100 per cent. The dummy variable assumes the value of 1 if the percentage of work done internally is between 20 per cent and 60 per cent (Likert = 2, 3, or 4), and 0 if it is over 60 per cent or under 20 per cent (Likert = 0, 1, or 5). Concurrent sourcing explores outsourcing strategies from a cognitive viewpoint, focusing on knowledge boundaries and the capabilities across firms.

The second variable evaluates the type of relationship with the supplier. We understand type of relationship as the contractual form adopted to regulate the exchange, as defined by law and mutual agreement among firms. Type of relationship defines organizational boundaries from a formal viewpoint, and captures the extent of the interactions between the firm and its supplier. Studies that focus on the types of relationships between partners identify a series of factors that influence the decision such as the length of the relationship, expected exchanges of knowledge and resources, and the need for efficiency and flexibility (Borys and Jemison, 1989; Argyres, 1996; Conner and Prahalad, 1996). The variable relationship with supplier captures the type of the firm's relationship with its suppliers measured on a nominal 1–5 scale (1 = contractor, 2 = preferred supplier, 3 = strategic alliance, 4 = partnership, 5 = joint venture). This variable investigates outsourcing strategies from an organizational viewpoint, identifying administrative and organizational boundaries.

In relation to the independent variables, we identified four factors that influence outsourcing strategies. The technological factors product modularity and process standardization are measured on a five-point Likert scale that investigates the use of modular products and standardized process in the outsourced activity based on the following items: modular products were used for these activities, and standardized operating procedures were followed in this activity. The technological factors are operationalized as follows: the variable frequency, indicating the frequency of provision is assessed using a five-point Likert scale and the following item: this activity is usually performed in every project in this company. The variable core indicates whether the activity is central to the type of the firm's offering and is measured on a five-point Likert scale through the item: this activity is a key activity in our business.

The distinction between strategic and technological factors has been tested empirically using principal component analysis, which is a statistical technique used for data reduction that allows us to explore similarities across identified elements. We identified two components (see Table 7.2) which confirm our theoretical distinction between strategic (core and frequency) and technological (modularity and standardization) factors. Factor loadings exceed the recommended cut-off value of 0.60. We performed an Analysis of Variance (ANOVA) to investigate the behaviour of the variables across activities (see Table 7.3). ANOVA is a statistical test for whether or not the means of several groups are equal. The use of multiple two sample t-tests would result in an increased chance of a type I error; since we are comparing seven groups, ANOVA is preferred. The results show that, for technological factors (product modularity and process standardization), the effects are significant (p = 0.058). This implies that the means differ more than would be expected by chance

Table 7.2. Principal component analysis

Scoring coefficients for orthogonal varimax rotation

Variable	Comp1	Comp2
Frequency	0.7089	−0.0259
Core	0.6794	−0.0038
Product Modularity	−0.1014	0.7790
Process Standardization	0.1596	0.6265

Table 7.3. One-way Anova

Strategy-related act. (comp1)		Tech-related act. (comp2)	
F ratio	Prob.>F	F ratio	Prob.>F
0.78	0.5887	2.52	0.0234
mean group differences are not significant		mean group differences are significant	

alone. Therefore, we can say that their values vary according to the types of activities, and that each activity implies a specific level of modularity or standardization originating from the nature of the activity. For the strategic factors (core and frequency), the effects are not significant ($p = 0.57$), and the differences between means are not sufficiently large to identify differences among the activities. This confirms our reasoning that technological factors are influenced by the underlying technology, and that their values differ according to the type of activity, while strategic factors are not dependent on the type of activity, and their values are not influenced by the characteristics of the activity.

The four control variables used in the models (increase in outsourcing, firm size, client size, and project length) are measured, respectively, as the difference between the percentage of outsourcing activities in the year of the analysis (2005) and five years previously (2000); the firm's annual turnover; the turnover of the solution's client; and the length of the project selected by the interviewee as representative of the firm's activities.

7.5.3 Data Analysis: Analytical Approach

We tested the data obtained from respondents for common method variance using Harman's single factor test (Podsakoff et al., 2003) and found no evidence of common method variance. The correlations are generally low (Table 7.4). We test the hypotheses by fitting an ordered logistic regression model (1) and a linear logistic regression model (2). Owing to the qualitative nature of the dependent variable, relationship with supplier, we used an

Table 7.4. Correlation matrix

		Mean	Std Dev.	1	2	3	4	5	6	7	8	9	10
1	Concurrent Sourcing	0.310	0.463	1.000									
2	Role Suppliers	2.470	1.103	0.008	1.000								
3	Process Standardization	3.940	1.066	-0.258	0.225	1.000							
4	Product Modularity	3.727	1.059	0.191	0.282	0.265	1.000						
5	Frequency	4.155	0.952	-0.016	0.064	0.216	0.258	1.000					
6	Core	4.322	0.960	0.028	0.143	0.153	0.238	0.381	1.000				
7	Increase of Outsourcing	0.023	0.172	0.227	0.021	-0.141	0.092	0.043	0.029	1.000			
8	Size of the firm	979	3.102	-0.002	-0.023	0.237	0.015	-0.116	-0.047	-0.037	1.000		
9	Client Size	2.195	0.856	-0.220	0.039	0.044	-0.121	-0.080	0.024	-0.046	0.259	1.000	
10	Project Length	1.968	0.814	0.122	-0.248	0.025	-0.270	0.023	-0.208	-0.138	0.188	0.154	1.000

Table 7.5. Ordered Logit Model 1 and Logit Model 2

	Model 1		Model 2	
	Dependent variable: Role of Supplier		Dependent variable: Concurrent Sourcing	
	Ordered Logistic Reg.		Logistic Reg.	
	Coeff.	S.E.	Coeff.	S.E.
Process Standardization	0.454***	0.148	−0.808***	0.210
Product Modularity	0.305**	0.140	1.054***	0.289
Frequency	−0.067	0.157	−0.373	0.273
Core	0.061	0.147	0.239	0.260
Increase of Outsourcing	0.037	0.749	2.563**	1.085
Size	−0.000	0.000	0.000	0.000
Client Size	0.224	0.159	−0.747***	0.247
Project Length	−0.416**	0.173	1.017***	0.293
N	*212*		*212*	
Log Likelihood	*−280.059*		*−86.527*	
PseudoR2	*0.055*		*0.260*	
LR chi2	*32.84*		*60.88*	

*p<0.10; **p<0.05; ***p<0.01

ordered logit model for Model 1. In Model 2, the dependent variable is binary (concurrent sourcing: 0; 1). Table 7.5 reports the results.

$$Y_1 = a + \beta_1 \, standardization + \beta_2 \, modularity + \beta_3 \, frequency$$
$$+ \beta_4 \, core + \beta_5 \, increase \; in \; outsourcing + \beta_6 \, firm \; size + \beta_7 \, client \; size \quad (7.1)$$
$$+ \beta_8 \, project \; length + \epsilon$$

$$Y_2 = a + \beta_1 \, standardization + \beta_2 \, modularity + \beta_3 \, frequency + \beta_4 \, core$$
$$+ \beta_5 \, increase \; in \; outsourcing + \beta_6 \, firm \; size + \beta_7 \, client \; size \quad (7.2)$$
$$+ \beta_8 \, project \; length + \epsilon$$

Model 1 (Table 7.5) yields the following results: two out of four independent variables have a significant effect on the dependent variable relationship with supplier. The two technological variables, standardization of processes (+0.454) and product modularity (+0.305), have a positive impact on the dependent variable role of suppliers, while the two strategic factors (the variables core and frequency) are not significant. Hypotheses 1 and 2 are not supported since the direction of the impact is opposite to the direction hypothesized. This finding contrasts with the previous literature. In the case of Model 2 (Table 7.5), analysis of the results of the logit regression shows that product modularity has a positive impact (+1.054) on the firm's choice to engage in concurrent sourcing, while the variable process standardization has a negative impact (–0.808). Similar to Model 1, none of the strategic factors, the variables core and frequency, is significant.

7.6 DISCUSSION OF RESULTS

Analysis of the two models, briefly discussed in Section 7.5.3, suggests the following. In the case of Hypothesis 1 (A 'faraway' outsourcing strategy is preferred in the case of modular products), we expected the variable product modularity to have a negative sign. However, product modularity has a positive impact in both models. The use of modularity facilitates the integration of different knowledge (Schilling, 2000); this pushes firms to increase their use of outsourcing. Moreover, modularity helps to resolve complex problems, enabling division of labour also in complex systems. However, such complexity requires strong integration with suppliers. Our results suggest that the use of modular products in a solution requires close integration among the players, because of the need to develop common interfaces to facilitate the functioning of different modules. Therefore, we can confirm that modularity acts in two steps. It facilitates the outsourcing of activities and, once the activities are outsourced, it requires close relationships with suppliers.

Hypothesis 2 (A 'faraway' outsourcing strategy is preferred in the case of highly standardized processes) is only partially supported. The variable process standardization has an impact on both dependent variables, but its role is ambiguous: in fact, it has a negative impact on the use of concurrent sourcing (Model 2). This supports Hypothesis 2, suggesting that standardization of processes increases division of labour: process standardization facilitates control and reduces the need to share knowledge and sensitive information. In Model 1, standardization of processes has a positive impact on the dependent variable role of suppliers, which does not support Hypothesis 2. The variable role of suppliers measures the structure of the firms' boundaries from an organizational viewpoint, while the variable concurrent sourcing is focused more on knowledge and information sharing. Our results suggest the existence of overlap in the organizational boundaries of companies: the standardization of processes (as in the case of product modularity) facilitates the use of outsourcing (as suggested by transaction cost economics), but, among all the possible configurations of outsourcing strategies, a strong relationship with partners is preferred.

The results of Models 1 and 2 do not support Hypothesis 3 (A 'so close' outsourcing strategy is preferred in the case of frequent activities) or

Hypothesis 4 (A 'so close' outsourcing strategy is preferred in the case of outsourcing core activities): the variables core and frequency are not significant. We tested the effect of these variables on the decision to outsource or not, and found a significant relation (details available from the authors upon request). However, these two variables play no role in influencing either the type of relationship with the suppliers or the use of concurrent sourcing. This is an important result: the variables frequency and core represent decisions taken by the firms; their lack of significance suggests that firms, on their own, have a minor impact on the outsourcing strategy. It would seem that outsourcing strategies are shaped mainly by the characteristics of the activities and much less by the strategic choices of firms. Our results suggest strong technological determinism: firms have little strategic discretion when defining the type of relations with the suppliers, and making decisions related to knowledge specialization and integration.

7.7 CONCLUSIONS

Outsourcing is a viable strategy that is being used by firms increasingly, to lower costs, to access new knowledge and capabilities, to gain flexibility, and to allow a focus on distinctive and core capabilities (Bettis et al., 1992; Brusoni et al., 2001; Mol et al., 2005; Rothaermel et al., 2006; Holcomb and Hitt, 2007). However, this strategy must be carefully considered. It carries risks and, in the long term, could lead to losses in core technologies and capabilities, and to the transfer of internal knowledge outside the firm's boundaries. It is crucial to understand the challenges related to knowledge integration.

The decision to outsource a specific activity is only the first in a series of important decisions about which knowledge to retain in house, which abilities to acquire, which specialized knowledge to keep, and which different organizational knowledge bases to integrate. The knowledge integration requirements related to implementing an outsourcing strategy were the central focus in this chapter.

There are two main findings from our investigation. First, high levels of product modularity and process standardization lead to close interactions among players, which is contrary to what we expected. Previous work suggests that the use of modular products and standardized processes facilitates division of labour: activities with these characteristics can be outsourced in a straightforward way from a technical perspective, but there is still a need for knowledge integration.

In the literature review we refer to the work of Mitchell (2006), who describes two different knowledge integration approaches—boundary spanning and integrative. Knowledge integration needs first to fulfil a boundary-spanning role to enable firms to import external knowledge (i.e. knowledge about the functioning of a specific component developed by external suppliers). This externally acquired knowledge needs to be recombined into a single bundle (Dawson et al., 2010). We believe that our results enhance this interesting classification: modularity and standardization operate as mechanisms facilitating the boundary-spanning role of knowledge integration and eliminating overlaps in firm and suppliers' knowledge. However, knowledge interactions are still required. Our results can be interpreted as technological factors act as boundary spanners, but integrative mechanisms are still needed. To implement integrative mechanisms, close interactions are needed among the players.

Second, our empirical results show clearly that strategic factors have a limited impact on the implementation of outsourcing strategies. The role of strategic factors in shaping firms' boundaries is generally accepted, and there is vast empirical evidence and theoretical justification for the central role played by the variables core and frequency in the decision to outsource or not. However, if we focus on how close firms want to be to their suppliers, and how they integrate the knowledge outsourced, this decision would seem to be independent of strategic factors. It would appear that the final configuration of the relationship is influenced much more by technological factors. Technological aspects and the characteristics of the productive process determine the knowledge integration strategy. This is coherent with Fixson and Park (2008: 1296), which points to 'the existence of multiple linkages between product architecture and industry structure'. Thus, the structure of the product influences the outsourcing strategy more than firms' internal characteristics. This reinforces the idea of technological determinism: firms have little strategic discretion in defining knowledge integration mechanisms.

Our results have some limitations. First, the analysis is based on a small sample, which might reduce their statistical power. The study's target population was narrowly defined to include a homogeneous set of firms, which could limit the generalizability of this research. Second, there are some data limitations: data were gathered at one point in time, so it is not possible conclusively to infer causality. Another consequence of our data-gathering approach is that whilst the analysis provides a very good static picture of the firms studied, it provides limited information on their evolution over time. Finally, our study does not evaluate firm performance. Our results refer to the decisions taken by the firms with no insight into the optimal decision from a performance viewpoint. These observations suggest several avenues for future research. Follow-up empirical studies are needed to confirm our hypotheses, and these should be extended to different industry sectors.

8

Knowledge, Uncertainty, and the Boundaries of the Firm

Evidence from a Study of Formula One Racing Constructors, 1950–2000

Fabrizio Castellucci and Gianluca Carnabuci

8.1 INTRODUCTION

A primary function of firms is to integrate diverse knowledge inputs in order to create economically valuable outputs (Barney, 1986; Prahalad and Hamel, 1990; Argyres, 1996; Teece et al., 1997). Prior literature emphasizes that learning to integrate knowledge across areas of specialization is crucial to gain competitive advantage (Grant, 1996) and to sustain a continuous stream of technological innovation (Kogut and Zander, 1992; Operti and Carnabuci, 2014). As the design, development, and manufacture of new technologies requires increasingly complex knowledge, firms often must complement their internal knowledge base with externally generated knowledge. Accordingly, understanding why some of the firm's critical technologies 'are developed and produced in house and why others are contracted out' (Brusoni et al., 2001: 597) is a central problem in knowledge-based theories of the firm and in organization theories more broadly.

In this chapter, we argue that the choice to either develop critical technologies in house or contract them out depends on the *kind* of uncertainty faced by the firm. Extant research suggests that uncertainty or the inability accurately to predict the future on the basis of the firm's existing knowledge (Beckman et al., 2004: 260), is a critical variable influencing whether the firm's knowledge integration processes occur within or across organizational boundaries. For example, prior studies argue that organizational decision-makers tend to adopt a vertically integrated structure to facilitate the exchange of relevant knowledge among employees (Kogut and Zander, 1992; Monteverde, 1995), which reduces the hazards associated with technological uncertainty (Kapoor and Adner, 2012). Similarly, Operti and Carnabuci (2014) suggest that although firms attempting to combine diverse knowledge inputs during innovative processes face significant uncertainty, vertical integration might help them reduce this uncertainty. Brusoni et al. (2001) posit that uncertainty ensues when the technologies involved in knowledge integration processes develop at uneven rates and that one way in which firms cope with such uncertainty is to build knowledge at the interface between organizational boundaries.

In this chapter, we seek to advance existing literature on knowledge integration by arguing that decisions concerning the locus of organizational boundaries are contingent on the source of uncertainty facing the organization. Specifically, we develop and empirically test three related hypotheses. First, we posit that organizations faced with general uncertainty at the field level will react by keeping the source of uncertainty outside their organizational boundaries. However, and second, when an organization faces uncertainty related to its internal conditions (i.e. firm-specific uncertainty), we argue that it will try to bring the source of uncertainty under direct administrative control. Third, because uncertainty produced by competitive interdependence exposes organizations to social influences from other organizations (Thompson, 1967), we hypothesize also that organizations will be more likely to emulate other organizations that provide legitimate benchmarks for role performance when deciding whether to develop a critical technology in house or to outsource it.

Previous studies examine the relation between knowledge, uncertainty, and scope of organizational boundaries (Pfeffer and Salancik, 1978; Williamson, 1991; Podolny, 1994) and we are not the first to distinguish among sources of uncertainty (Sutcliffe and Zaheer, 1998; Podolny, 2001). The present work extends the existing results in several ways. First, we emphasize that uncertainty is, in part, an endogenous outcome of competition among firms, to which firms respond by modifying the scope of their organizational boundaries and, hence, the locus of knowledge integration. This view highlights the role played by social influence in the diffusion of organizational design practices (Fligstein, 1990) and makes our theoretical framework consistent with contemporary studies that consider organizations as '[i]nterpreting one another's actions by comparing them with accepted role performances' (Zuckerman, 1999: 1398). Second, we clarify the link between uncertainty and knowledge integration by combining insights from classic organization theory with current knowledge-based views of the firm. The third contribution is methodological. Existing research mainly uses indirect measures of uncertainty derived from hypothetical scenarios or based on collective outcomes that are largely beyond the control of individual organizations. The conceptualization and measures of uncertainty we propose are closely tied to the concrete reality of the organizations under study and relate to each individual organization.

The empirical setting of our study is the field of Formula One car racing. This setting is appropriate to test our theoretical arguments since, despite being knowledge intensive, the organizations we study face considerable firm-level and field-level uncertainties. Furthermore, a key strength of this setting is that it allows us to measure more precisely than previously possible: i) the sources of organizational uncertainty; ii) how different types of uncertainty affect individual organizational design decisions; and iii) how these decisions reflect the processes of social influence among competing organizations. Because individual differences in performance are the essence of Formula One car races, our sample allows measures of performance that are simple, but unambiguous and meaningful. The chapter is organized as follows. Section 8.2 presents our hypotheses. Section 8.3 describes the research design, including the sample, variables, and empirical specification of our models. In Section 8.4, we report the results of our analyses. The chapter concludes in Section 8.5 with a discussion of how our proposed theory and findings affect current understandings of the relation between uncertainty, knowledge integration, and organizational boundaries.

8.2 THEORY AND HYPOTHESES

While firms strive to acquire, produce, store, and recombine their knowledge base in order to keep abreast of competitors (Grant, 1996; Spender and Grant, 1996; Carnabuci and Operti, 2013), their knowledge is inevitably incomplete and susceptible to obsolescence (Sanchez and Mahoney, 1996), which generates uncertainty. A well-established argument in organization theory posits that organizations attempt to reduce uncertainty by modifying their internal organizational structures and by building external exchange relations, particularly when this uncertainty threatens the firm's core activities (Selznick, 1949; Thompson, 1967; Meyer and Rowan, 1977; Pfeffer and Salancik, 1978; Williamson, 1991; Podolny, 1994). However, what is less well understood is how organizations reconfigure their boundaries to deal with the specific *kinds* of uncertainty they may confront in attempting to integrate knowledge across distinct areas of technological activity. There are two theoretical visions which seem to support opposite predictions about the role of uncertainty on the locus of organizational boundaries. According to the first, organizations react to uncertainty by incorporating recognized sources of uncertainty within their boundaries (Williamson, 1975). The consequence of this strategy is to transform problematic external resource dependencies into an internal coordination and control issue (Chandler, 1977). Walker and Weber (1987) provide some evidence supporting this view in the context of make-or-buy decisions involving suppliers. However, the second vision considers that organizations facing uncertain contingencies assume a more pronounced social orientation and tend to become more open to social influences from other organizations. This notion was first articulated by Thompson (1967), who suggested that organizations react to uncertainty by relying on 'social tests' of the soundness of their decisions. Building on this insight, Podolny (1994), for example, shows that uncertainty induces organizations to assume a more pronounced social orientation by exchanging more—rather than less—with other organizations.

However, the articulation of these alternative theoretical visions typically makes no reference to the fact that uncertainty is a complex construct that resists reduction to unique measures (Milliken, 1987). Several studies show that different aspects of uncertainty have different organizational design implications. For example, Sutcliffe and Zaheer (1998), using experimental data collected from 308 managers, find that primary and competitive uncertainty have a negative effect on the decision to vertically integrate, but that supplier uncertainty has the opposite effect. In this respect, the distinction between firm-specific and field-level uncertainty introduced by Beckman et al. (2004) seems particularly relevant. Firm-specific uncertainty stems from incomplete knowledge of the structure and direction of the cause–effect relations underlying core internal production processes and, hence, from ambiguities in the link between problems and solutions within organizations (Cohen et al., 1972). The inability to find internal solutions to problems posed by uncertainty reduction may convince organizations to enlarge their domains and incorporate new activities, perceived as direct causes of variance in organizational performance. This argument has a strong theoretical grounding in relation to organizations employing intensive technologies which are predicted to expand their domains by incorporating within their boundaries the object of their transformation (Thompson, 1967). These types of organizations tend to experience higher levels of learning by doing and, therefore, may be more easily convinced of the value of integrating new knowledge domains within their organizational boundaries. Indirect evidence supporting this view is provided in Beckman et al. (2004), which shows that firm-specific uncertainty stimulates exploration through the search for new partners. Translated into our framework, this finding suggests that the need to build new knowledge and capabilities triggers 'problemistic search' for new solutions (March, 1988). In turn, problems of uncertainty generated by idiosyncratic activities lead organizations to redraw their boundaries around the knowledge areas that are perceived as directly related to the new learning tasks. Furthermore, firm-specific uncertainty increases the hazard associated with reduced knowledge exchange and knowledge integration between a firm and its suppliers (Kapoor and Adner, 2012). Vertical integration reduces this hazard by promoting communication and introducing codes to facilitate knowledge exchange (Kogut and Zander, 1992; Monteverde, 1995), and by granting decision rights on the investment required for the solution search (Grossman and Hart, 1986). For these reasons, we hypothesize that:

Hypothesis 1: The greater the firm-specific uncertainty, the more likely that the organization will attempt to integrate the source of uncertainty within its boundaries.

While the sources of firm-specific uncertainty are essentially internal to and frequently are unique to the organization, field-level uncertainty is generalized, that is, it affects all organizations in the same field similarly (Beckman et al., 2004). The source of this generalized uncertainty is inherently difficult to detect since it stems from instabilities in specific market conditions, such as competitive actions (Burgers et al., 1993; Sutcliffe and Zaheer, 1998) and technological uncertainty (McGrath, 1997), which impair firms' ability to both interpret past events and forecast the evolution of the specific market conditions (March and Olsen, 1975). Therefore, organizations faced with field-level uncertainty generally will find it difficult to identify candidate sources for integration. In addition, because the sources of field-level uncertainty are largely exogenous to the firm, the levers of administrative control are unlikely to be effective, and the learning value of expanding the organization's boundaries is, at best, ambiguous. Consequently, under these conditions, expanding an organization's boundaries to integrate the sources of uncertainty is likely to be both costly and ineffective. Therefore, rather than attempting to reduce field-level uncertainty through organizational integration, the firm may opt for the reverse strategy, that is, it may decide to increase its structural flexibility in order to better adapt to the changing demands of its uncertain environment. Based on these arguments, we conjecture that field-level uncertainty might reduce the probability of observing attempts to draw boundaries around critical sources of uncertainty. This argument is summarized in our second hypothesis:

Hypothesis 2: The greater the field-level uncertainty, the less likely that the organization will attempt to integrate the source of this uncertainty within its boundaries.

Thus far, we have assumed that organizations respond to uncertainty without any particular guidance or any particular reference point. That is, we have argued that an organization's choice to expand or shrink its organizational boundaries varies depending only on the kind of uncertainty it faces during the knowledge integration process. Nevertheless, organizational choices are often influenced by the choices of other organizations. When critical cause–effect relations are poorly understood, organizations look to each other to learn and to shed light on their own unresolved problems. This is why organizations tend to assume a more pronounced social orientation precisely when they are confronted with uncertainty (Thompson, 1967). Obviously, not all organizations are equally useful knowledge sources (Operti and Carnabuci, 2014). It has been shown that successful organizations are more likely to act as the sources of a wide variety of social influence processes that shape the attitudes, behaviours, and performance of interdependent organizations (Haveman, 1994). Endorsement by prestigious supporters (Stuart et al., 1999), affiliation with well-known exchange partners (Podolny, 1993; Benjamin and Podolny, 1999) or with prominent organizations (Baum and Oliver, 1991), high-quality resource endowments and capabilities (Hallen, 2008), and exceptional performance (Rao, 1994; Ahuja, 2000), all signal organizational success. Overall, the empirical evidence strongly supports the claim that organizations regarded as successful in a given field act as uncertainty-reducing mechanisms in a wide variety of organizational decisions (Haunschild and Miner, 1997). Based on these arguments, we advance our final hypothesis:

Hypothesis 3: Organizations are likely to respond to conditions of competitive interdependence by implementing organizational design solutions adopted by successful organizations in their field.

8.3 RESEARCH DESIGN AND METHODS

8.3.1 Data

We tested our empirical predictions by examining the decision of Formula One racing constructors to integrate engine manufacturing activities in the Formula One racing car production process. Formula One, since its first race held in 1950, is considered by most people to be the pinnacle of autosport racing. It is governed by the Fédération Internationale de l'Automobile (FIA), which determines the set of rules—the 'formula'—that all participants and cars must meet to qualify for competition. The Formula One season consists of a series of races, known as Grands Prix, which are held either on purpose-built tracks or closed city streets, whose results are combined to determine two annual world championships, one for drivers and one for constructors. These championships are awarded to the driver and constructor scoring the highest championship points during the season, according to a points system based on Grand Prix results.

There are several features that make Formula One racing particularly appropriate to test our hypotheses. First, there are few contexts that provide clearer measures of performance than Formula One racing. In Formula One racing a limited number of constructors compete in a limited number of races. As constructors compete on the same tracks, are subject to the same racing conditions, have to adhere to the same sets of rules, and are awarded points based on the same points system, performance is easy to observe. As a result, both constructor-specific uncertainty and field-level uncertainty in a racing season are easily observed and assessed. In the case of constructor-specific uncertainty, if a constructor tends to score the same number of points for all the races in a racing season, its uncertainty about how its cars are positioned against the competition will be minimal. In other words, the constructor has developed a clear knowledge about how the different components of the car interact to produce a stable performance. On the other hand, if the performance of a constructor's cars varies widely across races, the constructor might have less clear knowledge, which will result in higher levels of uncertainty about how to remain or become competitive in future races. In the case of field-level uncertainty, racing seasons either demonstrate clear dominance of a constructor over competitors or not. If one constructor dominates the season, it is likely that it has developed superior knowledge about the optimal integration of the different car components with respect to its competitors. As the racing season unfolds, uncertainty among constructors about the results of the competition will be reduced. However, if no constructor has developed superior knowledge about how optimally to integrate the different components of their cars, the final result will remain uncertain.

Second, Formula One constructors need to manufacture at least the vehicle's chassis in order to be eligible for racing. The other components can be bought from the external suppliers of their choice or manufactured internally. In order to reach the limits of their performance, each component needs not only to be independently optimized but also and, in particular, needs to be integrated with all the other components. The principal of the Honda team described it thus: 'with a Formula One car it is the inter-relationships that are important rather than one specific area' (formula1.com, 2007b). BMW Sauber's technical director, Willy Rampf, maintains that whenever a team is looking for areas of improvement, 'It's not a single part, it's the interaction of the different areas that we need to look at' (formula1.com, 2008). Among the various components that can be outsourced to external suppliers, the most important one is the engine because, in conjunction with the chassis, it determines the weight, speed, ease of handling, and, ultimately, the car's performance during the race. Its importance is demonstrated also by the fact that engine–chassis integration, which is usually iterative and occurs through small improvements, is one of the key factors in the success or failure of a Formula One car (De Groote, 2003). Commenting on its Formula One car in the 2006 season, Toyota's senior general manager for engines, Luca Marmorini, explained that the lack of performance was due to the fact that 'during the year we suffered some issues in terms of how the engine worked with the rest of the car' (formula1.com, 2007a). The process of integration requires that the chassis and engine departments work together on their design, collect feedback from the car and the driver during both testing and racing, interpret this feedback, design the appropriate modification, and implement the new iteration of the integration process. Commenting on the car that allowed the Renault Formula One team to win both the driver and the constructor championships in 2006, technical deputy managing director Rob White explained that the very good performance of the car 'reflected not only the hard work we had done' with the engine department, 'but also the constant improvements in communication and collaboration with our colleagues [in the chassis department]' (formula1.com, 2006). The ability to increase integration between the knowledge bases of the two departments was 'considered crucial to the success' of Mercedes in 2014 (autosport.com, 2014). There is a need for knowledge integration because, in the words of Ferrari's assistant technical director, 'everything is now inter-related' in that there is 'a huge amount of technology to understand', which has 'pulled the chassis department and the engine department closer together. So there's a huge amount more interaction between the two groups' (formula1.com, 2014). Teams have developed different organizational solutions to manage this inter-action. These range from 'High levels of cooperation between separate engine and chassis bases' (autosport.com, 2014), to the creation of specific roles aimed at increasing 'Awareness of potential issues within the interaction of chassis/ engine control', to a 'strategy of complete technical integration of the inter-actions between the engine and the chassis' as in the case of Red Bull and its engine supplier (Total, 2014).

For these reasons this context is particularly well suited to test how firm-specific and competitive uncertainty affect a constructor's decision to vertically integrate the activities related to manufacturing the engine.

The hypotheses we developed are tested on competition among Formula One constructors between 1950 and 2007. Data were collected from *Auto-course*, an annual trade publication that records all Formula One events. Our data include 155 constructors (an average of twenty constructors per year) with a maximum of thirty-six in 1951 and a minimum of ten in 2004. This results in a panel of 676 constructor–year observations. Among these, 166 are constructors that vertically integrated their organizations to include engine manufacturing activities.

8.3.2 Dependent and Independent Variables

Our dependent variable is an indicator variable that takes the value 1 if the constructor is vertically integrated with the engine manufacturing activities, and 0 otherwise. We constructed our measure of field-level uncertainty based on the distribution of the scores obtained by the different constructors in the various races. Specifically, we use an index of diversity D derived from the Herfindahl index of concentration (Blau, 1977), which ranges between 0 and 1. The formula for the index is:

$$D = 1 - \sum_i \rho_i^2 \qquad (8.1)$$

where ρ_i^2 is the proportion of championship points scored by constructor i in a racing season. By indicating a high concentration of points in one or few dominant constructors, an index value close to 0 measures a low uncertainty situation in that the racing season shows a low level of competitiveness and the dominance of one or a few constructors. An index value close to 1 indicates a low concentration of points among constructors and, consequently, a situation of high uncertainty in that many constructors are competing for the final championship.

We constructed our measure of firm-specific uncertainty by considering the time variations in individual constructor performance. Specifically, we measure this uncertainty as the standard deviation of average car performance for a constructor within a racing season. Since constructors can enter more than one car per race, we averaged the points scored by the constructor for each race. We then compute the standard deviation of this average value across the different races in a racing season.[1]

A clear measure of success, which is easily observable for constructors in Formula One racing, is the award of Constructor Championship, assigned to the constructor scoring the most championship points in a racing season. We constructed an indicator variable, called vertically integrated champion, which takes the value 1 if the constructor that won the Constructor Championship was vertically integrated and 0 otherwise.

8.3.3 Empirical Model Specification and Control Variables

To test our hypotheses, we estimate a random-effects logistic regression for panel data using the following function:

$$\text{logit}(p_{it}) = \log\left(\frac{p_{it}}{1-p_{it}}\right) = a + U_i + \beta x_{it-1} + e_{ij} \qquad (8.2)$$

where p_{it} is the probability that constructor i-th is vertically integrated at time t, a is a constant term, U_i is a Gaussian random variable for each constructor,

---

[1] Despite their low correlation, it could be argued there still might be interdependencies between field and firm uncertainty, in that one or two teams dominate the championship over time. Although this is feasible, teams rarely dominate the championship for more than one or two seasons in a row. For instance, Williams dominated the 1997 season by scoring 47 per cent of the total points awarded and winning 28 per cent of the races, but its performance was mediocre in 1998 when it scored only 9 per cent of the total points and won no races. Conversely, McLaren dominated the 1998 season by scoring 32 per cent of total points and winning 56 per cent of races in 1998, following 23 per cent of total points and 18 per cent of races won in 1997.

denoted *i*, with mean 0 and variance v^2, β is a vector of coefficients and x_{it-1} are the explanatory variable at t–1. The unit of observation is the constructor at risk of being vertically integrated in each season, in a panel of fifty-seven racing seasons from 1950 to 2007. Using data from *Autocourse*, we assign a 1 for the constructor event entry of the event vector if the constructor was vertically integrated at time t, and 0 otherwise.

It should be noted that, since the decision to integrate is based on the information available, the explanatory variables are lagged one year. To account for possible unobserved heterogeneity, we estimate a random effects model (Neuhaus et al., 1994). We include the following control variables. Vertically integrated previous season is a dummy variable that takes the value 1 if the constructor was vertically integrated during the previous racing season. Firm age is the constructor's age measured in years since founding. Proportion of technical retirements measures the proportion of a constructor's cars that retired from a race owing to technical failures over the total number of cars that entered a race in a racing season. Constructor performance is measured as the average points scored by a constructor's cars during a racing season. The inherent structure of this racing series, where racing tracks are located on different continents, imposes costs on constructors related to the logistics involved in moving materials, equipment, personnel, cars, and spare parts around the world, which are in addition to race car participation fees. Historically, constructors decide to enter a number of cars and to participate only in a subset of the races in a season, depending on their budget. However, starting in the early 1990s, the FIA forces constructors to enter two cars in every race in the racing calendar. Failure to comply with this rule results in a fine imposed by the FIA. Despite this, constructors often decide not to participate in a race, or to enter only one car, since the saving in logistic costs is higher than the fine imposed by the FIA. For these reasons, we measure constructor resources as the sum of the cars a constructor entered during a racing season. We also include engine quality measured as the average number of points earned by all the constructors supplied by an engine supplier in the previous racing season. Proportion of vertically integrated measures the proportion of vertically integrated constructors over the total number of constructors in a racing season. Competitive crowding is measured as the number of constructors taking part in the Formula One championship during a racing season. Since Formula One has tended to evolve over the decades owing to rule changes and technical evolutions, we include indicator variables for decades.[2]

---

[2] It could be argued that both uncertainties might depend on changes to the points system over the years. In our sample, how points are assigned to drivers and constructors does not change in the following time periods: 1950–9, 1960, 1961–90, 1991–2002, and 2003–7. Although these time periods almost overlap with the indicator variables used to control for decades, we

8.4 RESULTS

Table 8.1 presents the descriptive statistics and a correlation matrix; Table 8.2 reports the results of our statistical test.

Model 1 is a baseline model including only control variables. As expected, the results show that constructors that were vertically integrated in the previous season tend to remain vertically integrated in the current season (and, similarly, constructors that were not integrated tend to remain not integrated). Net of this inertial process, two control variables appear to play a significant role. First, the probability that a constructor is vertically integrated in the current season increases with the constructor's average performance in the previous season. Second, the higher the level of competitive crowding among Formula One constructors in the previous racing season, the lower the likelihood that a constructor will be vertically integrated in the current season. It is interesting that there does not appear to be any 'bandwagon' effect; that is, the probability of a constructor being vertically integrated in the current season does not depend on the proportion of vertically integrated constructors in the previous season.

Model 2, which adds our variables of interest to Model 1, shows that the estimates are consistent with our three hypotheses. As predicted by Hypothesis 1, the higher the firm-specific uncertainty experienced by a constructor in the previous season, the higher the likelihood that the constructor will become vertically integrated. Although the estimate is only marginally significant, this result suggests that vertically integrated forms tend to be the preferred response to constructor-level uncertainty among Formula One constructors (the log odds of becoming vertically integrated in a given season increases by a factor of 1.12 for a one standard deviation increase in firm-level uncertainty). However, as predicted by Hypothesis 2, constructors react in an altogether opposite way to field-level uncertainty. Namely, the more hard-fought and uncertain the previous season's championship, the lower the probability that a constructor will become vertically integrated in the current season (a standard deviation increase in field-level uncertainty results in a 1.75 decrease in the log odds of becoming vertically integrated). Finally, as predicted by Hypothesis 3, constructors are more likely to implement design solutions adopted by successful organizations. If the winner of the constructor championship in the previous racing season was vertically integrated, the log odds of constructors becoming vertically integrated increase by 5.66.

replaced these indicator variables with alternative indicator variables for the periods when the points system did not change (the omitted variable is the indicator for the time period 1961–90). The sign and the level of significance of our estimates remains the same for this alternative operationalization.

Table 8.1. Variables descriptive statistics and first order correlation coefficients

Variable	Mean	St.dev	2	3	4	5	6	7	8	9	10	11
1. Firm age	11.311	11.574										
2. Proportion of vertically integrated	0.188	0.101	-0.07									
3. Vertically integrated previous season	0.244	0.430	0.31	0.29								
4. Constructor resources	25.226	13.492	0.36	-0.17	0.02							
5. Constructor performance	1.011	1.354	0.45	0.10	0.24	0.22						
6. Engine quality	26.720	35.451	0.42	0.09	0.23	0.32	0.60					
7. Proportion of technical retirements	0.327	0.217	-0.15	0.05	0.06	-0.16	-0.32	-0.26				
8. Competitive crowding	18.999	6.054	-0.31	-0.17	0.01	-0.38	-0.17	-0.25	0.12			
9. Firm-specific uncertainty	0.856	0.845	0.48	-0.02	0.24	0.40	0.73	0.54	-0.19	-0.31		
10. Field-level uncertainty	0.769	0.067	0.17	-0.22	-0.12	0.29	0.04	0.11	-0.13	-0.49	0.31	
11. Vertically integrated champion	0.447	0.498	-0.12	0.39	0.15	-0.23	0.03	-0.01	-0.02	0.28	-0.12	-0.28

n = 676. Correlations greater than |0.10| are significant at $p < 0.01$

Table 8.2. Random effect logit estimates of vertical integration

Variables	Coefficients	
	Model 1	Model 2
Firm age	0.049	0.061
	(0.044)	(0.051)
Proportion of vertically integrated	3.747	3.486
	(7.549)	(9.522)
Vertically integrated previous season	9.723***	13.085***
	(1.268)	(2.559)
Constructor resources	−0.008	−0.026
	(0.034)	(0.036)
Constructor performance	0.460*	0.280
	(0.263)	(0.521)
Engine quality	−0.001	−0.014
	(0.012)	(0.016)
Proportion of engine retirements	1.134	1.934
	(1.663)	(1.965)
Competitive crowding	−0.183*	−0.405***
	(0.094)	(0.146)
Firm-specific uncertainty		1.326*
		(0.791)
Field-level uncertainty		−26.163**
		(11.907)
Vertically integrated champion		5.663**
		(2.239)
Years 1960–9	−1.149	2.763
	(1.464)	(2.242)
Years 1970–9	−0.874	5.049
	(1.765)	(3.577)
Years 1980–9	−3.371	2.037
	(2.075)	(3.094)
Years 1990–9	−1.446	6.112
	(2.413)	(4.648)
Years 2000–7	−2.456	−2.573
	(2.161)	(2.636)
Constant	−0.794	13.285
	(4.028)	(9.667)
Log Likelihood	−38.775	−30.549
Chi2 (compared to Model 1)		16.449***
df		3
N	676	676

Note: Standard errors in parentheses
*p<0.1; **p<0.05; ***p<0.01

8.5 DISCUSSION AND CONCLUSIONS

According to Cyert and March (1963: 166): 'Uncertainty is a feature of organizational decision making with which organizations must live.' If this is true, it would be difficult to think of anything more crucial than how organizations deal with uncertainty by modifying the structure of their internal organizational design and external exchange relations. The results of our analysis are directly related to this concern. We have shown that different kinds of uncertainty have different implications for the organization's propensity to adjust its boundaries to either include or exclude the sources of uncertainty. More specifically, vertical integration is not a likely reaction to uncertainty generated by field-level factors affecting all organizations. However, we found also that vertical integration is more likely the greater the uncertainty generated by time variations in firm-specific performance. In addition, we showed that, regardless of the kind of uncertainty faced, the choice to extend the organization's boundaries becomes more likely if successful organizations have already made that choice.

These results are important because they add more detail to our understanding of how uncertainty affects organizational design choices, and sheds new light on the conditions that make it more likely that the organization will redraw its administrative boundaries to include the knowledge and technological inputs it needs to integrate. Our findings are consistent with the notion that organizations change their structure in order to cope with uncertainty (Thompson, 1967). However, we also found that different organizational design choices are made depending on the specific *kind* of uncertainty faced. When the uncertainty is endogenous to the firm, that is, it stems from its own operations, the firm's preferred strategy is to reduce uncertainty by developing the necessary knowledge and technological inputs within the organization's boundaries, in order to achieve tighter control of all key aspects of the knowledge integration process. Consistent with the received theory, we interpret this finding as evidence that organizations attempt to minimize variances and unexpected events that might disturb their technical core, by expanding the scope of administrative control and increasing the level of integration of the knowledge developed in different technical areas (Brusoni et al., 2001). But do organizations always respond to uncertainty by integrating the source of uncertainty within their boundaries? Our analysis suggests that integrating the source of uncertainty is an effective strategy only if two conditions are met jointly. First, that the source of uncertainty can be identified; if the locus of uncertainty is unknown, candidates for organizational integration are hard to detect. Second, that the lever of administrative control can effectively temper the uncertainty to which the organization is exposed. Since neither of these conditions is met when an organization faces field-specific uncertainty, organizational integration is not a viable strategy. We found that, rather than attempting to reduce field-level uncertainty, organizations tend to increase their structural flexibility in order to cope with the uncertainty. In this case, maintaining the perimeter of administrative control around the organization's core competencies, rather than expanding it to a broader domain of activities, would appear to be more functional.

Our study also considered the uncertainty-reducing role of social influence processes in organizational design decisions. The notion that organizations influence each other's choices and behaviours is well established. It is well known also that the organization's social orientation peaks under conditions of uncertainty (Podolny, 1993). In line with these arguments, we suggested and showed that the organizational design choices of those organizations that are regarded as exceptionally successful tend to be monitored and, to the extent possible, mimicked by other organizations. In addition to unveiling an unknown and important antecedent to organizational structure, this finding emphasizes that organizational design choices reflect objective conditions as much as they reflect social influence and isomorphism dynamics.

Attempts to go beyond the limitations of the current study could reveal several new research opportunities. The prior literature argues that a firm's ability to integrate complex knowledge inputs is critical for its ability to innovate (Kogut and Zander, 1992; Brusoni et al., 2001) and gain competitive advantage (Grant, 1996). Our research suggests that distinct knowledge integration strategies could enhance organizational performance depending on the source of the uncertainty faced by the firm. The study presented in this chapter documented how organizations react to different kinds of uncertainty, but neglected the issue of how the various reactions observed affect organizational performance by enhancing or stabilizing it. We hope that the arguments and findings presented here will stimulate research in this direction. Another limitation of this study is the almost exclusive focus on the engine at the expense of attention on other suppliers, which might be less relevant in the firm's overall knowledge-integration strategy. While this choice was driven by the need to focus on the most critical junction in the knowledge integration process, it does not tell us how organizations respond to interdependencies across the full range of technological activities implicated in the knowledge integration process. For example, Brusoni et al. (2001) show that unexpected interdependencies across technological areas are a prime source of uncertainty in complex knowledge integration processes, and that firms cope with such uncertainty by developing 'excess knowledge'—knowledge that firms have no immediate need for in their production process. Similarly, it would be interesting to integrate insights into the role of technological interdependencies in the theoretical arguments we have advanced with respect to the locus of organizational boundaries. Furthermore, we have not considered the role played by focal individuals in brokering and integrating knowledge. It has been shown that learning and articulating knowledge in diverse technological areas allows individuals to act as knowledge integrators (Brusoni and Prencipe, 2006). Arguably, the existence of knowledge integrators, mediating between teams and engine suppliers, might change the need for vertical integration among teams facing high firm-level uncertainty. Anecdotal evidence suggests that some teams require their engine suppliers to provide at least one engine engineer to work full time at the team site. This is clearly a team attempt to reduce the impact of firm-level uncertainty in a more flexible way than full vertical integration. It would be interesting to examine empirically the impact of these roles on the need for vertical integration. Finally, we must acknowledge that the sample selected for our study has a number of idiosyncratic features that might affect the generalizability of our findings. Nevertheless, the relation between uncertainty and organizational structure documented here, and the role of social influence in organizational design decisions, are likely to attract continuing research interest in relation to understanding the knowledge integration processes within and across organizational boundaries.

9

Struggling with Knowledge Boundaries and Stickiness

Case Studies of Innovating Firms in an Emerging Economy

Solmaz Filiz Karabag and Christian Berggren

9.1 INTRODUCTION

Research in international business has studied how multinational corporations in developed economies exploit their knowledge assets through alliances, joint ventures, or wholly owned subsidiaries, to establish a presence in new markets and to access local knowledge. This chapter takes the opposite perspective and investigates how emerging economy firms cross knowledge boundaries to access the advanced knowledge needed to build their own competitive capabilities. In this study of reverse boundary crossing and knowledge acquisition, we compare two emerging innovator firms. One started by signing licensing agreements with multinational corporations (MNCs) and then independently building innovation capabilities; the other built its innovation capabilities in the context of a joint venture with a multinational corporation. The study of independent capability building suggests that access to and assimilation of the required external knowledge depends on the existence of international technological discontinuities, knowledge transfer from suppliers and equipment makers, and collaboration with national and international universities. The analysis of capability building in joint ventures suggests that this context offers rich opportunities for crossing engineering-related knowledge boundaries, but also that interest-related boundaries within multinational corporations constrain the access of local firms to the knowledge needed to build full-scale development capabilities. This chapter exploits theories of knowledge boundaries (Carlile, 2004), knowledge stickiness (von Hippel, 1994; Szulanski, 2000), and technology upgrading (Hobday, 1995; Hobday et al., 2002; Amsden and Chu, 2003; Cantwell and Amann, 2012) to frame the analysis. Section 9.2 provides an overview of the literature on knowledge boundaries, Section 9.3 presents the empirical context and various approaches to catching up by emerging economies, and Section 9.4 describes the methods and data. Section 9.5 presents the two case studies, and Section 9.6 compares how the studied firms struggled to acquire and integrate the knowledge needed to succeed in international competition. Section 9.7 discusses the limitations to knowledge flows and boundary crossing in a supposedly global knowledge economy and the value of continuing research on emerging economy innovators.

9.2 KNOWLEDGE BOUNDARIES AND STICKINESS IN THE INNOVATION AND INTERNATIONAL BUSINESS LITERATURE

A key concept in mainstream organization theory is the notion of organizations as boundary maintaining systems (Hernes, 2003). Boundaries are seen as important to delimit and separate organizations, cultures, and knowledge domains, and to create order. They constrain 'the flow of new opportunities and ideas' and also constitute 'enabling mechanisms for individuals and groups to develop their distinctive strengths' and mobilize resources (Hernes, 2003: 36, 42). The boundary concept is related to the notion of stickiness, that is, the cost of acquiring, transferring, and using a piece of knowledge from one organization or area of application in another (von Hippel, 1994). Classical organization studies focus on boundary control (Aldrich, 2008), but recent decades have witnessed increasing interest in boundary crossing, networking, and ecosystems (Carlile, 2002; Santos and Eisenhardt, 2005). The management of knowledge across boundaries is assigned particular importance in the international business literature: 'The transfer of firm-specific resources, especially knowledge...has long been predicted as a key for the success of multinational corporations' (Jensen and Szulanski, 2004: 517); and a 'significant explanatory factor in the performance of multinational corporations' (Riusala and Smale, 2007: 17). Several researchers have analysed the stickiness of knowledge, that is, the cost and difficulty of transferring technological or organizational knowledge across boundaries, across countries, and across cultures, or among various subsidiaries. A long list of possible 'stickiness factors' has been suggested: the character of the knowledge concerned (e.g. complexity/ambiguity, codifiability and teachability), the characteristics of the source and of the recipient (motivation, absorptive capacity, etc.), and the features of the social and organizational context (e.g. trust and commitment). A consistent pattern emerges from these detailed investigations (Szulanski, 2000) and there are two factors that stand out: the qualities of the particular knowledge, especially its causal ambiguity (complexity); and the absorptive capacity of the recipient (Cohen and Levinthal, 1990, for more on this concept see Chapter 4 in this volume).

Studies of the transfer of organizational knowledge stress that such transfer 'should be regarded as a process in which the recipient organization needs to recreate and maintain the new knowledge' and, thus, should be conceived as 'a process of reconstruction rather than a mere act of transmission and reception' (Szulanski, 2000: 10, 23). In a study of the transfer of complex technical knowledge, von Hippel (1994: 431) emphasizes the amount of complementary information needed, noting that the 'anticipation and avoidance of all field problems that might affect a new airplane or a new process machine ... would require that a very large amount of information about the use environment be transferred to the development lab'.

The international business literature focuses on geographical and organizational boundaries, whereas research in innovation and new product development highlights the difficulty of overcoming discipline and domain boundaries. Various organizational set-ups have been suggested to transcend these innovation boundaries, for example, cross-functional teams, temporary co-location of relevant competencies, and articulation of boundary objects (see Carlile, 2002; Lakemond and Berggren, 2006). However, most studies fail to discriminate between different types of cognitive and social boundaries. In an in-depth analysis, Carlile (2004) distinguishes three different types of boundaries or asymmetries in the innovation process, which call for different modes of boundary-crossing mechanisms. The crossing of information-related or *syntactic* boundaries requires a common terminology or lexicon to handle information requirements in a consistent way. Interpretive or *semantic* boundaries call for a process of translation to develop a shared understanding of the ambiguities involved. Interest or *pragmatic* boundaries call for political processes of analysis and negotiation to uncover and reconcile the impact of dependencies and consequences across the involved disciplines and departments. Carlile's analysis (Carlile, 2004) is highly relevant for studying the acquisition and integration of technical knowledge across boundaries in international contexts, and inspires the analysis of emerging economy innovator firms in this chapter.

These firms do not enjoy the knowledge and network resources advantages that characterize international firms in established economies, which are able to combine multiple means, both formal and informal, to overcome barriers, and to transfer and integrate technological knowledge from distant locations (Hansen and Lövås, 2004). Compared to previous firm generations, emerging economy firms are able to exploit global knowledge flows more easily, but are obliged to enter crowded international markets and be exposed to global competition from almost the start of the journey from manufacturing to innovation. As a result, their progress to the knowledge frontier has to be speedier, and they have to cross different knowledge boundaries either simultaneously or in rapid succession, and devise fast tracks to leverage the knowledge acquired. The need for rapid boundary crossing, learning, and leveraging can be considered crucial qualities for capability building in emerging economies, and distinguishes their experience from that of upgrading firms in the history of established economies.

9.3 EMERGING ECONOMIES AND VARIOUS APPROACHES TO CATCH-UP

'Emerging economies' is the term used to describe countries starting from low per capita income and exploiting the process of globalization and market liberalization to grow rapidly (Sutton, 2007; Karabag et al., 2011; Kearney, 2012). The general features of emerging economies can be summarized as follows: they start with low cost manufacturing of simple products, and invest heavily in physical infrastructure and education to upgrade their economies. Although their systems of governance and regulation may not be fully developed, they receive recognition based on their increasing competitive power in the global market (Guillén and García-Canal, 2009). The Financial Times Stock Exchange (FTSE, 2014) suggests the classifications of advanced and secondary emerging economies. This chapter focuses on Turkey, which FTSE (2014) classifies as an advanced emerging economy, which is ranked sixteenth in the global ordering of economies based on purchasing power adjusted Gross Domestic Product (GDP) (Kearney, 2012). Since 1995, Turkey has been part of a customs union with the European Union (EU), which makes this country a particularly interesting case of an upgrading emerging economy. On the one hand, firms in Turkey have ample access to European markets and knowledge providers, but on the other hand, all of its manufacturing industries are directly exposed to international competition.

There is a vast literature on catch-up by latecomer countries and industries (Lall, 1992; Hobday, 1995; Amsden, 2001, Malerba and Nelson, 2011). However, with the exception of some Korean and Taiwanese cases, there are few studies of the innovation journey of specific firms, from low-end manufacturing to advanced product development, and the knowledge challenges involved in this process (Kim, 1998). As Mathews (2002, 2006) notes, the contexts of these firms and their degrees of strategic freedom differ profoundly from established competitors and their choice between being early versus late entrants (Zhao and Parry, 2012). Latecomer innovators enjoy none of the benefits of rare, non-imitable, and non-transferable resources (including advanced technological and management knowledge), which resource-based theories present as sources of competitive success (Barney, 1991). Instead, researchers emphasize the necessity for latecomer firms to acquire and integrate knowledge from external sources (Fu et al., 2011). This imperative has been integrated into several models of catch-up and technology upgrading, for example, the three step model suggested by Hobday (1995), and the linking/leverage/learning model proposed by Mathews (2002). However, as noted above, the absorptive capacity of the recipients, that is, the capabilities development of emerging economy firms, is crucial to their success in overcoming the internal and external knowledge boundaries they face.

According to some authors, the global markets for technology, advanced machinery, and equipment, have reduced entry barriers and made technological catch-up easier (Luo et al., 2011: 45). Studies of various linkage mechanisms reveal a more ambiguous pattern that includes early benefits and later difficulties in the overcoming of knowledge boundaries. Original equipment manufacturing (OEM) contracts, that is, contracts for the manufacture of components or entire products for developed economy brand names, have proved effective for diffusing production skills. However, these links may be negatively associated with efforts by the contract producer to develop own brands, owing to the 'constraints on inter-partner learning/resulting/from the power asymmetry' (Horng and Chen, 2008: 126). In similar vein, a study of knowledge transfer from transnational firms to suppliers in Poland shows that '[t]o create new knowledge, domestic suppliers rely on their own Research and Development (R&D) capability and the upgrading effort is not led by the buyer' (Simona and Axèle, 2012: 804).

Foreign licences have been suggested as another way to acquire external product knowledge. Several studies show that they are important for the acquisition of basic designs, but, as Mahmood and Zheng (2009: 1490) point out, the next technology level requires more specialized and difficult-to-acquire knowledge. In addition, licences tend to restrict knowledge transfer to mature technologies, and do not support catch-up to state-of-the-art technologies: 'closer to the frontier, licensing becomes more difficult and/or expensive' (Lee and Lim, 2001: 481). Another way to acquire technological and organizational knowledge is to recruit experienced researchers and managers from firms in advanced countries or multinational corporations operating in emerging economies, or to recruit researchers with doctorates from renowned universities. This approach was crucial at the start of independent capability building for one of our case firms.

International joint ventures represent a more controlled way to transfer knowledge across national and organizational boundaries, and constitute a prime strategy for emerging economy firms with aspirations to upgrade their capabilities. The main alternative to this dependence strategy is independent capability-building including the creation of proprietary technologies. In Korea and Japan, the first Asian countries to create broad-based innovation capabilities, independence was the strategy chosen, complemented by marginal joint ventures. In China, both alternatives were pursued, but seldom in the same sector. In the telecom equipment sector independent capability building dominates, and in the automotive sector international joint ventures are the preferred choice (Malerba and Nelson, 2011). Despite their importance, these two different ways to cross knowledge boundaries and access sticky knowledge are seldom compared. This chapter studies firms in Turkey pursuing these two alternative approaches: the joint venture approach in the automotive sector, and independent capability building in the white goods sector. It will be seen that both approaches involve combination, which has resulted in several different means of boundary crossing in rapid and overlapping sequences.

9.4 METHOD AND DATA

To understand the struggles endured by emerging economy firms to acquire external knowledge, we need detailed firm level information on the current situation and also the firm's past situation and its development process. Since there are several possible ways to cross external knowledge boundaries, the chapter studies firms in two industry sectors with different characteristics in terms of capital intensity and ownership structure. Case selection is critical to a qualitative research strategy (Flyvbjerg, 2007; Jensen, 2012) and various selection strategies have been suggested (Patton, 1990). To observe unusual manifestations (outstanding successes or notable failures) of the phenomena under investigation, this study employed the significant case selection method suggested by Shakir (2002). The first case is a study of the development of Arçelik from a domestic licence-based producer to one among leading firms in the international white goods industry. The second case studies Fiat Tofaş (Tofas), which is a firm in the automotive industry, and exemplifies the effort to build local innovation capabilities in the context of a joint venture with a foreign multinational corporation. Comparison of the two approaches within the same sector was impossible because of the lack of representative cases. There are several international joint ventures in the white goods sector in Turkey, but in none of these cases has the local partner sought to build innovation capabilities. On the other hand, the automotive sector is completely dominated by joint ventures, with no local firms choosing the route of independent capability formation. Both of the case firms are owned by Koç Holding, a huge diversified business group, known for its long-term orientation and research and development (R&D) investments (Colpan and Hikino, 2010; Koç Holding, 2011). The case firms can be seen as exemplars of a broader set of emerging economy innovators, involved in international competition with established industry leaders. Thus, the insights and implications from the study in this chapter differ from investigations of other innovations in resource-constrained economies such as 'bricolage', that is, making do with available resources (Cunha et al., 2014), or base-of the-pyramid innovations for local low-end markets (Lim et al., 2013; Viswanathan and Srinivas, 2012). We interviewed former company and group executives to explore the strategic choices and constraints faced by the studied companies, complemented by personal accounts of the early R&D history of Arçelik (Ureyen, 2010) and Tofas's company history (Kücükerman, 2008); we interviewed current R&D managers and academic specialists at Istanbul Technical University to discuss the role of specific projects for capability building; and we interviewed officers from the Department of Science, Technology, and Innovation Policy at Tubitak (the major public agency supporting science and innovation) to gather contextual knowledge regarding state support initiatives. Table 9.1 provides descriptive information regarding these interviews, including location and date. Complementary information on sales and product launches was gathered from annual reports, company publications, and Turkish PhD dissertations (Ilman, 2009; Tuncay-Celikel, 2009). The chief technology officer at Electrolux contributed an analysis of the new global competitive landscape, and Thomson Reuters provided an analysis of the patent performance of Turkish firms and selected white goods competitors (Thomson Reuters, 2014).

9.5 CASE STUDIES: TWO APPROACHES TO BOUNDARY CROSSING

9.5.1 Case 1. Arçelik's Struggle to Build Independent Innovation Capabilities

The production of white goods in Turkey started in 1959 when Arçelik assembled its first refrigerator (Esen, 2010). In 2013, the Turkish white goods industry consisted of five final product firms, two domestic companies (Arçelik and Vestel) and three controlled by German and Italian firms. In their early years, the white goods firms in Turkey competed in a highly protected domestic market and production expanded slowly. In the 1980s, Turkey's economic policy changed from import substitution to export promotion, culminating in a customs union with the EU in 1995. This altered the competitive conditions quite dramatically. Both domestic and foreign investment increased in the white goods industry, and production increased from

Table 9.1. Descriptive information of interviewees and overview of interviews

Firm/ Institution	Interviewee's position (years in positions)	Start of career at the firm/ institute	Date of interview/ correspondence	Location	Length (if face to face interview) in minutes
Arçelik	CEO (1983–91) Various coordinator positions at Koc Holding	1970	26 April 2012	Istanbul, Turkey	90
	R&D Manager(1987–2001)	1986	Mail correspond. in 2013	Istanbul, Turkey	NA (supplied twenty pages in response to the questions)
	R&D Manager (2003–7) - Innovation & System Development Manager (since 2007)	1994	19 April 2013	Istanbul, Turkey	140
Fiat/	CEO (2006–12)	2006	26 April 2013	Istanbul, Turkey	65
Koc Holding/ Tofas	R&D Manager (1990–2004)	1984	23 September 2014	Istanbul, Turkey	65
	Innovation and Technology Development Manager (since 2005)	1992	24 September 2014	Istanbul, Turkey	85
	Product Programme Manager (since 2009)	2001	26 September 2014	Bursa, Istanbul	70
	Transmission and Control Systems Manager (1996)	1999	26 September 2014	Bursa, Istanbul	55
	Product Programme Manager	2000	26 September 2014	Bursa, Istanbul	50
ITU	Researcher collaborating with Arçelik	1987	22 April 2013	Istanbul, Turkey	95
Tubitak	Head of Science, Technology and Innovation Policy Department Tubitak since 2011	2004	24 April 2013	Ankara, Turkey	90
Özaltın Group	Owner and manager of several enterprises including white goods and automotive	1969	20 April 2013	Adana, Turkey	120
Electrolux	The chief technology officer (2011)	2011	25 March 2015	Stockholm, Sweden	90

1 million units in 1985 to 21.5 million in 2012. Exports soared from 60,000 ovens and refrigerators in 1987 to 16 million units in 2012, making Turkey the fifth largest white goods exporter in the world.

When Arçelik built its first washing machines and refrigerators, the company used several external means to cross knowledge boundaries and access product and manufacturing knowledge. These included basic licences and know-how agreements with foreign white goods firms, visits to licensors and equipment makers, and knowledge brought by international component producers. To interpret and implement this basic knowledge, the company employed a few mechanical engineers, technical draftsmen, and prototyping technicians. In the 1980s, when European firms started to export novel products to Turkey, Arçelik signed OEM contracts with several international firms. This helped the Turkish firm to improve its capabilities in standardized production, quality control, and logistics (Mamulattan Markaya, 2001; Gülsoy et al., 2012). Arçelik managers identified inadequacies in their basic product knowledge and, in the mid-1980s, negotiated a licensing agreement with Bosch-Siemens to acquire knowledge related to new product technologies for several types of white goods. However, the agreement was based on technologies in the mature or declining stage of their life cycles, and excluded new or future products. Arçelik then tried to negotiate extensions to the licence agreement to include future products. This coincided with preparations for the customs union with the EU. Group managers realized that free trade would result in a complete transformation of the competitive landscape in Turkey, with cut-throat competition in prices and performance. The high cost of extending the licence agreement and the restrictions involved made negotiations difficult, and group managers sought the advice of various consultancies including McKinsey and Bain and Company. Their recommendation was to sell the company, since it was not possible for it to acquire the costly and advanced innovation and marketing knowledge needed for international competition. After lengthy deliberations, and parallel negotiations with international firms over licensing agreements, the Koç group and Arçelik executives decided to take a risk and invest in the development of their own innovation capabilities.

This effort encountered a host of difficulties, beginning with the dominant business logics in Turkish industry which perceived knowledge and technology as similar to any traded good, epitomized by the mantra 'pay the money, get the technology'. The lack of an innovation culture was evident in the attitude to idea creation and problem-solving at Arçelik. Under the licensing regime, engineers and/or managers were discouraged from suggesting ideas since it could be dangerous to implement changes in production methods or in the products themselves. To overcome these obstacles, Arçelik hired an R&D manager, previously employed by General Electric, to head its fledgling R&D department. This individual set out to recruit engineers with external knowledge, including engineers with PhD degrees awarded by universities in Germany and the US, and engineering graduates from well-known Turkish universities. The company also developed close cooperation with leading Turkish researchers who participated as project partners. The R&D staff increased rapidly, from three engineers in its early years in the 1990s, to 800 researchers and eight research centres in 2012.

A key issue for the R&D management was to identify strategic projects able to leverage the new department's scarce resources and reduce the difficulties involved in acquiring state-of-the-art knowledge. The international Montreal Protocol which requires refrigerator and freezer manufacturers to replace ozone-depleting gases such as chlorofluorocarbons with environmentally friendly coolants provided Arçelik with a rare opportunity. Across the world, companies were struggling to find a coolant substitute, and United Nations agencies and the World Bank were encouraging knowledge dissemination. This greatly facilitated the identification and acquisition of external knowledge for emerging innovators such as Arçelik (cf. Lee and Lim, 2001). The R&D engineers at Arçelik participated in major conferences to increase their knowledge, and met leading scientists whom they invited to Arçelik. Researchers and their graduate students from several Turkish universities also participated in what came to be known as the 'Montreal project'. When the US announced that after 1995 refrigerators containing harmful gases would be banned, the project became even more urgent, and R&D engineers at Arçelik collaborated closely with production engineers to meet the EU and US criteria. This effort proved the importance to the company of the new department in a major product category, and demonstrated its development of international competitive capabilities.

In the wet goods area there were no international regulatory challenges. R&D managers identified the company's 'walking washing machine' as a critical project: in order to compete with a popular rival product, Arçelik increased the machines' spin cycle speed, which created stability problems, making Arçelik machines infamous for their uncontrollable movement. The problem proved much more complex than envisaged by the production department, and had several possibly interacting causes, which led to the involvement of the new R&D department. By collaborating with university experts in machine dynamics and computer simulation, the instability problem was finally solved, and the value of the R&D department to the existing product development department was demonstrated in this product category.

Following the establishment of its in-house R&D department, Arçelik began to build an independent Intellectual Property Rights (IPR) portfolio, and in 2000 submitted twelve international patent applications. This number soon increased tenfold, which catapulted Arçelik into the top three innovative European companies in the white goods sector, overtaking established companies such as Miele and Whirlpool. In a 2014 comparison of patent performance, Arçelik was shown to have a substantial number of patents and patent applications in Europe and North America, but only half the number registered by the international leader, Electrolux. Compared to another emerging economy competitor, Haier in China, Arçelik stands out for its strong international protection, with 77 per cent of its applications and patents granted in Europe and the US. The IPR activities of the Chinese market leader are overwhelmingly domestic, with less than 4 per cent of patents and patent applications outside China (Thomson Reuters, 2014). An analysis of product categories shows particular Arçelik IPR strength in refrigerators and freezers, which may be related to its early efforts to leverage the international collaboration and boundary-crossing opportunities opened up by the Montreal Protocol, and the company's subsequent focus on energy efficient technologies. In other product categories, such as cooking appliances, the company has had less opportunity to access and leverage external knowledge, and its patent performance in this area is considerably weaker.

9.5.2 Case 2: Tofaş's Struggle with Knowledge Boundaries and Stickiness

The automotive industry is another major manufacturing sector in Turkey. During the import substitution regime in the 1960s and 1970s, international firms invested in local manufacturing and joint ventures in Turkey (Ansal, 1990), which pre-empted the emergence of independent automotive firms. The integration of Turkey in the EU via the customs union forged in 1995 was a watershed for the automotive industry. Car firms, such as Fiat, Ford, Hyundai, Renault, and Toyota, invested heavily to upgrade their manufacturing capacity and quality. Production in Turkey grew 260 per cent from 300,000 vehicles in 1999 to 1,125,000 vehicles in 2013, positioning Turkey sixteenth in the global ranking of automotive producers, with particular strengths in light commercial vehicles.

We focus on Koç Holding's Italian partnership Fiat Tofaş, the only Turkish light vehicle builder with documented innovation capabilities in the form of an international IPR presence. Tofaş was founded in 1968 to assemble light commercial vehicles for the local market, sometimes producing models that had long been discontinued in Italy. In the early 1980s, production was around 20,000 units per year, but following investments in automated machines and equipment, in a few years this production had quadrupled. To manage its investment, the company employed Turkish engineers with international experience in automated technologies and established a new industrial engineering division. Tofaş invested in and improved its production technologies, and the Turkish economy opened up for competition from the EU; however, new model licences were not forthcoming from Fiat Italy because of disagreements between the partners regarding the direction and control of the joint venture. These problems made it impossible to convince Fiat Italy to open an R&D unit in Turkey. A study of product development in the Turkish automotive industry by Tuncay-Celikel (2009: 79–80) notes that:

> Fiat's main goal was to make production in Turkey, but there was no thought of involving Tofaş in Fiat's R&D activities.... On the other hand, Tofaş was very ambitious to start R&D in Turkey. Tofaş definitely believed that establishing R&D would not only enable them to improve their product quality, but it would also increase the added value in new models.

The problems between the partners, competitive pressure from the EU majors, and the dynamic market conditions within Turkey encouraged Tofaş to establish a clandestine R&D division in one of its warehouses. At that time, all local adaptations and product modifications were required to be verified in Italy since there were no automotive test centres in Turkey. However, with government support, Tofaş invested in a local test centre. This increased operational efficiency by saving on the time and money spent in submitting adaptations to Italy and receiving verifications, and contributed also to the formation of local product development capabilities. In 1994, Tofaş R&D established a formal R&D division to assist the production and localization of components by Turkish suppliers. This allowed the R&D engineers to support production, conduct process verification, and test the performance of new products. With the Doblo project in 2002, a project to develop a new light commercial vehicle, the R&D division embarked on a complete product development process including prototype production (Karabag et al., 2011). As a result, Tofaş's responsibilities in subsequent development projects in-creased, and included the 'New Doblo' (2009), which is sold under several different brands in Europe. In 2014, Tofaş embarked on the development of its first vehicle concept (Kucuksuleymanoglu, 2014), although conceptual design remained in Italy. Supported by government incentives, the R&D centre expanded, and in 2013 employed 500 engineers. The increase in the number of R&D staff and the expanded role in new product development projects resulted in a growing number of patent applications. By 2012, the Tofaş portfolio consisted of seventy-seven filings, 70 per cent of them applying for or granted protection outside Turkey.

Compared to the challenges experienced by Arçelik to obtain access to external knowledge, Tofaş enjoyed the advantage of access to a multinational corporation partner. In addition to Fiat licences and assistance in production developments, Turkish engineers went to Italy for training and to participate in various projects, and Italian engineers were seconded to Turkey to support Tofaş when needed (in both cases around 50–100 per year). The joint venture arrangement also conferred some limitations. Senior managers at Tofaş noted that the multinational corporation resisted several attempts by Tofaş to build adaptation and development capabilities, and implemented an elaborate structure of organizational boundaries regarding product decisions and IPR. The Turkish partner is involved in the development of the upper body and interior design, and filing of patent applications related to these design activities. The development of core technologies, such as engines, chassis design, and styling, is conducted exclusively by Fiat in Italy. This division of labour represents huge boundaries to the R&D conducted at Tofaş, and has reduced its knowledge development possibilities (Lall, 1992) and the value of its IPR portfolio. In contrast to power-train patents, Tofaş's IPR refers to objects integral to the product and its manufacture, and have no real market value. This is confirmed by patent analysis. Among the patents assigned to Tofaş in 2000–11, more than half are classified as related to 'fabrication/assembly', 'general components', or 'personal accommodation' (i.e. seating). There is one application concerning an engine invention (Thomson Reuters, 2014). The above highlights the stickiness of core knowledge in this industry, and the difficulties encountered by new players in trying to cross organizational boundaries and access state-of-the-art knowledge. Turkey is not an exceptional case; very few firms have been able to use joint ventures as a stepping stone to autonomous capabilities building in this knowledge-intensive and capital-intensive industry. Hyundai in Korea stands out as the only real exception since the mid 1990s (Chung, 2009).

9.6 ANALYSIS AND COMPARISON OF THE TWO APPROACHES TO BOUNDARY-CROSSING

These case studies of knowledge stickiness and the difficulties involved in knowledge transfer highlight two factors: the absorptive capacity of the recipient; and the complexity of the knowledge (Szulanski, 2000). In the cases studied, both firms made substantial local investments in engineering, test centres, and R&D projects, and increased their capacity to absorb more advanced external knowledge. The analytical framework proposed by Carlile (2004) suggests a distinction between three types of knowledge and the corresponding knowledge boundaries: syntactic boundaries related to the absence of a common language or lexicon; semantic boundaries related to difficulties in the interpretation of ambiguous cause–effect problems; and pragmatic boundaries related to the different professional or organizational interests.

Interpreting the cases in the context of this framework, it could be argued that Arçelik faced several syntactic and semantic boundaries in its efforts to identify, transfer, and absorb the technological knowledge required to build independent development capabilities. The manufacturing contracts and licensing agreements in the 1980s helped the firm to overcome syntactic boundaries and to develop the language and lexicon necessary to absorb basic product knowledge. The expansion of tertiary education in Turkey and the large increase in the supply of university-trained electronics and mechanical engineers supported the crossing of these syntactic boundaries by creating a basic engineering language common across organizational and national boundaries.

Arçelik's subsequent efforts to develop proprietary products encountered new boundaries, as indicated in the wet goods example of the 'walking washing machine'. The lexicon acquired by its engineers in the previous step was insufficient to analyse the complexities involved in that problem, which could not be solved via trial and error efforts. Managers had to approach university scientists to jointly develop dynamic simulation models necessary to bridge this 'semantic boundary' and achieve a shared understanding of the solution across both the R&D and the production engineering departments. In other product areas, where collaboration with Turkish universities was not enough to acquire the needed knowledge, the Turkish innovation candidate faced pragmatic knowledge boundaries in relation to the international white goods industry. These boundaries were temporarily removed for an important product category, fridges and freezers, by the international Montreal Protocol that involved the rapid replacement of harmful coolants. This industry discontinuity exploited diverse interests to solve a common industry problem (Carlile, 2004). Arçelik, somewhat unexpectedly, was able to cross the advanced external knowledge boundary and feed the acquired knowledge into its independent R&D development. Strict deadlines for the phasing out of the banned coolant facilitated further boundary crossing within the firm, between the development and production engineers and their different origins and cultures.

In the automotive industry, engineers at Tofaş acquired the syntactic knowledge needed to build manufacturing plants and product adaptation facilities from their Fiat partner. They accumulated relevant knowledge through their own trial and error efforts, and repeated exchanges with Fiat engineers. Similar to Arçelik, this company also benefited from the rapidly increasing supply of university-trained engineers in Turkey. However, the complex knowledge required to participate in the development of new vehicles necessitated a higher level of interaction with home country engineers, and more advanced local efforts (Tenenbaum et al., 2012). Repeated transfer of engineers between Turkey and the multinational corporation's home country facilitated the initial crossing of this semantic knowledge boundary, but did not leverage Turkish capabilities to the level of complete vehicle and subsystem design. Here, knowledge acquisition involved the crossing of several semantic and pragmatic boundaries. As indicated above, the Turkish partner mastered some of the semantic boundaries through participation in development projects, but there are critical pragmatic boundaries related to different organizational interests between the multinational corporation home and host countries that remain to be crossed.

9.7 DISCUSSION

The challenge related to acquiring and transferring sticky knowledge across geographical and organizational boundaries has been a long-standing research theme in the international business literature. This chapter shifted the focus from established multinationals to firms in emerging economies and, in particular, manufacturing firms with aspirations to build innovation capabilities and compete in global markets with their own products. The literature on technological upgrading emphasizes that developing countries need to open up to international trade, invest in education, and create linkages with advanced knowledge centres. In the contemporary economy, developing economy firms can exploit global knowledge flows and recruit educated workers more easily than previous firm generations. However, they are also exposed more directly to global competition than before, and need to target state-of-the-art knowledge in order to be successful. This makes the issue of access to advanced external knowledge critical. However, the extant literature tends not to be specific about the knowledge boundaries these firms encounter. To cross the boundaries and gain access to external knowledge, the studied firms pursued contrasting strategies with different degrees of success. In the automotive industries of most emerging economies from Brazil to China, exploiting international joint ventures to build innovation capabilities has become the standard approach to the external knowledge problem (Malerba and Nelson, 2011). In Turkey, Koç Holding forged early joint venture agreements with several multinational corporations, including Fiat. From an initially domestic orientation, the joint venture with Fiat became a manufacturing operation with strong exports, supported by sustained local efforts to acquire and stepwise expand product development capabilities, although this was not the multinational corporation's original intention.

As illustrated in Tofaş's case, the joint venture partnership reduced the barriers to external knowledge acquisition, for example, by arranging exchanges of engineers between the multinational corporation's home country and the Turkish host country, and by investing in Turkey as a centre for the production of light commercial vehicles. It also demonstrates how a multinational corporation can impose strict pragmatic boundaries by limiting the product development and engineering mandate in the foreign partner. The case of Tofaş demonstrates how problematic it was for the local joint venture partner to cross the boundary to the technological knowledge frontier. The Arçelik route to independent capability building involved a highly risky decision by the business group management, and included establishment of a complex R&D system, selective external recruitment, collaborative university projects, and skilful exploitation of an unexpected international opportunity for boundary crossing. In terms of product and patent performance this approach has been successful, but Arçelik is still struggling to upgrade the brand value of its products to be able to command higher prices and support continuous upgrading of its R&D activities.

The literature on catch-up in emerging economies offers a wealth of cases of successful upgrading, such as wind turbines in India (Awate et al., 2012), telecom in China (Cantwell and Amann, 2012), and memory chips in Korea (Hobday et al., 2002), which together convey a picture of irresistible progress. The cases studied here suggest a more complex pattern of boundary-crossing efforts, influenced by external contingencies and constraints, which have resulted in uneven performance across firms and sectors. In some respects, emerging innovator firms are a reminder to established economy firms of their own histories of persistent external knowledge acquisition, development, and upgrading. However, whereas leaders in established economies, when confronted with problems, tend to make staff redundant and to relocate and recruit new competencies in other locations, emerging economy firms display an impressive determination to continue to upgrade and complement their primary workforce and locations even in the face of extremely high external barriers. Thus, their boundary crossing and capability-building efforts should provide important lessons for the future.

10

How Boundary Organizations Facilitate Collaboration across Diverse Communities

Markus Perkmann

10.1 INTRODUCTION

In this chapter, I examine how boundary organizations initiate and sustain knowledge-oriented collaboration among diverse knowledge producers. This collaboration constitutes a necessary antecedent to successful knowledge integration particularly in the context of industries with fast-developing knowledge bases, where the sources of knowledge are highly dispersed and firms routinely seek access to external knowledge (Powell et al., 1996). In many cases knowledge is dispersed not just within (Grant, 1996) or across firms (Grant and Baden-Fuller, 2004), but also across various types of communities such as academia, corporate research and development (R&D) users, or community producers (Berggren et al., 2011).

In this case, the successful integration of dispersed knowledge requires the crossing of social boundaries. Social boundaries 'are objectified forms of social differences' which establish distinct categories of people across social fields (Lamont and Molnar, 2002: 168). For instance, academia is a social system in which scientists accumulate social status by having the novelty and originality of their openly published work acknowledged by their peers. By contrast, in industry, staff conduct R&D within a system that ultimately prioritizes the utility of research outcomes for commercial application. Participants in these different social realms are oriented towards different institutional logics, which can be defined as the basic organizing principles through which actors interpret organizational reality, evaluate alternatives, and define their identities and actions (Kraatz and Block, 2008; Greenwood et al., 2011; Thornton et al., 2012). When actors are adhering to different institutional logics, this can result in significant complementarities which, in turn, generate opportunities for collaboration. For instance, in the academic system, the pursuit of novelty (precedence) is deeply institutionalized within the system of science (Merton, 1973), and drives the scientist's quest for scientific discovery in directions that are considered too risky in industry but may ultimately underpin commercially viable inventions.

Collaboration among participants from different social realms may be hampered by a divergence of world views, norms, and institutionalized objectives. Specifically, the collaboration is likely to be affected by two problems. The first problem affecting collaborations across social boundaries is that their governance can involve tensions and conflicts stemming from the structurally imposed divergence among participants' interests. To resolve this problem requires a governance structure that ensures the interests of all participants are accounted for and that no single participant's interests take precedence. The second problem refers to creating sufficient common ground initially to attract participants to the collaboration, and then to keep them motivated over time. If a potential collaboration does not fulfil the requirements of each of its participants, it will not come into existence or will break down because of the participants' lack of motivation to pursue it.

Previous research suggests that boundary organizations might represent an organizational solution and facilitate productive collaboration between 'unexpected allies' (O'Mahony and Bechky, 2008). Boundary organizations are entities founded specifically to operate at the boundary of two or more pre-existing communities or fields, such as between science and politics, academia and industry, or industry and open-source software communities (Guston, 2001; Miller, 2001; Schneider, 2009; Parker and Crona, 2012). Boundary organizations 'help actors with divergent goals further a sub-set of convergent interests' (O'Mahony and Bechky, 2008: 454) by allowing them to collaborate. Their role is broader than the roles of intermediaries which specialize in enabling transactions among dispersed actors (Howells, 2006; Sasson, 2008) or brokers that recombine resources or knowledge reaped from other actors (Hargadon and Sutton, 1997).

O'Mahony and Bechky (2008) investigated four open-source software project organizations, which brought together loosely organized communities of open-source software programmers with for-profit firms. They suggest that boundary organizations play a fourfold role in enabling diverse actors to collaborate: they govern the collaboration; they make decisions about membership; they attribute ownership of what is produced; and they control production. Thus, boundary organizations can enable participating parties to achieve goals that match their interests, and avoid destructive conflict and tension. While O'Mahony and Bechky (2008) emphasize the structural aspects of boundary organizations, they focus less on how boundary organizations 'win the hearts and minds' of the participating parties. Boundary organizations, no less than any other organization, operate also in the cognitive realm and influence their members by generating visions and strengthening organizational identity (Albert and Whetten, 1985; Kogut and Zander, 1996). This latter aspect can be particularly problematic, given that participants brought together by boundary organizations come from diverse social realms and, therefore, hold different notions of the organization's overall purpose.

In this study, I investigate how boundary organizations intervene, both structurally and cognitively, in order to enable collaboration across social domains. The research question I address is how do boundary organizations create a shared social space that makes social differences less salient and allows participants to collaborate productively without necessarily having to abandon or compromise their own interests and ways of working.

10.2 RESEARCH CONTEXT, DATA, AND METHODS

I carried out an inductive, qualitative study of the Structural Genomics Consortium (SGC), a joint initiative between pharmaceutical firms, charitable and government-funded organizations, and universities, which was established in 2004.[1] The SGC's objective was to identify the three-dimensional shapes of thousands of human proteins with potential relevance for drug discovery. The physical shape of proteins affects how they interact with other molecules in the human body; thus, knowledge about these 'structural' characteristics is important for identifying new drugs and exploring the biological mechanisms that underpin them.

10.2.1 The Structural Genomics Consortium

During the 2000s, decision-makers in the pharmaceutical industry were recognizing that, despite increased expenditure on R&D, research productivity measured by the number of new drugs being approved each year had stagnated (Paul et al., 2010). The large pharmaceutical companies responded by reducing their R&D expenditure and increasing external collaboration (Garnier, 2008). In this context, public–private partnerships seemed attractive, particularly as many industry insiders believed that a greater reliance on public science might help reduce the high rates of failure in drug development (Munos, 2009).

The initial impetus for establishing the SGC came from informal interactions between GlaxoSmithKline (GSK), one of the world's largest pharmaceutical

[1] In this section, I draw extensively on a previously published study (Perkmann and Schildt, 2015), which provides more details on the case context and the methods used.

companies, and the London-based Wellcome Trust, a leading medical research charity. The participants were inspired by the Human Genome Project, which, in the 1990s, had brought together a number of academic laboratories on a platform funded by large charitable and government research funders. Like the Human Genome Project, the SGC aimed to provide information on protein structures, on an industrial scale, and publish its results. However, the new initiative differed significantly from the Human Genome Project, which had not received any corporate funding and, instead, had competed against a similar private initiative (Collins et al., 2003).

The SGC was incorporated in 2003 as an independent, not-for-profit organization based in Toronto, Canada, with an annual budget of around US$30 million. The consortium operated by acquiring funding from charities, government organizations, and pharmaceutical companies to conduct a large-scale research programme at sites connected to world-class universities. Its funders included thirteen public and private organizations, including the Wellcome Trust, government funding organizations based in the UK, Canada, and Sweden, and pharmaceutical companies including GSK, Merck, and Novartis. Its chief executive officer (CEO) was an academic scientist, who had also been involved in some biotechnology start-ups and so was familiar with both the academic and commercial worlds. The CEO was supported by a small administrative team and was accountable to a board of directors of some fifteen individuals who represented SGC's sponsors. In addition, there was a scientific committee of ten scientists—some representing sponsors, others independent—who had oversight of all scientific decisions. The SGC operated at three sites renowned for world-class life science—the Universities of Toronto (Canada) and Oxford (UK), and the Karolinska Institutet in Stockholm (Sweden)—and employed approximately 180 staff. Each site hosted several teams led by principal investigators with oversight from a chief scientist. Each team worked on different subsets of the human proteome and most researchers had affiliations to departments in their respective universities. By 2010, the SGC had released 700 protein structures, and the contribution of the SGC to the total global number of protein structures released into the public domain in 2010 was 27 per cent.

In terms of its approach, the SGC proposed 'open data' as a new formula for how pharmaceutical companies should interact with universities and research funding organizations in this field (Perkmann and Schildt, 2015). While, traditionally, intellectual property protection had been a cornerstone for how pharmaceutical firms and universities interacted with each other in this field, the SGC actors proposed a mode of interaction that de-emphasized intellectual property and, instead, stressed open disclosure and stronger collaboration within the industry in order to avoid R&D duplication. In some ways similar to open-source software initiatives, open data science was designed to generate innovations by enlisting self-motivated innovators who could build freely on the work of other innovators (Edwards, 2008).

10.2.2 Data Collection and Analysis

I collected varied data from archival documents, interviews, informal conversations, and observations. The archival data consisted of the official, confidential minutes of sixteen meetings of key SGC bodies, including the board of directors, the business committee, the scientific committee, and the audit and risk committee, held between February 2005 and July 2007. Together with other SGC documentation, including the Memoranda on Articles of Association, the Funding Agreement, annual reports, and press communications, the archive word length was approximately 100,000. The second body of evidence was collected from twenty-two one hour long semi-structured interviews with SGC staff, members of the board and the scientific committee, senior management, and scientists. The interviews covered more than half of the individuals involved in the governance and management of the SGC, a sample of the researchers, and an external observer. Data collection was complemented by observations and informal conversations on various occasions, including SGC workshops in London and a field visit to Toronto, with individuals involved in the management of the SGC, representatives of the sponsors, and external observers, between 2007 and 2011.

I used an inductive approach to analyse the data. In the course of a previous study (Perkmann and Schildt, 2015), a narrative account had been generated, depicting the organization's emergence and development and its main structures and practices. For the present study, I went back to the raw evidence, and recoded it based on the new research question. I conducted a first, open round of coding to identify how the SGC made social differences less relevant, and how it succeeded (or failed) to enlist collaborators without forcing them to abandon their own organizational principles and working practices. This meant that the codes primarily captured actions and interventions on the part of the boundary organization; in concrete terms, the actions taken by the consortium's governing bodies and senior managers. For instance, I found that the SGC created various sets of rules to govern how the various participants were able to influence the consortium's work programme. The codes also included interventions of a more symbolic and discursive nature, such as attempts to frame the SGC's environment in terms of the structural crisis faced by the pharmaceutical industry ('diagnose crisis in drug discovery'). For each coding instance, I looked for validation across various individual informants and situations and discarded codes that I was unable to triangulate. I also focused specifically on what the boundary organization did and discarded codes that related to actions taken in isolation by various stakeholders.

Next, I moved to axial coding and established relationships between the open codes by searching for logical connections between them. This step resulted in five second level codes, which included, for instance, the SGC's intervention to 'facilitate sequential decision-making' and its efforts at 'establishing socio-political legitimacy' within its wider environment. Over the course of the coding exercise,

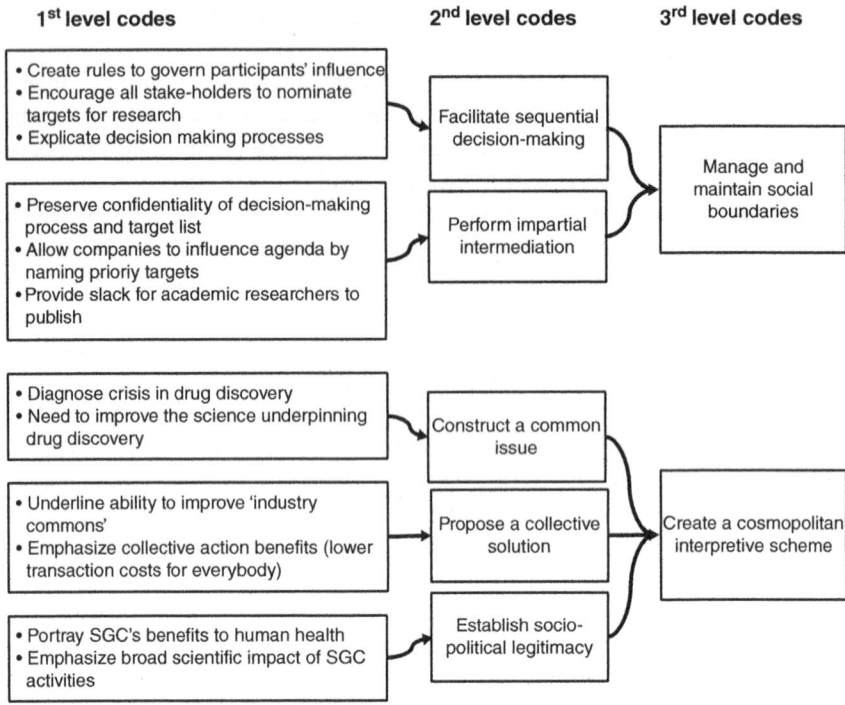

Figure 10.1. Coding structure

I realized that the second-level codes were converging into two third-level codes, one of which referred essentially to the SGC's structural interventions, while the other expressed SGC's more cognitive and symbolical activities. I grouped the second level categories into two overarching third-order categories, resulting in the two key processes underpinning a boundary organization's role: 'manage and maintain social boundaries' and 'create a cosmopolitan interpretive scheme'. Throughout these steps, I moved continuously backward and forward between the evidence and emerging categories, to produce results that were as robust as possible. The coding structure is depicted in Figure 10.1.

10.3 FINDINGS

10.3.1 Structural Dimension: Manage and Maintain Social Boundaries

The SGC's ability to operate was aided by its early choice to minimize direct interactions between the parties subscribing to different logics. The organization was able to maintain the boundaries between institutional logics, while effectively forming new interactions across them. This was achieved in two ways. First, the SGC avoided potential conflicts by sequencing the decision-making process into a set of separate issues that the different participants could address independently. Second, the SGC played a role as an intermediary, brokering mainly dyadic interactions with field constituents and positioning itself between the companies, academics, charities, and governments.

10.3.2 Facilitate Sequential Decision-Making

The SGC's decision-making processes were designed in order to enable the various constituents to influence interactions based on their core institutional logics. The process required sequential inputs from corporations, the academic community, charities, and individual research teams, which minimized the decisions that required negotiation across the boundaries between constituencies subscribing to potentially conflicting institutional logics.

The decision-making process centred on compiling a list of protein targets, which constituted the SGC's work programme. Every sponsor, including companies, foundations, and government agencies, was allowed to nominate a 'wish list' of 200 targets, twenty of which could be designated priority targets, and had the right to propose subsequent amendments to its list. Members of the academic community were also allowed to nominate targets. All nominations were examined by the scientific committee, which was responsible for producing a shortlist of proposed targets for final approval by the board. The list of targets at the time of the data collection included a few thousand proteins, providing a base from which the scientific teams could select those proteins they intended to work on. Whenever possible, this selection took account of the sponsors' priority targets.

For the pharma companies, the ability to shape the research agenda was a critical benefit of participating in the consortium, as expressed by a board member:

> [the SGC] was completely different from a grant where we just gave academics some money. It was very much about ensuring...that there was the ability to influence....pharma were quite insistent on having a set-up where they could have some influence.

The academic community was also allowed to nominate targets although a recipient and not a sponsor of resources. By soliciting research targets from academia, the SGC positioned itself as a credible player in the academic world and pleased those of its government sponsors that had an interest in the organization serving the research agendas of their domestic scientific communities. One representative explained that owing to 'the amount of public funding that's gone into it, we wanted to ensure that all researchers [in our constituency] had access to being able to nominate targets'. In this particular case, the government agency organized a workshop in collaboration with a local research institute to determine the targets that 'were of interest to our research community as they specialize in certain disease areas'.

As the final step in the sequential decision-making process, the individual researchers and research teams employed in the participating universities were able to choose which proteins they wanted to study from the target list. By sequencing sponsors' decisions on their target nominations and the SGC scientists' choice of research topics, the SGC was able to avoid direct negotiations that would have pitted the interests of the corporations against the interests of the academics and, thus, required 'hybrid' decision-making criteria. A key aspect of the decision-making process was its additive nature, in the sense that each constituent was given a say, but little interaction amongst them was required. Via the transparent, formalized process it put in place, the boundary organization aggregated the requests made by the various constituents into a work programme that reflected the diversity of the logics involved.

Naturally, conflict was not entirely absent even with the above provisions in place. However, it was usually not related to participants having to negotiate over performance criteria that combined industrial and academic concerns. Since the validity of the various sets of criteria valued by each of the constituents was not questioned, conflict ensued only when participants felt that too many of the decisions taken favoured the counterparty's interests. However, since these interests were represented equally in the SGC's decision-making bodies, which, moreover, were chaired by 'super parties' figureheads, these conflicts could be resolved more easily compared to micro-level negotiations over novel decision-making criteria aimed at synthesizing diverging interests.

10.3.3 Perform Impartial Intermediation

A significant difference between conventional university–industry collaboration and the novel interaction patterns promoted by the SGC was the almost complete lack of direct interaction of academic research teams with corporations, charities, or government funding bodies. Instead, all the involved actors interacted primarily via the SGC, which channelled funds to the research teams through universities, and monitored their performance. Sponsor representatives reported how they dealt with the SGC mainly through the board, and SGC scientists confirmed that interaction with their counterpart scientists at sponsor firms was rare.

This role can be characterized as 'intermediation', which I define as activities aimed at facilitating transactions and exchange between parties (Hirsch, 1972; Sasson, 2008). Such intermediation helped manage and maintain the boundaries that existed between institutional logics, thereby avoiding potential conflicts arising from direct coordination efforts between the parties subscribing to different and possibly contradictory institutional logics.

My analysis revealed that a central factor in the SGC's ability to position itself as an intermediary was its relative autonomy from the established institutional logics in the field. Situated at the boundaries between the various constituencies it brought together, the SGC operated relatively independently from each constituency. All sponsors I interviewed valued the fact that the SGC was not beholden to the interests and world views of the other sponsors. A board member representing a charitable foundation explained:

> The SGC was quite independent in that it wasn't linked to one university, so you had an independent board and independent pay scales and independent conditions about how it worked, which was a model that we liked . . . as it was separated from government and any other institutions.

The SGC's relative autonomy appealed to its charitable funders because it meant it was not controlled directly by the pharmaceutical companies. While organizational alternatives, such as contracting to private firms or establishing proprietary operations, had been considered by the private-sector sponsors, they maintained that the collective interest would be served best if the organization was given a reasonable amount of strategic and operational autonomy.

The handling of the target list of proteins compiled from sponsor requests exemplifies how intermediation enabled SGC to retain the boundaries between institutional logics. The corporate interest dictated that the wish lists submitted by the pharma companies would remain anonymous since a publicly demonstrated interest in a specific protein structure might reveal sensitive information to competitors about a company's research priorities. In other words, the pharma companies did not wish to disclose publicly which proteins they had proposed and prioritized. Because of its intermediary position between the sponsors, the SGC was able to ensure confidentiality of the wish lists submitted by individual companies. Only the CEO's office was privy to these wish lists, which were kept confidential, and were not available even to the board of directors and the scientific committee. Thus, a sponsor's interest in a particular protein was never revealed to fellow sponsors within the SGC nor, by implication, to the rest of the world. The office of the CEO combined the individual wish lists into a 'master list' that was circulated internally among the management, the board of directors, and the scientific committee. This master list provided no information on the identity of the sponsor that had suggested a specific target. As a further safeguard, once the master list had been agreed upon, it was passed on to the academic participants, but was not released to the public.

Another example of designing interactions to accommodate central interests was the SGC's decision to allow for organizational slack, which enabled the SGC scientists to make discoveries and publish them in peer-reviewed articles within the employment relationship sponsored through the SGC. Using the time and resources provided by SGC, scientists commonly pursued their interests—beyond the confines of the SGC's mandate—in the proteins they had discovered, and studied how they linked to and reacted with other molecules. For instance, scientists were encouraged to investigate how the focal proteins bind to inhibitors. This work was rewarded, but did not count towards the official targets established by SGC's performance management regime: 'Even though the primary focus of the SGC is to deliver structures, there is still an expectation by the community that the SGC scientists should publish in peer reviewed journals.' According to a pharmaceutical company member, the follow-on work was:

> one of the best ways in which the researchers can establish their careers by really creating detailed, high-quality publications. And those publications usually aren't based on one structure, but maybe a structure of the protein, a structure of an inhibited complex...and a series of follow-on structures.

Relatedly, an SGC scientist explained: 'There's some latitude, and the groups themselves have some capability to do their own research.... [Targets] are not prescribed down to "all these have to be done and none of the others".... There's some latitude that can allow both scientific curiosity'.

The above findings illustrate how the SGC performed intermediation, ensuring a degree of separation between all the parties involved, which, in turn, was instrumental for enabling the interactions in the first place. Inter-mediation allowed the SGC to reconcile the need for confidentiality, which was central to the corporate logic, with the workings of the academic logics which emphasized the ability to publish and relative freedom of research.

10.3.4 Create a Cosmopolitan Interpretive Scheme

Apart from engaging in structural interventions, the SGC also worked to establish a cosmopolitan interpretive scheme. An interpretive scheme is a cognitive schema that enables an actor to map their experience of the world, and identify its constituents and how they should be interpreted and under-stood (Ranson et al., 1980). The term 'cosmopolitan' is commonly used to describe an actor free from local or provincial attachment, and 'belonging to the world' (Gouldner, 1957). I use the notion of 'cosmopolitan interpretive scheme' to refer to an interpretive scheme that is not confined to specific local communities, but that provides meaning for a wider set of communities. Below, I outline the components of the SGC's interpretive scheme and how it enabled the boundary organization to link its *raison d'être* to the meaning systems of its diverse participants.

10.3.5 Construct a Common Issue

An issue is a development, event, or trend perceived as having significant implications for an organization or community (Dutton et al., 1983). The issue proposed by the SGC was that the current state of affairs in the pharmaceutical industry and, by implication, society at large, was untenable and should be changed. Key individuals associated with the SGC, notably its lead chief scientists, argued that insufficient basic scientific research was the main reason underpinning the research productivity crisis affecting the industry: 'The economics of small-molecule drug discovery, which is dominated by attrition, would improve most dramatically with a greater scientific understanding of human pathophysiology, pharmacology and heterogeneity' (Edwards, 2008: 731). They argued that at the root of the problem was the structural set-up of the industry and, specifically, the way the drug discovery process was organized. The CEO of the SGC maintained that 'in biomedicine, the *system* is the greatest hurdle to the discovery of innovative medicines. [So] why not *change* the system?' The SGC argued that resources for tackling the underlying scientific challenges were scarce because research was duplicated several times across corporations. This inefficiency was seen as being exacerbated by the fact that research programmes were pursued in secrecy, thus pharma companies were unable to learn from each other. The lead scientists argued that this system led scientists to invest their careers in solving problems that others had already solved or found to be dead ends. The CEO of the SGC warned,

> the predominant methods of drug research and discovery are too patent heavy, leading to duplicated effort and lost opportunities for significant productivity.... Intellectual property is killing the process of drug discovery.

The issue posed by the SGC and the solution proposed resonated with both industry and academic audiences. For the participating firms, their laboratories' stagnating product pipelines made the prospect of a structural alternative to in-house drug discovery attractive. For the academic scientists, a system where drug discovery would be pursued via an alternative system that prioritized collective, cumulative knowledge production promised a wealth of new opportunities for academic research.

10.3.6 Propose a Collective Solution

To address these issues, the SGC proposed that the drug discovery process be opened up to enable the participation of a large number of scientists by strengthening large-scale collaboration between pharmaceutical companies and academic science. This would involve shifting the frontier of pre-competitive science to include areas that presently were considered competitively sensitive within pharma companies. Instead of practising intellectual property protection via secrecy or patenting, the SGC argued that in these areas the pharmaceutical companies should pool their work with the commons of academic science. This would prevent widespread duplication of work across the industry and, simultaneously, would enhance the quality and quantity of the scientific work being carried out. As a result, the pharmaceutical industry would be able to benefit from deeper insight across the field and to develop drugs with a lower level of attrition and lower overall unit cost per developed drug: 'Research collaborations, transparency, and data in the public domain are essential to new drug development.' The consortium's CEO hinted at the scale of the intended change by claiming that 'pre-competitive projects can work to deliver science and change culture' and that 'discovering drugs without patents' constituted 'an open access revolution in progress'.

The SGC stressed how the money provided by the sponsors would catalyse the creation of an industry commons that otherwise would not exist, and would herald free access to basic research and data. The funding provided by charitable foundations would lead pharmaceutical companies to invest in the production of a public good. The pool of new public knowledge would have a greater effect on research than direct grants to individual researchers. Participants emphasized various ways in which openness constituted a positive step towards resolving the dearth of innovation within the industry. The companies saw the positive effects on the overall volume of 'follow-on' research stimulated through the open consortium, as compensating for the potential drawbacks of openness. As a board member representing a pharmaceutical sponsor explained: 'There was a recognition that we would all benefit from getting the process flowing in the public domain.'

10.3.7 Establish Sociopolitical Legitimacy

SGC also elaborated its general moral worth in order to gain sociopolitical legitimacy. The SGC portrayed its activities as having a broader impact on the scientific community and on drug development, and, thus, helping society at large. For instance, the leaders argued that the new model would result in an 'engaged citizenry that promotes science and acknowledges risk' and helps 'build a business community built on high value service'.

These efforts were particularly visible in relation to how the pharma sponsors rationalized their participation, emphasizing the 'greater good' from involvement in the consortium. A respondent said that: 'It feels right to have the link with academia in that it provides added value that feeds back into directing the initiative, the direct connection with utilization in the academic community, the propagation of the academic research...'.

Overall, my findings suggest that the SGC succeeded in creating an interpretive scheme that all of the participants were able to link to their communities' specific objectives and values. I refer to this type of scheme, created by the boundary organization, as 'cosmopolitan' because it provided meaning to both the industry and academic participants involved in the SGC. For industry, the SGC's interpretive scheme was linked to a major problem and implied a potential solution, albeit via unconventional means. The scheme allowed industry to interpret the contemporary environmental trends by diagnosing the problem and defining a possibly compelling solution with little downside risk. It also chimed with the recognition within the industry of the importance of corporate social responsibility vis à vis its broader audience. For academia, the boundary organization's interpretive scheme offered an academically inspired map for participation in scientific challenges. It outlined a greater role for 'open science' within the overall societal challenge of discovering novel drugs, promising opportunities for both resource acquisition and new research topics.

Overall, by constructing a common issue, proposing a collective solution, and generating sociopolitical legitimacy for itself, the SGC worked towards an interpretive scheme with which many of its diverse stakeholders could identify. The scheme was cosmopolitan in the sense that it was not narrowly 'industrial' or 'academic', but contained elements that both constituencies could agree with while still maintaining general adherence to their specific logics.

10.3.8 Discussion

I explored how the SGC, a boundary organization, initiated and sustained formal collaboration between industry firms and academic scientists aimed at generating new knowledge. The study focused on the organizational level of analysis and highlighted the mechanisms used by boundary organizations to tackle the two main challenges involved in collaborations across social boundaries: how to motivate diverse parties to engage in a collaboration and keep them engaged, and how to govern a collaboration and avoid conflicts arising from incompatible logics. Figure 10.2 summarizes the findings.

The findings suggest that the boundary organization operated via both structural and cognitive interventions. In structural terms, it managed the collaboration by guarding each of the participants' interests and maintaining the social boundaries between them. Rather than negotiating inputs and outputs collectively, the formalized decision process called for proponents of the various institutional logics to provide sequential inputs to the decision-making. This design feature reduced the potential for friction among actors adhering to different logics, by avoiding situations where one interest was

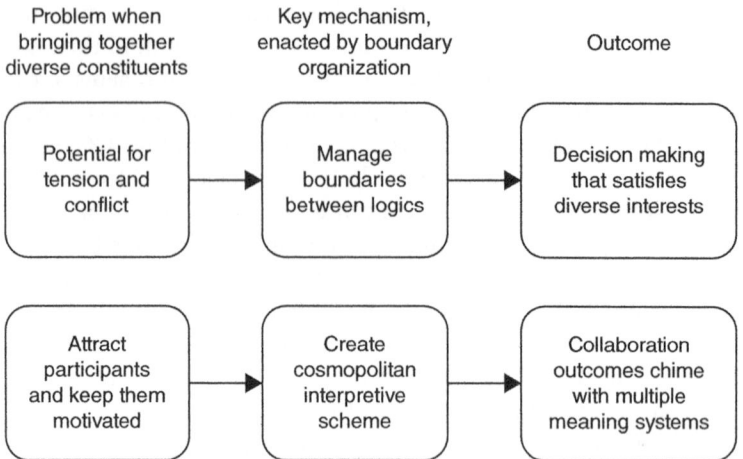

Figure 10.2. Key mechanisms enacted by boundary organizations

pitched against another, possibly degenerating into zero sum bargaining. Intra-organizational combination of logics can lead quickly to conflicts (Reay and Hinings, 2009; Battilana and Dorado, 2010), but because the governance of interactions was dealt with largely through rules set up at the level of SGC, the organizations were not confronted by internal political conflicts over decision-making authority, or primacy of a particular logic.

Previous studies emphasize the tensions arising when actors adhering to multiple logics come together, resulting in intraorganizational struggle and a rebalancing of power (D'Aunno et al., 1991; Pache and Santos, 2010) and requiring the creation of structural response mechanisms (Kraatz and Block, 2008; Reay and Hinings, 2009). Comparison with prior research on multiple logics helps to explain how a boundary organization can reduce one of the main problems arising from involving multi-community stakeholders in a collaboration, that is, the risk of tension and conflict. First, maintaining and managing the boundaries between stakeholders adhering to different logics reduces conflicts by lessening the need for ongoing bargaining, and compromises based on incompatible evaluation criteria. Second, the reach of the boundary organization into the participating individual organizations was limited. Thus, its constituents were shielded against having to change their own objectives and practices, which in turn maintained their legitimacy for their particular stakeholders. The boundary organization's maintenance of an equal distance from each of its constituents' logics strengthened its status as an independent arbiter and trustworthy intermediary.

The specific mandate of the SGC indicates a possible boundary condition on the extent to which the findings can be generalized to all boundary organizations. The task division in this particular collaboration was sequential and did not involve many reciprocal interdependencies between corporations and academia (Thompson, 1967). This made it easier structurally to maintain the social boundaries between the collaborating parties, which might be more difficult to accomplish in close-knit collaborations for tasks involving high mutual interdependencies throughout.

I found that the activities of the boundary organization are not confined to managing structural aspects. Having working governance mechanisms in place may ensure operational viability but may not suffice for addressing the second problem of enabling collaboration involving diverse communities, of attracting participants to engage in a common enterprise and maintain their commitment. In this respect, the study in this chapter suggests that the boundary organizations succeeded in creating a cosmopolitan interpretive scheme. An interpretive scheme is a shared cognitive map held by members of an organization, which is used by them to interpret and ascribe meaning to the organization's objectives and activities, and the environment in which it operates (Bartunek, 1984). In the present case, the SGC created and cultivated a cognitive scheme that allowed for significant overlaps with the interpretive schemes held by each of its constituents. This has two implications. First, to reflect its status of an autonomous organization with its own resource base and legally drawn organizational boundary, the boundary organization's interpretive scheme had to be distinct from its constituents' interpretive schemes. Thus, the SGC was not operating as an industry focused entity oriented exclusively to the pursuit of scientific research for ultimate commercial exploitation. Neither was the SGC a purely academic operation in which reality was interpreted in terms of the evolving frontier science. Rather, the SGC crafted an idiosyncratic scheme around the notion of 'open source science', which essentially constituted a novel business model aimed at bringing parts of the drug discovery process into the realm of not-for-profit organizational activity.

Second, the boundary organization's interpretive scheme had to contain elements that could be integrated easily with the respective interpretive schemes of its constituents. This resulted in the various parties involved not being required to make major concessions towards the other participants, for instance by having to adopt new practices or norms associated with an institutional logic that was foreign to them. Hence, the boundary organization allowed individual organizations to preserve their existing schemes, decreased the potential for resistance, and increased their motivation and interest.

To conclude, my study suggests that boundary organizations have specific organizational advantages that enable them to bring together constituents from diverse communities and enable them to collaborate to create novel knowledge. The main focus of the knowledge integration in the SGC case was to bring together representatives from different communities in industry and academia, so that they could determine together what knowledge should be produced. Thus, in this case, knowledge integration did not imply the integration of different bodies of expertise, but rather the integration of different communities' priorities for knowledge discovery. It is conceivable that this represents a further boundary condition in the context of the generalizability of this study. For example, boundary organizations may be more useful when the knowledge from different communities needs to be brought together in order to determine what further knowledge should be produced, compared to when different communities are brought together to produce that knowledge.

Similar to previous studies, I find that boundary organizations are able to govern such collaborations productively because of their ability to maintain a separation between the participating constituents and, thereby, control what is being decided and what is being produced (O'Mahony and Bechky, 2008). However, managing and maintaining social boundaries may be a necessary, but not sufficient condition for bringing diverse parties together. Creating an interpretive scheme that appeals equally to stakeholders with fundamentally different outlooks is important for motivating and reproducing collaboration.

11

Talking through Objects

The Sociopolitical Dynamics embodied in Boundary Objects in Architectural Work

Dmitrijs Kravcenko and Jacky Swan

11.1 INTRODUCTION

Understanding how knowledge can be integrated across specialist groups is an ongoing concern for scholars of organization studies (Brint, 1996; Okhuysen and Bechky, 2009). It is an especially important issue in the context of complex projects, such as construction projects, that rely on collaboration among distinct professional groups, sometimes from multiple organizations, in order to deliver project outcomes (Hobday, 2000; Swan et al., 2010). In such contexts, both knowledge and power are widely distributed, and the ability to exercise hierarchical or resource-based control over professionals is often limited (Swan and Scarbrough, 2005). Success, or otherwise, of knowledge integration therefore rests upon ongoing negotiation, communicative practices, and 'boundary work' among interacting specialists (Hardy et al., 2003; Carlile, 2004; Swan and Scarbrough, 2005; Bechky, 2006). Here boundary objects are found to play a critical role, enabling the integration of knowledge across diverse specialist groups by mediating communicative practices and smoothing and mitigating conflict.

This chapter explores a relatively neglected aspect of these sociopolitical dynamics of the work performed by boundary objects; that is, the communicative practices embodied within objects themselves when deployed across boundaries created by professional specialisms. We argue that previous research on the role of objects in knowledge integration privileges the social interaction and communicative practices that occur *around* objects over the communication that objects themselves embody; objects themselves are often 'blackboxed'. Yet many objects used by professionals in knowledge integration efforts, such as design drawings in architectural work (the focus of our study), embody text and talk (e.g. comment, description, and annotation) as well as visual representation (e.g. drawing). This chapter explores the sociopolitical dynamics embodied within objects and how these define the possibilities for coordinated action and knowledge integration in architectural work. In so doing, we address an important lacuna in boundary object literature, which is that it 'specifies communicative practices and the associated relations among participating communities. It does not, however, offer a compelling conceptualization of how the materiality of the medium interacts with recurrent and typified communication practices' (Østerlund, 2008: 6).

11.2 BOUNDARY OBJECTS AND KNOWLEDGE INTEGRATION

Early sociological studies of boundary work focused on the ways in which divisions between fields of knowledge (e.g. scientific versus non-scientific) are demarcated, contested, and defended by more or less powerful social groups (e.g. Gieryn, 1983; Abbott, 1988). 'Boundaries' here are viewed actively, (re) drawn by social groups in order to demarcate areas of specialist knowledge, defend professional and occupational jurisdictions, and establish claims to power. This stream of work highlights the discursive, often ideological, constructions of boundaries. It also highlights the important role of certain 'objects' in being able to bridge boundaries because they satisfy the needs of multiple social groups (Star and Griesemer, 1989). Following the original notion of Star and Griesemer (1989: 393), boundary objects are, thus, defined as:

> Objects which are both plastic enough to adapt to local needs and constraints of the several parties employing them, yet robust enough to maintain a common identity across sites. They are weakly structured in common use, and become strongly structured in individual-site use. They may be abstract or concrete. They have different meanings in different social worlds but their structure is common enough to more than one world to make them recognizable as a means of translation.

Boundary work and boundary objects were conceived of in this original work as socially constructed, entailing ongoing negotiation and power struggles among interacting groups.

The notion of 'boundary object' has since featured prominently in more recent literature on organization and management and, in particular, on knowledge integration across professional and occupational groups (e.g. Carlile, 2002; Levina and Vaast, 2005; Zeiss and Groenewegen, 2009; Nicolini et al., 2012, Lainer-Vos, 2013). In this research stream, objects are found to play a key role in negotiating and integrating knowledge across groups with differentiated specialist practices. Much of the reason for the success of the concept can be attributed to the so-called 'practice turn' in organization theory. Thus, from a practice view, specialist knowledge is both 'good' and 'bad' for the organization; it is required to accomplish organizational tasks, but, simultaneously, creates boundaries to coordination and knowledge integration across specialist 'communities of practice', which is central to innovation (Lave and Wenger, 1991; Swan, 2001; Carlile, 2002). As well as materially mediating social interaction (cf. Feldman and Orlikowski, 2011), objects help to resolve this 'paradox of specialist knowledge' by allowing knowledge to be shared across boundaries without necessitating those involved to become deeply knowledgeable in one another's specialisms. In short, boundary objects both cross and maintain specialist boundaries (Levina and Vaast, 2005). Whereas other work emphasizes the development of shared practice, mutual understanding, and common ground as a solution to the problem of integrating specialist knowledge (Levina and Vaast, 2005; Hsiao et al., 2012), boundary objects offer a more pragmatic alternative: 'rather than inducing consensus, boundary objects enable diverse groups to work to share knowledge and cooperate by constituting a *modus operandi* that does not demand substantial agreement' (Lainer-Vos, 2013: 516).

The pragmatic alternative to 'deep sharing' offered by boundary objects is especially important in complex project settings that rely on multidisciplinary specialists working together under constraining conditions (Majchrzak et al., 2012; Nicolini et al., 2012). In such projects, demands such as time pressure, deep specialization of tasks, long timespans, and geographical distribution do not permit 'full sharing' of information and knowledge (Newell et al., 2009), so objects play a critical role in knowledge integration (Czarniawska and Joerges, 1996). Indeed, as Star (2010: 604) reiterated recently, her 'initial framing of the concept was motivated by a desire to analyse the nature of cooperative work in the absence of consensus'. Boundary objects permit knowledge integration in the absence of consensus, first, because they materialize and decontextualize knowledge, thus providing a platform for coordination (Bechky, 2003b), and second, because they smooth communication and negotiation across pragmatic, politically invested boundaries that might otherwise be seen as challenging the knowledge claims and identities of the professional involved (Carlile, 2004; Barrett and Oborn, 2010). However, precisely how the materiality of objects works in relation to these sociopolitical dynamics is poorly understood (Østerlund, 2008).

11.3 SOCIOPOLITICAL DYNAMICS OF BOUNDARY OBJECT WORK

Struggles among professional groups to establish authority and expertise over knowledge claims in collaborative work are well documented in the literature on knowledge integration (e.g. Carlile, 2002; Lindkvist, 2005; Bechky, 2006; Kimble et al., 2010; Bruns, 2013). Organizational scholars identify such struggles as tied to misaligned interests and understandings, and professional norms and practices (Carlile, 2002; Kellogg et al., 2006; Nicolini et al., 2012; Bruns, 2013). Boundary objects have been found to play a critical role in mitigating these sociopolitical struggles (Carlile, 2002; Bechky, 2003b; Swan et al., 2007; Barrett et al., 2012; Nicolini et al., 2012; Quick and Feldman, 2014). For example, research has explored the use of objects in problem-solving across occupational and professional boundaries (Bechky, 2003b); the role of objects in reducing conflict and enhancing collaboration across professional disciplines (Keshet et al., 2013); the impact of power differences in helping or hindering object-centred collaboration (Levina and Orlikowski, 2009); the ways in which boundary objects help to reconfigure boundary relations among occupational groups (Barrett et al., 2012); the implications of such reconfigurations for the jurisdictions, status, and power of professional groups involved in interdisciplinary work (Levina and Arriaga, 2014); and the symbolic power of objects in legitimizing claims to knowledge and expertise (Swan et al., 2007). Thus, this research pays close attention to the ways in which a myriad of objects influence the social and power relations that unfold around them.

However, the same cannot be said about the sociopolitical dynamics embodied within objects themselves as communicative devices. With notable exceptions (e.g. Huvila, 2011; Levina and Vaast, 2014), boundary objects tend to be portrayed as more or less stable artefacts that enable social interaction by allowing differences and dependencies across interacting groups to be realized and worked through (Carlile, 2002). The work they perform is usually depicted as that of helping interacting specialists to recognize, smooth, and overcome potential sources of conflict and vested interests, allowing people to arrive at shared understandings. This, rather harmonious, portrayal of boundary object work is prevalent, despite the fact that it has long been noted that 'creating and reshaping boundary objects is an exercise of power that can be collaborative or unilateral' (Boland and Tenkasi, 1995: 362).

Recently, research on boundary spanning has begun to address the sociopolitical dynamics of boundary objects more explicitly (e.g. Levina and Vaast, 2005; Barrett and Oborn, 2010; Huvila, 2011; Lainer-Vos, 2013). Barrett and Oborn (2010), for example, emphasize the emergent nature of problems, boundaries, and boundary objects. They find that the use of boundary objects during transitions involves definitional control and redistribution of power and authority, thereby inhibiting knowledge sharing in cross-cultural development of software. Similarly, Levina and Vaast (2008), examine 'mutual adjustment' and the ways in which boundaries between interacting groups emerge through negotiation around objects in offshore collaboration. Hsiao et al. (2012) examine how experts employ boundary objects to identify knowledge ownership and collective responsibilities. Others have used an actor network theory lens to analyse the complex power relations in boundary activities including the agency of networks and objects (e.g. Fleischmann, 2006; Gasson, 2006). These studies look at how processes of translation in organizations and networks link to actor–object relations.

However, the empirical focus of this research is on how actors interact and communicate around a focal object (or objects). This contrasts with the small attention paid to the sociopolitical dynamics actually embodied within the object itself—albeit with objects recognized to be potentially dynamic and changing (see also Ewenstein and Whyte, 2009). The, essentially, socially constructed nature of objects emphasized in earlier sociologically spirited work, seems to have been 'lost' in favour of a focus on materially mediated interpersonal communication. Recent exceptions include studies that show how objects are constitutive of communicative genre in emergency rooms (Østerlund, 2008) and in evaluation practices in online hotel evaluations (Orlikowski and Scott, 2013). For example, drawing from practice studies and an empirical account of communication between doctors and nurses in an emergency room, Østerlund (2008) identifies three ways in which objects become part of communicative practices. First, they act as objects of evolution— that is, the focal subject of attention in an interaction (Carlile, 2002). Second, they themselves express communication—for example, a computer drawing might express higher status than one drawn on paper. Third, they are part of the 'actionable field' of communication—that is, they index the ways in which dialogue is produced and understood. For example, a whiteboard, in Østerlund's study, becomes part of the defining landscape in which communication occurred between doctors' and nurses' discussions of patient flow in and out of the emergency room. However, even in this case, the focus of attention was on talk around rather than through objects.

Yet many boundary objects embody 'talk and text'—the comment or 'red line' scrawled on a technical drawing, for example (Bechky, 2003b; Østerlund, 2008). Indeed this can be a major mechanism for sharing knowledge in complex projects, where specialists may not always be able to interact face to face. We argue too that text within objects is also politically invested. For example, Huvila's (2011) study of archaeological reports as boundary objects between specialists with conflicting interests shows how these objects acted as devices for creating and maintaining hegemonic power and achieving authority over marginal groups. Huvila's (2011: 2,537) study highlights that: 'boundary objects incorporate articulations of power even if a boundary object may appear as a seemingly neutral consensual device'. Precisely how power dynamics and negotiation occur *through objects themselves*, however, remains little understood; there have been recent calls for research on the interplay between discursive practices and materiality, and how power relations are brought to bear (Hardy and Thomas, 2014). In the succeeding sections we respond to these calls by exploring the ways in which particular visual objects—architectural design drawings—embody discursive practices and differ-ing viewpoints, and how this shapes the possibilities for knowledge integration across boundaries constructed by professional specialisms in a complex project setting.

11.4 RESEARCH METHODOLOGY

To help sketch out our argument, we draw on a year-long ethnographic study of a large architecture firm. The project we observed is a £30 million extension to an existing office building in the UK. Data collection for this particular project began concurrently with the onset of the construction stage, shortly after generous and virtually limitless research access was granted by the architecture firm and its client. By this time, the overall design had been approved and commissioned, and the building was set to undergo construc-tion for the next year and a half or so. As the project went on site, the amount of input from various specialists increased dramatically and their roles became more established. Overall, the project brought together 143 professionals working across four main organizations: the architecture firm, a construction company, and two engineering firms—one specializing in mechanical and electrical building services (ventilation, plumbing, electricity, etc.) and one in structural engineering. We focus on the use of design drawings in collaborative design development, during this stage, by a group of interdisciplinary and inter-organizational professionals.

Construction projects are largely distributed phenomena and, as such, they do not offer the convenience of a single location, requiring the researcher to navigate across different sites and episodes in space and time (Nicolini, 2009). We conducted the crux of our research activity while being embedded in the architecture firm responsible for the initial conception and the ongoing design of the building extension. We chose to concentrate on the architects not only because of their creative function with reference to the design of the building but also because they were responsible for administering the building contract by ensuring that what was being built was what the client had agreed to. This strategy proved quite fruitful, and we collected vast amounts of data relating to both the process of design and the management and power dynamics. The breadth of our collected findings is quantified in Table 11.1.

To analyse our data we followed the interpretive tradition with a particular focus on abductive analysis (Yanow and Schwartz-Shea, 2006; Timmermans and Tavory, 2012; Tavory and Timmermans, 2013, 2014). Abductive analysis is centred on the principle of iterative data analysis, emphasizing continuous movement between theory and data (Timmermans and Tavory, 2012). The context of our research setting and our research questions was particularly

Table 11.1. Empirical data collected

Data type	Total collected	Extension project	Share of total
Observations	1,120 hours	450 hours	40%
Research notes	720 pages	240 pages	33%
Emails	12,084	8,874	73%
Drawings/commented drawings	4,098/330	3,450/284	84%/86%
Artefacts	93 units	60 units	64%
Photographs	244 units	196 units	80%

conducive to using this form of analysis because abduction privileges both unexpected evidence and cultivation of multiple theoretical explanations based on the emerging research data, rather than working around one or more predetermined hypotheses. Since we had set out to explore the socio-political dynamics embodied within objects and how these define the possibilities for coordinated action and knowledge integration in architectural work, abductive analysis offered a helpful way of processing much of what we had not anticipated finding based on the existing literature.

Throughout this chapter, we use examples of drawings retrieved during data collection in order to help illustrate the argument. All the drawings we use are two-dimensional CAD (Computer Aided Design) generated drawings that show some particular part of the building. During design development these are passed around among the professionals as either commands (i.e. this is what this detail must look like), questions (i.e. is this what this detail should look like?), or reports (i.e. this is what has been done since the last command/question/report). Figure 11.1, for example, is an instance of a reporting drawing, while Figure 11.4 is clearly a drawing intended to accompany a question. While we do not concentrate explicitly on particular typologies of drawings, it should be noted that, in light of the volume of material collected (Table 11.1), we had to select what to include in this chapter carefully. Whereas some of the data encompassed the sociopolitical dynamics of knowledge integration entirely, other data displayed them over time and, perhaps, not in an entirely complete way. Either way, in order to communicate our findings in a format suitable for a book, we had to select those examples from the data which we considered the most revelatory. Accordingly, the drawings we chose to use to illustrate our arguments were chosen purely on the basis that they a) are drawings from the office extension project, and b) seem to provide the best illustration of the object of our argument.

11.5 TALKING THROUGH DESIGN DRAWINGS

We chose to concentrate on design drawings because they qualify as 'ideal' types of boundary objects (cf. Star and Griesemer, 1989) and play an important

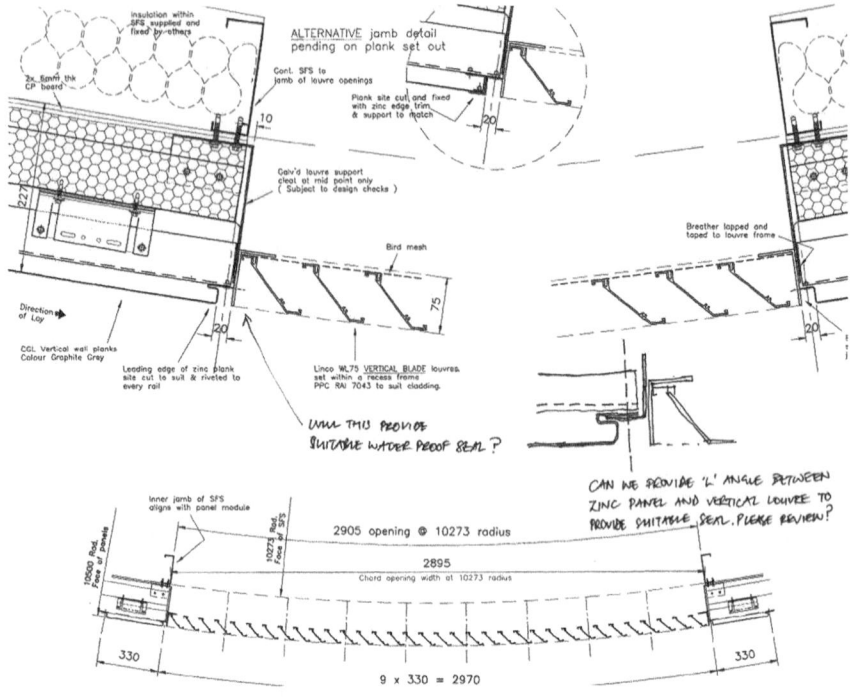

Figure 11.1. Example of a CAD drawing with comments by the architect

role in the circulation of knowledge among geographically and temporally dispersed specialists. Based on a common knowledge of building construction among distinct specialisms involved in the building construction and design, design drawings provide a practical means of cross-professional communication (Bechky, 2003b; Carlile, 2004; Levina and Vaast, 2014). For example, drawings are commonly passed between professionals to demonstrate and/or seek approval of the parts of work they are responsible for (Boland et al., 2007). Design drawings embody various kinds of communicative practices, including visuospatial, technical, and aesthetic (intended layout of the building), but also discursive (written text, sketches, queries, and annotations—Ewenstein and Whyte, 2009).

We focus, in particular, on these objects as they pass back and forth between the professionals on the project design team (e.g. architect to structural engineer and back), who 'edit' them based on their respective knowledge specializations and pragmatic concerns (Sahlin-Andersson, 1996). The purpose of design teams in construction is to integrate design drawings and other technical information into final instructions and plans, intelligible to those people who are putting together the actual building. During our time with the architecture firm, we observed a number of projects conducted by design teams, which always comprised professionals from the fields of architecture, construction, and accounting, as well as mechanical, electrical, and structural engineers. Occasionally, and depending on the stage of work, other relevant professional parties (i.e. environmental or acoustic consultants) and subcontractors would be invited to join and contribute to the design team. However, regardless of the composition of any one design team, we observed that design-related communication was always conducted via design drawings. Following Østerlund (2008), we identify and focus on design drawings that incorporate communicative practices in three respects: they act as an object for evaluation, they are expressive communication mediums, and they are part of an 'actional field' of communication.

11.6 BOUNDARY OBJECTS AS MATERIAL MEDIATORS OF COMMUNICATION

Design drawings are two-dimensional technical depictions of a building project, produced to a set of standards and conventions which render them recognizable and intelligible to practitioners. Not all design drawings qualify as boundary objects in architecture and construction, and even those that do facilitate the spanning of boundaries do so not by virtue of their being objects of a particular kind, but because they mediate those aspects of practice-related information that carry pragmatic meaning (Levina and Vaast, 2014). In other words, boundary objects can be seen as 'restricted agents' of work in as much as the mode of communication that they are capable of is very specific—design drawings, for example, allow limited textual communication around technical issues, among only those individuals with sufficient knowledge of the relevant practice. Figure 11.1 is an example of a design drawing, prepared by a cladding subcontractor and commented on by the architect, in one of the projects we observed.

Practitioners can physically interact with design drawings in a variety of ways—they are regularly printed out and collated in huge project folders, they can be drawn on (as in Figure 11.1), they can be passed around and sent between different individuals either directly or as email attachments, and they can be (and routinely are) torn, crushed, damaged, or disposed of in other physically damaging ways. For the duration of the project, design drawings are stored in digital and physical project folders, but after the project is completed and the building is 'signed off' by the client, they remain preserved in the archives of participating organizations either on blu-ray disks or in some other form for an additional ten years, as a record of collective work. On the face of it, they are different from more abstract objects, such as linguistic labels or

metaphors (cf. Czarniawska-Joerges and Joerges, 1990), in that design drawings objectify the information embedded in them for more than one person
and in a time enduring form. However, design drawings also embody material
manifestations of more abstract concepts and labels such as mathematical
formulae and building dimensions (see Figure 11.1). Thus, one observation is
that distinctions between concrete/physical and abstract objects (e.g. Star and
Griesemer, 1989; Carlile, 2002) may be considerably more blurred than
previous work would imply.

One point of using boundary objects in cross-professional work is to
communicate information and knowledge in a way that is intelligible to each
party. This is possible only if the object already embodies some commonly
held ideas and concepts to which different professionals can refer (Forty,
1986). The way design drawings work to this end is by communicating
information to one professional on the progress of another professional's
work. As discussed above, design drawings are physical objects, but they
refer to abstract concepts in restricted, concrete ways (i.e. design of a building
that does not yet exist). Referencing an abstract concept in a concrete way is
done by constructing a representational space where any relevant information
can be made intelligible, even across boundaries (Østerlund, 2008; Ewenstein
and Whyte, 2009).

Constructing this representational space—a drawing in our case—involves
two stages of work. First, the originating author must adhere to a set of
normative conventions that qualify the object they produce as a 'design
drawing'. This entails the use of an appropriate software suite, a particular
page size, and the use of institutionally and, sometimes, locally agreed upon
symbols and shapes for particular types of materials and arrangements.
Second, the author must encode information about the specific design
work performed, and arrange it in a way that will be intelligible by whom-
ever the drawing is intended for. As shown in Figure 11.1, on the one
hand, when the architect made a comment enquiring about whether a
particular angle 'between the zinc panel and the vertical louvre' is possible,
s/he did not sketch out the entire section of the building, only the element
in question. The information embedded in that very specific sketch was
deemed sufficient since it was provided in a context appropriate for the
cladding subcontractor to understand. On the other hand, the subcontract-
or did not draw out the entire building to contextually position the particular elements depicted in Figure 11.1 for the benefit of the architect.
Instead, the title of the drawing refers to the location of the relevant
elements within the building, on the assumption that this amount of
information will be enough for the architect to make sense of the design
drawing. Assumptions about which information to include, and in which
form, rest upon perceptions of the relative levels of expertise and authority
amongst participating parties.

Communications via design drawings reveal power dynamics by showing how, for example, a subcontractor, working on an element of a building, is in a position of less authority and expertise relative to the architect in the area of building design, but is in a position of high expertise (but still lower authority) on the technical specifications of the said element.

11.7 HOW BOUNDARY OBJECTS SUSTAIN CROSS-BOUNDARY POWER RELATIONS

In addition to materially mediating communication among practitioners, design drawings demarcate a set of specific roles and expectations that are deemed acceptable among participants on either side of the boundary. In other words, design drawings can carry, in themselves, information on which actions are possible for which participants (Østerlund, 2008). This means that, far from being an open space for collaboration, contestation, and integration of knowledge, design drawings sustain pre-established power relations and constrain knowledge integration in a number of ways. First, circulation of the information in the design drawings is exclusive to the sender and the recipient. The constraints of project work, and the specialized nature of the knowledge sometimes communicated in design drawings, prevent open dialogue around them. For example, a drawing by the cladding subcontractor (Figure 11.1) was sent only to the architect and the construction manager—to the architect in order to obtain approval that this particular design was in line with the general design of the building, and to the construction manager in order to confirm that the design was feasible. Other professionals on the design team were excluded a priori. Such point-to-point form of communication is not merely a by-product of the technology involved (email, in this case); it is an inherent feature of specialized work. The pattern of exclusion, along 'who needs to know' lines, is mirrored also in meeting spaces. When members of the design team gather to discuss ongoing progress and any arising issues, all the printed design drawing are openly available for anyone on the design team to scrutinize. However, as far as we observed during 120 hours of such meetings on one of the projects, those individuals with specialisms not directly relevant to the particular issue being discussed, quickly lost interest and, generally, refrained from engaging in the discussion. Similarly, the architects are not included in the conversations between different types of engineers, who share very technical, often tabulated, information with each other.

Second, there is an implicit hierarchy according to which professionals from different knowledge domains engage with the design drawing. When a drawing is sent to the construction manager and the architects, as in Figure 11.1, it is the architect who is the first to comment. Others follow thereafter. One outcome of the presence of such a hierarchy is that the architects on the project maintain virtually unchallenged editorial power (Sahlin-Andersson, 1996), meaning that they have the power to completely close off chosen drawings and other acts of communication. What we identify as a 'closed off drawing' is a potential boundary object, whose use has been made restricted by a powerful party. The restriction of drawings does not take place through hostile acts, such as isolation, destruction, or demarcation of some sort, but is achieved through a final 'stamp of approval'—a note, in large capitals, reading 'NO COMMENTS' (see Figure 11.2). Absence of comments from the architect has the effect of removing the drawing from the space of collective work and returning it to the specialist domain of the architect who originated it. While it can be argued that the whole point is that the architect should approve the subcontractor's work, once the drawing becomes closed, the communication medium that is embedded actually disappears from the space of collectively intelligible work.

Third, the communicative practice embodied in design drawings is dominated by expert power, which can be exercised in quite heavy-handed, coercive ways. As Figure 11.3 shows, the material space afforded by the object, far from depoliticizing communication among specialists (as shown by Carlile, 2002, and others), allows dominant professional groups (in particular, architects) to express themselves more assertively than might otherwise be tolerated within the usual norms of 'polite behaviour' and, sometimes, effectively to silence others. For example, red pen lines literally cross out, check, or correct others' suggestions. Annotations 'shout' orders ('UPDATE LOCATIONS!!!') and exhibit frustration ('CLASH WITH STRUCTURE!!'), sarcasm ('GOING THROUGH SHEAR [*sic*] WALL? NEED TO REROUTE'), and so on (see Figure 11.3). Conflict is clearly manifest in these visual objects. Yet, despite this, collaboration occurs through them—speedily and without offence. These visual boundary objects seem to allow for overt expression of power and conflict (in the text), but, at the same time, enable continued collaboration and knowledge sharing. This suggests that the oft-claimed opposition between conflict and collaboration, with boundary objects dampening the former and encouraging the latter, is too stark.

One reason for the lack of disruption to collaboration might be that the communicative practices embodied within the drawings (compared to the emails, telephone conversations, and face-to-face meetings surrounding them), whilst overtly political, are also depersonalized. In particular, comments are 'signed' not by named individuals but on behalf of participating organizations (e.g. 'Architects Ltd'). Use of such organizational demarcations in communicating through design drawings was a universally common feature of all the projects we observed. There is added weight justifying this since

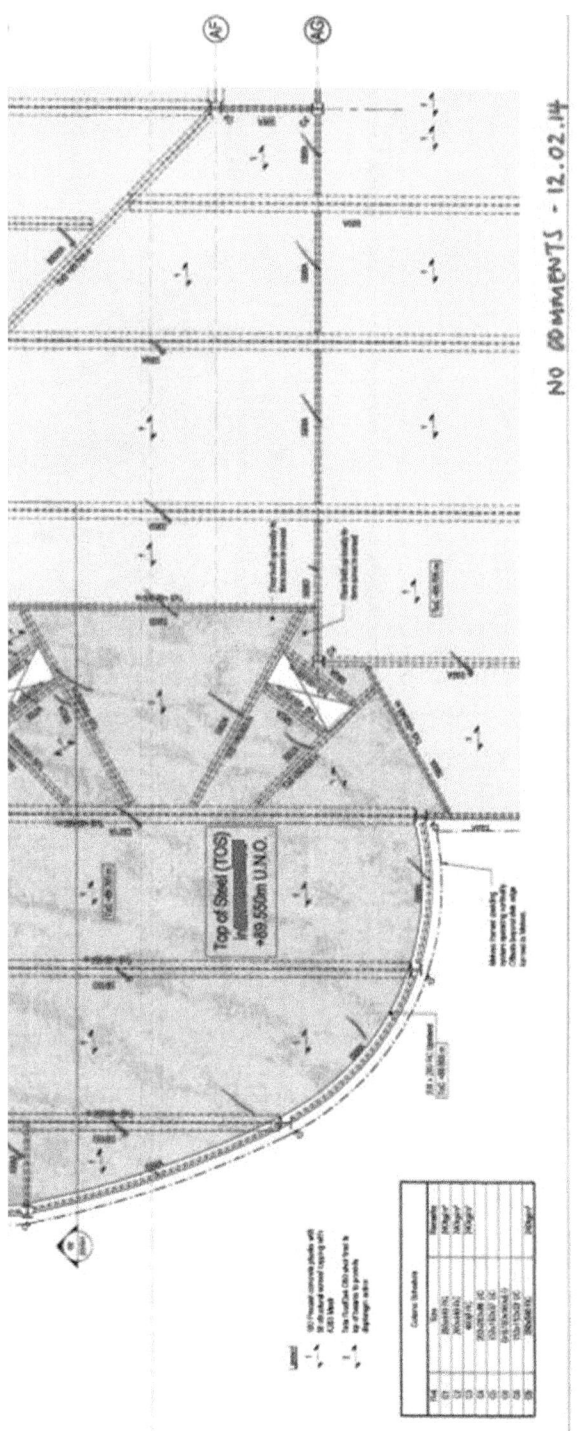

Figure 11.2. An example of a 'closed off' drawing

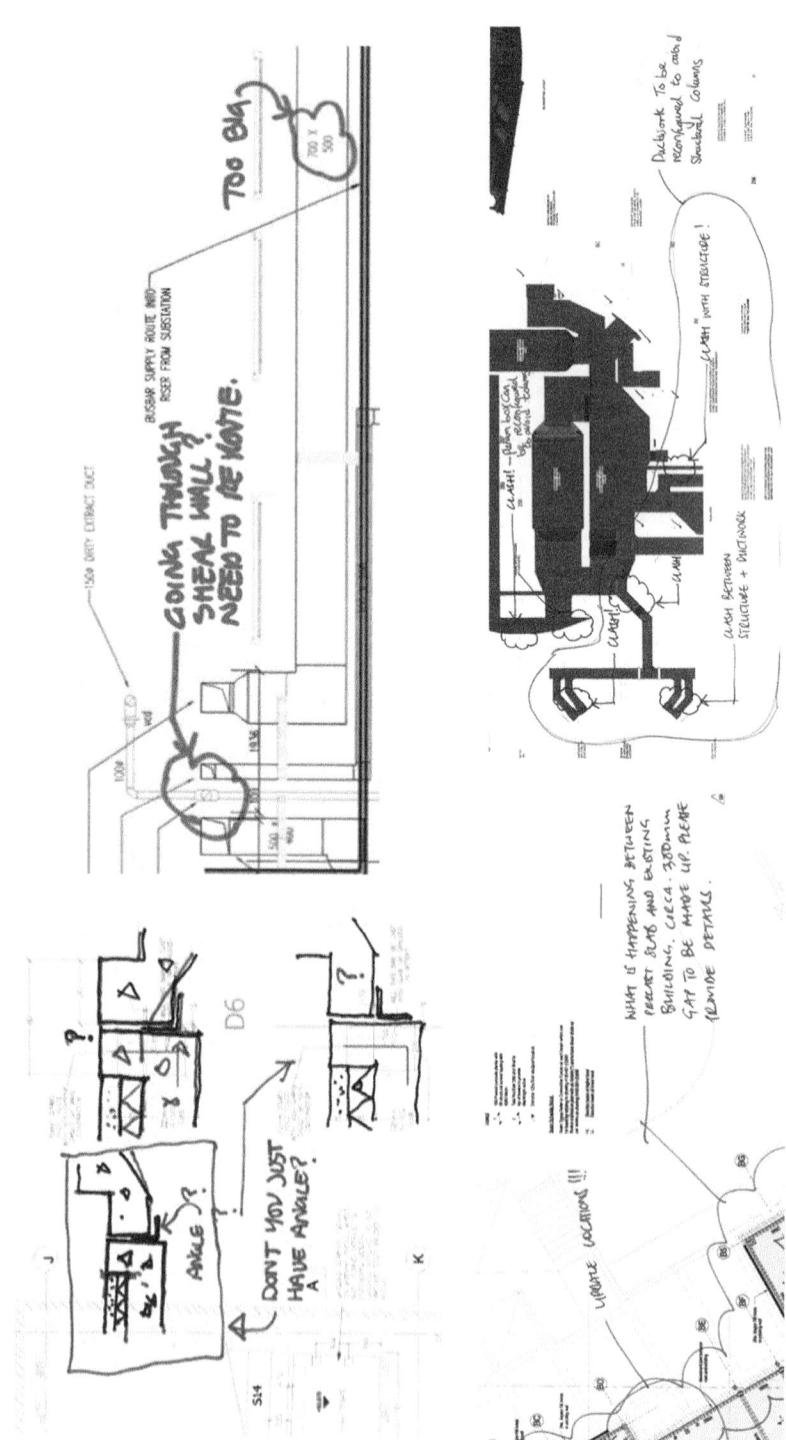

Figure 11.3. Examples of assertive communication

construction projects are structured around very long and detailed contracts, where areas of accountability and legal responsibility in the events of non-compliance are clearly defined among participating organizations. Furthermore, it is not uncommon for complex construction projects to extend over years in time—one of the projects we observed was entering the construction phase having been in design development since 2008. In this respect, using organizational affiliations rather than individuals' names provides the added benefit of continuity in case of staff turnover. This combination of demarcated liability and temporality in architectural work means that, as far as ongoing communication within a project is concerned, it is entire organizations not particular individuals that are seen to 'do' the communicating.

11.8 THE STRUGGLE FOR KNOWLEDGE INTEGRATION THROUGH DESIGN DRAWINGS

The power attributed to architects in construction projects is not illegitimate—the role they play in designing the building and, later, administrating the contract during construction, comes with a fair share of legal and commercial responsibility. Following various projects from the position of the architect *in vivo* for a year, we gained a degree of appreciation for the amount of commercial and legal responsibility resting on the project architect. We suggest that the authoritative way in which architects communicate with other specialists through material objects, such as design drawings, should be interpreted in light of these wider pressures inherent to their field of practice, as well as their jurisdictional control relative to that of other professionals.

Not all work on a project necessarily includes architects—different specialists also communicate with one another using design drawings. It is interesting to see how the dynamics change when two parties in relatively equal positions of power communicate. Figure 11.4 provides an example of communication between structural and mechanical engineers. This is a drawing by mechanical engineers sent over to structural engineers to ensure there are no issues with the way mechanical engineers were planning to install water drainage. The comments in pink are the initial response by the structural engineers, delivering some sharp critiques of proposed plans (e.g. 'it will be virtually impossible'). Mechanical engineers followed up with a response to the comments from the structural engineers, asserting some of the proposals presented initially, and commenting on the comments. Words such as 'need' and 'do not' were underlined for added poignancy, and some suggestions were made (e.g. 'would this help?'). The structural engineers' response to this appears to communicate some form of strong

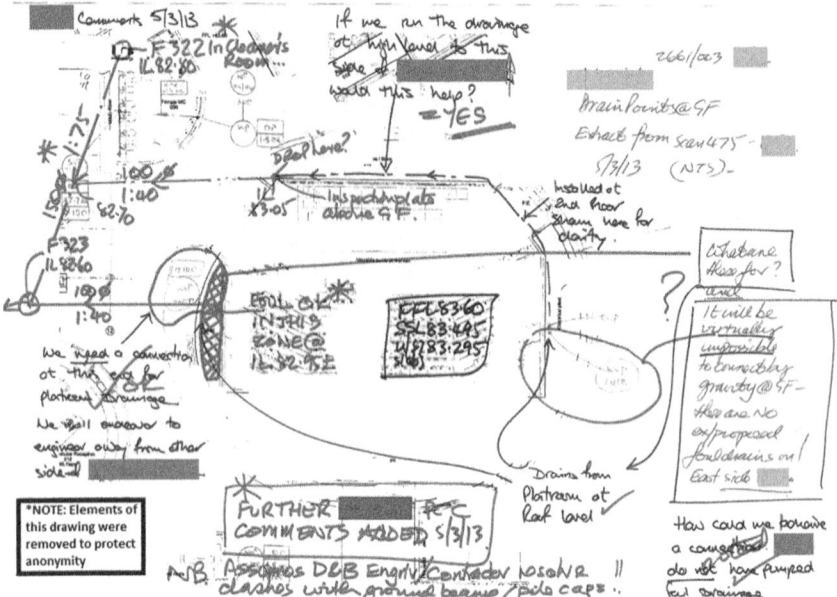

Figure 11.4. Example of communication without an obviously dominant group involved

emotion, using heavy red ink and making statements such as 'resolve clashes with ground beam/pole caps!!' and writing over the mechanical engineers' previous comments.

Compared to the situations above where an obviously dominant party was involved in knowledge integration, the situation presented in Figure 11.4 far more resembles a quarrel than a report. This is because, first, the two groups of engineers had difficulty constructing a common intelligibility space in which cross-boundary work might begin to take place. In other words, to communicate via a design drawing was not inherent to either of the parties (engineers have slightly different sets of work tools compared to architects), so the exact intent of communication may have been unclear, causing initial confusion as to what was going on or being proposed.

Second, the relative power and knowledge bases of each of the groups of engineers were not readily compatible—the mechanical engineers were enquiring about a mechanical issue, and the structural engineers were responding from a structural point of view. The content and context were not aligned, so apparently there was no mutually beneficial way out of this situation after the initial comments were returned. Third, neither party had, or was seeking, the authority to make any final decision on the validity of the ideas and knowledge embedded in this design drawing. Unlike the architects, who have a clear mandate for decision-making as far as the building design is concerned, neither of the engineer groups had legitimacy in this area of work. In this situation (Figure 11.4), the design drawing failed to integrate knowledge across boundaries between the two groups and, in fact, may have played a role in erecting a boundary between them.

Situations exemplified by Figure 11.4 are especially interesting because they suggest the need for power asymmetry between participating practices in order to enact boundary objects. There are at least two reasons for this: in a situation that includes a dominant party there are restrictions on how objects can be used, and in a situation where the distribution of power is most clearly established there is little need to (re)negotiate power bases. It should be noted that this is subject to particular ways of working, and that our observations are based on a highly professionalized, project-based setting. In the most basic sense this means that the individuals are coerced into collaborative work by the constraints of a project because, in the event of delays or defects, the liability is not restricted to any one party. With this in mind, however, it does appear that boundary objects actually require an imbalance of power in interdisciplinary work.

In a situation where a dominant party is present there are restrictions on how objects can be used to facilitate (or not) knowledge integration. The notion of dominance here is rooted mainly in specialist knowledge, although we did observe limited use of interpersonal power too. In the case of design drawings, architects enjoyed dominance over other professionals not least because the communication of information by way of design drawings is an inherently architectural way of doing work. Accordingly, and as we discussed in Section 11.6 (Figure 11.3), architects enjoyed ownership over what can be said and in which ways. Figure 11.2 is a good example of this—an engineer sent a drawing to the architect with the intention of *reporting* work conducted on a number of details; this use of a drawing was expected and sanctioned by the architect who used the 'No comment' cue to approve the work and *command* it to the next work stage. Overall, this seemingly eventless drawing actually served to integrate knowledge across a professional and spatio-temporal boundary—an engineer applied the object (a CAD drawing) in a way deemed appropriate by the architect (to *report* in this situation) who, in turn, received and processed the information and returned it with a 'stamp of approval'. Approval of design issues by the architect ensured continuation of the construction work. Figure 11.4, on the other hand, depicts a situation where lack of a dominant party removed clarity about how the object should be used in order to cross boundaries. As we described above, lack of clear authoritative demarcation when using an object to span an interdisciplinary boundary may work to erect further boundaries. The object of discussion in Figure 11.4 had to be resolved later by the engineers, over the phone, because the drawing itself had ceased to be useful by the time it reached the stage it is in in Figure 11.4.

A clear and established distribution of power is also a clear factor in interdisciplinary knowledge integration. This ties in very closely with the previous point about acceptable ways of using objects for cross-boundary work. This aspect, however, is important to illustrate that (re)negotiation of power over particular boundary objects and ways of doings things occurs through objects too. Elements of sarcasm, shown in Figure 11.3, for instance, are typical of when a new group of professionals enters the project or a new section of work begins. In both cases a process of establishing areas and degrees of power would take place. The use of multiple exclamation marks, sarcasm, and even the red pen were only observed as being employed by the architect as a means of establishing a clear hierarchy of authority over the use of particular objects. We observed an interesting example of this, albeit one beyond the scope of this chapter, when an architect exercised great distance from technical information on the ceiling layout produced by the mechanical engineer (using engineering work tools, mainly tabulated data), but felt much more comfortable exploring and examining the same data when it was produced in the form of a CAD drawing, thus using a very specific type of boundary object to engage in knowledge integration. Exploring how individuals and professional groups shape information and knowledge into objects relative to the power bases of participating parties is one area of collaborative work via boundary objects that is worth looking at in more detail.

11.9 DISCUSSION

Our observations highlight that the political dynamics and communicative practices embodied in boundary objects need to be understood with reference to the wider systems of practice in which objects are embedded. This goes beyond Østerlund's (2008) notion of 'actional fields' to include broader, institutionalized norms and tools of professional practice—the 'tools of the trade', so to speak. In other words, it is not enough for a boundary object to be something around which cross-boundary interaction can take place—a boundary object must not be alien to the broader environment in which the object of work is situated. In fact, we observed no boundary objects that were not also the work tools of either architects or engineers and, in every case, inherent to both. Accordingly, it might be worth thinking of boundary objects as boundary objects of work where *work* is emphasized and *boundary* is de-emphasized. Our research suggests that boundaries in interdisciplinary work emerge only as a consequence of the work being conducted through objects in a manner not deemed proper by whichever practice used the object in question as a work tool. To put it differently—we never observed failure of knowledge integration across boundaries when a design drawing was used the way architects use it.

In the case of construction projects, design drawings were used to enable and facilitate cross-boundary collaboration between different professional specialisms. However, drawings are an institutionalized tool in architectural practice and, as such, embody the architect's paradigmatic concerns—the emphasis is on the design information rather than the technical information, for example. Even the more technical drawings, of particular building details or arrangements of insulation, for instance, present information within a design paradigm, as opposed to tabulated textual or numerical data, used more often by other groups of specialists. Accordingly, we observed that design drawings that did facilitate knowledge integration did so when an architectural party was present, and those that hampered it (as in Figure 11.4) did so when an architect was not involved, but when the tool of architectural practice (the drawing) was being used by others.

In our case, an architect may be permitted to wield the 'red pen' at certain points in the knowledge integration process, and to open out or close down communication by virtue of their legitimate authority and their recognized responsibilities in the project (Schlaich, 2006). However, when the responsibilities and authority are contested—as in the example of the structural and mechanical engineers talking through objects—knowledge integration is more difficult to achieve (Figure 11.4). As Lainer-Vos (2013: 528), notes: 'examination of the making and functioning of boundary objects must take account not only of the objects themselves but also their immediate material and institutional positioning'), including their relation to professional identities and wider systems of power (cf. Gal et al., 2004).

Our investigation of design drawings in complex construction projects supports this claim as well as drawing attention to the idea that, material and institutional positioning notwithstanding, objects of work that become boundary objects are more than artefacts around which communication and interrelating happen. The sociopolitical dynamics of boundary work take place *within* the representational space provided by objects, just as in surrounding interaction. Boundary objects, then, should not be viewed solely as elements that are brought into the work in order to aid knowledge integration across boundaries. Instead, we argue that an appreciation of the power dynamics and discourse embodied within objects should accompany an examination of the consequences of their involvement in social interaction (cf. Hardy and Thomas, 2014). In other words, when looking at knowledge integration, it might be helpful to understand what kinds of representational work and communication are embodied in the object(s) before looking at how people communicate around them. For example, consideration of the construction projects we observed in terms of the professionals interacting around objects would seem to suggest that cross-boundary knowledge integration was 'successful' (at least in some cases), and that design drawings formed a large proportion of the boundary objects used to accomplish this. However, a closer look at how different professional parties engaged in communicative work *through* design drawings allowed observation of a hierarchy, and a machinery of power, which help to explain the detrimental effect of objects on knowledge integration alongside their more constructive effects, more commonly studied in previous work.

12

Bridging Scientists and Informal R&D Collaborations

Implications for Firm-Level Knowledge Integration and Patent Performance

Annapoornima M. Subramanian,
Kwanghui Lim, and Pek-hooi Soh

12.1 INTRODUCTION

Knowledge integration is the purposeful combination of specialized and complementary knowledge to achieve specific tasks (see Chapter 1 in this volume). The knowledge integration process involves collaboration among partners, each of which has specialized knowledge (Tell, 2011). In this chapter, we explore the extent to which formal and informal research and development (R&D) collaborations shape the ability of biotechnology firms to integrate specialized knowledge. R&D scientists and engineers play an important role in the knowledge integration process (Almeida et al., 2011; Johansson et al., 2011), but it is often difficult to distinguish empirically between informal and formal collaborations established by R&D staff. Research on knowledge integration describes it as a complex, multilevel process that requires firm-specific capabilities, frequently illustrating through case studies and small sample qualitative analysis (Berggren, et al., 2011). We overcome this limitation by employing empirical measures for formal and informal collaborations across a sample of 222 biotechnology firms. This approach enables us to examine when R&D collaboration affects firms' innovation performance. We show that both formal and informal collaborations matter, although we focus on informal collaborations since these are less well explored in the literature. Our research contributes the perspective that knowledge integration differs between university–firm and firm–firm collaborations, and that it is shaped by the firm's human capital, specifically by the presence of Pasteur bridging scientists who matter greatly for the knowledge integration process.

Knowledge integration is context specific and is shaped by knowledge structures, task characteristics, and relationships (Tell, 2011), and is particularly salient in technology-based industries. In biotechnology, R&D collaborations are important and shape the firm's ability to generate and integrate new knowledge (Zucker et al., 1998; Owen-Smith and Powell, 2004; Subramanian et al. 2013). Prior studies show that personal network ties to high-quality university scientists are important sources of external knowledge for biotechnology firms (Zucker et al., 1998; Gittelman and Kogut, 2003; Almeida et al., 2011). Gittelman and Kogut (2003) observe that 70 per cent of articles published by 116 US biotech firms between 1988 and 1994 are joint publications with external organizations, and that 92 per cent of research partners are universities, non-profit research institutions, and government laboratories. Furthermore, Liebeskind et al. (1996) show that research publications are associated more frequently with informal collaborations than with formal collaborations. Nevertheless, few studies have examined the interdependency between scientific human capital and informal R&D collaboration, a notable exception being Almeida et al. (2011).

Formal R&D collaboration relies on alliances, networks, and licensing structures to facilitate collaborative exchanges between organizations (Stuart et al., 2007; Lavie et al., 2010; Soh and Subramanian, 2014), while informal R&D collaboration relies on trust, status networks, and communications at the more personal level (Kreiner and Schultz, 1993; Liebeskind et al., 1996; Powell et al., 1996). While both forms of collaborations are important, informal collaborations are by nature more difficult to characterize and track. As a consequence, researchers often need to make a choice between in-depth case studies and surveys to obtain deep, rich, project-level data, and use of less refined proxy measures to observe changes across a large number of firms and over time.

We build on our earlier research on 'bridging scientists' or boundary-spanning scientists working in firms, who engage in both patenting and publishing activities (Subramanian et al., 2013). In that research, we distinguished between Pasteur bridging scientists and Edison bridging scientists, the former being more inclined towards fundamental research compared to the latter. We showed that both types of bridging scientists are complements to R&D alliances between focal firms and other firms, but that the fundamental research orientation of Pasteur scientists makes them a substitute for R&D alliances between the focal firm and universities.

In this chapter, we focus on the extent to which a firm's informal collaborations affect patent performance, which is an important outcome of knowledge integration in the biotechnology industry. Furthermore, we examine how a firm's Pasteur bridging scientists affect this relationship. In terms of knowledge integration in the context of biotechnology, the role of such scientists is particularly interesting because they act as important boundary spanners between the worlds of scientific exploration and commercially valuable patented drugs (Gittelman and Kogut, 2003; Baba et al., 2009; Breschi and Catalini, 2010).

In our study, formal R&D collaborations refer to the number of R&D alliances in which the focal firm engages, while informal collaborations refer to the number of joint research publications between the focal firm's scientists and external scientists who are *not* employees of the organizations with which the focal firm has had formal R&D collaborations. In other words, we measure the extent to which a firm's scientists collaborate on scientifically productive projects with organizations that are not the firm's past and present formal alliance partners.

We analyse patent, publication, and alliance data from biotechnology firms. Our results show that informal R&D collaborations between the focal firm and universities have a significant positive effect on patent performance. However, informal R&D collaborations between the focal firm and other firms are detrimental to patent performance. This is likely to be because if both parties are firms, there is a tension between collaborators and the need for each party to protect proprietary knowledge. However, we find that a firm's Pasteur bridging scientists not only enhance the patent-related benefits of informal university collaborations but also diminish the negative effect on patent performance of informal firm collaborations.

Our work suggests that the boundary-spanning activities of firm scientists are important for shaping knowledge integration outcomes. We adopt a multilevel approach, linking scientists in firms with interorganizational collaboration mechanisms that facilitate knowledge integration. By distinguishing between informal and formal collaboration, our study complements the innovation literature on technological specialization and interorganizational knowledge integration, including work by Brusoni et al. (2005), Dibiaggio (2007), and Lavie and Drori (2012).

12.2 PRIOR RESEARCH AND HYPOTHESES

The process of knowledge integration varies at various levels within a firm and depends also upon the type of partner involved (see Preface and Chapter 1 in Berggren et al., 2011). This perspective—that knowledge integration is an intricate and complex organizational process—highlights the need to understand how organizations combine complementary knowledge from internal and external sources, often through iteration over time, in order to generate novel and useful products, services, systems, and solutions (Berggren et al.,

2011: 9). A holistic view of knowledge integration is particularly relevant in technology-intensive industries, such as biotechnology, which rely upon absorbing and integrating complex external scientific knowledge in order to generate new solutions to difficult medical problems.

The literature suggests an important distinction between process and outcome (Okhuysen and Eisenhardt, 2002). The process of knowledge integration is shaped by the type of knowledge, type of relationship with the outside partner, and the knowledge management process (Berggren et al., 2011). In much of the existing research, the context and the organizational factors influencing the knowledge integration process are weakly linked to the outcomes of that process (Berggren et al., 2011, Fig. 1.1). We attempt to bridge this divide by analysing how a firm's R&D collaborations and scientists (both important to the knowledge integration process), and the context of its external collaborations (university/firm partner), relate to its output of patented innovations.

12.2.1 Knowledge Integration, Boundary Spanning and Bridging Scientists

Prior research on knowledge integration covers a broad range of industry contexts and management sub-fields (e.g. Iansiti and Clark, 1994; Okhuysen and Eisenhardt, 2002; Dibiaggio, 2007; Singh, 2008; Tiwana, 2008a), making it difficult to systematize the key findings in the literature. The need for knowledge integration arises because of knowledge specialization (Tell, 2011: 21): specialization generates efficiency, but, as a consequence, value creation activities require the integration of knowledge among these specialist organizations.

Within an organization, effective knowledge integration requires the surmounting of barriers arising from misaligned incentives among the actors, and the construction of mechanisms to facilitate coordination among the actors (Gebert et al., 2010; Cheung et al., 2011; Majchrzak et al., 2012). While these organizational processes are important, we are interested in interorganizational activities, among which boundary spanning is important.

One of the keys to successful knowledge integration is the ability to bridge across specialist knowledge boundaries (Carlile, 2004; Bercovitz and Feldman, 2011; Gardner et al., 2012; Majchrzak et al., 2012). According to Tell (2011), focusing only on knowledge transfer is insufficient; knowledge integration is shaped also by the ability to exploit similar or related knowledge across boundaries, and knowledge complementarity. This view is consistent with other authors who emphasize the importance of knowledge overlap (e.g. Cohen and Levinthal, 1990; Sapienza et al., 2004; Ahuja and Katila, 2001) and complementarity (e.g. Cassiman and Veugelers, 2006; Tiwana, 2008; Hess and Rothaermel, 2011).

The literature describes two major types of boundaries that must be spanned, the first being the boundaries between knowledge domains and the second being the boundaries between organizational structures. Hargadon and Sutton (1997), Hargadon (1998), and Hsu and Lim (2014) explore the factors affecting knowledge brokering across knowledge domains, and Rafols and Meyer (2010) capture interdisciplinarity in the wider sense of knowledge integration. Prior research shows the importance of also spanning organizational boundaries (e.g. March, 1991; Rosenkopf and Nerkar, 2001; Burt, 2005).

In line with the capabilities view, those firms that are successful boundary spanners and are able to integrate knowledge, achieve a performance advantage (Henderson and Cockburn, 1994; Iansiti and Clark, 1994; Grant, 1996; Verona and Ravasi, 2003). Organizations with scarce scientific human capital and difficult-to-imitate integration routines are better placed to absorb external knowledge, and to combine it with its own superior human capital to produce beneficial outcomes, thus making knowledge integration a potential source of competitive advantage relative to rivals.

Boundary spanning can be facilitated by the firm scientists, especially bridging scientists who are able to span both organizational and knowledge domain boundaries. However, scientists are often faced with conflicting choices, for example, to pursue proprietary commercial success or build scientific reputation among academic researchers (who tend to favour open science). In Sections 12.2.2 and 12.2.3, we explore the scientist's roles in formal versus informal collaborations and analyse the importance of Pasteur bridging scientists in the firm's collaborations with universities and other firms.

12.2.2 Formal and Informal R&D Collaboration

Prior research shows the importance of R&D alliances between universities and industry, and strong collaboration networks with firms (Rothaermel and Deeds, 2004; Stuart et al., 2007; Markman et al., 2008; Baba et al., 2009; Lavie and Drori, 2012). Formal R&D collaborations, which include joint research, sponsored research, and licensing agreements, are the primary vehicles for the transfer of university intellectual property to industry partners with the capabilities to develop and commercialize innovations.

Compared to the large literature on strategic alliances, joint ventures, and university technology licensing, empirical research on informal collaborations, which largely involve individual scientists exchanging ideas and knowledge that may be unpublished or more tacit in nature, is quite scarce (Almeida et al., 2011). This is probably because it is more difficult to observe and measure informal collaboration on a large scale (Bouty, 2000). Many of the insights in prior work stem from excellent observational research and qualitative case studies. For example, Andersson and Berggren (2011) trace knowledge integration by individual innovators in three large technology-oriented firms. They identify several elements that facilitate boundary spanning: leveraging personal knowledge and experience to span knowledge domains; participating in diverse discussions with colleagues and contacts outside the organization's boundaries; and conducting informal prototyping and testing, often with external collaborators.

In general, formal and informal collaborations involving R&D activities can be distinguished by the motivations for knowledge exchange and the knowledge governance norms (see Table 12.1 for a summary). First, formal collaborations between organizations are driven by economic incentives for the participating firms such as leveraging external sources of knowledge, skills, and capabilities, which are costly to create and maintain internally (Robinson and Stuart, 2007). In contrast, informal collaborations between individual scientists in co-publishing activities are motivated by the desire to share ideas, solve complex problems, facilitate learning, and achieve higher status within the scientific community (Liebeskind et al., 1996; Almeida et al., 2011). Second, the norms of knowledge governance in formal collaborations exist to protect and appropriate the value of the intellectual property produced by the partnership, usually through contractual agreements. This contrasts with knowledge exchange and problem-solving in informal collaborations which is governed by the norms of trustworthy behaviour—reciprocity, respect, and honesty in research (Liebeskind et al., 1996)—although the outcome, often joint publications, might still have a subsequent impact on the firm's patented innovations.

In the case of formal collaborations, we would expect firms to rely on different governance mechanisms and dedicated organizational functions to manage alliances and to ensure that alliance partners contribute with relevant complementary capabilities, conduct deep and broad search for new knowledge, and mobilize diverse participants from boundary-spanning networks linked to their partner organizations (Davis and Eisenhardt, 2011). These mechanisms ensure the transfer and integration of knowledge, which underlies successful innovation in a collaborative context. In contrast, informal collaborations are often initiated by individual scientists (or groups) with the aim of advancing the particular body of scientific knowledge. Rather than relying on proprietary and structured knowledge transfer means, informal collaborations rely on such mechanisms as exchange and hiring of students, co-supervision of researchers, informal conversations during conferences and meetings, collaborative research between former laboratory colleagues, and so on (Agrawal and Henderson, 2002). Typically, the knowledge that is transferred through informal collaborations is generated by laboratory work or theory development, which, potentially, is more publishable and less prone to conflicts of interest between competing organizations. The firm's scientists facilitate the acquisition and integration of new knowledge, which has the potential for creating impactful innovations.

Table 12.1. Formal and informal R&D collaborations in the biotechnology industry

	Formal R&D collaborations	Informal R&D collaborations
Definition	Joint R&D activities between firms and with research institutions. The focus is on the commercial success of a new drug.	Collaborative R&D activities between internal and external scientists. The focus is on knowledge exchange, problem-solving, and co-publishing.
Motivations of knowledge exchange	• Integrate and appropriate internal and external intellectual capital. • Access to intellectual property rights to scientific discoveries owned by others through contracts and legal mechanisms. • Access to complementary resources (scientific labs, instruments, tools, as well as scientists) and possibly functional knowledge (product testing, production, marketing, and distribution). • Gain organizational legitimacy in new markets, especially for small and new ventures.	• Sharing of scientific knowledge, unpublished and tacit knowledge. • Access to external experts and academic scientists. • Enhanced learning through interpersonal relationships. • Signalling of firm scientist's status within the scientific community.
Mechanisms of knowledge exchange	• Interorganization: mergers and acquisitions, R&D alliances, research contracts, joint ventures, and other equity-based arrangements. • Cross-boundary collaborative settings: cross-functional teams.	• Interorganization: co-authoring relationships with scientists from other firms or institutions (including former colleagues, post-doctorates, and existing university students). • Cross-boundary collaborative settings: conferences, seminars, etc.
Attributes of knowledge governance	• Commercialization of scientific discoveries is governed by norms of proprietary science. • The value of discoveries is protected by patents and captured through explicit provisions in formal contracts. • Research publication is feasible only when knowledge is patentable or not strategically important.	• Knowledge exchange is governed by norms of trustworthy behaviour, including reciprocity and honesty. • Intellectual property is respected through seminar/conference presentations and co-authorship. • Less structural, cultural, and cognitive barriers since scientists are free to discuss and exchange new ideas.
Examples	• Networks of alliances (e.g. licensing and joint ventures) between biotech and pharmaceutical firms (Barley et al., 1992; Powell et al., 1996; Baum et al., 2000). • Vertical alliances (Pisano, 1991; Rothaermel and Deeds, 2004; Stuart et al., 2007).	• Boundary-spanning social networks through interpersonal relationships (Liebeskind et al., 1996; Bouty, 2000; Zucker et al., 2002). • Joint publications (Hicks, 1995; Cockburn and Henderson, 1998; Almeida et al., 2011). • Co-authoring relationships fostered through scientist recruitment and mobility (Song et al., 2003; Lim, 2004; Tzabbar, 2009).

Scientists' formal and informal collaborations are likely to be important for integrating knowledge across firms, and empirical evidence shows that recruitment and mobility of scientists are mechanisms that foster the integration of distant knowledge (Song et al., 2003; Lim, 2004; Tzabbar, 2009). Thus, continued informal collaboration by the firm's scientists with former university supervisors or former colleagues in other firms is likely to affect the focal firm's scientific research activities. However, there are few empirical studies that link the role of scientists and the context of informal collaboration to the firm's innovation outcomes. According to prior research on formal collaboration, the type of the firm's scientists and the collaborative context combined have implications for when external knowledge can most effectively be transferred and integrated with internal knowledge (Baba et al., 2009; Hess and Rothaermel, 2011; Subramanian et al., 2013). We would argue that, depending upon the collaborative context, informal collaboration via co-authorship relations among bridging scientists could influence knowledge integration and the firm's patenting performance. The context of the collaboration (such as collaborating with firms vs universities) can influence the expectations and decisions of the focal firm's scientists related to exchanging knowledge (Bouty, 2000). In the remainder of this section, we develop hypotheses on the performance impact of informal R&D collaborations.

12.2.3 Hypotheses

Studies of informal R&D collaboration show that joint publication efforts involving academic and firm scientists facilitate knowledge exchange and flexible learning, which benefits industrial firms. Collaboration with academic scientists provides access to frontier scientific research and signals R&D quality (Zucker et al., 1998; Audretsch and Aldridge, 2009). Firm scientists who are active members of scientific networks through joint publications are more likely to gain access to star scientists at universities and research institutes which make commercially valuable discoveries (Liebeskind et al., 1996).

Zucker et al. (1998) and Gittelman and Kogut (2003) argue that personal ties in networks of high-quality university scientists and via joint publications are important for biotechnology firms. This includes joint publications with universities, non-profit research institutions, and government labs.

Hypothesis 1a: The number of informal collaborations with universities has a positive effect on the focal firm's patenting performance.

The aforementioned mechanisms of informal knowledge transfer are effective in the context of informal R&D collaborations between the focal firm and universities. This is because universities are oriented towards open science and their key goals are centred around producing impactful publications and shaping academic networks; these goals are well aligned to engagement in informal collaborations. Further, universities have an abundant supply of scientists in training (i.e. graduate students), who are considered to be the predominant knowledge transfer channel (Agrawal and Henderson, 2002).

Unlike informal collaborations with universities, informal collaborations between firms include none of these mechanisms, suggesting that there are limits to the benefits to be derived from such collaborations. The risk of opportunism and the coordination costs associated with informal collaborations with other firms are high relative to the potential benefits. Thus, in the context of informal collaboration between the focal firm and other firms, we expect the value of knowledge integration and innovation performance to be low because of significant information asymmetry problems. These problems apply particularly to informal collaborations that involve proprietary science. Prior research shows that *ex ante* asymmetric positions between partners give rise to competitive behaviour, leading to collaboration failure if there is an expectation of pure private benefits (Khanna et al., 1998; Park and Ungson, 2001; Lavie, 2007). This inhibits knowledge integration. Hence, we hypothesize that:

Hypothesis 1b: The number of informal collaborations with other firms has a negative effect on the focal firm's patenting performance.

Unlike formal R&D collaborations, informal R&D collaborations with universities follow the norms of open science with the result that there are fewer coordination, redundancy, and information asymmetry problems. Collaborating with academic institutions enhances the firm's learning flexibility and signals to others the quality of the focal firm's scientific capability (Hicks, 1995; Zucker et al., 1998; Murray, 2002; Audretsch and Aldridge, 2009). These advantages are more pronounced for firms that rely upon basic research in their innovation process and which employ boundary-spanning scientists (Cassiman and Veugelers, 2006; Hess and Rothaermel, 2011). Since firms with more Pasteur bridging scientists are at an advantage in terms of being able to leverage academic scientists' informal networks (Subramanian et al., 2013), we predict that high investment in Pasteur bridging scientists will enhance the focal firm's boundary-spanning role in open scientific networks:

Hypothesis 2a: As the proportion of Pasteur bridging scientists in the focal firm increases, the positive influence of informal collaborations with universities on the focal firm's patenting performance is reinforced.

Turning to informal collaborations with other firms (rather than universities), we predict that the boundary-spanning activities of the focal firm's Pasteur bridging scientists will exacerbate information asymmetry problems and spillovers of valuable internal knowledge, thereby compromising the overall quality of the knowledge production. Therefore, we hypothesize that a high level of investment in Pasteur bridging scientists will increase the negative influence of informal collaborations with other firms on knowledge integration:

Hypothesis 2b: As the proportion of Pasteur bridging scientists in the focal firm increases, the negative influence of informal collaborations with other firms on the focal firm's patenting performance increases.

In contrast, Edison bridging scientists have a lower preference for fundamental science and a lower willingness to collaborate in open science. Therefore, we do not expect Edison scientists to alter the benefits that the focal firm derives from informal collaborations. However, Edison scientists are included as a control variable in our analysis.

12.3 DATA AND METHODS

In order to test our hypotheses, we collected data from the biotechnology industry, a highly innovation-intensive industry (Sorenson and Stuart, 2000). Our sample firms were extracted from Plunkett's Directory, which includes 436 public listed biotechnology and pharmaceutical firms. Following Subramanian et al. (2013), we collected data on patents, publications, alliances, and the financial performance of the sample firms, from the NUS-MBS patent database, the Web of Science ISI Science Citation Index, Recombinant Capital, and Compustat Global. We excluded firms with missing data for the period 1990–2000. The final sample includes 222 firms.

12.3.1 Dependent Variables

We measure patent performance using two well-established variables from the literature: a) patent forward citations, and b) patent originality. A patent's forward citations are a good proxy for its economic value (Trajtenberg, 1990) and, in our study, this variable is calculated as the cumulative number of forward citations received by each patent up to 2004. Patent originality is calculated by measuring the breadth of the technology classes that a patent cites. Specifically, for each patent it is calculated as 1 (Herfindahl concentration index of the technology classes of backward cited patents). Patent originality captures the breadth of the technologies that are recombined to develop a new patent, and is a proxy for the patent's scientific novelty. It ranges between 0 and 1, where a higher number signifies that the knowledge contained in the focal patent is more original than the knowledge contained in other patents with a lower score, which, therefore, make smaller, incremental improvements to the prior technology (Trajtenberg et al., 1997). Thus, a higher patent originality score suggests an attempt to foster the emergence of new technologies.

12.3.2 Independent Variables

The firm's collaborative efforts beyond R&D alliances can be captured using the number of joint research publications between the focal firm's scientists and external scientists who are not employees of organizations with which the focal firm has formal R&D alliances (Subramanian et al., 2013). We use this measure to proxy for informal collaborations. We identify whether the external scientists are from universities or other firms in order to separate informal university collaborations and informal firm collaborations.

Similar to Gittelman and Kogut (2003), we classify bridging scientists as scientists who engage in both patenting and publishing. Specifically, the bridging scientists variable in our study refers to the firm's proportion of patenting inventors whose names appear on both patents and publications. We denote the proportion of bridging scientists with above average levels of publishing and patenting Pasteur bridging scientists. A detailed description of this measure can be found in Subramanian et al. (2013).

12.3.3 Control Variables

Since patenting performance might be influenced by the firm's scientific capability, we control for this effect using two variables—publishing intensity and number of citations. Publishing intensity is the ratio of publications produced by a firm in a particular year divided by the firm's R&D expenditure in that year. Number of citations is a variable representing the normalized citation count for the firm's publications in a particular year, and is used also by Gittelman and Kogut (2003).

A technologically strong firm can apply for large numbers of overlapping patents, which improves its patenting performance. We control for this effect using the cumulative number of patents applied for by the firm in a year that are within the same technology class as the focal patent. We control for other firm-level factors that might influence patent performance, including number of inventors, Edison bridging scientists, R&D expenditure, firm size (measured by number of employees), and firm age (measured by number of years since founding). Since patenting performance relies also on external R&D inputs, we control for this using the number of the firm's formal R&D collaborations with universities and other firms. The rest of the control variables are patent age, a dummy variable to differentiate biotechnology firms from pharmaceutical firms, a dummy variable for patent technology class, and year fixed effects.

12.4 RESULTS

Since the patent forward citation measure exhibits over-dispersion, we chose negative binomial regressions for the models that include this variable as the dependent variable. For models that include patent originality as the dependent variable we employed ordinary least square regressions. Most of our quantitative findings were very similar when a Tobit model was used. The unit of analysis is the individual patent, but several other of our variables are firm level; to account for this, we include in the regression models robust standard errors clustered by firm.

The results of the regression analysis are presented in Table 12.2. Model 1 presents the main effects of informal university collaborations, informal firm collaborations, and Pasteur bridging scientists on patent forward citations. Model 2 includes tests for the interaction term between informal collaborations and Pasteur bridging scientists; similar to Model 1 it uses forward citations as the dependent variable. Model 3 is similar in structure to Model 2, but uses patent originality as an alternative dependent variable.

Models 2 and 3 show that informal university collaborations have a significant positive association with both patent forward citations and patent originality ($p < 0.01$), which provides support for Hypothesis 1a. In contrast, informal firm collaborations have a significant negative association with both patent forward citations and patent originality ($p < 0.05$, $p < 0.10$). Thus, Hypothesis 1b cannot be rejected. Table 12.2 shows also that formal collaborations (with both universities and other firms) are positively correlated with patent performance.

Comparing Models 2 and 3, we observe that informal firm collaborations have a weaker negative influence on patent originality ($p < 0.1$) than on patent forward citations ($p < 0.05$). This suggests that the problem of information asymmetry associated with informal firm collaborations is less significant if the firm is working on more scientifically original innovations.

Across these models, Pasteur bridging scientists have a positive and significant effect on patent performance, reinforcing our prediction that they play an important role in knowledge integration and, thus, innovation outcomes. Moreover, the interaction term between Pasteur bridging scientists and informal university collaborations is positive and significant in both Model 2 (forward patent citations) and Model 3 (patent originality). This supports Hypothesis 2a, that the boundary-spanning activities of Pasteur bridging scientists strengthen the patent-related benefits from informal university collaborations.

In Model 2, the interaction term between informal firm collaborations and Pasteur bridging scientists is negatively associated with forward citations (-0.0293, $p < 0.05$). This negative interaction term, coupled with the negative main effect of informal firm collaborations (-0.0145, $p < 0.05$), supports

Table 12.2. Pasteur bridging scientists, informal collaborations on forward citations of patents and patent originality

Dependent Variable	Forward Citations		Patent Originality
Variables	Model 1 (Negative Binomial)	Model 2 (Negative Binomial)	Model 3 (OLS)
Independent Variables			
Informal University Collaborations	0.0545**	0.1412***	0.0232***
	[0.0236]	[0.0322]	[0.0021]
Informal Firm Collaborations	−0.0149***	−0.0145**	−0.0005*
	[0.0065]	[0.0071]	[0.0002]
Pasteur Bridging Scientists	0.5936***	0.8004***	0.0578***
	[0.2010]	[0.2186]	[0.0069]
Interaction between Pasteur Bridging Scientists and Informal Collaborations			
Pasteur Bridging Scientists* Informal University Collaborations		0.1921***	0.0216***
		[0.0560]	[0.0029]
Pasteur Bridging Scientists* Informal Firm Collaborations		−0.0293**	0.0027***
		[0.0117]	[0.0003]
Control Variables			
Edison Bridging Scientists	0.4402***	0.3510*	0.0067
	[0.1929]	[0.1683]	[0.0097]
Formal University Collaborations	0.1919***	0.1921***	0.0020***
	[0.0563]	[0.0560]	[0.0004]
Formal Firm Collaborations	0.0223***	0.0221***	0.0001
	[0.0023]	[0.0022]	[0.0001]
Publication Intensity	−0.0001	−0.0001	−0.0000
	[0.0002]	[0.0002]	[0.0000]
Publication Citation	−0.0453*	−0.0402	0.0069***
	[0.0251]	[0.0281]	[0.0013]
Technological	−0.0024***	−0.0024***	0.0001
Focus	[0.0008]	[0.0008]	[0.0001]
Number of Inventors	0.0310***	0.0351***	0.0022***
	[0.0128]	[0.0128]	[0.0006]
Patent age	0.1670***	0.1674***	0.0009
	[0.0194]	[0.0197]	[0.0006]
R&D Expenditure	0.0143	0.0137	0.0179***
	[0.0302]	[0.0307]	[0.0009]
Firm size	0.0454	0.0451	0.0161***
	[0.0357]	[0.0357]	[0.0007]
Firm age	−0.2592***	−0.2751**	0.0114
	[0.0875]	[0.0891]	[0.0117]
Bio/Pharma Dummy	−0.0260	−0.0161	0.0082
	[0.1665]	[0.1783]	[0.0093]
Constant	−0.4588	−0.4369	−0.1625***
	[0.4144]	[0.4179]	[0.0138]
No. of Observations	7,670	7,670	7,670

Note: Technology class dummy variables and year fixed effect were included but not reported. Standard errors appear in parentheses.
*p<0.1; **p<0.05; ***p<0.01

Hypothesis 2b. However, in Model 3 the interaction term between informal firm collaborations and Pasteur bridging scientists is positively associated with patent originality (0.0027, p <0.01). This positive interaction term, when combined with the negative main effect of informal firm collaborations (–0.0005. p <0.1), does not support Hypothesis 2b. In summary, we find mixed results for Hypothesis 2b depending upon which dependent variable is used.

Comparing the interaction terms in Model 3, we observe that the moderating influence of Pasteur bridging scientists is larger in magnitude when it is interacted with informal university collaborations than when it is interacted with informal firm collaborations. This reflects the emphasis of Pasteur bridging scientists on engaging in research that is more closely associated with the research conducted at universities compared to other firms.

12.5 DISCUSSION AND CONCLUSION

To summarize, we find that informal collaborations involving boundary-spanning scientists play an important role in the firm's knowledge integration. Informal collaborations with universities are positively correlated with the patent performance of the firm. In contrast, informal collaborations with other firms have a negative influence on the firm's patent performance. The focal firm's Pasteur bridging scientists enhance the patent-related benefits from informal collaborations with universities, and reduce the negative effects of informal collaborations with other firms on patenting performance.

Our findings are consistent with the view that knowledge integration is complex and involves the interplay of factors at multiple levels, including the collaboration choices made by individual scientists, firm-level alliances, and other formal relationships, and the types of external partners involved (universities vs other firms). These factors shape the way firms integrate and recombine knowledge with measurable performance outcomes. While probably well-intentioned and rational at the individual level, not all external collaborations are positively associated with improved firm innovation performance.

In addition, the role of individuals cannot be assumed to be uniform, with Pasteur bridging scientists having a disproportional impact. They have a positive direct effect on performance, but their impact via informal collaborations depends on the type of partner: our results are positive for university collaborations, but mixed for collaborations with firms. This is in line with our expectations that Pasteur bridging scientists have an affinity for the types of research conducted at academic institutions and reinforce the relationships that facilitate firm attempts to tap these sources of external knowledge. This raises questions about the types of contingencies that make Pasteur bridging scientists more effective at knowledge integration, for example, geographic proximity, the need for complementary human capital to facilitate collaboration, and incentives for participating in fundamental research.

We conclude with a provocative conjecture for future research. While previous work on knowledge integration focuses on the activities of large firms (e.g. see Preface in Berggren et al., 2011), it might be equally important for smaller firms, but exist in more informal and fluid forms. We observe that, at least in the biotechnology industry, knowledge integration is important for a broad range of firms from tiny start-ups to established behemoths. Knowledge integration is also motivated by competition and the highly fragmented knowledge specialization across scientific domains and organizational boundaries. However, in a small start-up knowledge integration is likely to depend much more on informal collaborations than in a large firm, which has formal organizational routines in place alongside formal communication and external tie structures.

13

Knowledge Integration at Work

Individual Project Competence in Agile Projects

Karin Bredin, Cecilia Enberg, Camilla Niss,
and Jonas Söderlund

13.1 INTRODUCTION

Most research and development (R&D) projects are carried out by temporary organizations that depend heavily on the integration of numerous disciplinary knowledge domains for their successful completion (Carlile and Rebentisch, 2003). The issue of knowledge integration as a key factor in R&D projects has received considerable attention in recent years (Berggren et al., 2011; Majchrzak et al., 2012). There is a substantial body of research focusing on projects as knowledge integration arenas (see, e.g., Nonaka and Takeuchi, 1995; Söderlund, 2002) and on knowledge integration processes in projects (see, e.g., Okhuysen and Eisenhardt, 2002; Enberg, 2007; Söderlund, 2010; Wahlstedt, 2014). This work offers profound insights into the mechanisms involved in successful integration of knowledge across knowledge boundaries.

Most prior research takes single projects or project-based organizations as the unit of analysis; we argue that there is a need for more focus on the individual level of analysis. A few studies address the individual competencies and skills needed by project members (e.g. Zika-Viktorsson and Ritzén, 2005; Söderlund and Bredin, 2011) and offer valuable insights into individual-level knowledge integration processes and project work. However, in our view, they have two important gaps. Firstly, they do not address the disciplinary knowledge needed by individuals to provide input into knowledge integration processes (cf. Leonard-Barton et al., 1994). Rather, they tend to emphasize the competencies and skills that support collaboration and project-based work more generally. Secondly, extant research fails to offer firm conclusions about the variations across different project contexts and the implications of new forms of project organization for knowledge integration processes. In particular, there is a lack of a more elaborate understanding of how different types of projects influence the competencies and skills required of individual project members.

In this chapter, we contribute to the emerging stream of research on the individual as a contributor to knowledge integration processes and address the differences among various project contexts. We highlight individual project competence as a key element in knowledge integration processes in different kinds of projects. Our arguments related to the individual and contextual turns in knowledge integration rest on two observations and trends, related to the important role of individuals in knowledge integration processes and to novel logics for project organizing.

13.2 INDIVIDUAL PROJECT COMPETENCE AND NEW LOGICS OF PROJECT ORGANIZING

The first observation is the crucial role of individuals in the integration of knowledge (see, e.g., Enberg, 2007; Enberg et al., 2010). We argue that there is a need for more research to further our understanding about what goes on in projects and project teams. Given the importance of specialized disciplinary knowledge and the need to integrate this knowledge to facilitate the development of new products and systems (Grant, 1996), the disciplinary knowledge and skills that individuals need to master to contribute to knowledge integration in projects are particularly relevant. These competences and skills are essential components of what prior research describes as 'individual project competence' (Zika-Viktorsson and Ritzén, 2005). By focusing on the individual as a contributor to knowledge integration processes in projects, we can define this competence as the individual's ability to manage his/her contribution to knowledge integration processes in projects.

Based on the distinctions in prior research (see, e.g., Iansiti, 1995; Zika-Viktorsson and Ritzén, 2005), we suggest that individual project competence consists of two central elements: 1) *disciplinary knowledge*, that is, the knowledge and skills related to a particular disciplinary domain; and 2) *supportive knowledge*, that is, the skills and abilities required by project members alongside their specialized disciplinary knowledge to allow them to contribute efficiently to the knowledge integration process. Prior research primarily includes supportive knowledge in analyses of individual project competence. However, since knowledge integration inherently requires the integration of several disciplinary knowledge domains, disciplinary knowledge, by definition, must be a central element in individual project competence. We extend previous definitions of individual project competence to include disciplinary knowledge.

The second observation is that new project organizing logics, such as agile methodologies, are emerging and diffusing through the organizational landscape (e.g. Muduli, 2013). These new logics are setting a new context for knowledge integration in projects, and research is needed to compare the requirements of different project contexts and understand the variations in requisite individual project competence. This chapter focuses on the increasingly popular agile project methodologies, arguing that a better understanding of agile projects should allow more insights into the individual project competence requirements related to different kinds of projects. We suggest that deeper investigation of the distinction between disciplinary and supportive knowledge is particularly important.

Against this background, we analyse what constitutes individual project competence in agile projects, comparing them with more traditional projects based on their representations in the literature. Drawing on empirical accounts derived from interviews with respondents from three firms that had recently implemented agile project management, we focus on two main dilemmas related to individual project competence. Both are linked to the trade offs from breaking down versus maintaining knowledge boundaries. We posit that these 'boundary dilemmas' influence individual project competence in agile projects. The first dilemma relates to the difficulties involved in maintaining depth in disciplinary knowledge whilst encouraging a higher degree of flexibility and breadth in project workers' disciplinary skills. The second dilemma concerns the balancing of short-term with long-term interests. These two boundary dilemmas are essential for understanding individual project competence requirements in agile projects, and provide a useful base for a comparison with traditional projects.

13.3 LITERATURE REVIEW

As already mentioned, previous research identifies individuals as central contributors to knowledge integration in projects, but there have been calls for more research at the individual level of analysis with respect to the knowledge integration processes that take place in projects. Zika-Viktorsson and Ritzén (2005: 193) argue that project competence has been discussed as an organizational level competence related to the ability of 'upper management [to manage] project portfolios according to strategies and demands from the surrounding world'. This applies to several studies performed by Söderlund and Tell on the dynamics of project competence in P-form organizations (see, e.g., Söderlund, 2005, 2008; Söderlund and Tell, 2009). Moreover, research on project competence at the individual level has addressed the knowledge, skills, and abilities of project managers to 'manage formalized processes, and to plan, monitor and co-ordinate' project work (Zika-Viktorsson and Ritzén, 2005: 193). These studies tend to emphasize the role of the project manager to orchestrate knowledge integration, which results in a leadercentric model of knowledge integration in projects. This might work well in some traditional industries and in projects that rely on traditional methods for project management, but is ill suited to knowledge integration in agile projects. Indeed, some studies discuss individual project competence in relation to what is required from individual project members. However, most existing work refers to what we call supportive knowledge and pays scant attention to the linkages between different kinds of knowledge and the particular context.

13.3.1 Individual Project Competence—Supportive Knowledge

Zika-Viktorsson and Ritzén's (2005) study is based on evidence from line managers, project managers, and designers engaged in R&D projects. The authors identify two main sets of project competencies: planning competence and interpersonal competence. Planning competence involves the abilities to manage time and to cope with change. Interpersonal competence includes ability to manage a team whose members are jointly responsible for the entire work process and team performance by supporting an open climate, managing negotiations and conflicts, and acting self-confidently. Zika-Viktorsson and Ritzén's findings support prior studies which emphasize social skills and team abilities as important for the ability to contribute to knowledge integration in project work (see, e.g., Pauget and Wald, 2013). Their study is in line also with research that highlights the need for project members to develop self-confidence and self-management skills to enable competent representation of a specific disciplinary domain in multidisciplinary collaborations (e.g. Bredin and Söderlund, 2011). In particular, Zika-Viktorsson and Ritzén (2005) include the management of time and coping with change: abilities that are reasonable effects of being part of a temporary organization. Other abilities necessitated by the temporary nature of projects include being able to establish relationships quickly, understand socialization processes, and manage uncertainties (Söderlund and Bredin, 2011).

Söderlund and Bredin (2011) approach the issue of knowledge integration from an individual perspective, adopting a somewhat different stance. They focus on the participants in knowledge integration processes and identify five main activities that members of R&D project teams engage in and which are critical for knowledge integration processes: rule following, relating, role carving, reflection, and reframing. These activities require exploitation of existing contextual rules and individual social capital in the focal project, understanding and shaping individual roles in dynamic and ambiguous social settings, reflecting on technical aspects to cope with new problem-solving situations, and reframing complex problems. The ability to manage these activities is an important part of what Borg and Söderlund (2014) describe as 'liminality competence', which is considered essential for project members to manage their contributions to knowledge integration in projects. Söderlund and Bredin (2011: 97) emphasize that project members need 'to understand how to make use of other people's knowledge, to know how, and, not least, when to contribute their own uniquely held knowledge to other people's problem-solving processes'—an ability tied as much to the supportive knowledge as to the disciplinary knowledge needed to contribute to a successful project outcome.

13.3.2 Individual Project Competence—Disciplinary Knowledge

Projects are generally set-up as cross-functional, that is, to include different knowledge bases as inputs to the knowledge integration process in projects. Project members are allocated to projects based on their expertise within a particular disciplinary knowledge domain. Disciplinary knowledge can be defined more specifically as the scientific and/or technical qualities that enable particular project members to conduct specific tasks, and endow them with abilities and skills that distinguish them from their colleagues with other disciplinary identities (cf. Collinson, 2001). According to previous research, project members with disciplinary expertise 'are particularly well suited to attack narrowly defined problems within their area of expertise and, consequently, they can offer superior local search for incremental improvements on particular components' (Melero and Palomeras, 2015: 156). However, multiple project team members with deep disciplinary expertise in different areas pose challenges to knowledge integration, and it has been suggested, much in line with Söderlund and Bredin's (2011) proposal, that project participants must be able to relate their particular disciplinary knowledge to that of other project team members (Iansiti, 1993; Leonard-Barton, 1995).

Hence, to contribute meaningfully to knowledge integration processes in projects, individual project members need more than expertise within their own disciplinary knowledge domain. As discussed in prior research on traditional projects, individuals need to develop 'T-shaped skills' (Iansiti 1993:139), which provide the capability for members to engage in 'convergent, synergistic thinking' and to 'apply knowledge across situations' (Leonard-Barton 1995: 76). T-shaped skills are developed through interaction and learning among team members and are crucial for successful knowledge integration in projects (Enberg and Bredin, 2015). However, this framework does not suggest that project members should acquire in-depth *content* or *practice* of the disciplinary knowledge of their colleagues in the project. As Grant (1996) suggests, the integration of knowledge requires that the disciplinary knowledge remains differentiated among project members—otherwise there is no knowledge to integrate. Rather, what improves the potential for knowledge integration in projects, is common knowledge at 'the intersection of their [team members'] individual knowledge sets', which enables project team members to 'integrate aspects of knowledge which are *not* common between them' (Grant, 1996: 115—original emphasis).

This difference between knowing about something and knowing how to do something is articulated by Collins (2004: 127), who makes the distinction between 'interactional' and 'contributory' expertise. Interactional expertise is based on the idea that one can learn by 'linguistic socialization', that is, by 'spending enough time talking with the practitioners of the relevant domains without actually practising the practices'. The result of this type of learning provides the ability to 'speak the language' without being able to 'practice the corresponding physical activities' (Collins, 2004: 127). In contrast, according to Collins (2004), contributory expertise is ability to practise the practices. Therefore, drawing on Iansiti (1993, 1995) and Grant (1996), effective knowledge integration requires individuals with contributory expertise in one particular disciplinary knowledge domain combined with interactional expertise within several domains, in order to create a certain level of common knowledge.

Although the amount of common knowledge needed for efficient knowledge integration has been debated in previous research on knowledge integration in projects (see, e.g., Schmickl and Kieser, 2008), scholars agree that a project team's disciplinary knowledge should remain specialized and differentiated. This body of work generally focuses on traditional project forms. However, given the recent popularity of agile project methods, which to some extent change fundamental ideas about what defines a project and a project team, the relevance of these models for knowledge specialization, and a minimum level of common knowledge, could be questioned.

13.3.3 Individual Project Competence as Situated in a Particular Project Context

Previous work addresses the specific nature of projects as temporary organizations. In many cases, this is pertinent given the recurrent shifts across projects, with collaboration occurring among relative strangers (Lindkvist, 2005; Bechky, 2006). The traditional view of projects is that they are temporary in relation to both tasks and teams; a team is formed to work on a particular task and, when the task is completed, the team is dissolved and individual members move on to new projects. Previous research discusses a number of challenges associated with such project organizing, including lack of knowledge transfer (Prencipe and Tell, 2001), problems related to establishing trust (Söderlund, 2000), and the costs of coordination (Bechky, 2006). A growing number of firms are trying to sidestep some of these problems by applying agile project management methods, which allow for a more flexible approach to task completion.

Agile methods are designed to respond to sudden changes in demand during the development process, and are based on the ideal of less initial planning and flexible, incremental development with tight feedback loops involving the customer during the process (see, e.g., Drury-Grogan, 2014; Serrador and Pinto, 2015). The core of the development process is usually small, cross-functional, and co-located development teams with high levels of discretion for deciding about and managing their own development and knowledge integration process. These teams normally work with short, well-defined deliveries, followed by check-ups and new decisions. Drury-Grogan (2014: 508) describes agile team work as an 'interactive group process with a multidisciplinary team working together from start to finish', where team members 'rotate roles and share leadership across the team' (see also Nerur et al., 2005). Our respondents were all employed in firms that had implemented agile project methods. For all these firms, this had resulted in the fading out of the previous line-based structures that hosted different disciplinary domains, and the establishment of multidisciplinary agile teams as more stable units. Thus, the traditional understanding of projects as involving temporary teams which are dissolved after project completion, and individuals being reallocated to new project teams, is less valid in agile project contexts. Moreover, the problem-solving logic in agile projects is more flexible and incremental compared to traditional projects (Drury-Grogan, 2014).

Addressing different project contexts, we can on the one hand identify projects conducted by more or less permanent teams and on the other identify projects that follow a problem-solving logic that is more or less agile. We believe that this might have quite different implications for individual project competences. We assume that working in a temporary team is quite different from working in a permanent team. We assume also that working according to an agile approach is quite different from a more traditional approach. The latter constitutes a knowledge collectivity (Lindkvist, 2005) and requires people to rely on 'swift trust' (Meyerson et al., 1996), owing to its temporariness. A knowledge collectivity acts on differentiated and distributed knowledge and, therefore, it is important that its members know who knows what in order for them to connect to the appropriate person once a problem is encountered. In agile project contexts, the logics are quite different.

Firstly, Enberg and Bredin (2015) provide empirical examples of how agile project methodologies are implemented, involving the creation of project

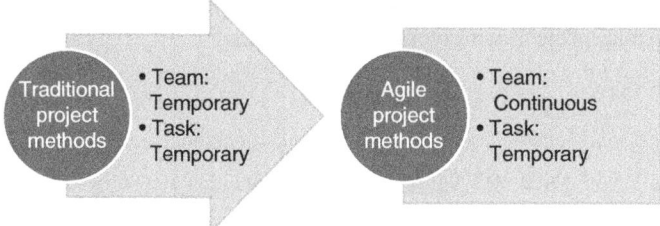

Figure 13.1. A trend from traditional project methods towards agile project methods

teams that are permanent over extended periods of time. In contrast to more traditional project structures, these teams are not dissolved once the project is completed; rather the team takes on a new project task. Hence, although the project task is temporary, the project team is not, which means that it cannot be seen as a knowledge collectivity as defined by Lindkvist (2005) (see Figure 13.1).

Secondly, agile projects seem to foster other qualities related to the disciplinary knowledge of project members, compared to traditional projects. For example, role interchangeability is encouraged within agile project teams, which means that members are also encouraged to broaden their repertoire of skills and disciplinary knowledge to increase the team's ability to be self-sufficient in knowledge. For example, Nerur et al. (2005: 75) argue that, in agile teams, 'team members, empowered with more discretionary and decision-making powers, are not confined to a specialized role', something which 'increases the diversity/variety of the teams'. In addition, Muduli (2013) suggests that the use of agile project management methods requires project participants to exhibit higher levels of flexibility and adaptability in comparison to a more traditional project context.

To summarize, we suggest that individual project competence should be understood as consisting of supportive as well as disciplinary knowledge. Hence, in order to develop our understanding of individual project competence in different contexts, both these aspects need to be considered. Furthermore, previous studies of individual project competence focus primarily on traditional project settings, characterized by task and team temporality, and individuals who are highly specialized within particular disciplinary domains. Although research on agile projects is scarce, some studies indicate that agile projects represent a quite different work context, incorporating, for example, permanent project teams and less specialized individuals. This has implications for the disciplinary knowledge of project members, but also, as Muduli (2013) suggests, for supportive knowledge. Taken together, this suggests that the application of agile project management methods will have implications for individual project competence requirements.

13.4 RESEARCH METHODOLOGY

The study reported in this chapter is based on an interview study involving project team members and managers in project-based organizations that rely on agile project methodologies. In order to capture knowledge integration processes at the individual level, we collected data from the core actors involved. Given our particular interest in individual project competence, the interviews focused on capturing individual experiences regarding the knowledge, skills, and abilities required to perform in an agile project team. Previous work pays scant attention to the elements of disciplinary knowledge when addressing individual project competence. Therefore, we highlighted this aspect in the interviews. Our respondents had experience of working in more traditional as well as agile project settings, and the interviews were also aimed at capturing perceived changes in requirements related to working in agile projects compared to traditional ones.

We conducted a total of thirty-five interviews across three firms (twelve, nine, and fourteen interviews respectively), corresponding to a total of twenty-seven hours. The three firms are project-based, and employees are involved in advanced product and systems development (see Box 13.1).

Common to these firms is that most employees involved in projects have at least a Master's in engineering, and some have doctoral degrees. Another commonality is that knowledge integration among project participants in cross-functional and co-located teams is essential for project success. At the time of our study, all the firms had relatively recently implemented agile project management methods as a way to organize their product development work. This constituted major shifts in how knowledge integration was organized in the product development process.

For this chapter, all interviews were transcribed and analysed as a single dataset (for more details on the empirical findings for each firm and cross-case analysis, see Enberg and Bredin, 2015). The parts of the transcriptions that involved topics related to individual project competence were selected into a focused dataset, coded, and categorized. Two primary empirical patterns related to individual project competence were identified. We have described these empirical patterns as 'boundary dilemmas' since both highlight the conflicting requirements of *integration*—breaking down and crossing existing boundaries, and *specialization*—maintaining and nurturing boundaries required as inputs into knowledge integration processes.

Box 13.1 Respondents' employing firms—a brief description

Software Inc. develops advanced software products and systems and is among the top three companies worldwide in its industry. It offers a wide range of customized software-based products and systems for customers in areas such as media, transport, automotive, and utilities. The company has over 100,000 employees worldwide, but the respondents participating in our study were all working in a development unit located in Sweden, which employs around 2,200 people.

Sentio is a world-leading developer and manufacturer of sensor systems. The company offers a wide range of vision products for industrial applications such as vision sensors, smart cameras, and 3D cameras, which are customized and integrated in customers' existing production systems. The company has around 5,500 employees worldwide, and the respondents contributing to this study all work in one of Sentio's R&D units in Sweden, which employs around fifty-five people.

MedTech is a Swedish market-leading developer and seller of products and services in the area of medical information technology (IT). The company offers a wide range of products comprising IT solutions, software licences, service and upgrading agreements, consultancy services, and training. The company has delivered some of the largest radiology IT installations worldwide to customers in the healthcare sector. Their products are integrated with customers' existing systems and are developed in close collaboration with customers. MedTech employs around 500 people, and the respondents in this study were all employed in the R&D unit, which employed about seventy employees.

13.5 BOUNDARY DILEMMAS IN AGILE PROJECTS

The two boundary dilemmas discussed here, illustrate: 1) the simultaneous need for depth and breadth in disciplinary knowledge (see also Iansiti 1993); and 2) the simultaneous need for both a short- and a long-term perspective. These boundary dilemmas are essential problems, representing constant balancing acts that project members have to manage in order to contribute meaningfully to the knowledge integration processes. We would argue also that, although these dilemmas are at the individual level, they are important for the organization's long-term knowledge-integration capabilities. As the discussion will show, these dilemmas can be identified in previous research on project-based organizing and knowledge integration—these balancing acts are not specific to agile projects. However, the empirical study in this chapter clearly suggests that agile projects put these dilemmas in a new light, and emphasize other aspects of individual project competence compared to traditional projects.

13.5.1 Boundary Dilemma 1—Knowledge
Breadth versus Knowledge Depth

Our empirical observations showed that project members were frequently required to broaden their disciplinary knowledge in order to contribute to the knowledge integration process. While the logic in more traditional projects tends to imply that this 'broadening' mainly involves developing a common language to enhance collaboration in temporary teams (e.g. Grant, 1996), our empirical study, involving agile team members, highlighted the need for greater flexibility, including taking on assignments not within their primary disciplinary knowledge domain. For example, system developers might be required to conduct testing or installation work. In other words, project workers in agile projects, in which the teams are continuous and relatively self-managed, not only need to develop disciplinary knowledge in several different disciplinary knowledge domains to enhance collaboration; they also need to develop a certain depth of disciplinary knowledge within those domains in order to make the team more self-sufficient in knowledge, and less vulnerable to absences and varying knowledge domain needs. The respondents often referred to the particularities of agile projects, and the agile team's joint responsibility to develop the knowledge and abilities required to solve team assignments, as driving forces for the development of knowledge within more than one disciplinary domain. This was described by a team coach responsible for supporting the agile teams:

> I think that this [the agile project setting] makes it easier to broaden one's knowledge, it becomes kind of mandatory. You get a feature which affects several areas and there's no one else who's supposed to do it. In that way, it facilitates. And you give the team the responsibility to make it on its own, instead of [...] telling someone to do it. So it's more a situation when the team says, OK, what do we need to learn to manage this feature?

Although this flexibility in disciplinary knowledge among individual project members can be seen as highly beneficial for the team's common abilities, it clearly constitutes a boundary dilemma. On the one hand, project members are required to leave their comfort zone in terms of their particular expertise, and to learn more about what others know, in order to meet project deadlines and optimize the effectiveness of teamwork. On the other hand, several respondents questioned the sense of individuals having to take on tasks that they were not good at. One project member argued:

> My personal opinion has always been that it's ineffective to work in cross-functional teams [...] because often, you find yourself doing tasks which you're not good at ... [...]. And I really think that the basic principles of [agile project methods] are completely wrong because it seems as if the basic idea is that it's more important just to get a task over and done with than to get the task done

by the right person. [...] In any other discipline or profession—medical doctors, electricians or plumbers [...]—the one person best suited to do it will do it, but that's not the case in [agile project methods].

Project members also said that the need to broaden their knowledge into other disciplinary domains reduced the possibilities for them to further their primary disciplinary domain. The need for flexibility in the team outweighed individuals' desires to strengthen their disciplinary specialization. One project member expressed this clearly:

> When I talked to my manager a while ago, I told him that I wanted to go back to working more with design. But then we had a discussion in the team and we came to the conclusion that for the team, it's much better that I learn system verification. If I had been able to decide 100% on my own, I would have chosen design. But it's not like [...] I'm walking around dissatisfied with me learning system verification instead.

In sum, flexibility, agile work methods, and self-management of the project team require project workers to deepen their knowledge in various disciplinary domains. On the one hand, this means that individuals become more flexible and more able to contribute in several disciplinary domains, making the team stronger and less vulnerable. On the other hand, there is a risk that an individual's primary disciplinary specialization may be eroded by a focus on broadening knowledge into other disciplinary domains. This primary disciplinary specialization is especially difficult to maintain in settings with very few arenas for disciplinary peers to share experience and work together on problem-solving (Enberg and Bredin, 2015).

This first boundary dilemma represents a fundamental problem for all R&D organizations, especially concerning how much to invest in the development of deep disciplinary knowledge and how much to invest in broadening knowledge domains (Brusoni et al., 2001). At firm level, research indicates the criticality that firms need to know more than they can make to be able to integrate new knowledge and to understand how they should adjust to absorb related knowledge and technologies. A similar idea, we suggest, applies to the individual level.

13.5.2 Boundary Dilemma 2—Short-Term versus Long-Term Perspectives

All respondents work at companies which rely on agile projects to develop new products and systems. This has led to an increased short-term focus where teams take responsibility for work packages and deliver in short, so-called 'sprints', which, in turn, implies a higher degree of autonomy for the teams. Hence, there is a high degree of temporality in project work as new work packages come and go. In parallel with this short-term focus, the project teams that the respondents worked in were designed to be relatively stable over time. Thus, project tasks come and go, whilst the team remains stable. Making project teams less temporary was aimed generally at enhancing more lasting ties among members and promoting the flexibility required. Most respondents considered this stability to be beneficial, since it allows the team to develop better collaboration and become more effective. However, there are some drawbacks to stable teams which were raised by several respondents. One drawback is the risk that team members over time will develop too similar knowledge profiles and, hence, the value of cross-functional teamwork is lost. The following extract from one of our interviews with a project member explains the implications of belonging to a stable team for eighteen months:

> The longer time a team works together, the more we all know increasingly similar things. In our team, we have worked together for about a year and a half now. So, now we know pretty much the same thing in relation to what we are working with. But before that, we contributed with more different competencies.

Another commonly expressed concern was that project members felt there were few arenas where they could work together with others with the same expertise, which potentially could affect individuals' possibilities to maintain sufficient depth of knowledge within their primary disciplinary domain, and which also could affect the quality of the solutions:

> My greatest concern is that since I and [a disciplinary peer] are located with different teams, we will not work together. That is the greatest risk. I hope the teams can be flexible enough to make exceptions from the principles of agile project management and scrum, that you should always have interdisciplinary teams working together [...] it's quite difficult, you often need several eyes on our type of [disciplinary-related] problems as they are really tricky [...] to keep up the quality...

In the companies employing the respondents, line managers' roles had changed from taking responsibility for building technical leadership to a focus mostly on human resources management. However, given the relatively high level of autonomy and self-management in agile teams, competence development is driven to a great extent by the project team and by the individual project workers, with the support of managers and team coaches. Since agile teams are driven mostly by short-term goals, individual invest-ments in more long-term learning are often described by respondents as difficult to prioritize. Several respondents expressed the importance of stra-tegic direction and the role of managers to support choices that are important in a long-term perspective although they are hard to prioritize in every-day work. While from a long-term perspective, competence development is necessary for both the individual and the company, taking time for such activities was seen as being disloyal to the team in the short run:

> You feel that you kind of deceive them—they are struggling while you're trying to learn something, reading a book or something. You really have to...I don't know...disconnect the person's, what could I say, sense of duty, to make it happen...

The second boundary dilemma related to balancing short- and long-term perspectives is a well-known dilemma in the management of organizations in general, and project-based organizations in particular. However, the study of project members in an agile project context highlights that in agile project settings the content of this dilemma is different compared to what we know from traditional projects. Firstly, the short term needs of integrating different knowledge bases in an efficient way through more stable teams that promote the development of 'supportive knowledge' is made more difficult by the risk that team members will develop too similar knowledge profiles in the long run. Secondly, the need for short-run internal flexibility in stable agile teams is complicated by the need for long-run individual development, particularly within the primary disciplinary domain. In the following section, we discuss these dilemmas in more depth.

13.6 DISCUSSION

Drawing on the existing literature and the discussion of empirical boundary dilemmas, we analyse how individual project competence can be understood and conceptualized in traditional and in agile projects. The discussion is rooted in the two proposed main elements of individual project competence— supportive and disciplinary knowledge. These elements are discussed based on previous research and the empirical foundation described by the two boundary dilemmas. We show that these boundary dilemmas are highly relevant in both types of projects, but that they have quite different implications for individual project competence.

13.6.1 Individual Project Competence: Variance in Supportive Knowledge

Based on research into project-based organizing and discussions of traditional projects, it is clear that project members in these settings need to develop certain competencies and skills that are not directly related to their disciplinary knowledge area, that is, they need to develop supportive knowledge. This supportive knowledge is linked tightly to the particularities of the project setting and, as we will show, can serve as a tool to enable individuals to better manage the balance between short-term and long-term needs. In other words, it enhances individual abilities to address the second boundary dilemma.

In traditional projects, project teams are temporary—meaning that project members collaborate and interact during a limited time period and, when the project is closed, move on to participate in a new project and in a new team. Sometimes they may be working with team members they have collaborated with previously; however, in general project teams are unique and involve novel tasks and groups of people. This form of temporary organizing calls for 'liminality competence' (Borg and Söderlund, 2014), requiring the ability to operate at organizational boundaries while also developing practices that make it easier to move into and out of projects. Project members in such traditional project settings need also to develop abilities for 'swift socialization' (Lindkvist, 2005: 1190) in order to rapidly develop enough common knowledge to enable the integration of knowledge. Studies that compare traditional and agile projects generally stress that traditional projects rely heavily on initial planning and life-cycle models for product development, including traditional project management tools and methods focused on controlling the processes, activities, and tasks (Nerur et al., 2005). Hence, project members in traditional projects need extensive planning competence (Zika-Viktorsson and Ritzén, 2005).

We argue that the supportive knowledge required in traditional projects is primarily a tool to enable individuals to handle the balance between short-term and long-term perspectives. In other words, it enhances their abilities to address the second boundary dilemma at the individual level. Project members need to build supportive knowledge to meet the work situation and to enable them to become competent project workers over time by building liminality competence, planning competence, and swift socialization competence. Our findings for agile projects show that these boundary dilemmas have quite different implications for the type of supportive knowledge needed.

The empirical study shows that the respondents worked in cross-functional, agile teams which are stable over time and across projects. Teams that are more stable and also more autonomous need team members who are flexible and adaptable in relation to assuming different roles and performing different tasks. Hence, in agile teams, flexibility is likely to be a more useful competence than liminality competence, since team members are not operating at organizational boundaries to the same extent as in traditional project settings. Moreover, the development process in agile projects is emergent rather than planned, and is guided by product features rather than activities and tasks (Nerur et al., 2005). The empirical study shows that agile teams are required to assume greater responsibility for delivery, which requires team members to manage an emerging project plan with short feedback loops and continuous new decisions about future directions (cf. Serrador and Pinto, 2015). Rather than high levels of planning competence, in the sense of initial planning of tasks and activities, agile projects require teams (and team members) that can participate in managing the internal team activities and making decisions based on feedback and changes of direction during the development process. This is in line with Muduli (2013), who argues that agile project members are generally more empowered in terms of decision-making within the team. Agile projects hence require the individual to possess managerial competence and the ability to participate in and contribute to self-management, more reactive planning, and decision-making.

As already discussed in this chapter, prior research shows the importance of supportive competence in the form of relational competence (Pauget and Wald, 2013, termed 'interpersonal competence' by Zika-Viktorsson and Ritzén, 2005). The empirical study confirms the importance of these competencies, but shows also that, in agile project settings in which teams are more stable over time, the focus of relational competence is not primarily on swift socialization. Rather, project members need to build long-standing relationships and to work on continuous improvement in team collaboration. In addition, in traditional projects, interactions are based mainly on individuals' predefined and stable roles, which might imply a more predictable relational pattern based on swift trust (Meyerson et al., 1996). In agile projects interpersonal relations are based on the more fluid roles of individual project members.

Based on the empirical findings, we suggest that individuals in agile project settings will benefit from developing flexibility competence, managerial competence, and relational competence for building long-term relations and continuous improvement in teams' internal collaboration. Thus, the type of supportive knowledge needed for agile projects differs from the supportive knowledge needed for traditional projects, although it is generally related to handling the challenges involved in balancing short- and long-term needs. Individuals in traditional project settings need to develop supportive knowledge which makes them excel in temporary teams and tasks, conducted over extended periods of time. Individuals in agile project settings, need to develop the type of supportive knowledge that allows optimum performance in stable, cross-functional teams over time, while simultaneously managing a development process characterized by short deadlines, continuous feedback loops, and decision-making at short notice.

13.6.2 Individual Project Competence: Variance in Disciplinary Knowledge

As described, members of traditional projects 'comprise a mix of individuals with highly specialized competences, making it difficult to establish [...] a common knowledge base and can thus be considered as knowledge collectivities'

(Lindkvist, 2005: 1190). Within these temporary projects, individual members contribute specialized expertise which needs to be integrated by exploiting the expertise of other project team members. Thus, members of traditional project teams need to develop 'T-shaped' skills (Iansiti, 1993: 139), that is, skills that are 'deep in one area, broad in many' (Iansiti, 1995: 536).

Building on Collins's (2004) terminology, we suggest that members of traditional project teams need to deliver a certain depth of 'contributory expertise'. The differences in contributory expertise among project members promotes knowledge integration. Iansiti's (1993) model of T-shaped skills (see Figure 13.2), in combination with Collins's (2004) terminology, can be used to illustrate the profile of disciplinary knowledge often aimed for in traditional project settings. The stem of the T shows that the profile has depth of contributory expertise within one disciplinary knowledge domain while the cross-bar of the T makes the disciplinary knowledge profile broader, indicating a certain amount of interactional expertise; that is, sufficient knowledge about other disciplinary areas to be able to communicate and understand how they relate to one's own area of expertise. In traditional projects, owing to their temporary character, members interact over a limited time. Thus, the development of interactional expertise in such projects is based on short-term interactions.

In agile projects, team members 'are not confined to a specialized role', which allows teams to 'self-organize and respond with alacrity to emergent situations' (Nerur et al., 2005: 75). Our findings show that members of agile project teams are expected to move outside their comfort zones as constituted by their primary disciplinary domains and take on tasks in other domains whenever necessary. More stable interdisciplinary teams combined with high levels of team autonomy and self-management, however, engendered that it was not enough for team members to develop interactional expertise. Team members also needed to develop contributory expertise within several disciplinary domains, in order to achieve high team performance over the long run.

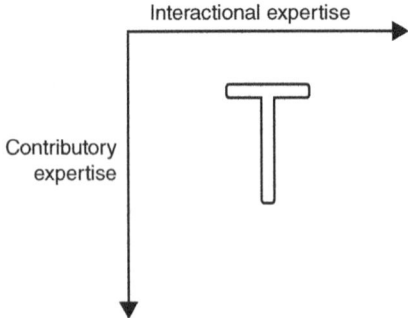

Figure 13.2. T-shaped disciplinary knowledge for traditional projects (authors' own illustration, based on Collins, 2004, and Iansiti, 1993, 1995)

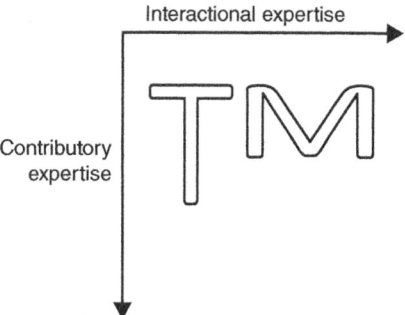

Figure 13.3. M-shaped disciplinary knowledge for agile projects (authors' own illustration, drawing on Collins, 2004, and Iansiti, 1993, 1995)

This allowed the team to cope with temporary absences and periods of both high and low work intensity. In traditional project settings, most project team members are affiliated to a functional line organization, which allocates resources to the project and can provide extra resources and particular disciplinary knowledge when necessary. However, in the agile setting described by our respondents, this did not happen. Hence, we would argue that while a T-shaped disciplinary knowledge profile might be beneficial in a traditional project setting, individuals in agile project settings need to develop M-shaped profiles (see Figure 13.3).[1] The M-shape denotes a disciplinary knowledge profile with contributory expertise in several areas, combined with interactional expertise.

In line with Collins (2004), we argue that the required interactional expertise can be developed in linguistic interactions among the members of agile project teams. That is, it can be developed without project workers actually practising the disciplines of their team colleagues. In fact, given the stability of agile teams, this is likely to develop over time without much effort. However, to develop contributory expertise requires practice and recurrent experience (Collins, 2004). This applies to the secondary disciplinary knowledge domains that individuals need to master in order to contribute, but applies also to the primary disciplinary knowledge domain. Our empirical study shows that this issue is linked closely to balancing knowledge depth and breadth. Working in stable cross-functional teams and learning to contribute to more disciplinary domains reduces the possibilities for deepening and developing the primary knowledge domain. Leonard-Barton (1995), in her discussions of T-shaped skills, highlights the risk of knowledge breadth being developed at the expense

---

[1] Social media include numerous discussions on different knowledge profiles such as I-shaped, comb-shaped, E-shaped, M-shaped, and π-shaped. These discussions highlight the relevance of these phenomena for practitioners, although the research community seems not to have found them important in relation to disciplinary knowledge so far.

of knowledge depth. She argues that this might lead to a situation where everyone becomes a generalist and no one possesses specialized knowledge. This risk seems relevant to the development of M-shaped knowledge profiles, which involves broadening of both interactional *and* contributory expertise. Leonard and Sensiper (1998) suggest that it takes at least ten years to develop deep skill. As a result, they suggest that most people develop a 'single bank of expertise', though a 'particularly talented or ambitious individual may develop deep skills in two or more arenas' (Leonard and Sensiper, 1998: 117). This is related to the argument in Grant (1996: 112), which suggests that 'experts are (almost) invariably specialists, while jacks-of-all-trades are masters-of-none'. As the empirical boundary dilemmas illustrate, there is a possibility that members of agile teams will develop individual project competence which will make them jacks of all trades. Hence, Figure 13.3 shows, and we argue, that M-shaped knowledge profiles will most likely lead to less depth in contributory expertise across all domains compared to a T-shaped profile. This might not be a significant problem if the products or technologies involved do not require narrow and deep contributory expertise for the knowledge integration process. However, our findings show that individual project workers were worried about loss of depth in their primary knowledge domain and a weakening of their disciplinary identity.

That each project member develops contributory expertise in more than one discipline also implies a risk that agile team members might develop similar disciplinary profiles. Leonard and Sensiper (1998: 118) suggest that 'when a group of diverse individuals addresses a common challenge, each skilled person frames both the problem and its solution by applying mental schemata and patterns he or she understands best'. Such variety of perspectives fosters 'creative abrasion', defined as 'intellectual conflict between diverse viewpoints producing energy that is channelled into new ideas and products' (Leonard and Sensiper, 1998: 118). This is related also to the argument in Grant (1996), which emphasizes the importance of specialized experts for knowledge integration processes. Thus, the development of M-shaped knowledge profiles among project members is likely to improve the effectiveness of teamwork and smooth collaboration, but might lead also to reduced knowledge integration capability within the team and, hence, reduced innovation capability in the organization.

13.7 CONCLUSIONS AND FUTURE RESEARCH

Our research adds to the prior literature by suggesting and problematizing the situated characteristics of individual project competence. Extant research on project-based work documents the importance of supportive competences such as planning competence and interpersonal competence (Zika-Viktorsson and Ritzén, 2005; Pauget and Wald, 2013). We suggest that traditional and agile projects imply different requirements with respect to individual project competence. For instance, agile projects have a greater requirement for 'flexibility competence' since individuals in such settings are expected to possess contributory expertise within several disciplinary domains. Agile teams also require managerial competence to master emergent planning and empowered team-based decision-making to allow project members to manage their work and changing work roles on a continuous and frequent basis. In contrast, members of traditional project teams require liminality competence, since project members move in and out of projects on a continuous basis, and planning competence, to facilitate the use of traditional, life-cycle-based planning tools and methods. Our empirical findings are summarized in Table 13.1.

In traditional project contexts, relations are built on swift trust and the ability to socialize rapidly based on predefined roles according to each individual's disciplinary knowledge. In agile projects, relationships are built over longer periods of time since teams are not dissolved after completion of a project task. They are shaped also by individual project members' abilities to act and contribute knowledge within a number of different disciplinary domains.

We argue that the conventional emphasis on supportive knowledge and skills should be complemented and combined with perspectives on the characteristics of the required disciplinary knowledge. We further suggest that the conceptualization of T-shaped and M-shaped skills, combined with the notion of interactional and contributory expertise, enhance our understanding of different forms of disciplinary knowledge and their complementarity in different

Table 13.1. Individual project competence matrix

Individual project competence	Traditional projects	Agile projects
Supportive knowledge	• Liminality competence • Planning competence • Interpersonal competence with focus on swift socialization	• Flexibility competence • Managerial competence • Interpersonal competence with focus on building long-term relations
Disciplinary knowledge	T-shaped • Interactional expertise required for short-term interactions in temporary project teams • Contributory expertise in one discipline	M-shaped • Interactional expertise required for long-term interactions in continuous project teams • Contributory expertise in several disciplines

project-based contexts. In discussing the types of disciplinary knowledge needed for the two types of projects addressed here, we introduced the concept of M-shaped skills in contrast to T-shaped skills (Iansiti, 1995). We suggested that, in both agile and traditional projects, individuals are expected to have interactional expertise in several disciplinary domains, but in agile projects they also need to develop contributory expertise in several areas as suggested by the concept and discussion of M-shaped skills. However, the development of expertise in several areas carries some risks which need further research. For example, we identified a cognitive trade off between learning in one or several disciplinary domains, which prompts the question of whether it is viable, over time, to master knowledge in more than one disciplinary domain or whether this could lead to a team made up of many generalists and few specialists. More research is needed on the consequences of different ways of organizing projects, and their implications for individual project competence and the firm's ability to conduct successful R&D projects over the longer term. We need to continue to investigate the individual contributions to the processes of knowledge integration in different kinds of projects.

14

Retrieval of Knowledge across Team Boundaries

Role of Transactive Memory Systems in a Restructuring Global Organization

Sirkka L. Jarvenpaa and Yongsuk Kim

14.1 INTRODUCTION

In today's global economy, organizations face greater volatility in their organizational designs, routines, and processes as they seek to meet new demands for flexibility, speed, and uncertainty (Galbraith, 2010). Team-based structures are often favoured because of their fast, flexible, and adaptive responses (Kozlowski and Bell, 2003). Teams are able to adapt quickly to changes while functioning as a robust and well-coordinated system, as long as they are able to harness and integrate knowledge (Galbraith, 1973; Van de Ven et al., 1976). Integration of specialized knowledge to perform a task or a project has been long viewed as the essence of organizational capability (Grant, 1996; Enberg et al., 2006).

One of the key knowledge integration challenges facing teams is to bring both the knowledge they own and the knowledge they can access from the rest of the organization to the conduct of their tasks. A prerequisite for effective knowledge integration is to know who has the required knowledge and expertise, or who can serve as an efficient external memory holder (Paoli and Prencipe, 2003). In knowledge retrieval, individuals seek knowledge held by others that is complementary to and can be combined with their own specialized knowledge.

Transactive memory systems theory argues that each individual has his or her own memory system, consisting of two components: internal memory (i.e. knowledge held in the mind of the individual) and external memory (i.e.

knowledge not possessed by the individual, but retrievable from others via a directory) (Wegner, 1987, 1995; Lewis, 2003). Members of a team can be the external memory holders of other team members. Efficient allocation and storage of knowledge within a team are based on who in the team has the expertise or task relevant to the knowledge. Teams with well-developed transactive memory systems can easily access and combine their specialized knowledge and bring it to bear on team tasks (Hollingshead, 1998; Alavi and Tiwana, 2002; Lewis, 2004; Lewis et al., 2005; Reagans et al., 2005; Pearsall and Ellis, 2006). If members have shared directories of who knows what, transactive memory systems maximize the efficiency of allocation and retrieval of knowledge (done in a coordinated manner) within teams (Liang et al., 1995; Lewis, 2003; Brandon and Hollingshead, 2004). Their shared understanding of who knows what allows members to minimize duplication and overlap of specialized knowledge, and quickly retrieve one another's knowledge for integration.

Organizational transactive memory systems extend the scope of knowledge directories to the organizational level in terms of knowing who knows what outside the team. They promote shared awareness of distributed expertise in the overall firm (Anand et al., 1998). Although it is argued that an organization-wide meta-directory can only be partially developed in a large organization (Nevo and Wand, 2005), it has been suggested also that an organizational transactive memory system can be better developed and maintained with the advancement of technology (e.g. Wu, 2013), and within a stable working environment with routines and stable membership in place (Moreland and Argote, 2003).

The existing literature on knowledge integration rarely considers transactive memory systems explicitly, although the ability to locate and access the knowledge is a key condition for integration. The transactive memory system literature focuses on transactive memory systems as enablers of knowledge coordination, which, in turn, facilitates combinative knowledge integration (Ren and Argote, 2011). In this chapter, we argue that organizational transactive memory systems can be viewed as a prerequisite for effective knowledge integration in and across teams. When tasks require members of different teams to work together, knowledge integration needs to go beyond single team boundaries and include boundary crossing of geography and time (Kellogg et al., 2006; O'Leary et al., 2011). Knowledge retrieval can occur through chains of transactive memory systems if a member of one team contacts a member of another team who is able to retrieve the sought-after knowledge on behalf of the seeker, using the team transactive memory system (Jackson and Klobas, 2008). The seeker then updates his or her organizational directory about who knows what and who does what in the organization.

During organizational restructuring, existing routines and procedures undergo changes that require much ad hoc problem-solving across team boundaries, which often requires the ability to locate and access the knowledge of others across different teams, geography, and functions. However, little is known about how teams and their members manage to locate and retrieve the required knowledge during organizational restructuring (Donaldson, 2001). Organizational restructuring involves internal administrative structure changes and is associated with an intentional management change programme (McKinley and Scherer, 2000). Although organizational restructuring can create clarity and order at the upper levels of management, the rest of the organization's employees can experience significant levels of disorder and ambiguity. Restructuring brings changes in tasks, group memberships, and interaction modes, all of which can significantly disrupt existing transactive memory systems and render them unreliable (Anderson and Lewis, 2014). An unreliable organizational transactive memory system, attributed to inaccurate and incomplete directory updates, can delay or harm the process of knowledge integration. An important question that arises is how teams and their members cope with the disruptive effects of restructuring on organizational transactive memory systems.

Nascent work examines the disruption to transactive memory systems resulting from organizational restructuring (e.g. Anderson and Lewis, 2014). Some studies suggest that team membership changes (Lewis et al., 2007; Ren and Argote, 2011) and task changes (Ren et al., 2006) lead to distorted transactive memory system structures and inefficient transactive memory system processes. In a simulation study, Anderson and Lewis (2014) found that transactive memory systems were damaged particularly by turnover and reorganization. Organizational restructuring brings about task and team membership changes and can increase physical separation and virtual interactions between individuals and teams (Griffith et al., 2003; Lewis, 2004; Fulk et al., 2005). Admittedly, there is some evidence that frequent task-oriented communication in the early stages of team tasks mitigates some of the negative effects of distance and virtual interactions (Kanawattanachai and Yoo, 2007). Furthermore, during restructuring, the assumption of expertise–responsibility alignment (i.e. that people who are responsible for specific knowledge have the right expertise) might not hold. Someone taking on a new role might not have an adequate level of expertise for the job. This incongruence between expertise and task responsibilities can create uncertainties in shared directories. During restructuring, frequent directory updates are critical (Griffith and Neale, 2001; Brandon and Hollingshead, 2004). However, given the pace and scale of changes, updates are subject to inaccuracy and incompleteness, making organizational transactive memory systems unreliable. When people rely on obsolete (thus, unreliable) transactive memory systems, knowledge integration is likely to suffer (Akgun et al., 2006).

In summary, organizational restructuring triggers volatility in tasks, team memberships, and communication. Restructuring is likely to make updating

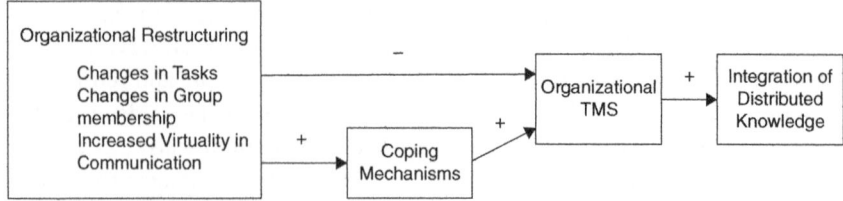

Figure 14.1. Framework of effects of organizational restructuring on organizational transactive memory system

of organizational directories slow, inaccurate, and incomplete, thus rendering organizational transactive memory systems unreliable. The global scale of organizational restructuring can exacerbate these volatilities (Berggren et al., 2011). However, little is known about how teams and their members manage to locate and retrieve external knowledge outside their team boundaries in order to get things done in a restructuring organization. Therefore, it is of great interest and importance to understand the coping mechanisms employed to restore or improve the reliability of organizational transactive memory systems in the midst of much organizational change (Figure 14.1).

14.2 RESEARCH APPROACH

We followed a US-based high-tech company (hereafter called ITechCo), which had nearly 90,000 employees globally. The operations of interest for our study dealt with ITechCo's global demand planning and supply chain management. At the time of our data collection, ITechCo's focus was on expanding into a retail channel beyond its existing direct sales channels. In conjunction with this change, the company was undergoing a major restructuring, including offshoring its manufacturing and relocating the control tower of its global supply chain operations to Asia. This major organizational restructuring triggered changes in tasks, team membership, and interaction on an unprecedented scale.

We visited five different global locations, including a site in the US, two in Asia, and two in Europe. Our observations included plant tours, on-site interviews, and both face-to-face and teleconference meetings involving members from different global locations. We interviewed over forty employees from supply chain governance and analytics, supply chain tools and enablement configuration management, inventory control, logistics, human resources, and information technology.

Our data analysis followed the guidelines for qualitative research (Miles and Huberman, 1994; Yin, 2003). Some coding categories were established in the transactive memory system literature; others emerged during the analysis.[1] A theoretical saturation point for each broad category was reached when no more unique codes were identified across interview transcripts.

14.3 ORGANIZATIONAL RESTRUCTURING AND ITS DISRUPTION OF ORGANIZATIONAL TRANSACTIVE MEMORY SYSTEMS

Before the restructuring, the operations organization had been decentralized, with considerable regional autonomy. Regional business executives met their regional demand directly from their own regional manufacturing facilities. After the restructuring, many regional teams became part of the 'global' organizational structure within which they operated as global teams. Many teams started coordinating tasks with their counterparts in other regions of the world. Regional executives in operations were facing mounting pressure to standardize local business processes and tools so that global contractors could process regional orders seamlessly. The globalization of demand planning and manufacturing put a premium on coordination and knowledge integration across regions. However, neither global processes nor tools existed to accomplish this type of global coordination and integration. New teams were also formed to deal with global demand planning, manufacturing operations, and supply chain activities. The organizational restructuring led to a large number of job transfers and staff turnover.

Employees experienced ambiguity in relation to their tasks and team membership. A senior manager explained:

> In the past we had a common understanding. Now, we are not coming from the same starting point. We have very different expectations and interpretations. We have different views of how restructuring has changed things and what is the best way to proceed. We don't clearly understand what each of these steps now means and what they don't. Eliminating options is the hardest part. These debates and conversations are 'interesting' [irony implied] when you don't really know who is at the other end of the telephone line.

In the following sections, we highlight the similarities to and differences from the current literature that we identified in the course of our study on organizational transactive memory systems in the wake of organizational restructuring. We report on the four coping mechanisms which we identified organizational

---

[1] The coding scheme and the common set of interview questions can be provided by the authors on request.

team members as employing to deal with unreliable organizational transactive memory systems.

14.3.1 Structure of Organizational Transactive Memory Systems

ITechCo's global operations were organized into multiple global teams working together—similar to the overall structure of an organizational transactive memory system reported in Anand et al. (1998) and Peltokorpi (2014), which conceptualize an organization as a group of groups.[2] An important characteristic of ITechCo's operations was its heavy reliance on outcome-driven metrics. The organization's motto was, 'If you cannot measure it, you cannot manage it.' There were 'metrics for everything' (e.g. number of units per hour, number of units per line, number of units per inch, and on-time order shipping). Outcome metrics were viewed as a flexible and adaptable way to manage a large company in a hypercompetitive environment. During the restructuring, teams increasingly found that their metrics were affected by other teams' actions. For instance, the actions of a customer services team would affect the master schedule and order services teams. In the past, these teams had operated in local sites or regions. Now, many of them had global responsibilities. Global team members did not necessarily know one another well, or meet face to face. As task interdependencies increased, so did conference calls and emails. In global conference calls, members discovered the existence of new members on their teams of whom they had no prior awareness.

The organizational transactive memory system in our study was similar to Austin's (2003) 'external relationship transactive memory', which is included as part of a group's transactive memory system and concerned with who knows whom outside the team. We found teams to be the basic directory structure. Teams, rather than individuals, and the expertise and roles and responsibilities of teams were typically encoded in individuals' organizational directories. Teams changed more slowly than individuals—teams' roles and responsibilities changed less frequently than did individuals. Teams did not enter the organization (formation of new teams) and leave the organization (dissolution of teams) with the same speed and frequency as individuals. In addition, there was much more information available about teams and their roles and responsibilities than about the members of these teams at any particular moment. Once individuals in other teams had identified the right team to contact, their first point of contact was often the team leader.

---

[2] We use the terms 'teams' and 'groups' interchangeably.

14.3.2 Processes of Organizational Transactive Memory Systems: Encoding, Storage, and Retrieval

As reported by post-bureaucratic organization studies (e.g. Kellogg et al., 2006), individuals commonly work in multiple and partially overlapping teams (O'Leary et al., 2011), and this was true of ITechCo. For instance, members of the Production Control team reported to the same manager, but maintained directories with little overlap because they interacted with different product teams and external partners. Although some members had common contacts, their directories included a large number of distinctive team contacts. Knowledge about who knows what, does what, and is responsible for what, was not necessarily shared openly within a team. Often, members informed only their team leader of relevant directory updates. Thus, team leaders became the central nodes in both social and task networks. Team members identified themselves most closely with their team leaders. Many teams were referred to by the team leader's name (e.g. 'Jeff's team', 'Susan's team'). When outsiders sought information from a team, they usually started with the team leader.

For example, when members searched for knowledge to solve a problem, they had two primary questions: What is the key issue and who 'owns' it (i.e. who has the closest role and responsibility). In relation to finding the right person to talk to about a given issue, 'who knows what' mattered less than 'who is primarily responsible for the issue', and 'whose job is it to take care of it' (i.e. whose team metrics are most affected). A team member explained: 'For example, for transfer cost issues, one would ask, who owes that transfer cost? Whose metric is impacted, if there is a metric? That will determine who to talk to. We usually will get the lead for each team into the path.'

Individual members struggled with their inability to update organizational directories in a timely and accurate fashion. It was difficult to keep up with changes in membership and roles and responsibilities (though less frequent) in other teams. As one member remarked, '[m]ost of us are unsure about who owns what'. Unless they kept in touch with their contacts on a regular basis, people's directory knowledge soon became obsolete.

Much of the literature assumes that directories are updated as a by-product of carrying out work (Ren and Argote, 2011). However, we observed more active and mindful updating of directories, including others' directory knowledge. Members regularly broadcast their information to 'let others know who I am, what I am working on, and what my role and responsibilities are'. During conference calls, members learned who had jobs relevant to theirs—both within and outside their team. In particular, if new members assumed another member's previous role, they sent out emails to their possible future contacts. The contact list was usually retrieved from the previous holder of the role.

Employees knew that they were dependent on other employees for knowledge related to the company.

According to transactive memory system theory, effective teams strive to maximize the efficiency of knowledge allocation and storage by allocating detailed knowledge based on members' expertise so that knowledge overlap or duplication can be minimized. Other teams simply update their directories according to the team's topic and location (Brandon and Hollingshead, 2004). We found little evidence of this type of efficiency in the case of knowledge storage. Rather, much overlap and duplication of knowledge storage occurred because people were concerned that frequent changes of tasks and team membership would make it difficult to access others' knowledge when it was needed. Because members could not rely with confidence on others for effective knowledge storage and retrieval, many members stored knowledge even outside their roles and responsibilities 'just in case'.

Because their organizational directories were inaccurate and incomplete, members would cast a wide net when searching for knowledge to retrieve from others. As previously noted, requests were sent out to specific individuals or teams, not just on the basis of their expertise but also on the basis of their roles and responsibilities. All team leaders and members whose roles and responsibilities seemed to be relevant, even if only remotely, typically were included in email exchanges. This approach naturally exacerbated information overload, but also helped eventually to locate the required knowledge. Such broad information seeking was undertaken not for the sake of efficiency, but to increase the effectiveness of knowledge retrieval.

Because of the difficulty of keeping directories up to date, knowledge retrieval was an 'everyday struggle'. 'Fishing around' for the right person, with the right roles and responsibilities, was far more important than locating a real subject expert. Owing to the frequent changes in tasks and team membership, roles and responsibilities were not necessarily aligned with real expertise. Even when the right expert was identified, people often hesitated to use the expert's knowledge without it being validated by the task (issue) owner, who had the right role and responsibility.

14.3.3 Coping Mechanisms to Deal with Incomplete and Unreliable Organizational Transactive Memory Systems

We identified several coping mechanisms employed by individuals to deal with incomplete and inaccurate organizational directories, which render transactive memory systems unreliable. These mechanisms included patching, knowledge redundancy, social networks, and hierarchy (see Table 14.1).

Table 14.1. Coping mechanisms dealing with unreliable organizations transactive memory systems

---

• *Patching*: mapping and remapping, adding, splitting, transferring, and combining directory knowledge;

• *Knowledge redundancy*: processing and retrieving broad knowledge (allowing overlap and duplication), rather than minimizing information overload;

• *Social networks*: maintaining personal connections with others even when professional ones no longer existed;

• *Hierarchy*: relying on team leaders or more senior managers with better organizational visibility and better directory knowledge.

Patching

Patching was a strategy that involved continuous mapping and remapping of roles and responsibilities and adding names to communication loops while, along the way, also splitting, forwarding, and combining communications. A team member explained that patching involved much trial and error:

> So, it's common in this environment that someone or a team who should be involved in the email circulation [the decision-making process] was not aware of [what was going on] and was not included in the first place.... Then later, a lot of 'patching' follows. Patching after patching after patching, again and again. It's typical.

As a result of incomplete organizational directories, some key personnel or entire teams were often left out of urgent decision-making. Moreover, despite information overload, some key information was not sent to or received by the right people. Patching was used to ensure that the right people were later added to the communication loop for follow-ups. Patching was not an efficient knowledge-allocation mechanism, but it was needed to cope with unreliable directories in a large organization in the midst of major transitions. Members were acutely aware of their incomplete directories and almost took patching for granted.

During restructuring, agility was valued more highly than deliberate planning. The general view was that 'extinguishing a fire' by doing something immediately on the spot, such as identifying and involving key people with task accountability as soon as possible, was better than making sure everyone who should be involved was included in decision-making. Once a solution good enough to put out the fire was implemented, the solution was refined through continuous patching, bringing in those who initially had been left out. While creating inefficiency of knowledge allocation and retrieval, patching was necessary to deal with inaccurate organizational directories and to increase the effectiveness of integration over time.

Knowledge Redundancy

Restructuring created much uncertainty and ambiguity, and revealed many alternative ways in which operations could be handled or problems could arise. As the options increased, so did the importance of the knowledge that had to be considered and integrated in decision-making. The inaccuracy of organizational directories instilled fear in people that the right information would not be allocated or provided to the right people at the right time. Frequent changes of tasks and team membership exacerbated these concerns. To avoid the problem, much more information than was necessary was sent and received. Some team leaders were receiving 500 to 1,000 emails a day. As previously noted, information requests were typically sent to a large number of people. In addition, potential recipients constantly asked to be kept in various communication loops: 'Put me in the mailing list', and 'please cc me'. At times, people were unsure of their own roles and responsibilities, which further exacerbated the need to know 'just in case'. Although people complained about receiving too many emails, the anxiety about missing out on relevant information outweighed these complaints. Much overlap and duplication of knowledge storage occurred, creating a lot of inefficiency. However, this excess was seen as necessary to minimize the risk of failing to provide or access the right knowledge because of others' inaccurate organizational directories.

Social Networks

Social networks had been important for organizational transactive memory systems before the restructuring, and this importance did not flag during the restructuring. The social network approach is aligned to the relational view of information seeking (Moreland, 1999). Team members relied heavily on others they knew from their past roles and responsibilities to locate and retrieve knowledge outside their teams. In fact, the importance of social networks intensified because of the uncertainty and ambiguity of roles and responsibilities and task coordination during restructuring. Past and present team leaders were an important part of members' social networks.

Smooth knowledge retrieval is assumed once a source is located (Brandon and Hollingshead, 2004). However, during restructuring, those who had the required knowledge were not always available to help because they were occupied by other urgent matters. Prior research shows that increased job security concerns during organizational restructuring can reduce the motivation to respond to information retrieval requests (Balogun and Johnson, 2014). People at ITechCo had to leverage their social networks and apply social pressure when knowledge retrieval from the identified knowledge source took too much time or was unsatisfactory.

Hierarchy

Even in team-based structures, hierarchy still mattered. As previously noted, knowledge retrieval was mainly pursued on the basis of task (or issue) responsibility (roles and responsibilities), rather than actual expertise. People tried to determine which team was responsible for which task. When updating their organizational directories, some people included not only someone's name, team, and role but also information on those people two ranks above and one rank below them. This hierarchy information was useful when dealing with dynamic membership changes, reflecting the idea that the roles of teams are more stable than those of individual members.

When people were unclear about which team to contact, they turned to the top person in the broader area. Hierarchy in the organization was associated with holding a better organizational directory. External memory aids (e.g. organization chart, email lists) were often used to shorten the path to the right team and person in charge. Some people started their information search by contacting the top management person in the closest area, hoping that the director would route their email to the right team lead in their reporting lines. This 'shoot from the top' approach was regarded with mixed feelings. In particular, people with managerial and supervisory responsibilities were bombarded with emails starting with: 'Do you know who I should contact regarding...?'. Nevertheless, this approach worked quite well. Generally, managers were generous and responsive to enquiries. Rarely could anyone recall having received the response: 'that's not part of my job'.

14.4 FROM EFFICIENT TRANSACTIVE MEMORY SYSTEMS TO RELIABLE TRANSACTIVE MEMORY SYSTEMS

Our study describes how people in a restructuring organization rely on organizational transactive memory systems to get things done. Restructuring requires that teams and their members leverage and integrate distributed knowledge beyond team boundaries to deal with ad hoc problems. Knowledge had to be coordinated across time and geography, crossing a wide variety of boundaries. The shift from regional to global operations made it paramount for teams to be able to coordinate distributed knowledge across teams. The directories of organizational transactive memory systems played a vital role in enabling this integration.

Transactive memory systems are not immune to the disruptive effects of restructuring, such as task and membership volatilities (e.g. Moreland and Argote, 2003; Anderson and Lewis, 2014). People in a restructuring organization struggle with incomplete and inaccurate organizational transactive memory systems, as our findings—not surprisingly—show. Organizational directories that are incomplete and inaccurate lead to inefficiencies in encoding, storage, and transfer of knowledge. Yet, in the case of ITechCo, coping mechanisms led to good enough directories for team members to locate and retrieve the required knowledge to complete the task without major failures. Directories were not necessarily shared, but were held individually. However, they were dependable enough for action.

Our case study integrates the literatures on organizational transactive memory systems and knowledge integration. While the knowledge integration literature rarely considers transactive memory systems explicitly, the ability to locate and retrieve distributed knowledge has been recognized as a key condition for knowledge integration (e.g. Paoli and Prencipe, 2003). We discuss organizational transactive memory systems as a key antecedent to knowledge integration. Organizational transactive memory systems increase in significance during organizational restructuring since problem-solving and knowledge collaboration requires greater knowledge integration beyond team boundaries. Teams and their members locate and retrieve knowledge with the help of organizational directories of who knows what. As key business functions are increasingly being managed globally rather than regionally, knowledge is distributed across different global sites, teams, and individuals. The directories of organizational transactive memory systems provide the meta-knowledge of the organization's distributed cognition.

We found that people encoded organizational directories differently from what is suggested in the transactive memory system literature (e.g. Brandon and Hollingshead, 2004). In our study, the basic unit of a directory was the team rather than the individual (member). Similarly, Moreland and Argote (2003), regarding organizational transactive memory systems, suggest that the team is a more stable basis for a directory in a dynamic organization because the roles and responsibilities of teams change more slowly than those of individuals. The literature argues also that expertise serves as the basis for knowledge allocation, but we found that the notion of task responsibility was central to the structure of an organizational transactive memory system. Instead of choosing who to contact based purely on expertise, people considered whose roles and responsibilities were most closely related to the given task or issue. In a restructuring organization, expertise and roles and responsibilities are not always aligned because of membership and task changes. When seeking knowledge, in order to ensure that the knowledge was from a reliable source, people had to distinguish between who had the actual expertise and who had the formal accountability. Although we cannot tease out the extent to which these differences can be attributed to the effects of restructuring —rather than to the development of an organizational level transactive memory system—the findings advance our understanding of how people construct their organizational directories to produce more reliable organizational transactive memory systems.

We identified several mechanisms—patching, knowledge redundancy, social networks, and hierarchy—on which people in a dynamic organization relied in order to cope with incomplete and inaccurate organizational directories. At first glance, these mechanisms—particularly patching and knowledge redundancy—might seem inefficient, but we argue that they can be effective for restoring dependability and reliability to directories. Employees can avoid errors and mistakes in knowledge retrieval and integration in a dynamic organization, which can lead to organizational decline and downward spirals (Roberts, 1990; McKinley et al., 2014).

Finally, our findings point to the central role of team leaders in supplementing the directory knowledge held by individuals. In contrast to previous transactive memory system research, which assumes that everyone in the group has shared directory knowledge (cf. Mell et al., 2014), we found that directory knowledge was unevenly shared within teams, and that team leaders' directories were much superior to those of other team members. This finding is aligned with Mell et al. (2014), who found that in situations where knowledge is disconnected and distributed across members who are not necessarily aware of knowledge interdependences, superior performance is enabled by one central member with a better directory than the rest. This central member is able to facilitate connections among the members who have disconnected knowledge. In the organization we studied, team leaders played a critical role as the retainers of the most up-to-date directory knowledge within and outside their teams. They had the most comprehensive understanding of how their teams were positioned in the organization in terms of task and outcome interdependencies with other teams, and of who had what expertise and task ownership in their team and beyond. Team leaders did not necessarily have comprehensive working-level expertise, but they had the broadest and most accurate organizational directories because of their visibility in the organization and their network centrality within the team.

The superior organizational directories held by team leaders strengthened their authority in the organization. Members approached their team leaders to exploit their influence in encouraging others to provide them with information in a timely manner. Team leaders also changed often during the restructuring and new, competent team leaders were expected to learn quickly about who did/knew/owned what, in their teams and beyond. Our findings extend the results in Peltokorpi (2014), which shed light on the role of team leaders as coordinators of expertise in organizations.

Our collective findings suggest that in organizations that undergo major transitions, the reliability—not the shared nature—of organizational directories is emphasized in the context of effective retrieval and integration of distributed knowledge. Reliability might have parallels with organizational resilience at times of major organizational change or jolts (Farjoun, 2010). Resilience is the capacity to avoid mistakes and errors. In our study, people did not possess highly accurate and complete organizational directories, but they used several mechanisms, at the cost of efficiency, to make their directories reliable and dependable enough to retrieve the required knowledge in the end. From the resilience point of view, reliability ensures the absence of major failure in the face of major disturbance (Farjoun, 2010).

We would suggest that although transactive memory systems, and directories in particular, are often assessed in terms of efficiency, the reliability of directories at times of major organizational changes requires inefficiencies— including duplication, overlap, and exploration. As we have shown, the awareness that directories were incomplete and inaccurate led people to use several coping mechanisms to make their organizational transactive memory systems sufficiently reliable. Hence, our study emphasizes a reliability logic for transactive memory systems over an efficiency logic as a prerequisite for knowledge integration during times of organizational restructuring.

Our findings should be considered with some of the study's limitations in mind. Our case study is based on a single company headquartered in the US, with operations in Asia, Europe, and South America. Although cultural issues were outside the scope of this study, they were clearly present and relevant. For example, hierarchy manifested itself differently, depending on the local culture. In locations such as Asia, where the culture is arguably more hierarchical than in the other regions, members found that they often had to justify their requests for information from other teams. In contrast, in North America and Europe, members generally expended less effort in justifying their access to knowledge. This finding suggests that some coping mechanisms may be culturally dependent—an area for future research.

15

Boundary Spanning, Boundary Objects, and Innovation

Andrew Van de Ven and Shaker A. Zahra

15.1 INTRODUCTION

This book addresses a central knowledge management question: how to integrate knowledge across boundaries. The KITE (Knowledge Integration and Innovation in Transnational Enterprise) research programme and the previous chapters in this book provide a relatively clear answer to this question. There is convergence on the need for absorptive capacity and boundary objects for integrating knowledge across different boundaries and contexts. The degree and types of complexities involved in crossing knowledge boundaries, and the variety of boundary objects that might be used in order to stimulate technological, product, and administrative innovations, render this answer interesting.

This chapter builds on these insights and examines two propositions related to how knowledge boundary complexity influences the likelihood of innovation. We propose: first, that *there is a curvilinear relationship between the complexity of spanning knowledge boundaries and innovation novelty*; and second, that *boundary objects moderate this relationship*. These propositions seem to capture key inferences from the KITE research programme. Our argument is based on conceptual reasons, empirical evidence, and context-dependent findings from the KITE programme and related research studies. Further research into different types of innovations and settings is needed to test our propositions.

Throughout this chapter we focus on knowledge at the boundaries, that is, knowledge at the intersection of different activities, within or across levels in a firm, or across firms. This knowledge is rarely an amalgam of the knowledge domains from which it springs. It often develops and evolves with its own vocabulary, terms, and grammar rules with the result that those familiar with the original domains would find it difficult to understand or use this 'boundary' knowledge.

Section 15.1 defines the key concepts and develops the first proposition. Section 15.2 relies heavily on the other chapters in this book, authored by KITE researchers and others, to discuss the moderating effects of boundary knowledge by introducing a typology of different boundary objects for the integration of knowledge across boundaries. Section 15.3 provides a concluding discussion on the implications of this typology for integrating knowledge across boundaries and outlines key research issues to be explored in the future.

15.2 BOUNDARY SPANNING AND INNOVATION

Boundary spanning is the process by which organizational actors sense, identify, learn about, and gather information on developments outside their domain of expertise (Allen and Cohen, 1969). Boundary-spanning activities often transcend knowledge domains that have the capacity to be recombined in novel ways to create innovations. Boundary spanning typically entails considerable technical, organizational, and social learning about customers, markets, and technologies. This learning usually crosses and encompasses multiple knowledge domains (i.e. areas of specialized expertise). In acquiring this diverse, domain-specific knowledge, boundary spanners often reflect the characteristics and skills of the different organizational levels and roles that they occupy (Tushman and Scanlan, 1981). Boundary spanners are connected to others within and across disciplinary communities and typically engage in tasks that would exceed the capabilities and resources of single individuals. Hence, the need for 'engaged scholarship' (Van de Ven, 2007) among different specialists and disciplines to understand complex phenomena.

Boundary spanners are usually able to connect with diverse personalities and appreciate diverse views. This ability to connect and network allows them to amass considerable amounts of information that could be useful to their companies (Galbraith, 1974). These boundary-spanning activities can be organized through formal organizational structure and roles, or through informal arrangements (Aldrich and Herker, 1977). The empirical studies in this book show that boundary spanning comprises a wide variety of mechanisms, which are not necessarily performed by the same person. Further, as Lindkvist and Bengtsson's review of Nonaka's model in Chapter 5 suggests, the acquired knowledge and learning is often tacit in nature, and boundary spanners may not be fully aware of what they know and why, or to whom it matters. This suggests the need for boundary spanners to capture, share, translate, and integrate the knowledge if it is to be useful for organizational purposes. Integrating the knowledge from these diverse actors, at different organizational levels and in different units, provides a foundation for converting knowledge into mental models and prototypes, which can facilitate developing innovations.

In Chapter 1, Tell et al. discuss knowledge integration, defined as 'the purposeful combination of specialized and complementary knowledge to achieve specific tasks, [which] is becoming increasingly important for an expanding array of organizations facing rapidly changing institutional environments, globalized markets, and fast-paced technological development'. A dominant theme of this book is that this integration is central to organizational learning, adaptability, and innovation. Most innovations (e.g. iPods, digital cameras) combine different types of knowledge that have been developed in globally dispersed networks (Yoo et al., 2006; Arthur, 2009). These networks emerge in different regions, countries, and communities of practice, for historical, resource, or national policy reasons (Nelson, 1993), exemplified by the rise of India's software and Singapore's information technology industries. The growing globalization of research and development (R&D), and the widespread use of international joint ventures and alliances, research consortia, and supply chains, as well as the emergence of the open innovation movement, reflect an awareness of the advantages of collaboration to gain access to knowledge from different networks (Gibbons et al., 1994; Nohria and Ghoshal, 1997; Nowotny et al., 2001; Chesbrough, 2003b; Perkmann, 2007; Van de Ven et al., 2008). All these sources allow companies to gain access to very different types of knowledge needed to develop their innovations. This knowledge usually embodies different codes, heuristics, and scientific conventions, which require understanding and resolution to effect their integration. This knowledge is complex in content, making it difficult to transfer, understand, and share. Much of it is tacit in nature, and its transfer requires interaction and communication across boundaries.

A number of chapters in this book adopt Carlile's (2004) framework to examine this boundary complexity in terms of the difference, dependence, and understanding of domain-specific knowledge among people attempting to communicate across a boundary.[1] *Difference* refers to unique amounts of capabilities (e.g. as between novices and experts) and types of specialized domain-specific knowledge of people at a knowledge boundary. If there is no difference in people's domain-specific knowledge, there is no communication boundary. However, as the difference in domain-specific knowledge increases among people, the effort required to share and assess each other's knowledge increases. *Dependence* is the degree to which people working across boundaries perceive the need to take account of the other's views if they are to

---

[1] Because our dependent variable is innovation novelty, for simplicity we relabel Carlile's novelty dimension to focus on his definition of novelty as ambiguity in understanding domain-specific knowledge among the parties involved at the knowledge boundary.

achieve their goals. In the absence of this dependence, difference is no longer important. The management and coordination of dependence among people working at a boundary requires the capacity to develop adequate common knowledge as resources and tasks change. The greater the interdependence, the greater the requirement for coordination through more intensive and rich communication. The rapid co-specialization in technological and business fields is making companies increasingly interdependent in terms of the supply and demand for knowledge that could fuel innovation.

Understanding refers to either lack of common knowledge owing to the different disciplinary specialties, cultures, and contexts of individuals working at a boundary, or new domain-specific knowledge owing to technological advances and new scientific research findings. Low levels of understanding usually lead to a lack of the common knowledge required to share and assess domain-specific knowledge.

Postrel (Chapter 3) points out that these dimensions of knowledge complexity can become a 'thick stack' of social, cognitive, and artifactual layers that may cause people to be at cross purposes. In addition, Bengtsson et al. (Chapter 6) discuss how, in order to develop the various components needed for their innovations, innovating firms often need to cross the boundaries between multiple organizations and professions with specialized capabilities and technologies. This search across boundaries, which is triggered by need and curiosity, often leads to connections with existing and emerging networks where the required knowledge resides; however, this knowledge can be hard to transfer because it is sticky (Postrel, Chapter 3). Sometimes complexity is derived from the attributes of the knowledge itself, as in the case of pharmaceutical products or advanced scientific discoveries. At other times, it is because the knowledge is intangible and tacit, as discussed by Lindkvist and Bengtsson in Chapter 5 in relation to Nonaka's SECI (Socialization, Externalization, Combination, Internalization) model. Bredin et al. (Chapter 13) discuss the different competencies of project managers in terms of their technical and interactive skills, which makes it possible to consider combining different ways of boundary spanning. For example, these boundary spanners could reorganize heterogeneous knowledge from different networks (Hardagon and Douglas, 2001; Baron and Ensley, 2006) in order to develop new combinations that generate innovations. This recombined knowledge comprises different knowledge strands, which, together, can be used to create innovative products, goods, and services, for example (Arthur, 2009). It is knowledge integration that facilitates these outcomes.

Given the benefits and costs of boundary spanning, Postrel (Chapter 3) poses two key managerial questions: *(1) How much time and effort should units dedicate to spanning in breadth across boundaries at the expense of accumulating disciplinary depth and solving specialized problems within boundaries? (2) How should managers structure interactions across*

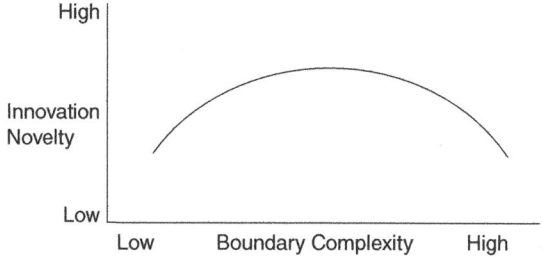

Figure 15.1. Proposed curvilinear relationship between boundary complexity and innovation

boundaries? In response to the first question we draw on Bengtsson et al.'s finding (Chapter 6) of a curvilinear relationship between boundary spanning and innovation. They show that while crossing knowledge boundaries is positively related to innovation performance, this relationship turns negative if too many boundaries are involved. They found also that this curvilinear relationship appears to shift or be moderated by the objects used to cross boundaries and the context of knowledge integration. The remainder of this chapter discusses how the chapters in this volume address these two managerial questions.

To address question 1, we propose *a curvilinear (inverted U-shaped) relationship between the complexity of spanning knowledge boundaries and innovation novelty*. Figure 15.1 shows that when knowledge boundaries are simple, that is there is little difference or dependence, and there is clear understanding among the parties involved, this similar knowledge is unlikely to promote radically novel recombinations. A moderate level of boundary complexity will result in novel and non-obvious recombinations because the parties involved are likely to recognize that their specialized knowledge is different, complementary, and interdependent, yet understandable. Postrel (Chapter 3) discusses how higher levels of boundary complexity create communication difficulties that can inhibit knowledge production. Professional and scientific communities tend to develop specialized languages, which often make it difficult for outsiders to understand what they do, how they do it, and why they are doing it. These specialized languages become intertwined with unique processes and structures, which render innovation practices context-specific and increasingly difficult for outsiders to decipher (Bengtsson et al., Chapter 6). These practices can frustrate boundary spanners' efforts to understand and make use of specialized knowledge flows in these networks, resulting in only a small part of this domain-specific knowledge crossing boundaries. For example, Bengtsson et al. state that 'the gains from crossing boundaries are eaten up by the costs of the efforts required to integrate the external knowledge' (Chapter 6).

15.2.1 Objects or Mechanisms for Communicating across Boundaries

Previous chapters examine a variety of boundary objects or mechanisms that can be used for integrating knowledge across boundaries. These boundary objects provide ways to extend or expand the curvilinear relationship referred to in Proposition 1. Specifically, they suggest that *boundary objects moderate the curvilinear relationship between boundary complexity and innovation novelty* (Proposition 2). In Table 15.1, boundary objects are grouped according to how they address Carlile's (2004) three types of linguistic barriers (syntactic, semantic, and pragmatic) and the degrees of knowledge complexity (i.e. difference, dependence, and understandability) for people at boundaries. This provides a typology of boundary objects or mechanisms for integrating knowledge across progressively more complex boundaries. They range from knowledge transfer, translation, and transformation modes of communication at increasing levels of boundary complexity. Transfer refers to the sharing of existing knowledge and making it accessible to others. Translation is interpreting that knowledge to make it comprehensible to others. Transformation renders the knowledge pragmatically usable across different boundaries.

Although in Figure 15.1 these boundary objects are clearly demarcated, the transition from one to another is often not easily identified by the actors involved. Moreover, these boundary objects reflect a Guttman (1950) scale.

Table 15.1. Boundary objects or mechanisms for communicating across knowledge boundaries

		Types of Boundary Complexity		
		Knowledge Transfer across syntactic boundary	Knowledge Translation across semantic boundary	Knowledge Transformation across pragmatic, political boundary
Degree of Boundary Complexity	High	Computerized CAD/CAM and simulation models.	Project teams and organizations	Intermediary organizations
	Medium	Modular designs, components, and prototypes	Interactive expertise and absorptive capacities of boundary spanners	Problem-solving task forces and conflict resolution teams Competitive review and selection
	Low	Process standardization drawings, pictures, blueprints, and routines	Direct communications among parties to clarify interpretations	Direct interpersonal negotiations of interests

Increasing boundary complexity assumes ever-greater capacities for knowledge transfer, translation, and transformation (see Table 15.1). The ranking of the boundary objects in Table 15.1 is such that the use of a medium- or high-complexity mechanism assumes mastery of less complex mechanisms. Finally, we view the boundary objects as mechanisms for preventing coordination failures rather than technical glitches. Postrel (Chapter 3) observes that it is important to distinguish glitches, which refer to the technical uncertainty of not knowing what the other party can do, from coordination failures, which can be addressed by better communication, planning, and organizing among the parties involved.

We review the boundary objects related to expanding the capacities of knowledge transfer, translation, and transformation, which are examined in the previous chapters.

15.2.2 Knowledge Transfer Mechanisms

Crossing a knowledge boundary is typically understood as a knowledge transfer process in which communication is considered from an information processing perspective (Galbraith, 1974). Carlile (2004) notes that this form of communication is 'unproblematic' if the parties at the boundary have a common syntax and lexicon, allowing the knowledge to be transferred using conventional and standardized forms of information processing. Kravcenko and Swan (Chapter 11) show that these standardized knowledge transfer methods can be represented in drawings, pictures, or blueprints, and, as Ceci and Prencipe (Chapter 7) show, in terms of product modularity and process standardization.

The major challenge in knowledge transfer is identifying a communication medium that is able to transmit the richness in the information being conveyed (Daft and Lengel, 1984). Some forms and channels of communication cannot adequately convey the richness of the message and, hence, parties at the boundary may receive a simplified, reduced, or filtered message. This can result in misperception or misunderstanding of its meaning or relevance. As Subramanian et al. discuss in Chapter 12, knowledge integration is context specific and, while informal methods of external collaboration with universities may have a positive effect on patent performance, they can have a detrimental effect in the case of transferring and sharing very complex knowledge requiring highly specialized processes for its creation. In the latter case, more formal collaboration mechanisms are required. Hence, Bengtsson et al. (Chapter 6) and Postrel (Chapter 3) call for a matching between the complexity of the knowledge medium and the message. They echo Galbraith's (1974) model, which uses mechanisms that process more information if the task is highly uncertain. Organizations seeking to transfer ambiguous knowledge across boundaries may need to invest in increased 'vertical integration systems' (Galbraith, 1974) that enhance knowledge transfer across boundaries through the building of specialized languages that promote effective communication of that knowledge. This is illustrated by Jarvenpaa and Kim's discussion (Chapter 14) of transactive memory systems for transferring knowledge across highly complex knowledge boundaries.

Table 15.1 depicts some of the mechanisms or boundary objects that can be employed to transfer knowledge across boundaries. It shows the increasingly costly mechanisms involved in moving from low, to medium, to high levels of boundary complexity. In the next section we discuss how the information-processing capacities of standardized boundary objects can be expanded through direct horizontal contacts, teams, task forces, liaison positions, and intermediary organizations.

15.2.3 Mechanisms for Knowledge Translation

A semantic boundary can develop if people using the same language interpret it differently—even in a context of relatively close knowledge domains. For example, Nonaka and Takeuchi (1995) discuss how established pharmaceutical companies were unable to understand how biotechnology start-ups conducted their research, despite both groups being focused on similar drug families. Biotech firms developed and used different drug-making methods, which delayed pharmaceutical companies' learning. Consequently, a knowledge translation perspective is necessary to recognize that people from different domains (i.e. different thought worlds) interpret things differently. In this case, communication often requires people to talk so that they can create 'shared meanings' (Dougherty, 1992), 'reconcile discrepancies in meanings' (Nonaka and Takeuchi, 1995: 67), or use bridging scientists based on informal collaboration, as discussed by Subramanian et al. (Chapter 12) in relation to the biotechnology industry.

Crossing more complex boundaries typically requires boundary spanners to develop greater absorptive capacity (Cohen and Levinthal, 1990), in order to develop the interactive expertise (Collins, 2004) required to translate knowledge across boundaries (Berggren et al. (Chapter 4)). Bredin et al. (Chapter 13) discuss some of the requirements for individual development of interactive expertise, and Postrel (Chapter 3) notes that development of absorptive capacity requires exposure to and engagement with different types of knowledge, as well as time to develop, refine, and use it.

Berggren et al. (Chapter 4) insightfully point out that the concepts of knowledge integration and absorptive capacity are partly opposing in the context of boundary crossing. Whereas knowledge integration requires expanding the breadth of knowledge across the different boundaries being integrated, absorptive capacity focuses on the path-dependent process of knowledge deepening in order to stay abreast of new knowledge within specific domains. Drawing on Giddens's (1984) structuration theory, Berggren et al. propose a synthesis, viewing the knowledge boundaries being integrated as social structures which are continuously created and reproduced by the absorptive capacities of agents. This synthesis provides a much-needed temporal appreciation of how the dynamic capabilities of knowledge integration and absorptive capacity change as boundaries are socially reconstructed.

The studies in Chapters 6–14 offer examples supporting this knowledge integration and absorptive capacity synthesis. The studies illustrate that alliances, joint ventures, and technology consortia provide companies with ways to both cross and deepen their knowledge over time, in domains seen as important. Firms also invest in building the knowledge of their employees (the foundations of absorptive capacity) to allow them to capture, assimilate, and translate incoming knowledge from their own and other industries. This exposure requires connections to diverse internal and external sources of knowledge, and the spanning of multiple boundaries, as discussed by Bengtsson et al. (Chapter 6). In addition to expanding the capabilities of individual boundary spanners, Table 15.1 suggests that project teams and organizations provide collective boundary objects for knowledge translation (Kravcenko and Swan, Chapter 11) and for building inter-team transactive memory processes (Jarvenpaa and Kim, Chapter 14) to expedite and improve knowledge translation. Building collective boundary objects useful for knowledge translation requires attention to team development, cross-functional training, sharing of expertise, and an appreciation that individual and team absorptive capacity contributes to a more encompassing, organization-wide capability.

Gibbons (2008) replaces the metaphors of knowledge transfer or translation with those of knowledge exchange, which he views as a process of engagement among specialists (researchers and practitioners) in all the phases of knowledge production and distribution. Boundary work is essential for knowledge exchange. It starts with boundary objects, which create a transaction space or trading zone in which specialists can interact to transform an issue into a possible set of activities resembling a project. This is nicely illustrated in Kravcenko and Swan's (Chapter 11) discussion of the use of drawings at the boundaries between professional specialists.

Postrel relies on Collins and Evans (2007) to explain why a pidgin language is needed for specialists to communicate at the boundary. He maintains that it is impossible to study a scientific or knowledge domain without interactional expertise, which indicates an in-depth understanding of the subject matter without the capacity necessarily to practise it. Interactional expertise is necessary for understanding a subject; most innovators, entrepreneurs, and researchers have to learn how to communicate about a domain without being able to practise it. Bredin et al. (Chapter 13) point out that interactional expertise is a prerequisite for boundary work and requires learning how to cross the different communication barriers identified by Carlile (2002). Thus, boundary spanning entails more than a structural hole in a network (as Burt, 1992, argues); it entails interactional expertise, which increases credibility with diverse actors and leads to a better understanding of the knowledge being exchanged, as well as its value.

Although people with interactional expertise may be unable to perform a specific job in a given domain, they are able to communicate and engage with specialists in fruitful cross-disciplinary conversations (Collins, 2004). Entrepreneurs and innovators who have honed their interactional expertise skills know how to relate to specialists (e.g. physicists and chemists) in ways that encourage them to share what they know, its technical content, and possible uses. This expertise allows the boundary-spanning entrepreneur to recognize specialists' views, motives, interests, and knowledge, and to exploit opportunities to convert and use this knowledge to create innovations. This increases the slope of innovation novelty in Figure 15.1 before its maximum. In other cases, it might widen and deepen the curve in Figure 15.1 by allowing the actors to benefit more quickly from knowledge translation.

15.2.4 Mechanisms for Knowledge Transformation

Beyond the syntactical and semantic barriers is a pragmatic boundary constituted by the different interests of the actors in a distributed innovation network. Lindkvist and Bengtsson (Chapter 5) draw on Nonaka and Takeuchi's (1995) argument that knowledge management involves more than articulating what the key actors in a network know (moving from tacit to explicit knowledge). It includes three related processes: acquiring relevant and heterogeneous knowledge, integrating this knowledge by capitalizing on their own creativity and other cognitive skills, and iteratively translating this knowledge. As integrators of knowledge, boundary spanners translate the domain-specific knowledge they gather in order to master its content and to allow its integration with other knowledge. If this integration process is successful, the boundary spanner can translate it for potential users. Some describe translation as a process of conversion in which knowledge is transformed in ways that makes it easier to deploy in products, goods, or services (Hansen and Birkinshaw, 2007; Zahra et al., 2007). Perkmann's (Chapter 10) structural genome consortium case shows that considerable orchestration and negotiation are needed to gain the allegiance of diverse specialists, along with a willingness among participants to improvise, but not to compromise their interests. Throughout this iterative knowledge translation or knowledge conversion process, boundary spanners test, revise, and validate their assumptions and understandings through activities that connect them to different actors, possibly increasing their awareness of the opportunities to exploit this knowledge through firm creation. These are not mechanical processes, since different organizational actors focus on different particular parts or qualities of the knowledge. This sets the stage for perceiving or conceiving different combinations with different degrees of novelty.

The case studies presented by Perkmann (Chapter 10) and Kravcenko and Swan (Chapter 11) show that knowledge is power, and there is much 'at stake' for those actors who have developed it (Carlile, 2002). An actor's success in knowledge production and exploitation could undermine another actor's position, reducing the latter's willingness to change. Carlile (2004: 559) explains that:

> When interests are in conflict, the knowledge developed in one domain generates negative consequences in another. Here the costs for any actor are not just the costs of learning about what is new, but also the costs of *transforming* 'current' knowledge being used (i.e., common and domain-specific knowledge). These costs negatively impact the willingness of an actor to make such changes. (emphasis added)

Recognizing the consequences of an actor's decision for others, and working with them to identify ways to avert or reduce potential side effects, can improve knowledge production.

Table 15.1 suggests that as the degree of boundary complexity increases, specific task forces, problem-solving teams, and intermediary organizations are called on to address divergent goals, conflicts, and incentives among those unwilling to work across boundaries. Perkmann (Chapter 10) examines the case of the Structural Genomics Consortium, which is at the high end of boundary complexity. His discussion nicely illustrates how an intermediate organization is used to develop a cosmopolitan interpretive scheme of shared meanings. However, the value of knowledge to actors at the boundary differs. Perkmann (2007) examines knowledge production as an exchange relationship, which is enabled by the presence of differentials among actors—that is, the difference in value or level of interest in the bits of knowledge held by the exchange partners. Applying this logic, Kravcenko and Swan (Chapter 11) discuss the political use of boundary objects in communications among architects and engineers on a large construction project. The case suggests that exchange is more likely to occur if one party values some piece of knowledge more highly than the other. These differentials provide a basis for intellectual arbitrage. Entrepreneurs can connect these different exchange parties and create structural holes (Burt, 1992), which are an important foundation for business creation. Berggren et al. (Chapter 4) and Karabag and Berggren (Chapter 9) provide examples and a discussion of how this requires well-developed absorptive capacity among the actors (or teams) which take the 'converted' knowledge to its next logical designation: to use and deploy it in generating novel innovations.

15.3 CONCLUDING DISCUSSION

Knowledge integration is a crucial organizational activity that cuts across levels. It focuses on transferring, translating, and transforming different strands of knowledge, which vary in complexity, during the innovation journey (Van de Ven et al., 2008). We have proposed that knowledge boundaries have an inverted U-shaped relationship with innovation novelty (Figure 15.1). The magnitude of this relationship varies with the effort dedicated to knowledge transfer, translation, and transformation—a process that requires the use of very different organizational mechanisms (Table 15.1). These relationships are subject to several contingences.

Contingencies. Bengtsson et al. (Chapter 6) maintain that there is no single best knowledge integration practice; different practices are effective for different kinds of boundaries. They vary also with culture and region. Institutional or national norms of cooperativeness or competitiveness can influence boundary complexity and the mechanisms used to span boundaries. For example, Vasudeva et al. (2013) found that boundary spanners from collective and cooperative-oriented corporatist contexts were more capable in crossing diverse structural holes and were more innovative. Vasudeva et al. suggest that these capabilities could be knowledge and absorptive capacity related, or relationally focused on managing multiple divergent interests. This is consistent with Dyer and Singh (1998), who emphasized the benefits of strong relational skills for crossing boundaries in strategic alliances. The growing use of open innovation alliances and joint ventures requires consideration of the subtle, but powerful, influence of power when knowledge boundaries are crossed. We also need to explore more effective ways to cross boundaries to acquire, transfer, translate, and transform this knowledge, and to identify and examine the mechanisms of knowledge integration.

Knowledge integration processes are likely to be as complicated within firms as across them. Units in the same company develop different cultures, espouse different priorities and goals, and develop their own languages. Rivalries can erupt among these units, complicating communication and knowledge sharing and transfer (Szulanski, 1996). These problems are endemic in established companies, but can also affect young entrepreneurial ventures. The latter could derive considerable gains in the form of technological learning and product innovation from engagement in knowledge integration (Zahra et al., 2000).

The good news is that the cognitive and relational skills required to manage the boundary objects depicted in Figure 15.1 can be learned, acquired, and shared within the same context. The bad news is that, given the global nature of the knowledge required for innovation, the individuals or firms holding complementary knowledge may occupy different institutional contexts which exacerbate the complexity of boundary crossing. For example, Vasudeva et al.

(2013) found that when a firm's strategic alliance partners (or ego-network members) come from different institutional or national contexts, the focal firm is less innovative than if these partners belonged to the same domain.

Our discussion underlines the importance of organizational design for effective knowledge integration. Table 15.1 shows that adjustments to the organization design might be essential to promote knowledge transfer, translation, and transformation. However, these adjustments may be temporary, since companies engaged in the production of diverse and novel innovations need to integrate different and highly complex knowledge, which may require changes to the structure of their operations.

15.3.1 Contributions and Future Research

This book has highlighted the role of boundary spanning for gathering and sharing knowledge at the boundary, and discussed the importance of this knowledge for inducing variety and novelty in organizational outcomes, especially innovation. It has discussed the importance of knowledge complexity for defining boundary objects that are useful for knowledge transfer, translation, and transformation. The discussion in this chapter has also highlighted the critical role of boundary spanning for developing and reinforcing absorptive capacity. At the individual level, this capacity enhances 'interactional expertise'; at the firm level, it allows the firm to address knowledge complexity in ways that bring novelty to the firm's operations.

The discussion in this chapter suggests several avenues for future analysis and study. Our proposed framework (Table 15.1), while logical, requires empirical testing and validation. The typology reflects a key finding by KITE and other researchers that boundary objects are central mechanisms for integrating knowledge across different boundaries and contexts. The typology places knowledge complexity at the centre of the analysis and has the potential to guide future studies and managerial action intended to facilitate knowledge integration. It would be useful to establish empirically the veracity of our theory-derived claims and the robustness of the analysis. Such research will likely require engaged scholarship (Van de Ven, 2007) in longitudinal field studies. To measure and analyse the relationships between boundary objects and boundary complexity, we suggest that researchers should directly observe and engage with boundary spanners in order to determine how they perceive and understand the knowledge transfer, translation, and transformation boundaries they are crossing. These perceptions will change because boundary spanning entails a learning process. As a consequence, we expect the relative use of boundary-spanning objects to change over time.

We have proposed that knowledge complexity encourages knowledge integration. Other conditions might have similar effects, and it is important to identify these conditions. For instance, product complexity (e.g. iPhones and medical drugs) might encourage the integration of the knowledge in countless applications (or components). Intellectual property regimes might have a similar impact as companies integrate the knowledge contained in their products to avert leakage of trade secrets. No doubt other market and strategic variables might affect the need for and intensity of knowledge integration, and we need to identify these variables and study their influence.

Our dependent variable is the novelty of the innovations resulting from crossing knowledge boundaries. We proposed that knowledge integration moderates this relationship. However, crossing boundaries might have more pervasive and stronger effects on business definition as companies become aware of the potential for redefining themselves by introducing novel innovations. Crossing knowledge boundaries might also affect how and where companies compete. It might also alter the way companies recruit employees, by placing greater value on the ability to work at the intersection. These outcomes are subject to the influence of knowledge integration and deserve analysis.

The KITE research has refocused attention on the crucial role of boundary spanners in the firm. These people employ different lenses and possess different skills, which allow them to connect with diverse knowledge sources within and across organizations. They are able to employ transactional expertise to capture, translate, reframe, and transform data into knowledge that is useful for commercial and other purposes. We add to the literature by clarifying the various mechanisms by which knowledge at the boundaries is shared, translated, and transformed. Table 15.1 provides a fairly detailed description of these tools, and suggests that boundary objects expand the positive effects of boundary spanning on innovation novelty.

References

Abbott, A. (1988) *The System of Professions: An Essay on the Division of Labor*, Chicago: University of Chicago Press.

Agrawal, A. and Henderson, R. (2002) Putting Patents in Context: Exploring Knowledge Transfer from MIT, *Management Science*, 48(1): 44–60.

Ahuja, G. (2000) Collaboration Networks, Structural Holes, and Innovation: A Longitudinal Study, *Administrative Science Quarterly*, 45(3): 425–55.

Ahuja, G. and Katila, R. (2001) Technological Acquisitions and the Innovation Performance of Acquiring Firms: A Longitudinal Study, *Strategic Management Journal*, 22(3): 197–220.

Akgun, A. E., Byrne, J. C., Keskin, H., and Lynn, G. S. (2006) Transactive Memory System in New Product Development Teams, *IEEE Transactions on Engineering Management*, 53(1): 95–111.

Alavi, M. and Tiwana, A. (2002) Knowledge Integration in Virtual Teams: The Potential Role of KMS, *Journal of the American Society for Information Science and Technology*, 53(12): 1029–37.

Albert, S. and Whetten, D. A. (1985) Organizational Identity, in L. Cummings and B. Staw (eds.), *Research in Organizational Behavior*, Stamford, CT: JAI Press.

Aldrich, H. (2008) *Organizations and Environments*, Stanford, CA: Stanford University Press.

Aldrich, H. and Herker, D. (1977) Boundary Spanning Roles and Organization Structure, *Academy of Management Review*, 2(2): 217–30.

Allen, T. J. (1977) *Managing the Flow of Technology: Technology Transfer and the Dissemination of Technological Information within the R&D Organization*, Cambridge, MA: MIT Press.

Allen, T. J. and Cohen, S. I. (1969) Information Flow in Research and Development Laboratories, *Administrative Science Quarterly*, 14(1): 12–19.

Almeida, P., Hohberger, J., and Pedro, P. (2011) Individual Scientific Collaborations and Firm-Level Innovation, *Industrial and Corporate Change*, 20(6): 1571–99.

Amsden, A. H. (2001) *The Rise of 'the Rest': Challenges to the West from Late Industrializing Economies*, New York: Oxford University Press.

Amsden, A. H. and Chu, W. W. (2003) *Beyond Late Development: Taiwan's Upgrading Policies*, Cambridge, MA: MIT Press.

Anand, V., Manz, C., and Glick, W. (1998) An Organizational Memory Approach to Information Management, *Academy of Management Review*, 23(4), 796–809.

Ancori, B., Bureth, A., and Cohendet, P. (2000) The Economics of Knowledge: The Debate about Codification and Tacit Knowledge, *Industrial and Corporate Change*, 9(2): 255–87.

Anderson, E. G. and Lewis, K. (2014) A Dynamic Model of Individual and Collective Learning Amid Disruption, *Organization Science*, 25(2): 356–76.

Andersson, D. A. and Tell, F. (2016) Patent Agents and the Emerging Market for Patenting Services in Sweden, 1885–1914, *Enterprises et Histoire*, 25(82/April): 11–31.

Andersson, H. and Berggren, C. (2011) Inventors as Innovators and Knowledge Integrators, in C. Berggren, A. Bergek, L. Bengtsson, M. Hobday, and J. Söderlund (eds.), *Knowledge Integration and Innovation: Critical Challenges Facing International Technology-Based Firms*, Oxford: Oxford University Press.

Andersson, U., Dellerstrand, H., and Pedersen, T. (2014) The Contribution of Local Environments to Competence Creation in Multinational Enterprises, *Long Range Planning*, 47(1–2): 87–99.

Ansal, H. K. (1990) Technical Change and Industry Policy—The Case of Truck Manufacturing in Turkey, *World Development*, 18(11): 1513–28.

Argyres, N. (1996) Evidence on the Role of Firm Capabilities in Vertical Integration Decisions, *Strategic Management Journal*, 17(2): 129–50.

Arora, A. and Gambardella, A. (2010) Ideas for Rent: An Overview of Markets for Technology, *Industrial and Corporate Change*, 19(3): 775–803.

Arthur, B. (1994) *Increasing Returns and Path Dependence in the Economy*, Ann Arbor, MI: The University of Michigan Press.

Arthur, W. B. (2009) *The Nature of Technology: What it Is and How it Evolves*, New York: Free Press.

Athreye, S. and Kapur, S. (2009) Introduction: The Internationalization of Chinese and Indian Firms—Trends, Motivations and Strategy, *Industrial and Corporate Change*, 18(2): 209–21.

Audretsch, D. B. and Aldridge, T. (2009) Scientist Commercialization as Conduit of Knowledge Spillovers, *The Annals of Regional Science*, 43(4): 897–905.

Austin J. R. (2003) Transactive Memory in Organizational Groups: The Effects of Content, Consensus, Specialization, and Accuracy on Group Performance, *Journal of Applied Psychology*, 88(5): 866–78.

autosport.com (2014) *Ferrari F1 team Needs More Integration Says Chief Marco Mattiacci*, <http://www.autosport.com/news/report.php/id/114498>.

Awate, S., Larssen, M., and Mudambi, R. (2012) EMNE Catch-Up Strategies in the Wind Turbine Industry?, *Global Strategy Journal*, 2: 205–23.

Baba, Y., Shichijo, N., and Sedita, S. R. (2009) How Do Collaborators with Universities Affect Firms' Innovative Performance? The Role of 'Pasteur Scientists' in the Advanced Materials Field, *Research Policy*, 38(5): 756–64.

Balconi, M, Pozzali, A., and Viale, R. (2007) The 'Codification Debate' Revisited: A Conceptual Framework to Analyze the Role of Tacit Knowledge in Economics, *Industrial and Corporate Change*, 16(5): 823–49.

Baldwin, C. Y. and Clark, K. B. (2000) *Design Rules–The Power of Modularity*, Cambridge, MA: MIT Press.

Balogun, J. and Johnson, G. (2014) Organizational Restructuring and Middle Manager Sensemaking, *Academy of Management Journal*, 47(4): 523–49.

Barley, S., Freeman, J., and Hybels, R. (1992) Strategic Alliances in Commercial Biotechnology, in N. Nohria and R. Eccles (eds.), *Networks and Organizations*, Boston, MA: Harvard University Press.

Barley, W. C. (2015) Anticipatory Work: How the Need to Represent Knowledge Across Boundaries Shapes Work Practices Within Them, *Organization Science*, 26 (6): 1612–28.

Barney, J. B. (1986) Strategic Factor Markets: Expectations, Luck, and Business Strategy, *Management Science*, 32(10): 1231–41.

Barney, J. B. (1991) Firm Resources and Sustained Competitive Advantage, *Journal of Management*, 17: 99–120.

Baron, R. A. and Ensley, M. D. (2006) Opportunity Recognition as the Detection of Meaningful Patterns: Evidence from Comparisons of Novice and Experienced Entrepreneurs, *Management Science*, 52(9): 1331–44.

Barrett, M. and Oborn, E. (2010) Boundary Object Use in Cross-Cultural Software Development Teams. *Human Relations*, 63(8): 1199–221.

Barrett, M., Oborn, E., Orlikowski, W. J., and Yates, J. (2012) Reconfiguring Boundary Relations: Robotic Innovations in Pharmacy Work, *Organization Science*, 23(5): 1448–66.

Bartley, W. W. (1987) Alienation Alienated. The Economics of Knowledge versus the Psychology and Sociology of Knowledge, in G. Radnitzky and W. W. Bartley (eds.), *Evolutionary Epistemology, Rationality and the Sociology of Knowledge*, La Salle, IL: Open Court.

Bartley, W. W. (1990) *Unfathomed Knowledge, Unmeasured Wealth*, La Salle, IL: Open Court.

Bartunek, J. M. (1984) Changing Interpretive Schemes and Organizational Restructuring: The Example of a Religious Order, *Administrative Science Quarterly*, 29(3): 355–72.

Bathelt, H., Malmberg, A., and Maskell, P. (2004) Clusters and Knowledge: Local Buzz, Global Pipelines and the Process of Knowledge Creation, *Progress in Human Geography*, 28(1): 31–56.

Battilana, J. and Dorado, S. (2010) Building Sustainable Hybrid Organizations: The Case of Commercial Microfinance Organizations, *Academy of Management Journal*, 53(6): 1419–40.

Baum, J. A. C., Calabrese, T., and Silverman, B. S. (2000) Don't Go It Alone: Alliance Network Composition and Startups' Performance in Canadian Biotechnology, *Strategic Management Journal*, 21(3): 267–94.

Baum, J. A. C. and Oliver, C. (1991) Institutional Linkages and Organizational Mortality, *Administrative Science Quarterly*, 36(2): 187–218.

Bechky, B. A. (2003a) Object Lessons: Workplace Artifacts as Representations of Occupational Jurisdiction, *American Journal of Sociology*, 109(3): 720–52.

Bechky, B. A. (2003b) Sharing Meaning across Occupational Communities: The Transformation of Understanding on a Production Floor, *Organization Science*, 14(3): 312–30.

Bechky, B. A. (2006) Gaffers, Gofers, and Grips: Role-Based Coordination in Temporary Organizations, *Organization Science*, 17(1): 3–21.

Becker, G. S. and Murphy, K. M. (1992) The Division of Labor, Coordination Costs, and Knowledge, *Quarterly Journal of Economics*, 107(4): 1137–60.

Becker, M. C. (2004) Organizational Routines: A Review of the Literature, *Industrial and Corporate Change*, 13(4): 643–78.

Beckman, C. M., Haunschild, P. R., and Phillips, D. J. (2004) Friends or Strangers? Firm-Specific Uncertainty, Market Uncertainty, and Network Partner Selection, *Organization Science*, 15(3): 259–75.

Beimborn, D., Gleisner, F., Joachim, N., and Hackethal, A. (2009) The Role of Process Standardization in Achieving IT Business Value, in *Proceedings of the 42nd Hawaii International Conference on System Sciences (HICCS 2009)*, Hawaii, HI: IEEE.

Belderbos, R., Cassiman, B., Faems, D., Leten, B., and van Looy, B. (2014) Co-Ownership of Intellectual Property: Exploring the Value-Appropriation and Value-Creation Implications of Co-Patenting with Different Partners, *Research Policy*, 43(5): 841–52.

Bengtsson, L., Dabhilkar, M., and von Haartman, R. (2011) Knowledge Integration Challenges when Outsourcing Manufacturing, in C. Berggren, A. Bergek, L. Bengtsson, M. Hobday, and J. Söderlund (eds.), *Knowledge Integration and Innovation: Critical Challenges Facing International Technology-Based Firms*, Oxford: Oxford University Press.

Bengtsson, L., Lakemond, N., and Dabhilkar, M. (2013) Exploiting Supplier Innovation through Knowledge Integration, *International Journal of Technology Management*, 61(3/4): 237–53.

Bengtsson, L., Lakemond, N., Lazzarotti, V., Manizini, R., Pellegrini, L., and Tell, F. (2015) Open to a Select Few? Matching Partners and Knowledge Content for Open Innovation Performance, *Creativity and Innovation Management*, 24(1): 72–86.

Bengtsson, M. and Lindkvist, L. (2013) *Stylistic Replication Strategy: A Case Study of Visual Merchandising at Fashion Retailer H&M*, Linköping University, mimeo.

Benjamin, B. A. and Podolny, J. M. (1999) Status, Quality, and Social Order in the California Wine Industry, *Administrative Science Quarterly*, 44(3): 563–89.

Bensaou, M. and Venkatraman, N. (1995) Configurations of Interorganizational Relationships: A Comparison, *Management Science*, 41(9): 1471–92.

Berchicci, L. (2013) Towards an Open R&D System: Internal R&D Investment, External Knowledge Acquisition and Innovative Performance, *Research Policy*, 42(1), 117–27.

Bercovitz, J. and Feldman, M. (2011) The Mechanisms of Collaboration in Inventive Teams: Composition, Social Networks, and Geography, *Research Policy*, 40(1): 81–93.

Berends, H., Garud, R., Debackere, K., and Weggeman, M. (2011) Thinking Along: A Process for Tapping into Knowledge across Boundaries, *International Journal of Technology Management*, 53(1): 69–88.

Bergek, A., Berggren, C., Magnusson, T., and Hobday, M. (2013) Technological Discontinuities and the Challenge for Incumbent Firms: Destruction, Disruption or Creative Accumulation?, *Research Policy*, 42: 1210–24.

Berger, P. and Luckmann, T. (1966/1991) *The Social Construction of Reality–A Treatise in the Sociology of Knowledge*, London: Penguin Books.

Berggren, C., Bergek, A., Bengtsson, L., Hobday, M., and Söderlund, J. (eds.) (2011) *Knowledge Integration and Innovation: Critical Challenges Facing International Technology-Based Firms*, Oxford: Oxford University Press.

Berggren, C., Magnusson, T., and Sushandoyo, D. (2015) Transition Pathways Revisited: Established Firms as Multi-Level Actors in the Heavy Vehicle Industry, *Research Policy*, 44(5): 1017–28.

Bertrand, O. and Mol, M. J. (2013) The Antecedents and Innovation Effects of Domestic and Offshore R&D Outsourcing: The Contingent Impact of Cognitive Distance and Absorptive Capacity, *Strategic Management Journal*, 34(6): 751–60.

Bettis, R. A., Bradley, S. P., and Hamel, G. (1992) Outsourcing and Industrial Decline. *Academy of Management Executive*, 6(1): 7–22.

Birnholtz, J. P., Cohen, M. D., and Hoch, S. V. (2007) Organizational Character: On the Regeneration of Camp Poplar Grove, *Organization Science*, 18(2): 315–32.

Blau, P. M. (1970) The Formal Theory of Differentiation in Organizations, *American Sociological Review*, 35, April: 201–18.

Blau, P. M. (1977) *Inequality and Heterogeneity: a Primitive Theory of Social Structure*, New York: Free Press.

Blomkvist, K., Kappen, P., and Zander, I. (2010) Quo Vadis? The Entry into New Technologies in Advanced Foreign Subsidiaries of the Multinational Enterprise, *Journal of International Business Studies*, 41(9): 1525–49.

Blumer, H. (1969) *Symbolic Interactionism: Perspective and Method*, Upper Saddle River, NJ: Prentice-Hall.

Boland Jr, R. J., Lyytinen, K., and Yoo, Y. (2007) Wakes of Innovation in Project Networks: The Case of Digital 3-D Representations in Architecture, Engineering, and Construction, *Organization Science*, 18(4), 631–47.

Boland Jr, R. J. and Tenkasi, R. V. (1995) Perspective Making and Perspective Taking in Communities of Knowing, *Organization Science*, 6(4), 350–72.

Bonaccorsi, A. and Lipparini, A. (1994) Strategic Partnerships in New Product Development: An Italian Case Study, *Journal of Product Innovation Management*, 11(2), 134–45.

Borg, E. and Söderlund, J. (2014) Liminality Competence: An Interpretative Study of Mobile Project Workers' Conception of Liminality at Work, *Management Learning*, 46(3): 260–79.

Borys, B. and Jemison, D. B. (1989) Hybrid Arrangements as Strategic Alliances: Theoretical Issues in Organizational Combinations, *Academy of Management Review*, 14: 234–49.

Boschma, R. (2005) Proximity and Innovation: A Critical Assessment, *Regional Studies*, 39(1): 61–74.

Boschma, R. and Frenken, K. (2010) *The Spatial Evolution of Innovation Networks: A Proximity Perspective*, Papers in Evolutionary Economic Geography #09.05, Urban & Regional Research Center Utrecht, Utrecht University.

Bottomley, S. (2014) *The British Patent System during the Industrial Revolution, 1700–1852*, Cambridge: Cambridge University Press.

Bounfour, A. (1999) Is Outsourcing of Intangibles a Real Source of Competitive Advantage? *International Journal of Applied Quality Management*, 2(2): 127.

Bouty, I. (2000) Interpersonal and Interaction Influences on Informal Resource Exchanges between R&D Researchers across Organizational Boundaries, *Academy of Management Journal*, 43(1): 50–65.

Bradach, J. L. (1997) Using the Plural Form in the Management of Restaurant Chains, *Administrative Science Quarterly*, 42(2): 276–303.

Bradach, J. L., and Eccles, R. G. (1989) Price, Authority and Trust: From Ideal Types to Plural Forms, *Annual Review of Sociology*, 15: 97–118.

Brady, T. and Davies, A. (2004) Building Project Capabilities: From Exploratory to Exploitative Learning, *Organization Studies*, 25(9): 1601–21.

Brandon, D. P. and Hollingshead, A. B. (2004) Transactive Memory Systems in Organizations: Matching Tasks, Expertise, and People, *Organization Science*, 15(6): 633–44.

Bredin, K. and Söderlund, J. (2011) *Human Resource Management in Project-Based Organizations: The HR Quadriad Framework*, Basingstoke: Palgrave Macmillan.

Breschi, S. and Catalini, C. (2010) Tracing the Links between Science and Technology: An Exploratory Analysis of Scientists' and Inventors' Networks, *Research Policy*, 39(1): 14–26.

Bresman, H., Birkinshaw, J. M., and Nobel, R. (1999) Knowledge Transfer in Acquisitions, *Journal of International Business Studies*, 30(4): 439–62.

Brint, S. (1996) *In an Age of Experts: The Changing Role of Professionals in Politics and Public Life*, Princeton, NJ: Princeton University Press.

Brown, J. S. and Duguid, P. (1991) Organizational Learning and Communities of Practice: Toward a Unified View of Working, Learning, and Innovation, *Organization Science*, 2(1): 40–57.

Bruns, H. (2013) Working Alone Together: Coordination in Collaboration across Domains of Expertise, *Academy of Management Journal*, 56(1): 62–83.

Brusoni, S., Criscuolo, P., and Geuna, A. (2005) The Knowledge Bases of the World's Largest Pharmaceuticals Groups: What Do Patent Citations to Non-Patent Literature Reveal?, *Economics of Innovation And New Technology*, 14(5): 395–415.

Brusoni, S., Jacobides, M. G., and Prencipe, A. (2009) Strategic Dynamics in Industry Architectures and the Challenges of Knowledge Integration, *European Management Review*, 6(4): 209–16.

Brusoni, S. and Prencipe, A. (2001) Unpacking the Black Box of Modularity: Technologies, Products and Organizations, *Industrial and Corporate Change*, 10(1): 179–205.

Brusoni, S. and Prencipe, A. (2006) Making Design Rules: A Multidomain Perspective, *Organization Science*, 17(2): 179–89.

Brusoni, S., Prencipe, A., and Pavitt, K. (2001) Knowledge Specialization, Organizational Coupling, and the Boundaries of the Firm: Why Do Firms Know More Than They Make? *Administrative Science Quarterly*, 46(4): 597–621.

Bulathsinhala, N.A. (2012) *Innovation Processes in the Energy Sector*, University of Southern Denmark, doctoral dissertation.

Burgelman, R. A. (2002) Strategy as Vector and the Inertia of Coevolutionary Lock-In, *Administrative Science Quarterly*, 47: 325–57.

Burger, M. and Sydow, J. (2014) How Inter-Organizational Networks can Become Path-Dependent: Bargaining Practices in the Photonics Industry, *Schmalenbach Business Review*, 66(1): 73–99.

Burgers, W. P., Hill, C. W. L., and Kim, W. C. (1993) A Theory of Global Strategic Alliances: The Case of Global Auto Industry, *Strategic Management Journal*, 14(6): 419–32.

Burhop, C. (2010) The Transfer of Patents in Imperial Germany, *Journal of Economic History*, 70(4): 921–39.

Burt, R. S. (1980) Models of Network Structure, *Annual Review of Sociology*, 6: 79–141.

Burt, R. S. (1992) *Structural Holes: The Social Structure of Competition*, Cambridge, MA: Harvard University Press.

Burt, R. S. (2005) *Brokerage and Closure: An Introduction to Social Capital*, New York: Oxford University Press.

Cantwell, J. and Amann, E. (2012) *Innovative Firms in Emerging Market Countries*, Oxford: Oxford University Press.

Capello, R. (1999) Spatial Transfer of Knowledge in High Technology Milieux: Learning Versus Collective Learning Processes, *Regional Studies*, 33(4): 353–65.

Carlile, P. R. (2002) A Pragmatic View of Knowledge and Boundaries: Boundary Objects in New Product Development, *Organization Science*, 13(4): 442–55.

Carlile, P. R. (2004) Transferring, Translating, and Transforming: An Integrative Framework for Managing Knowledge Across Boundaries. *Organization Science*, 15(5): 555–68.

Carlile, P. R. and Rebentisch, E. S. (2003) Into the Black Box: The Knowledge Transformation Cycle, *Management Science*, 49(9): 1180–95.

Carnabuci, G. and Bruggerman, J. (2009) Knowledge Specialization, Knowledge Brokerage, and the Uneven Growth of Knowledge Domains, *Social Forces*, 88: 607–42.

Carnabuci, G. and Operti, E. (2013) Where do Firms' Recombinant Capabilities Come From? Intraorganizational Networks, Knowledge, and Firms' Ability to Innovate through Technological Recombination, *Strategic Management Journal*, 34(13): 1591–613.

Cassiman, B. and Veugelers, R. (2006) In Search of Complementarity in Innovation Strategy: Internal R&D and External Knowledge Acquisition, *Management Science*, 52(1): 68–82.

Cattani, G. and Ferriani, S (2008) A Core/Periphery Perspective on Individual Creative Performance: Social Networks and Cinematic Achievements in the Hollywood Film Industry, *Organization Science*, 2008, 19(6): 824–44.

Cattani, G., Ferriani, S, Mengoli, S., and Mariani, M. (2013) Tackling the 'Galácticos' Effect: Team Familiarity and the Performance of Star-Studded Projects, *Industrial and Corporate Change*, 22(6): 1629–62.

Ceci, F. (2009) *The Business of Solutions*, Cheltenham: Edward Elgar.

Ceci, F. and Masini, A. (2011) Balancing Specialized and Generic Capabilities in the Provision of Integrated Solutions: Empirical Evidence from the IT Sector, *Industrial and Corporate Change*, 20(1): 91–132.

Ceci, F. and Prencipe, A. (2008) Configuring Capabilities for Integrated Solutions: Evidence from the IT Sector, *Industry & Innovation*, 15(3): 277–96.

Cerasale, M. and Stone, M. (2004) *Business Solutions on Demand*, London: Kogan Page.

Chandler Jr, A. D. (1977) *The Visible Hand: The Managerial Revolution in American Business*, Cambridge, MA: Harvard University Press.

Chandler Jr, A. D. (1990) *Scale and Scope: The Dynamics of Industrial Capitalism*, Cambridge, MA: The Belknap Press of Harvard University.

Chesbrough, H. and Bogers, M. (2014) Explicating Open Innovation: Clarifying an Emerging Paradigm for Understanding Innovation, in H. Chesbrough, W. Vanhaverbeke, and J. West (eds.), *New Frontiers in Open Innovation*, Oxford: Oxford University Press.

Chesbrough, H. W. (2003a) The Era of Open Innovation, *Sloan Management Review*, 44(3): 35–41.

Chesbrough, H. W. (2003b) *Open Innovation: The New Imperative for Creating and Profiting from Technology*, Cambridge, MA: Harvard Business School Publishing.

Cheung, M. S., Myers, M. B., and Mentzer, J. (2011) The Value of Relational Learning in Global Buyer–Supplier Exchanges: A Dyadic Perspective and Test of the Pre-Sharing Premise, *Strategic Management Journal*, 32(10): 1061–82.

Chiang, C-Y., Kocabasoglu-Hillmer, C., and Suresh, N. (2012) An Empirical Investigation of the Impact of Strategic Sourcing and Flexibility on Firm's Supply Chain Agility, *International Journal of Operations & Production Management*, 32(1): 49–78.

Chung, M. (2009) Hyundai–Is it Possible to Realise the Dream of Becoming a Top Five Global Automaker by 2010? in M. Freyssenet (ed.), *The Second Automobile Revolution*, Basingstoke: Palgrave Macmillan.

Clark, K. and Fujimoto, T. (1991) *Product Development Performance: Strategy, Organization, and Management in the World Auto Industry*, Cambridge, MA: Harvard Business School Press.

Coase, R. (1937) The Nature of the Firm, *Economica*, 4(16): 386–405.

Cockburn, I. M. and Henderson, R. (1998) Absorptive Capacity, Co-Authoring Behavior and the Organization of Research in Drug Discovery, *Journal of Industrial Economics*, 46(2): 157–82.

Coenen, L. Moodyson, J., and Asheim, B. T. (2004) Nodes, Networks and Proximities: On the Knowledge Dynamics of the Medicon Valley Biotech Cluster, *European Planning Studies*, 12(7): 1003–18.

Cohen, M. D. (1991) Individual Learning and Organizational Routine: Emerging Connections, *Organization Science*, 2(1), 135–9.

Cohen, M. D., March, J. G., and Olsen, J. P. (1972) A Garbage Can Model of Organizational Choice, *Administrative Science Quarterly*, 17: 1–25.

Cohen, W. M. and Levinthal, D. A. (1990) Absorptive Capacity: A New Perspective on Learning and Innovation, *Administrative Science Quarterly*, 35(1): 128–52.

Cohendet P. and Steinmueller, W. E. (2000) The Codification of Knowledge: A Conceptual and Empirical Exploration, *Industrial and Corporate Change*, 11(2): 195–209.

Collins, F. S., Morgan, M., and Patrinos, A. (2003) The Human Genome Project: Lessons from Large-Scale Biology, *Science*, 300(5617): 286–90.

Collins, H. (2004) Interactional Expertise as a Third Kind of Knowledge, *Phenomenology and the Cognitive Sciences*, 3(2): 125–43.

Collins, H. and Evans, R. (2007) *Rethinking Expertise*, Chicago: University of Chicago Press.

Collinson, S. (2001) Knowledge Management Capabilities in R&D: A UK–Japan Company Comparison, *R&D Management*, 31(3): 335–47.

Colpan, A. and Hikino, T. (2010) Foundations of Business Groups: Toward an Integrated Framework, in A. Colpan, T. Hikino, and J. Lincoln. (eds.), *Oxford Handbook of Business Groups*, Oxford: Oxford University Press.

Conner, K. R. and Prahalad, C. K. (1996) A Resource-Based Theory of the Firm: Knowledge Versus Opportunism, *Organization Science*, 7(5): 477–501.

Cooke, P. (2001) Regional Innovation Systems, Clusters and the Knowledge Economy, *Industrial and Corporate Change*, 10(4): 945–74.

Coombs, R. and Hull, R. (1998) Knowledge Management Practices and Path-Dependency in Innovation, *Research Policy*, 27: 237–53.

Cowan, R., David, P., and Foray, D. (2000) The Explicit Economics of Knowledge Codification and Tacitness, *Industrial and Corporate Change*, 9(2): 211–53.

Crescenzi, R., Rodriguez-Pose, A., and Storper, M. (1997) On the Geographical Determinants of Innovation in Europe and the United States, *Journal of Economic Geography* 7(6): 673–709.

Cross, R. and Sproull, L. (2004) More than an Answer: Information Relationships for Actionable Knowledge, *Organization Science*, 15(4): 446–62.

Cunha, M. P., Rego, A., Oliveira Rosado, P., and Habib, N. (2014) Product Innovation in Resource-Poor Environments: Three Research Streams, *Journal of Product Innovation Management*, 31(2): 202–10.

Cyert, R. and March, J. G. (1963) *A Behavioral Theory of the Firm*, Oxford: Blackwell.

Czarniawska, B. and Joerges, B. (1996) Travels of Ideas, in B. Czarniawska and G. Sevon (eds.), *Translating Organizational Change*, Berlin: de Gruyter.

Czarniawska-Joerges, B. and Joerges, B. (1990) *Organizational Change as a Materialization of Ideas*, unpublished manuscript, Stockholm School of Economics, Stockholm, Sweden.

D'Aunno, T., Sutton, R. I., and Price, R. H. (1991) Isomorphism and External Support in Conflicting Institutional Environments: A Study of Drug Abuse Treatment Units, *Academy of Management Journal*, 34(3): 636–61.

D'Eredita, M. A. and Barreto, C. (2006) How does Tacit Knowledge Proliferate? An Episode-Based Perspective, *Organization Studies*, 27(12): 1821–41.

Dabhilkar, M. and Bengtsson, L. (2011) Trade-offs in Make-Buy Decisions: Exploring Operating Realities of Knowledge Integration and Innovation, in C. Berggren, A. Bergek, L. Bengtsson, M. Hobday, and J. Söderlund (eds.), *Knowledge Integration and Innovation: Critical Challenges Facing International Technology-Based Firms*, Oxford: Oxford University Press.

Daft, R. L. and Lengel, R. H. (1984) Information Richness: A New Approach to Manager Information Processing and Organization Design, in B. Staw and L. L. Cummings (eds.), *Research in Organizational Behavior*, 6, Homewood, IL: JAI Press.

Daft, R. Y. and Lewin, A. (1993) Where are the Theories of New Organizational Forms? An Editorial Essay, *Organization Science*, 4(4): i–vi.

Dahlander, L. and Frederiksen, L. (2012) The Core and Cosmopolitans: A Relational View of Innovation in User Communities, *Organization Science*, 23(4): 988–1007.

Dahlander, L. and Gann, D. M. (2010) How Open is Innovation? *Research Policy*, 39: 699–709.

Dahlander, L. and O'Mahony, S. (2011) Progressing to the Center: Coordinating Project Work, *Organization Science*, 22(4): 961–79.

Dahlgren, J. and Söderlund, J. (2001) Managing Inter-Firm Industrial Projects—On Pacing and Matching Hierarchies, *International Business Review*, 10: 305–22.

Dalziel, M. (2007) A Systems-Based Approach to Industry Classification, *Research Policy*, 36: 1559–74.

Damasio, A. (1999) *The Feeling of What Happens*, New York: Harcourt Brace & Company.

Das, A., Narasimhan, R., and Talluri, S. (2006) Supplier Integration—Finding an Optimal Configuration, *Journal of Operations Management*, 24(5): 563–82.

David, P. A. (1985) Clio and the Economics of QWERTY, *American Economic Review*, 75: 332–7.

Davies, A. (2001) *Integrated Solutions*, The Knowledge Bridge.

Davies, A. (2004) Moving Base into High-Value Integrated Solutions: A Value Stream Approach, *Industrial and Corporate Change*, 13(5): 727–56.

Davies, A., Brady, T., and Hobday, M. (2006) Changing a Path toward Integrated Solutions, *MIT Sloan Management Review*, 47(3): 39–48.

Davis, J. P. and Eisenhardt, K. M. (2011) Rotating Leadership and Collaborative Innovation: Recombination Processes in Symbiotic Relationships, *Administrative Science Quarterly*, 56(2): 159–201.

Dawson, G., Watson, R., and Boudreau, M-C. (2010) Information Asymmetry in Information Systems Consulting: Toward a Theory of Relationship Constraints, *Journal of Management Information Systems*, 37(3): 143–77.

De Groote, S. (2003) *Engine Mock up to Test Integration*, <http://www.f1technical.net/features/680>.

Dedrick, J., Kraemer, K. L., and Linden, G. (2010) Who Profits from Innovation in Global Value Chains? A Study of the iPod and notebook PCs, *Industrial and Corporate Change*, 19(1): 81–116.

DeFillippi, R. J., Arthur, M. B., and Lindsay, V. J. (2006) *Knowledge at Work. Creative Collaboration in the Global Economy*, Malden, MA: Blackwell Publishing.

Demsetz, H. (1968) The Cost of Transacting, *Quarterly Journal of Economics*, 82(Feb.): 33–53.

Demsetz, H. (1991) The Theory of the Firm Revisited, in O. E. Williamson and S. G. Winter (eds.), *The Nature of the Firm: Origins, Evolution, and Development*, New York: Oxford University Press.

Dibiaggio, L. (2007) Design, Complexity, Vertical Disintegration, and Knowledge Organization in the Semiconductor Industry, *Industrial and Corporate Change*, 16 (2): 239–67.

Dibiaggio, L. and Nasiriyar, M. (2009) Knowledge Integration and Vertical Specialization in the Semiconductor Industry, *European Management Review*, 6(4): 265–76.

DiMaggio, P. J. and Powell, W. W. (1983) The Iron Cage Revisited: Institutional Isomorphism and Collective Rationality in Organizational Fields, *American Sociological Review*, 48: 147–60.

Dionysiou, D. D. and Tsoukas, H. (2013) Understanding the (Re)Creation of Routines from Within: A Symbolic Interactionist Perspective, *Academy of Management Review*, 38(2): 181–205.

Dittrich, K. and Duysters, G. (2007) Networking as a Means to Strategy Change: The Case of Open Innovation in Mobile Telephony, *Journal of Product Innovation Management*, 24(6): 510–21.

Donaldson, L. (2001) *The Contingency Theory of Organizations*, Thousand Oaks, CA: Sage.

Dosi, G. (1982) Technological Paradigms and Technological Trajectories–A Suggested Interpretation of the Determinants and Directions of Technical Change, *Research Policy*, 11: 147–62.

Dougherty, D. (1992) Interpretive Barriers to Successful Product Innovation in Large Firms, *Organization Science*, 3(2): 179–202.

Droge, C., Jayaram, J., and Vickery, S. K. (2004) The Effects of Internal versus External Integration Practices on Time-Based Performance and Overall Firm Performance, *Journal of Operations Management*, 22: 557–73.

Drury-Grogan, M. L. (2014) Performance on Agile Teams: Relating Iteration Objectives and Critical Decisions to Project Management Success Factors, *Information and Software Technology*, 56(5): 506–15.

Dunbar, K. (1997) How Scientists Think: On-Line Creativity and Conceptual Change in Science, in T.B. Ward, S. M. Smith, and J. Vaid (eds.), *Creative Thought: An Investigation of Conceptual Structures and Processes*, Washington: American Psychological Association.

Dutton, J. E., Fahey, L., and Narayanan, V. K. (1983) Toward Understanding Strategic Issue Diagnosis, *Strategic Management Journal* 4(4): 307–23.

Dyer, J. H. and Singh, H. (1998) The Relational View: Cooperative Strategy and Sources of Interorganizational Competitive Advantage, *Academy of Management Review*, 23(4): 660–79.

Edmondson, A. C., Bohmer, R. M., and Pisano, G. P. (2001) Disrupted Routines: Team Learning and New Technology Implementation in Hospitals, *Administrative Science Quarterly*, 46: 685–716.

Edwards, A. (2008) Open-Source Science to Enable Drug Discovery, *Drug Discovery Today* 13(17–18): 731–3.

Eisenhardt, K. M. and Martin, J. A. (2000) Dynamic Capabilities: What Are They?, *Strategic Management Journal*, 21: 1105–21.

Elmquist, M., Fredberg T., and Ollila, S. (2009) Exploring the Field of Open Innovation, *European Journal of Innovation Management*, 12(3): 326–45.

Enberg, C. (2007) *Knowledge Integration in Product Development Projects*, Linköping University, doctoral dissertation.

Enberg, C. and Bredin, K. (2015) *Sustaining and Developing Disciplinary Expertise in Project-Based Organizations: Balanced and Integrated Solutions*, Newtown Square: Project Management Institute.

Enberg, C., Lindkvist, L., and Tell, F. (2006) Exploring the Dynamics of Knowledge Integration: Acting and Interacting in Project Teams, *Management Learning*, 37(2): 143–65.

Enberg, C., Lindkvist, L., and Tell, F. (2010) Knowledge Integration at the Edge of Technology: On Teamwork and Complexity in New Turbine Development, *International Journal of Project Management*, 28(8): 756–65.

Eriksson, K., Majkgård, A., and Sharma, D.D. (2000) Path Dependence and Knowledge Development in the Internationalization Process, *Management International Review*, 4: 307–28.

Esen, B. (2010) *Turkish White Goods Industry Report* (in Turkish: Beyaz Eşya Endüstrisi Raporu), Ankara: İhracatı Geliştime Etüd Merkezi Publication.

Ewenstein, B. and Whyte, J. (2009) Knowledge Practices in Design: The Role of Visual Representations as Epistemic Objects, *Organization Studies*, 30(1): 7–30.

Faems, D., van Looy, B., and Debackere, K. (2005) Interorganizational Collaboration and Innovation: Toward a Portfolio Approach, *Journal of Product Innovation Management*, 22: 238–50.

Faraj, S. and Xiao, Y. (2006) Coordination in Fast-Response Organizations, *Management Science*, 52(8): 1155–69.

Farjoun, M. (1994) Beyond Industry Boundaries: Human Expertise, Diversification and Resource-Related Industry Groups, *Organization Science*, 5(2): 185–99.

Farjoun, M. (2010) Beyond Dualism: Stability And Change As A Duality, *Academy of Management Review*, 35(2): 202–25.

Feldman, M. (2000) Organizational Routines as a Source of Continuous Change, *Organization Science*, 11: 611–29.

Feldman, M. S. and Orlikowski, W. J. (2011) Theorizing Practice and Practicing Theory, *Organization Science*, 22(5): 1240–53.

Feldman, M. S. and Pentland, B. (2003) Reconceptualizing Organizational Routines as a Source of Flexibility and Change, *Administrative Science Quarterly*, 48 (1): 94–118.

Felin, T. and Zenger, T. R. (2014) Closed or Open Innovation? Problem Solving and the Governance Choice, *Research Policy*, 43(5): 914–25.

Ferraro, F. and Gurses, K. (2009) Building Architectural Advantage in the US Motion Picture Industry: Lew Wasserman and the Music Corporation of America, *European Management Review*, 6(4): 233–49.

Fixson, S. K. and Park, J. K. (2008) The Power of Integrality: Linkages between Product Architecture, Innovation, and Industry Structure, *Research Policy*, 37(8): 1296–316.

Fleischmann, K. R. (2006) Boundary Objects with Agency: A Method for Studying the Design–Use Interface, *The Information Society*, 22(2), 77–87.

Fligstein, N. (1990) *The Transformation of Corporate Control*, Cambridge, MA: Harvard University Press.

Flyvbjerg, B. (2007) Five Misunderstandings about Case-Study Research, in C. Seale, G. Gobo, J. F. Gubrium, and D. Silverman (eds.), *Qualitative Research Practice*, London and Thousand Oaks, CA: Sage.

Foote, N., Galbraith, J., Hope, Q., and Miller, D. (2001) Making Solutions the Answer, *The McKinsey Quarterly*, 3: 84–93.

Foray, D. and Steinmueller, W. E. (2003) The Economics of Knowledge Reproduction by Inscription, *Industrial and Corporate Change*, 12: 299–319.

formula1.com (2006) *Champions' Engine Guru on New Rules and Red Bull Supply*, <http://www.formula1.com/news/interviews/2006/12/5369.html>.

formula1.com (2007a) *Toyota's Vasselon & Marmorini on the TF107*, <http://www.formula1.com/news/interviews/2007/1/5483.html>.

formula1.com (2007b) *Exclusive Interview with Honda's Nick Fry*, <http://www.formula1.com/news/interviews/2007/4/5900.html>.

formula1.com (2008) *Exclusive Interview–BMW Sauber's Willy Rampf*, <http://www.formula1.com/news/interviews/2008/2/7375.html>.

formula1.com (2014) *FIA Friday Press Conference–China*, <http://formula1.com/news/headlines/2014/4/15739.html>.

Forty, A. (1986) *Objects of Desire: Design and Society from Wedgwood to IBM*, New York: Pantheon.

Forza, C. (2002) Survey Research in Operations Management: A Process-Based Perspective, *International Journal of Operations & Production Management*, 22(2): 152–94.

Foss, N. J., Husted, K., and Michailova, S. (2010) Governing Knowledge Sharing in Organizations: Levels of Analysis, Governance Mechanisms, and Research Directions, *Journal of Management Studies*, 47(3): 455–82.

Foss, N. J., Laursen, K., and Pedersen, T. (2011) Linking Customer Interaction and Innovation: The Mediating Role of New Organizational Practices, *Organization Science*, 22(4): 980–99.

Foss, N. J. and Mahoney, J. T. (2010) Exploring Knowledge Governance, *International Journal of Strategic Change Management*, 2(2): 93–101.

Franke, N., Poetz, M. K., and Schreier, M. (2013) Integrating Problem Solvers from Analogous Markets in New Product Ideation, *Management Science*, 60 (4), 1063–81.

Freeman, R. E. (1984) *Strategic Management: A Stakeholder Approach*, Boston, MA: Pitman.

Fridlund, M. (1999) *Den gemensamma utvecklingen: Staten, storföretaget och samarbetet kring den svenska elkraftstekniken*, Stockholm: Symposion.

FTSE (2014) *FTSE Country Classification Process*, available at <http://www.ftse.com/products/downloads/FTSE_Country_Classification_Paper.pdf>.

Fu, X., Pietrobelli, C., and Soete L. (2011) The Role of Foreign Technology and Indigenous Innovation in the Emerging Economies: Technological Change and Catching-up, *World Development*, 39(7): 1204–12.

Fulk, J., Monge, P., and Hollingshead, A. B. (2005) Knowledge Resource Sharing in Dispersed Multinational Teams: Three Theoretical Lenses, in D. Shapiro, M. A. V. Glinow, and J. Cheng (eds.), *Managing Multinational Teams: Cultural, Organizational, and National Influences*, Amsterdam: Elsevier.

Gal, U., Yoo, Y., and Boland, R. J. (2004) *The Dynamics of Boundary Objects, Social Infrastructures and Social Identities*, Case Western Reserve University, Sprouts: Working Papers on Information Systems, 4(11).

Galbraith, J. R. (1973) *Designing Complex Organizations*, Reading: Addison-Wesley.

Galbraith, J. R. (1974) Organization Design: An Information Processing View. *Interfaces*, 4(3): 28–36.

Galbraith, J. R. (2002) Organizing to Deliver Solutions, *Organizational Dynamics*, 31(2): 194–207.

Galbraith, J. R. (2010) The Multi-Dimensional and Reconfigurable Organization, *Organizational Dynamics*, 39(2): 115–25.

Gardner, H., Gino, F., and Staats, B. R. (2012) Dynamically Integrating Knowledge in Teams: Transforming Resources into Performance, *Academy of Management Journal*, 55(4): 998–1022.

Garnier, J-P. (2008) Rebuilding the R&D Engine in Big Pharma, *Harvard Business Review* 86(5): 68–77.

Garriga, H., von Krogh, G., and Spaeth, S. (2013) How Constraints and Knowledge Impact Open Innovation, *Strategic Management Journal*, 34(9): 1134–44.

Garud, R., Kumaraswamy, A., and Karnøe, P. (2010) Path Dependence or Path Creation? *Journal of Management Studies*, 47(4): 760–74.

Garud, R. and Nayyar, P.R (1994) Transformative Capacity: Continual Structuring by Intertemporal Technology Transfer, *Strategic Management Journal*, 15: 365–85.

Gary M. S., Wood R. E., and Pillinger T. (2012) Enhancing Mental Models, Analogical Transfer, and Performance in Strategic Decision Making, *Strategic Management Journal*, 33(11): 1229–46.

Gassmann, O. (2006) Opening Up the Innovation Process: Towards an Agenda, *R&D Management*, 36: 223–8.

Gassmann. O., Enkel. E., and Chesbrough, H. (2010) The Future of Open Innovation, *R&D Management*, 40(3): 213–21.

Gasson, S. (2006) A Genealogical Study of Boundary-Spanning IS Design, *European Journal of Information Systems*, 15(1): 26–41.

Gavetti, G., Levinthal, D. A., and Rivkin, J. W. (2005) Strategy Making in Novel and Complex Worlds: The Power of Analogy, *Strategic Management Journal*, 26: 691–712.

Gebert, D., Boerner, S., and Kearney, E. (2010) Fostering Team Innovation: Why is it Important to Combine Opposing Action Strategies?, *Organization Science*, 21(3): 593–608.

Geels, F. W. (2005) Processes and Patterns in Transitions and System Innovations: Refining the Co-Evolutionary Multi-Level Perspective, *Technological Forecasting and Social Change*, 72: 681–96.

Geels, F. W. and Schot, J. (2007) Typology of Sociotechnical Transition Pathways, *Research Policy*, 36: 399–417.

Gentner, D. (2002) Analogy in Scientific Discovery: The Case of Johannes Kepler, in L. Magnani and N. J. Nersessian (eds.), *Model-Based Reasoning: Science, Technology, Values*, New York: Kluwer.

Gerring, J. (1999) What Makes a Concept Good? A Criterial Framework for Understanding Concept Formation in the Social Sciences, *Polity*, 31(3): 357–93.

Gersick, C. J. G. (1994) Pacing Strategic Change: The Case of a New Venture, *Academy of Management Journal*, 37(1): 9–45.

Gibbons, M. (2008) *Why is Knowledge Translation Important? Grounding the Conversation*, KT08: Forum for the Future, Colloquium presentation, Banff, Canada.

Gibbons, M., Limoges, C., Nowotny, H., Schwartzman, S., Scott, P., and Trow, M. (1994) *The New Production of Knowledge: The Dynamics of Science and Research in Contemporary Societies*, London: SAGE.

Giddens, A. (1984) The Constitution of Society: Outline of the Theory of Structuration, Oakland: University of California Press.

Gieryn, T. F. (1983) Boundary-Work and the Demarcation of Science from Non-Science: Strains and Interests in Professional Ideologies of Scientists, *American Sociological Review*, 48(6): 781–95.

Gilley, K. M. and Rasheed, A. A. (2000) Making More by Doing Less: An Analysis of Outsourcing and its Effects on Firm Performance, *Journal of Management*, 26(4): 763–90.

Gittelman, M. and Kogut, B. (2003) Does Good Science Lead to Valuable Knowledge? Biotechnology Firms and the Evolutionary Logic of Citation Patterns, *Management Science*, 49(4): 366–82.

Giuliani, E. (2007) Toward an Understanding of Knowledge Spillovers in Industrial Clusters, *Applied Economics Letters*, 14: 87–90.

Goldratt, E. and Cox, J. (1992) *The Goal: A Process of Ongoing Improvement*, Great Barrington, MA: North River Press.

Göranzon, B., Ennals, R., and Hammarén, M. (2006) *Dialogue, Skill and Tacit Knowledge*, Chichester: Wiley.

Gouldner, A. W. (1957) Cosmopolitans and Locals: Toward an Analysis of Latent Social Roles, *Administrative Science Quarterly* 2(3): 281–306.

Gourlay, S. (2006) Conceptualizing Knowledge Creation: A Critique of Nonaka's Theory, *Journal of Management Studies*, 43(7): 1415–36.

Govindarajan, V., Trimble, C., and Nooyi, I. K. (2012) *Reverse Innovation: Create Far from Home, Win Everywhere*, Cambridge, MA: Harvard Business Review Press.

Grandori, A. (2001) Neither Hierarchy Nor Identity: Knowledge-Governance Mechanisms and the Theory of the Firm, *Journal of Management and Governance*, 5(3–4): 381–99.

Granstrand, O. (1999) *The Economics and Management of Intellectual Property*, Cheltenham: Edward Elgar Publishing.

Granstrand, O. and Oskarsson, C. (1994) Technology Diversification in 'Mul-Tech' Corporations, *IEEE Transactions on Engineering Management*, 41(4): 355–64.

Granstrand, O., Patel, P., and Pavitt, K. (1997) Multi-Technology Corporations: Why they have 'Distributed' rather than 'Distinctive Core' Competencies, *California Management Review*, 39(4): 8–25.

Grant, R. M. (1996) Toward a Knowledge-Based Theory of the Firm, *Strategic Management Journal*, 17(Winter Special Issue): 109–22.

Grant, R. M. and Baden-Fuller, C. (2004) A Knowledge Accessing Theory of Strategic Alliances, *Journal of Management Studies*, 41(1): 61–84.

Greenwood, R., Kodeih, F., Micelotta, E., Raynard, M., and Lounsbury, M. (2011) Institutional Complexity and Organizational Responses, *Annals of the Academy of Management*, 5(1): 317–71.

Griesbach, D. and Grand, S. (2013) Managing as Transcending: An Ethnography, *Scandinavian Journal of Management*, 29(1): 63–77.

Griffith, T. L. and Neale, M. A. (2001) Information Processing in Traditional, Hybrid, and Virtual Teams: From Nascent Knowledge to Transactive Memory, in B. M. Staw and R. I. Sutton (eds.), *Research in Organizational Behavior*, Stamford, CT: JAI Press.

Griffith, T. L., Sawyer, J. E., and Neale, M. A. (2003) Virtualness and Knowledge in Teams: Managing the Love Triangle of Organizations, Individuals, and Information Technology, *MIS Quarterly*, 27(2): 265–87.

Grönlund, J., Rönnberg Sjödin, D., and Frishammar, J. (2010) Open Innovation and the Stage-Gate Process: A Revised Model for New Product Development, *California Management Review*, 52(3): 106–31.

Grossman, S. J. and Hart, O. D. (1986) The Costs and Benefits of Ownership: A Theory of Vertical and Lateral Integration, *The Journal of Political Economy*, 94(4): 691–719.

Gruber, M., Harhoff, D., and Hoisl, K. (2012) Knowledge Recombination Across Technological Boundaries: Scientists vs. Engineers, *Management Science*, 59(4): 837–51.

Gueldenberg, S. and Helting, H. (2007) Bridging the Great Divide: Nonaka's Synthesis of 'Western' and 'Eastern' Concepts Reassessed, *Organization*, 14(1): 101–22.

Guillén, M. F. and García-Canal, E. (2009) The American Model of the Multinational Firm and the 'New' Multinationals from Emerging Economies, *Academy of Management Perspectives*, 23(2): 23–35.

Gulati, R. (1998) Alliances and Networks, *Strategic Management Journal*, 19(4): 293–317.

Gulati, R. and Puranam, P. (2009) Renewal through Reorganization: The Value of Inconsistencies between Formal and Informal Organization, *Organization Science*, 20(1): 422–40.

Gülsoy, T., Özkanlı, Ö., and Lynch, R. (2012) The Role of Innovation in the Effective International Expansion of an Emerging-Country Firm: The Case of Arçelik, *Procedia-Social and Behavioral Sciences*, 41: 116–29.

Guston, D. H. (2001) Boundary Organizations in Environmental Policy and Science: An Introduction, *Science, Technology, and Human Values*, 26(4): 399–408.

Guttman, L. (1950) The Basis for Scalogram Analysis. In S. A. Stouffer, L. Guttman, E. A. Suchman, P. F. Lazarsfeld, S. A. Star, and J. A. Clausen, *Measurement and Prediction*: 60–90, Princeton, NJ: Princeton University Press.

Haas, P. M. (1989) Do Regimes Matter? Epistemic Communities and Mediterranean Pollution Control, *International Organization*, 43(3): 377–403.

Haas, P. M. (1992) Introduction: Epistemic Communities and International Policy Coordination, *International Organization*, 46: 1–35.

Hagedoorn, J. (1993) Understanding the Rationale of Strategic Technology Partnering: Interorganizational Modes of Cooperation and Sectoral Differences, *Strategic Management Journal*, 14: 371–85.

Håkanson, L. (2007) Creating Knowledge: The Power and Logic of Articulation, *Industrial and Corporate Change*, 16(1): 51–88.

Håkanson, L. (2010) The Firm as an Epistemic Community: The Knowledge-Based View Revisited, *Industrial and Corporate Change*, 19(6): 1801–28.

Hallen, B. L. (2008) The Causes and Consequences of the Initial Network Positions of New Organizations: From Whom Do Entrepreneurs Receive Investments?, *Administrative Science Quarterly*, 53(4): 685–718.

Hamel, G. and Prahalad, C. K. (1994) *Competing for the Future*, Boston, MA: Harvard Business School Press.

Hansen, M. and Lovås, B. (2004) How do Multinational Companies Leverage Technological Competencies? Moving from Single to Interdependent Explanations, *Strategic Management Journal*, 25(8–9): 801–22.

Hansen, M. T. and Birkinshaw, J. (2007) The Innovation Value Chain, *Harvard Business Review*, 85(6): 121.

Hardy, C., Phillips, N., and Lawrence, T. (2003) Resources, Knowledge and Influence: The Organizational Effects of Interorganizational Collaboration, *Journal of Management Studies*, 40(2): 321–47.

Hardy, C. and Thomas, R. (2014) Strategy, Discourse and Practice: The Intensification of Power, *Journal of Management Studies*, 51(2): 320–48.

Hargadon, A. (1998) Firms as Knowledge Brokers: Lessons in Pursuing Continuous Innovation, *California Management Review*, 40(3): 209–27.

Hargadon, A. B. (2002) Knowledge Brokering: A Network Perspective on Learning and Innovation, *Research in Organizational Behavior*, 21: 41–85.

Hargadon, A. B. and Bechky, B. A. (2006) When Collections of Creatives become Creative Collectives: A Field Study of Problem Solving at Work, *Organization Science*, 17(4): 484–500.

Hargadon, A. B. and Douglas, Y. (2001) When Innovations Meet Institutions: Edison and the Design of the Electric Light. *Administrative Science Quarterly*, 46(3): 476–501.

Hargadon, A. B. and Sutton, R. I. (1997) Technology Brokering and Innovation in a Product Development Firm, *Administrative Science Quarterly*, 42(4): 716–49.

Harrigan, K. R. (1986) Matching Vertical Integration Strategies to Competitive Conditions, *Strategic Management Journal*, 7(6): 535–55.

Haunschild, P. R. and Miner, A. S. (1997) Modes of Interorganizational Imitation: The Effects of Outcome Salience and Uncertainty, *Administrative Science Quarterly*, 42: 472–500.

Haveman, H. A. (1994) *The Ecological Dynamics of Organizational Change: Density and Mass Dependence in Rates of Entry into New Markets*, New York: Oxford University Press.

Hayek, F. A. (1945) The Use of Knowledge in Society, *American Economic Review*, 35(4): 519–30.

Hayek, F. A. (1978) *New Studies in Philosophy, Politics, Economics and the History of Ideas*, Chicago: University of Chicago Press.

He, D. and Nickerson, J. A. (2006) Why do Firms Make and Buy? Efficiency, Appropriability and Competition in the Trucking Industry, *Strategic Organization*, 4(1): 43.

Hedlund, G. (1994) A Model of Knowledge Management and the N-form Corporation, *Strategic Management Journal*, 14 (Special Issue): 73–90.

Helfat, C. E., Finkelstein, S., Mitchell, W., Peteraf, M. A., Singh, H., Teece, D., and Winter, S. G. (2007) *Dynamic Capability: Understanding Strategic Change in Organizations*, Oxford: Blackwell.

Helfat, C. E. and Peteraf, M. A. (2003) The Dynamic Resource-Based View: Capability Lifecycles, *Strategic Management Journal*, 24: 997–1010.

Hellgren, B. and Melin, L. (1992) Business Systems, Industrial Wisdom and Corporate Strategies, in R. Whitley (ed.) *European Business Systems*, London: Sage.

Henderson, K. (1991) Flexible Sketches and Inflexible Data Bases: Visual Communication, Conscription Devices, and Boundary Objects in Design Engineering, *Science, Technology & Human Values*, 14(4): 448–73.

Henderson, R. (1994) The Evolution of Integrative Capability: Innovation in Cardiovascular Drug Discovery, *Industrial and Corporate Change*, 3(3): 607–30.

Henderson, R. and Clark, K. B. (1990) Architectural Innovations: The Reconfiguration of Existing Products and the Failure of Established Firms, *Administrative Science Quarterly*, 35(1): 9–30.

Henderson, R. and Cockburn, I. (1994) Measuring Competence? Exploring Firm Effects in Pharmaceutical Research, *Strategic Management Journal*, 15(1): 63–84.

Henderson, R. and Cockburn, I. (1996) Scale, Scope, and Spillovers: The Determinants of Research Productivity in Drug Discovery, *RAND Journal of Economics*, 27(1): 32–59.

Hernes, T. (2003) Enabling and Constraining Properties of Organizational Boundaries, in N. Paulsen and T. Hernes (eds.), *Managing Boundaries in Organizations: Multiple Perspectives*, New York: Palgrave Macmillan.

Hernes, T. Simpson, B., and Söderlund, J. (2013) Managing and Temporality, *Scandinavian Journal of Management*, 29(1): 1–6.

Hess, A. M. and Rothaermel, F. T. (2011) When are Assets Complementary? Star Scientists, Strategic Alliances, and Innovation in the Pharmaceutical Industry, *Strategic Management Journal*, 32(8): 895–909.

Hicks, D. (1995) Published Papers, Tacit Competencies and Corporate Management of the Public/Private Character of Knowledge, *Industrial and Corporate Change*, 4(2): 401–24.

Hillebrand, B. and Biemans, W. G. (2004) Links between Internal and External Cooperation in Product Development: An Exploratory Study, *Journal of Product Innovation Management*, 21: 110–22.

Hirsch, P. M. (1972) Processing Fads and Fashions: An Organization-Set Analysis of Cultural Industry Systems, *American Journal of Sociology*, 77(4): 639–59.

Hirschhorn, L. and Gilmore, T. (1992) The New Boundaries of the 'Boundaryless' Company, *Harvard Business Review*, 70(3): 104–15.

Hobday, M. (1995) *Innovation in East Asia: The Challenge to Japan*, Aldershot: Edward Elgar.

Hobday, M. (2000) The Project-Based Organisation: An Ideal Form for Managing Complex Products and Systems? *Research Policy*, 29(7): 871–93.

Hobday, M., Davies, A., and Prencipe, A. (2005) Systems Integration: A Core Competence of the Modern Corporation, *Industrial and Corporate Change*, 14(6): 1109–43.

Hobday, M., Rush, H., and Bessant, J. (2002) *Firm-Level Innovation in the Korean Economy*, Report to the World Bank, SPRU, University of Sussex.

Holcomb, T. R. and Hitt, M. A. (2007) Toward a Model of Strategic Outsourcing, *Journal of Operations Management*, 25: 464–81.

Hollingshead, A. B. (1998) Communication, Learning, and Retrieval in Transactive Memory Systems, *Journal of Experimental Social Psychology*, 34: 423–42.

Holweg, M., Reichhart, A., and Hong, E. (2011) On Risk and Cost in Global Sourcing, *International Journal of Production Economics*, 131(1): 333–41.

Holzner, B. (1968) *Reality Construction in Society*, Cambridge: Schenkman Publishing.

Holzner, B. and Marx, J. H. (1979) *Knowledge Application: The Knowledge System in Society*, Boston, MA: Allyn and Bacon.

Hoopes D. G. and Postrel S. (1999) Shared Knowledge, 'Glitches,' and Product Development Performance, *Strategic Management Journal*, 20(9): 837–65.

Horng, C. and Chen, W. (2008) From Contract Manufacturing to Own Brand Management: The Role of Learning and Cultural Heritage Identity, *Management and Organization Review*, 4(1): 109–33.

Howells, J. (2006) Intermediation and the Role of Intermediaries in Innovation, *Research Policy*, 35(5): 715–28.

Hsiao, R. L., Tsai, D. H., and Lee, C. F. (2012) Collaborative Knowing: The Adaptive Nature of Cross-Boundary Spanning, *Journal of Management Studies*, 49(3): 463–91.

Hsu, D. H. and Lim, K. (2014) Knowledge Brokering and Organizational Innovation: Founder Imprinting Effects, *Organization Science*, 25(4): 1134–53.

Huang, F. and Rice, J. (2013) Does Open Innovation Work Better in Regional Clusters? *Australasian Journal of Regional Studies*, 19(1): 85–120.

Huber, G. P. (1991) Organizational Learning: The Contributing Processes and the Literatures, *Organization Science*, 2(1): 88–115.

Hughes, T. P. (1983) *Networks of Power: Electrification in Western Society 1880–1930*, Baltimore, MD: The Johns Hopkins University Press.

Huizingh, E. K. R. E. (2011) Open Innovation: State of the Art and Future Perspectives, *Technovation*, 31: 2–9.

Humphrey, J. and Schmitz, H. (2001) Governance in Global Value Chains, *IDS Bulletin*, 32, 3: 19–29.

Huvila, I. (2011) The Politics of Boundary Objects: Hegemonic Interventions and the Making of a Document, *Journal of the American Society for Information Science and Technology*, 62(12): 2528–39.

Hwang, E. W, Singh, P. V., and Argote, L. (2015) Knowledge Sharing in Online Communities: Learning to Cross Geographic and Hierarchical Boundaries, *Organization Science*, 26(6): 1593–611.

Iansiti, M. (1993) Real-World R&D: Jumping the Product Generation Gap, *Harvard Business Review*, 71(3): 138–47.

Iansiti, M. (1995) Technology Integration: Managing Technological Evolution in a Complex Environment, *Research Policy*, 24(4): 521–42.

Iansiti, M. and Clark, K. B. (1994) Integration and Dynamic Capability: Evidence from Product Development in Automobiles and Mainframe Computers, *Industrial and Corporate Change*, 3(3): 557–605.

Ilman, A. (2009) *Enabling Innovative Companies in Emerging Economies: Insights from the Turkish Innovation System and Turkish Consumer Electronics Companies*, University of St Gallen, doctoral dissertation.

Jackson, P. and Klobas, J. (2008) Transactive Memory Systems in Organizations: Implications for Knowledge Directories, *Decision Support Systems*, 44(2): 409–24.

Jacobides, M. and Winter, S. G. (2005) The Co-Evolution of Capability and Transaction Costs: Explaining the Institutional Structure of Production. *Strategic Management Journal*, 26(5): 395–413.

Jacobides, M. G. (2005) Industry Change through Vertical Disintegration: How and Why Markets Emerged in Mortgage Banking, *Academy of Management Journal*, 48(3): 465–98.

Jakubik, M. (2011) Becoming to Know. Shifting the Knowledge Creation Paradigm, *Journal of Knowledge Management*, 15(3): 374–402.

Jensen, P. D. Ø. (2012) A Passage to India: A Dual Case Study of Activities, Processes and Resources in Offshore Outsourcing of Advanced Services, *Journal of World Business*, 47(2): 311–26.

Jensen, R. and Szulanski, G. (2004) Stickiness and the Adaptation of Organizational Practices in Cross-Border Knowledge Transfers, *Journal of International Business Studies*, 35(6): 508–23.

Jensen, R. J. and Szulanski, G. (2007) Template Use and the Effectiveness of Knowledge Transfer, *Management Science*, 53: 1716–30.

Johansson, M., Axelson, M., Enberg, C., and Tell, F. (2011) Knowledge Integration in Inter-Firm R&D Collaboration: How Do Firms Manage Problems of Coordination and Cooperation?, in C. Berggren, A. Bergek, L. Bengtsson, M. Hobday, and J. Söderlund (eds.), *Knowledge Integration and Innovation: Critical Challenges Facing International Technology-based Firms*, Oxford: Oxford University Press.

Joskow, P. (1988) Asset Specificity and the Structure of Vertical Relationships: Empirical Evidence, *Journal of Law Economics and Organization*, 4(1): 95–117.

Kanawattanachai, P. and Yoo, Y. (2007) The Impact of Knowledge Coordination on Virtual Team Performance over Time, *MIS Quarterly*, 31(4): 783–808.

Kaplan, S. (2008) Framing Contests: Strategy Making Under Uncertainty, *Organization Science*, 19: 729–52.

Kapletia, D. and Probert, D. (2010) Migrating from Products to Solutions: An Exploration of System Support in the UK Defense Industry, *Industrial Marketing Management*, 39 (4): 582–92.

Kapoor, R. and Adner, R. (2012) What Firms Make vs. What They Know: How Firms' Production and Knowledge Boundaries Affect Competitive Advantage in the Face of Technological Change, *Organization Science*, 23(5): 1227–48.

Karabag, S. F., Tuncay-Celikel, A., and Berggren, C. (2011) The Limits of R&D Internationalization and the Importance of Local Initiatives: Turkey as a Critical Case, *World Development*, 39(8): 1347–57.

Katkalo, V. S., Pitelis, C., and Teece, D. J. (2010) Introduction: On the Nature and Scope of Dynamic Capabilities, *Industrial and Corporate Change*, 19(4): 1175–86.

Katz, R. (1982) The Effects of Group Longevity on Project Communication and Performance, *Administrative Science Quarterly*, 27(1): 81–104.

Kauffman, S. A. (1993) *The Origins of Order: Self-Organization and Selection in Evolution*, New York: Oxford University Press.

Kearney, C. (2012) Emerging Markets Research: Trends, Issues and Future Directions, *Emerging Markets Review*, 13(2): 159–83.

Kellogg, K., Orlikowski, W., and Yates, J. (2006) Life in the Trading Zone: Structuring Coordination across Boundaries in Postbureaucratic Organizations, *Organization Science*, 17(1): 22–44.

Keshet, Y., Ben-Arye, E., and Schiff, E. (2013) The Use of Boundary Objects to Enhance Interprofessional Collaboration: Integrating Complementary Medicine in a Hospital Setting, *Sociology of Health & Illness*, 35(5): 666–81.

Khanna, T., Gulati, R., and Nohria, N. (1998) The Dynamics of Learning Alliances: Competition, Cooperation, and Relative Scope, *Strategic Management Journal*, 19 (3): 193–210.

Kim, L. (1998) Crisis Construction and Organizational Learning: Capability Building in Catching-Up at Hyundai Motor, *Organization Science*, 9: 506–21.

Kimble, C., Grenier, C., and Goglio-Primard, K. (2010) Innovation and Knowledge Sharing across Professional Boundaries: Political Interplay between Boundary Objects and Brokers, *International Journal of Information Management*, 30(5): 437–44.

Knoben, J. and Oerlemans, L. A. G. (2006) Proximity and Inter-Organisational Collaboration: A Literature Review, *International Journal of Management Reviews*, 8(2): 71–89.

Knott, A. M. (2003) The Organizational Routines Factor Market Paradox, *Strategic Management Journal*, 24: 929–43.

Koç Holding (2011) *Annual Report of Koç Holding in 2011*, Istanbul: Koc Holding Yayinlari.

Koestler, A. (1964) *The Act of Creation*, London: Hutchinson.

Kogut, B. (2000) The Network as Knowledge: Generative Rules and the Emergence of Structure, *Strategic Management Journal*, 21: 405–25.

Kogut, B. and Zander, U. (1992) Knowledge of the Firm, Combinative Capabilities, and the Replication of Technology, *Organization Science*, 3(3): 383–97.

Kogut, B. and Zander U. (1996) What Firms Do? Coordination, Identity, and Learning, *Organization Science*, 7(5): 502–18.

Kotabe, M., Mol, M., and Murray, J. Y. (2008) Outsourcing, Performance, and the Role of E-Commerce: A Dynamic Perspective, *Industrial Marketing Management*, 37(1): 37–45.

Koufteros, X., Vonderembse, M., and Jayaram, J. (2005) Internal and External Integration for Product Development—The Contingency Effects of Uncertainty, Equivocality and Platform Strategy, *Decision Sciences*, 36(1): 97–133.

Koufteros, X. A., Rawski, G. E., and Rupak, R. (2010) Organizational Integration for Product Development: The Effects on Glitches, On-Time Execution of Engineering Change Orders, and Market Success, *Decision Sciences*, 41(1): 49–80.

Kozlowski, S. W. J. and Bell, B. S. (2003) Work Groups and Teams in Organizations, in W. C. Borman, D. R. Ilgen, and R. J. Klimoski (eds.), *Handbook of Psychology: Industrial and Organizational Psychology*, London: Wiley.

Kraatz, M. S. and Block, E. S. (2008) Organizational Implications of Institutional Pluralism, in R. Greenwood, C. Oliver, K. Sahlin, and R. Suddaby (eds.), *Handbook of Organizational Institutionalism*, Los Angeles, CA: Sage, 243–75.

Kreiner, K. and Schultz, M. (1993) Informal Collaboration in R & D. The Formation of Networks across Organizations, *Organization Studies*, 14(2): 189–209.

Kücükerman, Ö. (2008) Turkish Automotive Industry and 40th Year of Tofas (1968–2008), Istanbul: Tofas Publication.

Kucuksuleymanoglu, E. (2014) *The Collaboration between Tofas and Universities* (in Turkish: Tofaş Ar-ge Üniversite Sanayi İşbirlikleri), paper presented at the 10 RLC Gunler: Yildiz Technical University, Istanbul, 25–7 February 2014.

Lachmann, L. (1977) *Expectations, and the Market Process: Essays on the Theory of the Market Economy*, Kansas City, MO: Sheed Andrews and McMeel.

Lainer-Vos, D. (2013) Boundary Objects, Zones of Indeterminacy, and the Formation of Irish and Jewish Transnational Socio-Financial Networks, *Organization Studies*, 34(4): 515–32.

Lakemond, N., Bengtsson, L., Laursen, K., and Tell, F. (2016) Match & Manage: The Use of Knowledge Matching and Project Management to Integrate Knowledge in Collaborative Inbound Open Innovation, *Industrial and Corporate Change*, 25(2), in press.

Lakemond, N. and Berggren, C. (2006) Co-Locating NPD? The Need for Combining Project Focus and Organizational Integration, *Technovation*, 26:807–19.

Lakemond, N., Berggren, C., and van Weele, A. (2006) Coordinating Supplier Involvement in Product Development Projects: A Differentiated Coordination Typology, *R&D Management*, 36(1): 55–66.

Lall, S. (1992) Technological Capabilities and Industrialization, *World Development*, 20(2): 165–86.

Lamont, M. and Molnar, V. (2002) The Study of Boundaries in the Social Sciences, *Annual Review of Sociology*, 28(1): 167–95.

Lane, P. J., Koka, B. R., and Pathak, S. (2006) The Reification of Absorptive Capacity: A Critical Review and Rejuvenation of the Construct, *Academy of Management Review*, 31(4): 833–63.

Lane, P. J. and Lubatkin, M. (1998) Relative Absorptive Capacity and Interorganizational Learning, *Strategic Management Journal*, 19(5): 461–77.

Laureiro-Martínez, D., Brusoni, S., Canessa, N., and Zollo, M. (2015) Understanding the Exploration-Exploitation Dilemma: An fMRI Study of Attention Control and Decision-Making Performance, *Strategic Management Journal*, 36(3): 319–38.

Laursen, K. (2012) Keep Searching and You'll Find: What do we Know about Variety Creation through Firms' Search Activities for Innovation?, *Industrial and Corporate Change*, 21(5): 1181–220.

Laursen, K., Masciarelli, F., and Prencipe, A. (2012) Regions Matter: How Localized Social Capital affect External Knowledge Acquisition and Innovation, *Organization Science*, 23(1): 177–93.

Laursen, K., Reichstein, T., and Salter, A. (2011) Exploring the Effect of Geographical Proximity and University Quality on University–Industry Collaboration in the United Kingdom, *Regional Studies*, 45(4): 507–23.

Laursen, K. and Salter, A. (2006) Open for Innovation: The Role of Openness in Explaining Innovation Performance among UK Manufacturing Firms, *Strategic Management Journal*, 27 (2): 131–50.

Laursen, K. and Salter, A. (2014) The Paradox of Openness: Appropriability, External Search and Collaboration, *Research Policy*, 43(5): 867–78.

Lave, J. and Wenger, E. (1991) *Situated Learning: Legitimate peripheral participation*, Cambridge: Cambridge University Press.

Lavie, D. (2007) Alliance Portfolios and Firm Performance: A Study of Value Creation and Appropriation in the US Software Industry, *Strategic Management Journal*, 28(12): 1187–212.

Lavie, D. and Drori, I. (2012) Collaborating for Knowledge Creation and Application: The Case of Nanotechnology Research Programs, *Organization Science*, 23(3): 704–24.

Lavie, D., Kang, J., and Rosenkopf, L. (2010) Balance Within and Across Domains: The Performance Implications of Exploration and Exploitation in Alliances, *Organization Science*, 22(6): 1517–38.

Lawrence, P. R. and Lorsch, J. W. (1967) *Organization and Environment: Managing Differentiation and Integration*, Boston, MA: Division of Research Graduate School of Business Administration, Harvard University.

Lawson, B., Petersen, K. J., Cousins, P. D., and Handfield, R. B. (2009) Knowledge Sharing in Interorganizational Product Development Teams: The Effect of Formal and Informal Socialization Mechanisms, *Journal of Product Innovation Management*, 26: 156–72.

Lazzarotti, V., Manzini, R., and Pellegrini, L. (2011) Firm-Specific Factors and the Openness Degree: A Survey of Italian Firms, *European Journal of Innovation Management*, 14(4): 412–34.

Lechner, C. and Dowling, M. (2003) Firm Networks: External Relationships as Sources for the Growth and Competitiveness of Entrepreneurial Firms, *Entrepreneurship & Regional Development: An International Journal*, 15(1): 1–26.

Lee, K. and Lim, C. (2001) Technological Regimes, Catching-Up and Leapfrogging: Findings from the Korean Industries, *Research Policy*, 30(3): 459–83.

Leiponen, A. and Helfat, C. E. (2011) Location, Decentralization, and Knowledge Sources for Innovation, *Organization Science*, 22(3): 641–58.

Leonard, D. and Sensiper, S. (1998) The Role of Tacit Knowledge in Group Innovation, *California Management Review*, 40(3): 112–32.

Leonard-Barton, D. (1992) Core Capabilities and Core Rigidities: A Paradox in Managing New Product Development, *Strategic Management Journal*, 13: 111–25.

Leonard-Barton, D. (1995) *Wellsprings of Knowledge: Building and Sustaining the Sources of Innovation*, Boston; MA: Harvard Business School Press.

Leonard-Barton, D., Bowen, H. K., Clark, K. B., Holloway, C. A., and Wheelwright, S. C.. (1994) How to Integrate Work and Deepen Expertise, *Harvard Business Review*, 72(5): 121–30.

Levi-Strauss, C. (1962) *The Savage Mind*, Chicago: University of Chicago Press.

Levina, N. and Arriaga, M. (2014) Distinction and Status Production on User-Generated Content Platforms: Using Bourdieu's Theory of Cultural Production to Understand Social Dynamics in Online Fields, *Information Systems Research*, 25(3): 468–88.

Levina, N. and Orlikowski, W. J. (2009) Understanding Shifting Power Relations Within and Across Organizations: A Critical Genre Analysis, *Academy of Management Journal*, 52(4): 672–703.

Levina, N. and Vaast, E. (2005) The Emergence of Boundary Spanning Competence in Practice: Implications for Implementation and Use of Information Systems, *MIS Quarterly*, 29(2): 335–63.

Levina, N. and Vaast, E. (2008) Innovating or Doing as Told? Status Differences and Overlapping Boundaries in Offshore Collaboration, *MIS Quarterly*, 32(2): 307–32.

Levina, N. and Vaast, E. (2014) A Field-of-Practice View of Boundary-Spanning in and across Organizations, in J. Langan-Fox and C. L. Cooper (eds.), *Boundary Spanning in Organizations: Network, Influence, and Conflict*, New York: Routledge.

Levinthal, D. A. (1997) Adaptation on Rugged Landscapes, *Management Science*, 43(7): 934–50.

Levinthal, D. A. and March, J. G. (1981) A Model of Adaptive Organizational Search, *Journal of Economic Behavior & Organization*, 2: 307–33.

Levinthal, D. A. and March, J. G. (1993) The Myopia of Learning, *Strategic Management Journal*, 14 (Winter Special Issue): 95–112.

Levitt, B. and March, J. G. (1988) Organizational Learning, *Annual Review of Sociology*, 14: 319–40.

Lewin, A., Massini, S., and Peeters, C. (2011) Microfoundations of Internal and External Absorptive Capacity Routines, *Organization Science*, 22(1): 81–98.

Lewis, K. (2003) Measuring Transactive Memory Systems in the Field: Scale Development and Validation, *Journal of Applied Psychology*, 88(4): 587–604.

Lewis, K. (2004) Knowledge and Performance in Knowledge-Worker Teams: A Longitudinal Study of Transactive Memory Systems, *Management Science*, 50(11): 1519–33.

Lewis, K., Belliveau, M., Herndon, B., and Keller, J. (2007) Group Cognition, Membership Change, and Performance: Investigating the Benefits and Detriments of Collective Knowledge, *Organizational Behavior and Human Decision Processes*, 103 (2): 159–78.

Lewis, K., Lange, D., and Gillis, L. (2005) Transactive Memory Systems, Learning, and Learning Transfer, *Organization Science*, 16(6): 581–98.

Liang, D. W., Moreland, R., and Argote, L. (1995) Group versus Individual Training and Group Performance: The Mediating Role of Transactive Memory, *Personality and Social Psychology Bulletin*, 21(4): 384–93.

Liebeskind, J. P., Oliver, A. L., Zucker, L., and Brewer, M. (1996) Social Networks, Learning, and Flexibility: Sourcing Scientific Knowledge in New Biotechnology Firms, *Organization Science*, 7(4): 428–43.

Lim, C., Han, S., and Ito, H. (2013) Capability Building through Innovation for Unserved Lower End Mega Markets, *Technovation*, 33(12): 391–404.

Lim, K. (2004) The Relationship between Research and Innovation in the Semiconductor and Pharmaceutical Industries (1981–1997), *Research Policy*, 33(2): 287–321.

Lim, K. (2009) The Many Faces of Absorptive Capacity: Spillovers of Copper Interconnect Technology for Semiconductor Chips, *Industrial and Corporate Change*, 18 (6): 1249–84.

Lin, B-W. and Chen, C-J. (2006) Fostering Product Innovation in Industry Networks: The Mediating Role of Knowledge Integration, *International Journal of Human Resource Management*, 17(1): 155–73.

Lind, F., Holmen, E., and Pedersen, A-C. (2012) Moving Resources across Permeable Project Boundaries in Open Network Contexts. *Journal of Business Research*, 65(2): 177–85.

Lindkvist, L. (2004) Governing Project-Based firms, Promoting Market-Like Process in Hierarchies, *Journal of Management and Governance*, 8(1): 3–25.

Lindkvist, L. (2005) Knowledge Communities and Knowledge Collectivities: A Typology of Knowledge Work in Groups, *Journal of Management Studies*, 42(6): 1189–210.

Lindkvist, L. (2008) Epistemic Communities, in S. R. Clegg and J. R. Bailey (eds.), *International Encyclopedia of Organization Studies*, Thousand Oaks, CA: Sage.

Lindkvist, L. (2012) Knowledge Integration in Projects: A Contingency Framework, in P. Morris, J. Pinto, and J. Söderlund (eds.), *The Oxford Handbook of Project Management*, Oxford: Oxford University Press.

Lindkvist, L., Bengtsson, M., and Wahlstedt, L. (2011) Knowledge Integration and Creation in Projects: Towards a Progressive Epistemology, in C. Berggren, A. Bergek, L. Bengtsson, M. Hobday, and J. Söderlund (eds.), *Knowledge Integration and Innovation: Critical Challenges Facing International Technology-Based Firms*, Oxford: Oxford University Press.

Lindkvist, L., Söderlund, J., and Tell, F. (1998) Managing Product Development Projects—On the Significance of Fountains and Deadlines, *Organization Studies*, 19(6): 931–51.

Lissoni, F. (2010) Academic Inventors as Brokers, *Research Policy*, 39(7): 843–57.

Liu, J., Chaminade, C., and Asheim, B. (2013) The Geography and Structure of Global Innovation Networks: A Knowledge Base Perspective, *European Planning Studies*, 21: 1–18.

Lopez-Vega, H., Tell, F., and Vanhaverbeke, W. (2016) Where and How to Search? Search Paths in Open Innovation, *Research Policy*, 45(1): 125–36.

Luo, Y., Sun, J., and Wang, S. L. (2011) Emerging Economy Copycats: Capability, Environment, and Strategy, *Academy of Management Perspectives*, 25(2): 37–56.

McGrath, R. G. (1997) A Real Options Logic for Initiating Technology Positioning Investments, *Academy of Management Review*, 22(4): 974–96.

Macher, J. T. (2006) Technological Development and the Boundaries of the Firm: A Knowledge-Based Examination in Semiconductor Manufacturing, *Management Science*, 52(6): 826–43.

McIvor, R. (2008) What is the Right Outsourcing Strategy for your Process? *European Management Journal*, 26: 24–34.

McIvor, R. (2009) How the Transaction Cost and Resource-Based Theories of the Firm inform Outsourcing Evaluation, *Journal of Operations Management*, 27(1): 45–63.

McKinley, W., Latham, S., and Braun, M. (2014) Organizational Decline and Innovation: Turnarounds and Downward Spirals, *Academy of Management Review*, 39(1): 88–110.

McKinley, W. and Scherer, A. G. (2000) Some Unanticipated Consequences of Organizational Restructuring, *Academy of Management Review*, 25(4): 735–52.

Mahmood, I. P. and Zheng, W. (2009) Whether and How: Effects of International Joint Ventures on Local Innovation in an Emerging Economy, *Research Policy*, 38 (9): 1489–503.

Majchrzak, A., More, P. H. B., and Faraj, S. (2012) Transcending Knowledge Differences in Cross-Functional Teams, *Organization Science*, 23(4): 951–70.

Malerba, F. and Nelson, R. (2011) Learning and Catching Up in Different Sectoral Systems: Evidence from Six Industries, *Industrial and Corporate Change*, 6: 1645–76.

Mamulattan Markaya (2001) *From Production to Brand: Arçelik Company History 1955–2000* (in Turkish: Mamulattan Markaya: Arçelik Kurum Tarihi 1955–2000), Istanbul: Arçelik Publication.

March, J. G. (1988) *Decisions and Organizations*, Oxford: Blackwell.

March, J. G. (1991) Exploration and Exploitation in Organizational Learning, *Organization Science*, 2(1): 71–87.

March J. G. (1995) *Learning Processes are Powerful Tools of Organizational Adaptation*, Helsinki: Tvön Tuuli Aikakauskirja.

March, J. G. and Olsen, J. P. (1975) The Uncertainty of the Past: Organizational Learning Under Ambiguity, *European Journal of Political Research*, 3: 147–71.

March, J. G., Schulz, M., and Zhou, X. (2000) *The Dynamics of Rules: Change in Written Organizational Codes*, Stanford, CA: Stanford University Press.

March, J. G. and Simon, H. A. (1958) *Organizations*, Oxford: Blackwell.

Markman, G. D., Siegel, D. S., and Wright, M. (2008) Research and Technology Commercialization, *Journal of Management Studies*, 45(8): 1410–23.

Maskell, P., Pedersen, T., Petersen, B., and Dick-Nielsen, J. (2007) Learning Paths to Offshore Outsourcing: From Cost Reduction to Knowledge Seeking, *Industry and Innovation*, 14(3): 239–57.

Mathews, J. (2006) Catch-Up Strategies and the Latecomer Effect in Industrial Development, *New Political Economy*, 11(3): 313–35.

Mathews, J. A. (2002) Competitive Advantages of the Latecomer Firm: A Resource-Based Account of Industrial Catch-Up Strategies, *Asia-Pacific Journal of Management*, 19: 467–88.

Mead, G. H. (1934) *Mind, Self, and Society*, ed. C. W. Morris, Chicago: University of Chicago Press

Melero, E. and Palomeras, N. (2015) The Renaissance Man is not Dead! The Role of Generalists in Teams of Inventors, *Research Policy*, 44(1): 154–67.

Mell, J. N., Van Knippenberg, D., and Van Ginkel, W. P. (2014) The Catalyst Effect: The Impact of Transactive Memory System Structure on Team Performance, *Academy of Management Journal*, 57(4): 1154–73.

Merton, R. K. (1973) *The Sociology of Science. Theoretical and Empirical Investigations*, Chicago and London: University of Chicago Press.

Meyer J. and Rowan, B. (1977) Institutionalized Organizations: Formal Structure as Myth and Ceremony, *American Journal of Sociology*, 83(2): 340–63.

Meyerson, D., Weick, K. E., and Kramer, R. M. (1996) Swift Trust and Temporary Groups, in R. M. Kramer and T. R. Tyler (eds.), *Trust in Organizations*, Thousand Oaks, CA: Sage.

Miles, M. B. and Huberman, M. A. (1994) *Qualitative Data Analysis: An Expanded Sourcebook*, Thousand Oaks, CA: Sage.

Milgrom, P. and Roberts, J. (1992) *Economics, Organization, and Management*, Englewood Cliffs, NJ: Prentice Hall.

Miller, C. (2001) Hybrid Management: Boundary Organizations, Science Policy, and Environmental Governance in the Climate Regime, *Science, Technology & Human Values*, 26(4): 478–500.

Miller, J. and Roth, A. (1988) Manufacturing Strategies, *Operations Management Review*, 6(1): 285–304.

Milliken, F. J. (1987) Three Types of Perceived Uncertainty about the Environment: State, Effect, and Response Uncertainty, *Academy of Management Review*, 12(1): 133–43.

Miozzo, M. and Grimshaw, D. (2011) Capabilities of Large Services Outsourcing Firms: The 'Outsourcing Plus Staff Transfer Model' in EDS and IBM, *Industrial and Corporate Change*, 20(3): 909–40.

Mitchell, V. L. (2006) Knowledge Integration and Information Technology Project Performance, *MIS Quarterly*, 30(4): 919–39.

Mohammed, S. and Nadkarni, S., (2011) Temporal Diversity and Team Performance: The Moderating Role of Temporal Leadership, *Academy of Management Journal*, 54 (3): 489–508.

Mol, M. J., van Tulder, R. J. M., and Beije, P. R. (2005) Antecedents and Performance Consequences of International Outsourcing, *International Business Review*, 14(5): 599–617.

Monteiro, L. F. (2015) Selective Attention and the Global Knowledge-Sourcing Process, *Journal of International Business Studies*, 46(5): 505–27.

Monteverde, K. (1995) Technical Dialog as an Incentive for Vertical Integration in the Semiconductor Industry, *Management Science*, 41(10): 1624–38.

Moreland, R. L. (1999) Transactive Memory: Learning who Knows What in Work Groups and Organizations, in L. Thompson, D. Messick, and J. Levine (eds.), *Shared*

Cognition in Organizations: The Management of Knowledge, Hillsdale, NJ: Lawrence Erlbaum.

Moreland, R. L. and Argote, L. (2003) Transactive Memory in Dynamic Organizations, in R. S. Peterson and E. A. Mannix (eds.), *Leading and Managing People in the Dynamic Organization*, Mahwah, NJ: Erlbaum.

Morgan, K. (2004) The Exaggerated Death of Geography: Learning, Proximity and Territorial Innovation Systems, *Journal of Economic Geography*, 4: 3–21.

Muduli, A. (2013) Workforce Agility: A Review of Literature, *IUP Journal of Management Research*, 12(3): 55–65.

Munos, B. (2009) Lessons from 60 Years of Pharmaceutical Innovation, *Nature Reviews Drug Discovery*, 8(12): 959–68.

Murray, F. (2002) Innovation as Co-Evolution of Scientific and Technological Networks: Exploring Tissue Engineering, *Research Policy*, 31(8–9): 1389–403.

Murtic, A. (2016) *Soaking Up Knowledge: A Multi-Level Analysis and Conceptualization of Absorptive Capacity*, Stockholm School of Economics, doctoral dissertation.

Nadkarni, S. and Chen, J. (2014) Bridging Yesterday, Today, and Tomorrow: CEO Temporal Focus, Environmental Dynamism, and Rate of New Product Introductions, *Academy of Management Journal*, 57(6): 1810–33.

Narula, R. and Martinez-Noya, A. (2014) *International R&D Alliances by Firms: Origins and Development*, Discussion Paper Number JHD-2014-06, John H Dunning Centre for International Business, Henley Business School, University of Reading.

Nelson R. R. (1993) *National Innovation Systems: A Comparative Analysis*, New York: Oxford University Press.

Nelson, R. R. and Winter, S. G. (1982) *An Evolutionary Theory of Economic Change*. Cambridge, MA: The Belknap Press.

Nerur, S., Mahapatra, R., and Mangalaraj, G. (2005) Challenges of Migrating to Agile Methodologies, *Communications of the ACM*, 48(5): 73–8.

Nesta, L. and Saviotti, P-P. (2006) Firm Knowledge and Market Value in Biotechnology, *Industrial and Corporate Change*, 15(4): 625–52.

Neuhaus, J. M., Kalbfleisch, J. D., and Hauk, W. W. (1994) A Comparison of Cluster-Specific and Population-Averaged Approaches for Analyzing Correlated Binary Data, *International Statistical Review*, 59: 25–35.

Nevo, D. and Wand, Y. (2005) Organizational Memory Information Systems: A Transactive Memory Approach, *Decision Support Systems*, 39(4): 549–62.

Newell, S., Robertson, M., Scarbrough, H., and Swan, J. (2009) *Managing Knowledge Work and Innovation* (2nd ed.), Basingstoke: Palgrave.

Nicholas, T. and Shimizu, H. (2013) Intermediary Functions and the Market for Innovation in Meiji and Taishō Japan, *Business History Review*, 87(1): 121–49.

Nickerson, J. A. and Zenger, T. R. (2004) A Knowledge-Based Theory of the Firm—The Problem-Solving Perspective, *Organization Science*, 15(6): 617–32.

Nicolini, D. (2009) Zooming In and Zooming Out: A Package of Method and Theory to Study Work Practices in S. Ybema, D. Yanow, H. Wels, and F. Kamsteeg (eds.), *Organizational Ethnography: Studying the Complexities of Everyday Life*, London: Sage.

Nicolini, D., Mengis, J., and Swan, J. (2012) Understanding the Role of Objects in Cross-Disciplinary Collaboration, *Organization Science*, 23(3): 612–29.

Nightingale, P. (2003) If Nelson and Winter are Only Half Right about Tacit Knowledge, Which Half? A Searlean Critique of Codification, *Industrial and Corporate Change*, 12 (2): 149–83.

Nisbet, R.A. (1969) *Social Change and History: Aspects of the Western Theory of Development*, London: Oxford University Press.

Nohria, N. and Ghoshal, S. (1997) *The Differentiated Network: Organizing Multinational Corporations for Value Creation*, San Francisco, CA: Jossey-Bass.

Nonaka, I. (1991) The Knowledge-Creating Company, *Harvard Business Review*, November/December: 96–104.

Nonaka, I. (1994) A Dynamic Theory of Organizational Knowledge Creation, *Organization Science*, 5(1): 14–37.

Nonaka, I. and Takeuchi, H. (1995) *The Knowledge-Creating Company—How Japanese Companies Create the Dynamics of Innovation*, New York: Oxford University Press.

Nonaka, I. and Toyama, R. (2005) The Theory of the Knowledge-Creating Firm: Subjectivity, Objectivity and Synthesis, *Industrial and Corporate Change*, 14(3): 419–36.

Nonaka, I., Toyama, R., and Konno, N. (2000) SECI, Ba and Leadership: A Unified Model of Dynamic Knowledge Creation, *Long Range Planning*, 33(1): 5–34.

Nonaka, I. and von Krogh, G. (2009) Tacit Knowledge and Knowledge Conversion: Controversy and Advancement in Organizational Knowledge Creation Theory, *Organization Science*, 20(3): 635–52.

Nooteboom, B. (1997) Path Dependence of Knowledge: Implications for the Theory of the Firm, in L. Magnusson and J. Ottosson (eds.), *Evolutionary Economics and Path Dependence*, Cheltenham: Edward Elgar.

North, D. C. (1990) *Institutions, Institutional Change and Economic Performance*, Cambridge: Cambridge University Press.

Nowotny, H., Scott, P., and Gibbons, M. (2001) *Re-Thinking Science: Knowledge and the Public in an Age of Uncertainty*, Cambridge: Polity Press.

O'Leary, M. B., Mortensen, M., and Woolley, A. W. (2011) Multiple Team Membership: A Theoretical Model of its Effects on Productivity and Learning for Individuals and Teams, *Academy of Management Review*, 36(3): 461–78.

O'Mahony, S. and Bechky, B. A. (2008) Boundary Organizations: Enabling Collaboration among Unexpected Allies, *Administrative Science Quarterly*, 53(3): 422–59.

Okhuysen, G. and Bechky, B. (2009) Coordination in Organizations: An Integrative Perspective, *Academy of Management Annals*, 3(1): 463–502.

Okhuysen, G. A. and Eisenhardt, K. (2002) Integrating Knowledge in Groups: How Formal Interventions Enable Flexibility, *Organization Science*, 13(4): 370–86.

Oliva, R. and Kallenberg, R. (2003) Managing the Transition from Products to Services, *International Journal of Service Industry Management*, 14(2): 160–72.

Operti, E. and Carnabuci, G. (2014) Public Knowledge, Private Gain: The Effect of Spillover Networks on Firms' Innovative Performance, *Journal of Management*, 40(4): 1042–74.

Orlikowski, W. J. and Scott, S. V. (2013) What Happens When Evaluation Goes Online? Exploring Apparatuses of Valuation in the Travel Sector, *Organization Science*, 25(3): 868–91.

Orr, J. (1996) *Talking about Machines: An Ethnography of a Modern Job*, Ithaca, NY: Cornell University Press.

Østerlund, C. (2008) The Materiality of Communicative Practices, *Scandinavian Journal of Information Systems*, 20(1) 7–40.

Owen-Smith, J. and Powell, W. W. (2004) Knowledge Networks as Channels and Conduits: The Effects of Spillovers in the Boston Biotechnology Community, *Organization Science*, 15(1): 5–21.

Pache, A-C. and Santos, F. M. (2010) When Worlds Collide: The Internal Dynamics of Organizational Responses to Conflicting Institutional Logics, *Academy of Management Review*, 35(3): 455–76.

Paoli, M. and Prencipe, A. (2003) Memory of the Organization and Memories within the Organization, *Journal of Management and Governance*, 7: 145–62.

Park, S. H. and Ungson, G. R. (2001) Interfirm Rivalry and Managerial Complexity: A Conceptual Framework of Alliance Failure, *Organization Science*, 12(1): 37–53.

Parker, J. and Crona, B. (2012) On Being All Things to All People: Boundary Organizations and the Contemporary Research University, *Social Studies of Science*, 42(2): 262–89.

Parmigiani, A. (2007) Why do Firms both Make and Buy? An Investigation of Concurrent Sourcing, *Strategic Management Journal*, 28: 285–311.

Parmigiani, A. and Howard-Grenville, J. (2011) Routines Revisited: Exploring the Capabilities and Practice Perspectives, *Academy of Management Annals*, 5(1): 413–53.

Parmigiani, A. and Mitchell, W. (2009) Complementarity, Capabilities, and the Boundaries of the Firm: The Impact of Within-Firm and Interfirm Expertise on Concurrent Sourcing of Complementary Components, *Strategic Management Journal*, 30(10): 1065–91.

Parmigiani, A. and Rivera-Santos, M. (2011) Clearing a Path through the Forest: A Meta-Review of Interorganizational Relationships, *Journal of Management*, 37 (4): 1108–36.

Paruchuri, S. (2010) Intraorganizational Networks, Interorganizational Networks, and the Impact of Central Inventors: A Longitudinal Study of Pharmaceutical Firms, *Organization Science*, 21(1): 63–80.

Patel, P. and Pavitt, K. (1997) The Technological Competencies of the World's Largest Firm: Complex and Path-Dependent, but Not Much Variety. *Research Policy*, 26(2): 141–56.

Patel, P. C., Fernhaber, S. A., McDougall-Covin, P. P., and Van Der Have, R. P. (2014) Beating Competitors to International Markets: The Value of Geographically Balanced Networks for Innovation, *Strategic Management Journal*, 35(5): 691–711.

Patton, M. (1990) *Qualitative Evaluation and Research Methods* (2nd ed.), Newbury Park, CA: Sage.

Pauget, B. and Wald, A. (2013) Relational Competence in Complex Temporary Organizations: The Case of a French Hospital Construction Project Network, *International Journal of Project Management*, 31(2): 200–11.

Paul, S. M., Mytelka, D. S., Dunwiddie, C. T., Persinger, C. C., Munos, B. H., Lindborg, S. R., and Schacht, A. L. (2010) How to Improve R&D Productivity: The Pharmaceutical Industry's Grand Challenge, *Nature Reviews Drug Discovery*, 9(3): 203–14.

Pear, R., LaFranere, S., and Austen, A. (2013) From the Start, Signs of Trouble at Health Portal, *New York Times*, 10/12 <http://www.nytimes.com/2013/10/13/

us/politics/from-the-start-signs-of-trouble-at-health-portal.html?_r=0>. Accessed 19 December 2014.

Pearsall, M. and Ellis, A. (2006) The Effects of Critical Team Member Assertiveness on Team Performance and Satisfaction, *Journal of Management*, 32(4): 575–94.

Peltokorpi, V. (2014) Transactive Memory System Coordination Mechanisms in Organizations: An Exploratory Case Study, *Group and Organization Management*, 39(4): 444–71.

Perkmann, M. (2007) *Intellectual Arbitrage in Exchange Relationships across Institutional Domains*, Working paper, Wolfson School of Mechanical and Manufacturing Engineering, Loughborough University.

Perkmann, M. and Schildt, H. (2015) Open Data Partnerships between Firms and Universities: The Role of Boundary Organizations, *Research Policy* 44(5): 1133–43.

Perrow, C. (1970) *Organizational Analysis: A Sociological Review*, Belmont, CA: Wadsworth.

Petersen, K. J., Handfield, R. B., and Ragatz, G. L. (2003) A Model of Supplier Integration into New Product Development, *Journal of Product Innovation Management*, 20: 284–99.

Pfeffer, J. and Salancik, G. R. (1978) *The External Control of Organizations: A Resource Dependence Perspective*, New York: Harper and Row.

Pierson, P. (2000) Increasing Returns, Path Dependence, and the Study of Politics, *American Political Science Review*, 94(2): 251–67.

Pisano, G. P. (1991) The Governance of Innovation: Vertical Integration and Collaborative Arrangements in the Biotechnology Industry, *Research Policy*, 20(2): 237–49.

Pisano, G. P. and Teece, D. J. (2007) How to Capture Value from Innovation: Shaping Intellectual Property and Industry Architecture, *California Management Review*, 50 (1): 278.

Pitsis, T. S., Sankaran, S., Gudergan, S., and Clegg, S. R. (2014) Governing Projects under Complexity: Theory and Practice in Project Management, *International Journal of Project Management*, 32(8): 1285–90.

Plewa, C., Korff, N., Baaken, T., and Macpherson, G. (2013) University–Industry Linkage Evolution: An Empirical Investigation of Relational Success Factors, *R&D Management*, 43: 365–80.

Podmetina, D. and Smirnova, M. (2013) R&D Cooperation with External Partners and Implementing Open Innovation, *Journal of Innovation Management*, 1(2): 103–24.

Podolny, J. M. (1993) A Status-Based Model of Market Competition, *American Journal of Sociology*, 98(4): 828–72.

Podolny, J. M. (1994) Market Uncertainty and the Social Character of Economic Exchange, *Administrative Science Quarterly*, 39(3): 458–83.

Podolny, J. M. (2001) Networks as the Pipes and Prisms of the Market, *American Journal of Sociology*, 107(1): 33–60.

Podsakoff, P., MacKenzie, S., Lee, J-Y., and Posakoff, N. (2003) Common Method Biases in Behavioural Research: A Critical Review of the Literature and Recommended Remedies, *Journal of Applied Psychology*, 88(5): 879–903.

Polanyi, M. (1958/1998) *Personal Knowledge: Towards a Post-Critical Philosophy*, London: Routledge.

Polanyi, M. (1966) *The Tacit Dimension*, Gloucester, MA: Peter Smith.

Popper, K. R. (1963/1989) *Conjectures and Refutations—The Growth of Scientific Knowledge*, 5th ed., London: Routledge.

Popper, K. R. (1972) *Objective Knowledge: An Evolutionary Approach*, Oxford: Clarendon Press.

Popper, K. R. (1975) The Rationality of Scientific Revolutions, in R. Harré (ed.) *Problems of Scientific Revolutions*, Oxford: Clarendon Press.

Popper, K. R. (1994) *Knowledge and the Body-Mind Problem. In Defence of Interaction*, London: Routledge.

Porac, J. F., Thomas, H., and Baden-Fuller, C. (1999) Competitive Groups as Cognitive Communities: The Case of Scottish Knitwear Manufacturers, *Journal of Management Studies*, 26(4): 397–416.

Porter, M. E. (1990) *The Competitive Advantage of Nations*, New York: Free Press New York.

Postrel, S. (2002) Islands of Shared Knowledge: Specialization and Mutual Understanding in Problem-Solving Teams, *Organization Science*, 13(3): 303–20.

Postrel, S. (2009) Multitasking Teams With Variable Complementarity: Challenges for Capability Management, *Academy of Management Review*, 34(2): 273–96.

Powell, W. W., Koput, K., and Smith-Doerr, L. (1996) Interorganizational Collaboration and the Locus of Innovation: Networks of Learning in Biotechnology, *Administrative Science Quarterly*, 41(1): 116–45.

Praest Knudsen, M. and Bøtker Mortensen, T. (2011) Some Immediate – but Negative – Effects of Openness on Product Development Performance, *Technovation*, 31: 54–64.

Prahalad, C. K. and Hamel, G. (1990) The Core Competence of the Corporation, *Harvard Business Review*, 68(3): 79–91.

Prencipe, A. (1997) Technological Competencies and Product's Evolutionary Dynamics: A Case Study from the Aero-Engine Industry, *Research Policy*, 25(8): 1261–76.

Prencipe, A., Davies, A., and Hobday, M. (2003) *The Business of Systems Integration*, Oxford: Oxford University Press.

Prencipe, A. and Tell, F. (2001) Inter-Project Learning: Processes and Outcomes of Knowledge Codification in Project-Based Firms, *Research Policy*, 30(9): 1373–94.

Pugh, D., Hickson, D., Hinings, C., and Turner, C. (1968) Dimensions of Organizational Structure, *Administrative Science Quarterly*, 13(1): 65–105.

Puranam, P., Raveendran, M., and Knudsen, T. (2012) Organization Design: The Epistemic Interdependence Perspective, *Academy of Management Review*, 37(3): 419–40.

Quick, K. and Feldman, M. (2014) Boundaries as Junctures: Collaborative Boundary Work for Building Efficient Resilience, *Journal of Public Administration Research and Theory*, 31: 272–90.

Radjou, N., Prabhu, J., Ahuja, S., and Roberts, K. (2012) *Jugaad Innovation: Think Frugal, Be Flexible, Generate Breakthrough Growth*, New York: Wiley.

Rafols, I. and Meyer, M. (2010) Diversity and Network Coherence as Indicators of Interdisciplinarity: Case Studies in Bionanoscience, *Scientometrics*, 82(2): 262–87.

Ranson, S., Hinings, B., and Greenwood, R. (1980) The Structuring of Organizational Structures, *Administrative Science Quarterly*, 25(1): 1–17.

Rao, H. (1994) The Social Construction of Reputation: Certification Contests, Legitimation, and the Survival of Organizations in the American Automobile Industry: 1895-1912, *Strategic Management Journal*, 15: 29–44.

Rao, H. and Drazin, R. (2002) Overcoming Resource Constraints on Product Innovation by Recruiting Talent from Rivals: A Study of the Mutual Fund Industry, 1986–94, *Academy of Management Journal*, 45(3): 491–507.

Reagans, R., Argote, L., and Brooks, D. (2005) Individual Experience and Experience Working Together: Predicting Learning Rates from Knowing Who Knows What and Knowing How to Work Together, *Management Science*, 51(6): 869–81.

Reay, T. and Hinings, C. R. (2009) Managing the Rivalry of Competing Institutional Logics, *Organization Studies*, 30(6): 629–52.

Ren, Y. and Argote, L. (2011) Transactive Memory Systems: An Integrative Framework of Dimensions, Antecedents and Consequences, *Academy of Management Annals*, 5: 189–230.

Ren Y., Carley K. M., and Argote L. (2006) The Contingent Effects of Transactive Memory: When is it More Beneficial to Know what Others Know?, *Management Science*, 52(5): 671–82.

Rittiner, F. and Brusoni, S. (2013) Out of the Garbage Can? How Continuous Improvement Facilitators Match Solutions to Problems, in G. von Krogh, H. Takeuchi, K. Kase, and C. G. Cantón (eds.), *Towards Organizational Knowledge. The Pioneering Work of Ikujiro Nonaka*, Basingstoke: Palgrave Macmillan.

Riusala, K. and Smale, A. (2007) Predicting Stickiness Factors in the International Transfer of Knowledge through Expatriates, *International Studies of Management and Organization*, 37(3): 16–43.

Roberts, J. (2001) The Drive to Codify: Implications for the Knowledge-Based Economy, *Prometheus*, 19(2): 99–116.

Roberts, K. (1990) Some Characteristics of One Type of High Reliability Organization, *Organization Science*, 1(2): 160–76.

Robinson, D. T. and Stuart, T. E. (2007) Network Effects in the Governance of Strategic Alliances, *Journal of Law, Economics & Organization*, 23(1): 242–73.

Roettgers, J. (2014) A Failed Experiment: How LG Screwed Up its WebOS Acquisition, *Gigaom*, 8/28/14. <http://gigaom.com/2014/08/28/a-failed-experiment-how-lg-screwed-up-its-webos-acquisition/>. Accessed 21 September 2015.

Rosenkopf, L. and Nerkar, A. (2001) Beyond Local Search: Boundary-Spanning, Exploration, and Impact in the Optical Disk Industry, *Strategic Management Journal*, 22(4): 287–306.

Rothaermel, F. T. and Deeds, D. L. (2004) Exploration and Exploitation Alliances in Biotechnology: A System of New Product Development, *Strategic Management Journal*, 25(3): 201–21.

Rothaermel, F. T., Hitt, M. A., and Jobe, L. A. (2006) Balancing Vertical Integration and Strategic Outsourcing: Effects on Product Portfolio, Product Success, and Firm Performance, *Strategic Management Journal*, 27(11): 1033–56.

Rumelt, R. P. (1991) How Much Does Industry Matter? *Strategic Management Journal*, 12(3): 167–85.

Sahlin-Andersson, K. (1996) Imitating by Editing Success: The Construction of Organizational Fields, in B. Czarniawska and G. Sevón (eds.), *Translating Organizational Change*, Berlin and New York: De Gruyter.

Salmon, F. (2009) Recipe for Disaster: The Formula That Killed Wall Street, *Wired Magazine*, 17.03 23 February 2009. <http://archive.wired.com/techbiz/it/magazine/17-03/wp_quant?currentPage=all>. Accessed 9/21/15.

Salunke, S., Weerawardena, J., and McColl-Kennedy J. R., (2013) Competing Through Service Innovation: The Role of Bricolage and Entrepreneurship in Project-Oriented Firms, *Journal of Business Research*, 66(8): 1085–97.

Sanchez, R. and Mahoney, J. (1996) Modularity, Flexibility, and Knowledge Management in Product and Organization Design, *Strategic Management Journal, 17* (Winter Special Issue): 63–76.

Sanchez-Gonzalez, G., Gonzalez-Alvarez, N., and Nieto, M. (2009) Sticky Information and Heterogeneous Needs as Determining Factors of R&D Cooperation with Customers, *Research Policy*, 38(10): 1590–603.

Santos, F. M. and Eisenhardt, K. M. (2005) Organizational Boundaries and Theories of Organization, *Organization Science*, 16(5): 491–508.

Sapienza, H. J., Parhankangas, A., and Autio, E. (2004) Knowledge Relatedness and Post-Spin-Off Growth, *Journal of Business Venturing*, 19(6): 809–29.

Sasson, A. (2008) Exploring Mediators: Effects of the Composition of Organizational Affiliation on Organization Survival and Mediator Performance, *Organization Science*, 19(6): 891–906.

Schiele, H., Pulles, N., and Veldman, J. (2011) *Recognizing Innovative Suppliers: Empirical Study of the Antecedents of Innovative Suppliers within the Buyer-Suppliers Relationship*, Proceedings of the 20th Ipsera Conference, 10–13 April, Maastricht.

Schilling, M. (2000) Toward a General Modular System Theory and its Application to Interfirm Product Modularity, *Academy of Management Review*, 25(2): 312–34.

Schilling, M. A. and Steensma, H. K. (2001) The Use of Modular Organizational Forms: An Industry-Level Analysis, *Academy of Management Journal*, 44(6): 1149–68.

Schlaich, J. (2006) Engineer and Architect, *DETAIL Review of Architecture*, 1: 6–9.

Schmickl, C. and Kieser, A. (2008) How Much do Specialists have to Learn from Each Other when they Jointly Develop Radical Product Innovations?, *Research Policy*, 37 (6/7): 1148–63.

Schmiele, A. and Sofka, W. (2007) *Internationalizing R&D Co-Opetition: Dress for the Dance with the Devil*, ZEW–Centre for European Economic Research Discussion Paper No. 07-045.

Schneider, A. L. (2009) Why do some Boundary Organizations result in New Ideas and Practices and Others Only Meet Resistance?, *The American Review of Public Administration*, 39(1): 60–79.

Schot, J. and Geels, F. W. (2008) Strategic Niche Management and Sustainable Innovation Journeys: Theory, Findings, Research Agenda, and Policy, *Technology Analysis & Strategic Management*, 20(5): 537–54.

Schreyögg, G. and Kliesch-Eberl, M. (2007) How Dynamic can Organizational Capabilities Be? Towards a Dual-Process Model of Capability Dynamization, *Strategic Management Journal*, 28(9): 913–33.

Schreyögg, G., Sydow, J., and Holtmann, P. (2011) How History Matters in Organizations–The Case of Path Dependence, *Management & Organization History*, 6: 81–100.

Schumpeter, J.A. (1911/1934) *The Theory of Economic Development: An Inquiry into Profits, Capital, Credit, Interest, and the Business Cycle*, Translated from the German by Redvers Opie, New Brunswick, NJ: Transaction Publishers.

Scott, W. R. (2008) *Institutions and Organizations: Ideas, Interests, and Identities*, 2nd ed., Thousand Oaks, CA: Sage.

Selznick, P. (1949) *TVA and the Grass Roots; A Study in the Sociology of Formal Organization*, Berkeley: University of California Press.

Senyard, J., Baker, T., Steffens, P., and Davidsson, P. (2014) Bricolage as a Path to Innovativeness for Resource-Constrained New Firms, *Journal of Product Innovation Management*, 31(2): 211–30.

Serrador, P. and Pinto, J. K. (2015) Does Agile Work?—A Quantitative Analysis of Agile Project Success, *International Journal of Project Management*, 33(5): 1040–51.

Shakir, M. (2002) The Selection of Case Studies: Strategies and their Applications to IS Implementation Case Studies, *Research Letters in the Information and Mathematical Sciences*, 3:191–8.

Shipp, A. J., Edwards, J. R., and Schurer Lambert, L. (2009) Conceptualization and Measurement of Temporal Focus: The Subjective Experience of the Past, Present, and Future, *Organizational Behavior and Human Decision Processes*, 110: 1–22.

Shreve, S. (2008) Don't Blame the Quant<. Forbes, 8 October 2008 <http://www.forbes.com/2008/10/07/securities-quants-models-oped-cx_ss_1008shreve.html>. Accessed 6 January 2015.

Sieg, J. H., Wallin, M. W., and Von Krogh, G. (2010) Managerial Challenges in Open Innovation: A Study of Innovation Intermediation in the Chemical Industry, *R&D Management*, 40(3): 281–91.

Simard, C. and West, J. (2006) Knowledge Networks and the Geographic Locus of Innovation, in H. Chesbrough, W. Vanhaverbeke, and J. West (eds.), *Open Innovation: Researching a New Paradigm*, Oxford: Oxford University, Oxford.

Simon, H. (1991) Bounded Rationality and Organizational Learning, *Organization Science*, 2(1): 125–34.

Simon, H. A. (1969) *The Sciences of the Artificial*, Cambridge, MA: MIT Press.

Simona, G. L. and Axèle, G. (2012) Knowledge Transfer from TNCs and Upgrading of Domestic Firms: The Polish Automotive Sector, *World Development*, 40(4): 796–807.

Singh, J. (2008) Distributed R&D, Cross-Regional Knowledge Integration and Quality of Innovative Output, *Research Policy*, 37(1): 77–96.

Söderlund, J. (2000) Temporary Organizing: Characteristics and Control Forms, in R. A. Lundin and F. Hartman (eds.), *Projects as Business Constituents and Guiding Motives*, Boston, MA: Kluwer Academic Press.

Söderlund, J. (2002) Managing Complex Development Projects: Arenas, Knowledge Processes and Time, *R&D Management*, 32(5): 419–30.

Söderlund, J. (2005) Developing Project Competence: Empirical Regularities in Competitive Project Operations, *International Journal of Innovation Management*, 9(4): 451–80.

Söderlund, J. (2008) Competence Dynamics and Learning Processes in Project-Based Firms: Shifting, Adapting and Leveraging, *International Journal of Innovation Management*, 12(1): 41–67.

Söderlund, J. (2010) Knowledge Entrainment and Project Management: The Case of Large-Scale Transformation Projects, *International Journal of Project Management*, 28(2): 130–41.

Söderlund, J. and Bredin, K. (2011) Participants in the Process of Knowledge Integration, in C. Berggren, A. Bergek, L. Bengtsson, M. Hobday, and J. Söderlund (eds.), *Knowledge Integration and Innovation: Critical Challenges Facing International Technology-Based Firms*, Oxford: Oxford University Press.

Söderlund, J. and Tell, F. (2009) The P-Form Organization and the Dynamics of Project Competence: Project Epochs in Asea/ABB, 1950–2000, *International Journal of Project Management*, 27(2): 101–12.

Soh, P. H. and Subramanian, A. M. (2014) When Do Firms Benefit from University-Industry R&D Collaborations? The Implications of Firm R&D Focus on Scientific Research and Technological Recombination, *Journal of Business Venturing*, 29(6): 808–21.

Sokoloff, K. L. and Lamoreaux, N. R. (1999) Inventors, Firms, and the Market for Technology in the Late Nineteenth and Early Twentieth Centuries. In N. R. Lamoreaux, D. M. G. Raff, and P. Temin (eds.), *Learning by Doing in Markets, Firms, and Countries*, Chicago: University of Chicago Press.

Somaya, D. (2012) Patent Strategy and Management: An Integrative Review and Research Agenda, *Journal of Management*, 38(4): 1084–114.

Song, J., Almeida, P., and Wu. G. (2003) Learning-By-Hiring: When is Mobility More Likely to Facilitate Interfirm Knowledge Transfer?, *Management Science*, 49(4): 351–65.

Sorenson, J. and Stuart, T. (2000) Aging, Obsolescence and Organizational Innovation, *Administrative Science Quarterly*, 45(1): 81–112.

Spender, J. C. and Grant, R. M. (1996) Knowledge and the Firm: Overview, *Strategic Management Journal*, 17(S2): 5–9.

Star, S. L. (2010) This is Not a Boundary Object: Reflections on the Origin of a Concept, *Science, Technology & Human Values*, 35(5): 601–17.

Star, S. L. and Griesemer, J. R. (1989) Institutional Ecology, 'Translations' and Boundary Objects: Amateurs and Professionals in Berkeley's Museum of Vertebrate Zoology, *Social Studies of Science*, 19(3): 387–420.

Steinle, C. and Schiele, H. (2008) Limits to Global Sourcing?: Strategic Consequences of Dependency on International Suppliers: Cluster Theory, Resource-Based View and Case Studies, *Journal of Purchasing and Supply Management*, 14(1): 3–14.

Stuart, T. E., Hoang, H., and Hybels, R. C. (1999) Interorganizational Endorsements and the Performance of Entrepreneurial Ventures, *Administrative Science Quarterly*, 44(2): 315–49.

Stuart, T. E., Ozdemir, S. Z., and Ding, W.W. (2007) Vertical Alliance Networks: The Case of University–Biotechnology–Pharmaceutical Alliance Chains, *Research Policy*, 36(4): 477–98.

Subramanian, A. M., Lim, K., and Soh, P. H. (2013) When Birds of a Feather Don't Flock Together: Different Scientists and the Roles they Play in Biotech R&D Alliances, *Research Policy*, 42(3): 595–612.

Subramaniam, M. and Venkatraman, N. (2001) Determinants of Transnational New Product Development Capability: Testing the Influence of Transferring and Deploying Tacit Overseas Knowledge. *Strategic Management Journal*, 22(4), 359–78.

Sutcliffe, K. M. and Zaheer, A. (1998) Uncertainty in the Transaction Environment: An Empirical Test, *Strategic Management Journal*, 19(1): 1–23.

Sutton, J. (2007) *Quality, Trade and the Moving Windows: Competitiveness and the Globalization Process*, London School of Economics, available at <http://economics.uchicago.edu/pdf/sutton_042407.pdf>.

Swan, J. (2001) *Knowledge Management in Action: Integrating Knowledge across Communities*, System Sciences, 2001: Proceedings of the 34th Annual Hawaii International Conference on IEEE.

Swan, J., Bresnen, M., Newell, S., and Robertson, M. (2007) The Object of Knowledge: The Role of Objects in Biomedical Innovation, *Human Relations*, 60(12): 1809–37.

Swan, J. and Scarbrough, H. (2005) The Politics of Networked Innovation, *Human Relations*, 58(7): 913–43.

Swan, J., Scarbrough, H., and Newell, S. (2010) Why Don't (or Do) Organizations Learn from Projects?, *Management Learning*, 41(3): 326–44.

Sydow, J., Lindkvist, L., and DeFillippi, R. (2004) Project-Based Organizations, Embeddedness and Repositories of Knowledge, *Organization Studies*, 25(9): 1475–89.

Sydow, J., Schreyögg, G., and J. Koch (2009) Organizational Path Dependence: Opening the Black Box, *Academy of Management Review*, 34(4): 689–709.

Sydow, J., Windeler, A., Schubert, C., and Möllering, G. (2012) Organizing R&D Consortia for Path Creation and Extension: The Case of Semiconductor Manufacturing Technologies, *Organization Studies*, 33(7): 907–36.

Szulanski, G. (1996) Exploring Internal Stickiness: Impediments to the Transfer of Best Practice within the Firm, *Strategic Management Journal*, 17(S2): 27–43.

Szulanski, G. (2000) The Process of Knowledge Transfer: A Diachronic Analysis of Stickiness, *Organizational Behavior and Human Decision Processes*, 82(1): 9–27.

Szulanski, G. and Jensen, R. J. (2006) Presumptive Adaptation and the Effectiveness of Knowledge Transfer, *Strategic Management Journal*, 27: 937–57.

Takeishi, A. (2002) Knowledge Partitioning in the Interfirm Division of Labor: The Case of Automotive Product Development, *Organization Science*, 13(3): 321–38.

Tavory, I. and Timmermans, S. (2013) A Pragmatist Approach to Causality in Ethnography, *American Journal of Sociology*, 119(3): 682–714.

Tavory, I. and Timmermans, S. (2014) *Abductive Analysis: Theorizing Qualitative Research*, Chicago: University of Chicago Press.

Teece, D. J. (1982) Towards an Economic Theory of the Multiproduct Firm, *Journal of Economic Behavior and Organization*, 3: 39–63.

Teece, D. J. (2007) Explicating Dynamic Capabilities: The Nature and Microfoundations of (Sustainable) Enterprise Performance, *Strategic Management Journal*, 28 (13): 1319–50.

Teece, D. J. and Pisano, G. (1994) The Dynamic Capabilities of Firms: An Introduction, *Industrial and Corporate Change*, 3(3): 537–56.

Teece, D. J., Pisano, G., and Shuen, A. (1997) Dynamic Capabilities and Strategic Management, *Strategic Management Journal*, 18(7): 509–33.

Tell, F. (2004) What Do Organizations Know? Dynamics of Justification Contexts in R&D Activities, *Organization*, 11(4): 443–71.

Tell, F. (2011) Knowledge Integration and Innovation: A Survey of the Field, in C. Berggren, A. Bergek, L. Bengtsson, M. Hobday, and J. Söderlund (eds.), *Knowledge Integration and Innovation: Critical Challenges Facing International Technology-based Firms*, Oxford: Oxford University Press.

Tell, F. (2014) Knowledge Articulation, in D. J. Teece and M. Augier (eds.), *The Palgrave Encyclopedia of Strategic Management*, New York: Palgrave/Macmillan.

Tenenbaum, J. B., Kaelbling, L. P., Littman, M. L., and Wingate, D. (2012) *Acquiring and Exploiting Rich Causal Models for Robust Decision Making*, Massachusetts Institute of Technology Cambridge: available at <http://www.dtic.mil/dtic/tr/fulltext/u2/a566219.pdf>.

Tessarolo, P. (2007) Is Integration Enough for Fast Product Development? An Empirical Investigation of the Contextual Effects of Product Vision, *Journal of Product Innovation Management*, 24: 69–82.

Thompson, J. D. (1967) Organizations in Action: Social Science Bases of Administrative Theory, New York: McGraw-Hill.

Thomson Reuters (2014) *Technology Intelligence Data and Analysis of White Goods and Automotive* [Data and general technology analysis]. Stockholm: Patent Search Service of Thomson Reuters.

Thornton, P. H., Ocasio, W., and Lounsbury, M. (2012) *The Institutional Logics Perspective*, Oxford: Oxford University Press.

Timmermans, S. and Tavory, I. (2012) Theory Construction in Qualitative Research from Grounded Theory to Abductive Analysis, *Sociological Theory*, 30(3): 167–86.

Tiwana, A. (2008a) Do Bridging Ties Complement Strong Ties? An Empirical Examination of Alliance Ambidexterity, *Strategic Management Journal*, 29(3): 251–72.

Tiwana, A. (2008b) Does Technological Modularity Substitute for Control? A Study of Alliance Performance in Software Outsourcing, *Strategic Management Journal*, 29 (7): 769–80.

Total (2014) *Press release Formula 1*, <http://204.92.52.209/Competition/pdf/F1/Total-DP2014F1-UK-EXE.pdf>.

Trajtenberg, M. (1990) A Penny for Your Quotes: Patent Citations and the Value of Innovations, *RAND Journal of Economics*, 21(1): 172–87.

Trajtenberg, M., Henderson, R., and Jaffe, A. (1997) University versus Corporate Patents: A Window on the Basicness of Invention, *Economics of Innovation and New Technology*, 5(1): 19–50.

Trott, P. and Hartmann, D. (2009) Why 'Open Innovation' Is Old Wine in New Bottles, *International Journal of Innovation Management*, 13(4): 715–36.

Tsoukas, H. (2003) Do we Really Understand Tacit Knowledge?, in M. Easterby and M. A. Lyles (eds.), *The Blackwell Handbook of Organizational Learning and Knowledge Management*, Oxford: Blackwell.

Tsoukas, H. (2009) A Dialogical Approach to the Creation of New Knowledge in Organizations, *Organization Science*, 20(6): 941–57.

Tsoukas, H. and Vladimirou, E. (2001) What Is Organizational Knowledge?, *Journal of Management Studies*, 38(7): 973–93.

Tuertscher, P., Garud, R., and Kumaraswamy, A. (2014) Justification and Interlaced Knowledge at ATLAS, CERN, *Organization Science*, 25(6): 1579–608.

Tuncay-Celikel, A. (2009) *Factors Affecting Research and Development (R&D) Collaboration of Multinational Enterprises (MNCs) and their Local Partner Firms: A Case Study of Turkish Automotive Industry*, doctoral dissertation, Istanbul: Işık University Press.

Tushman, M. L. and Scanlan, T. J. (1981) Characteristics and External Orientations of Boundary Spanning Individuals, *Academy of Management Journal*, 24(1): 83–98.

Tversky, A. and Kahneman, D. (1974) Judgment under Uncertainty: Heuristics and Biases, *Science*, 185(4157): 1124–31.

Tzabbar, D. (2009) When Does Scientists Recruitment Affect Technological Repositioning?, *Academy of Management Journal*, 52(5): 873–96.

Ullman, D. (2010) *The Mechanical Design Process*, 4th ed., New York: Mc-Graw-Hill.

Ulrich, K. (1995) The Role of Product Architecture in the Manufacturing Firm, *Research Policy*, 24(3): 419–40.

Un, C. A., Cuervo-Cazurra, A., and Asakawa, K. (2010) R&D Collaborations and Product Innovation, *Journal of Product Innovation Management*, 27: 673–89.

UNCTAD (2013) *World Investment Report 2013, Global Value Chains: Investment and Trade for Development*, Geneva: United Nations.

Ureyen, R. (2010) An R&D Story, *Mühendislik Mimarlık Öyküleri*, 4:75–102.

Van de Ven, A. H. (2007) *Engaged Scholarship: A Guide for Organizational and Social Research*, Oxford: Oxford University Press.

Van de Ven, A. H., Delbecq, A. L., and Koenig, R. (1976) Determinants of Coordination Modes Within Organizations, *American Sociological Review*, 41: 322–38.

Van de Ven, A. H., Polley, D. E., Garud, R., and Venkataraman, S. (2008) *The Innovation Journey*, New York: Oxford University Press.

Van Huyck, J., Battalio, R., and Beil, R. (1990) Tacit Coordination Games, Strategic Uncertainty, and Coordination Failure, *American Economic Review*, 80(1): 234–48.

Vanhaverbeke, W., Van de Vrande, V., and Chesbrough, H. (2008) Understanding the Advantages of Open Innovation Practices in Corporate Venturing in Terms of Real Options, *Creativity and Innovation Management*, 17(4): 251–8.

Varian, H. (1978) *Microeconomic Analysis*, New York: W.W. Norton.

Vasudeva, G., Zaheer, A., and Hernandez, E. (2013) The Embeddedness of Networks: Institutions, Structural Holes, and Innovativeness in the Fuel Cell Industry, *Organization Science*, 24(3): 645–63.

Vergne, J-P. and Durand, R. (2011) The Path of Most Persistence: An Evolutionary Perspective on Path Dependence and Dynamic Capabilities, *Organization Studies*, 32(3): 365–82.

Verona, G. and Ravasi, D. (2003) Unbundling Dynamic Capabilities: An Exploratory Study of Continuous Product Innovation, *Industrial and Corporate Change*, 12(3): 577–606.

Viswanathan, M. and Srinivas, S. (2012) Product Development for the BoP: Insights on Concept and Prototype Development from University-Based Student Projects in India, *Journal of Product Innovation Management*, 29(1): 52–69.

Volberda, H. W., Foss, N. J., and Lyles, M. A. (2010) Perspective—Absorbing the Concept of Absorptive Capacity: How to Realize its Potential in the Organization Field, *Organization Science*, 21(4): 931–51.

von Hippel, E. (1994) 'Sticky Information' and the Locus of Problem-Solving: Implications for Innovation, *Management Science*, 40(4): 429–39.

von Krogh, G., Nonaka, I., and Rechsteiner, L. (2012) Leadership in Organizational Knowledge Creation: A Review and Framework, *Journal of Management Studies*, 49 (1): 240–77.

Wagenstetter, N., Kalogerakis, K., Kersten, K., and Herstatt, C. (2013) *A New Approach to Innovation for Logistics Service Providers based on Inventive Analogies*, paper presented at the IEEE International Technology Management Conference.

Wahlstedt, L. (2014) *Dynamic Knowledge Integration: A Field Study of an Information Systems Development Project*, Linköping University, doctoral dissertation.

Walker, G. and Weber, D. (1987) Supplier Competition, Uncertainty, and Make-or-Buy Decisions, *Academy of Management Journal*, 30(3): 589–96.

Ward, T., Smith, S. M., and Vaid, J. (1997) Conceptual Structures and Processes in Creative Thought, in T. Ward, S. M. Smith, and J. Vaid (eds.), *Creative Thought: An Investigation of Conceptual Structures and Processes*, Washington, DC: American Psychological Association.

Wegner, D. M. (1987) Transactive Memory: A Contemporary Analysis of the Group Mind, in B. Mullen and G. R. Goethals (eds.), *Theories of Group Behavior*, New York: Springer.

Wegner, D. M. (1995) A Computer Network Model of Human Transactive Memory, *Social Cognition*, 13(3): 319–39.

Weick, K. E. (1993) The Collapse of Sensemaking in Organizations: The Mann Gulch Disaster, *Administrative Science Quarterly*, 38(4): 628–52.

Weick, K. E. (2001) *Making Sense of the Organization*, Oxford: Blackwell.

Wenger, E. (1998) *Communities of Practice: Learning, Meaning and Identity*, Cambridge: Cambridge University Press.

Wenger, E. and Snyder, W. M. (2000) Communities of Practice: The Organizational Frontier, *Harvard Business Review*, Jan–Feb: 139–45.

Williamson, O. E. (1975) *Markets and Hierarchies, Analysis and Antitrust Implications: A Study in the Economics of Internal Organization*, New York: Free Press.

Williamson, O. E. (1985) *The Economic Institutions of Capitalism*, New York: Free Press.

Williamson, O. E. (1991) Comparative Economic Organization: The Analysis of Discrete Structural Alternatives, *Administrative Science Quarterly*, 36(2): 269–96.

Windahl, C., Andersson, P., Berggren, C., and Nehler, C. (2004) Manufacturing Firms and Integrated Solutions: Characteristics and Implications, *European Journal of Innovation Management*, 7(3): 218–28.

Windahl, C. and Lakemond, N. (2006) Developing Integrated Solutions: The Importance of Relationships within the Network, *Industrial Marketing Management*, 35(7): 806–18.

Winter, S. G. (1991) On Coase, Competence, and the Corporation, in O. E. Williamson and S. G. Winter (eds.), *The Nature of the Firm: Origins, Evolution, and Development*, New York: Oxford University Press.

Winter, S. G. (2010) The Replication Perspective on Productive Knowledge, in H. Itami, K. Kusunoki, T. Numagami, and A. Takeishi (eds.), *Dynamics of Knowledge, Corporate Systems and Innovation*, Berlin Heidelberg: Springer.

Winter, S. G. and Szulanski, G. (2001) Replication as Strategy, *Organization Science*, 12(6): 730–43.

Woodward, J. (1965) *Industrial Organization: Theory and Practice*, New York: Oxford University Press.

Wu, L. (2013) Social Network Effects on Productivity and Job Security; Evidence from the Adoption of a Social Networking Tool, *Information Systems Research*, 24(1): 30–51.

Wu, L.-W. and Lin, J.-R. (2013) Knowledge Sharing and Knowledge Effectiveness: Learning Orientation and Co-production in the Contingency Model of Tacit Knowledge, *Journal of Business & Industrial Marketing*, 28(8): 672–86.

Wüllenweber, K., Beimborn, D., Weitzel, T., and König, W. (2008) The Impact of Process Standardization on Business Process Outsourcing Success, *Information Systems Frontiers*, 10(2): 211–24.

Yakura, E. K. (2002) Charting Time: Timelines as Temporal Boundary Objects, *Academy of Management Journal*, 45(5): 956–70.

Yanow, D. and Schwartz-Shea, P. (2006) *Interpretation and Method: Empirical Research Methods and the Interpretive Turn*, New York: M. E. Sharpe.

Yayavaram, S. and Ahuja, G. (2008) Decomposability in Knowledge Structures and its Impact on the Usefulness of Inventions and Knowledge-Base Malleability, *Administrative Science Quarterly*, 53(2): 333–62.

Yin, R. K. (2003) *Case Study Research: Design and Methods*, Beverly Hills, CA: Sage.

Yoo, Y., Boland Jr, R. J., and Lyytinen, K. (2006) From Organization Design to Organization Designing, *Organization Science*, 17(2): 215–29.

Zahra, S., Ireland, D. R., and Hitt, M. (2000) International Expansion by New Venture Firms: International Diversity, Mode of Market Entry, Technological Learning and Performance, *Academy of Management Journal*, 43(5): 925–50.

Zahra, S., Van de Velde, E., and Larrañeta, B. (2007) Knowledge Conversion Capability and the Performance of Corporate and University Spin-Offs, *Industrial and Corporate Change*, 16(4): 569–608.

Zahra, S. A. and George, G. (2002) Absorptive Capacity: A Review, Reconceptualization, and Extension, *Academy of Management Review*, 27(2): 185–203.

Zeiss, R. and Groenewegen, P. (2009) Engaging Boundary Objects in OMS and STS? Exploring the Subtleties of Layered Engagement, *Organization*, 16(1): 81–100.

Zhao, Y. L. and Parry, M. E. (2012) Mental Models and Successful First-mover Entry Decisions: Empirical Evidence from Chinese Entrepreneurs, *Journal of Product Innovation Management*, 29(4): 590–607.

Zika-Viktorsson, A. and Ritzén, S. (2005) Project Competence in Product Development, *Research in Engineering Design*, 15(4): 193–200.

Zirpoli, F. and Camuffo, A. (2009) Product Architecture, Inter-Firm Vertical Coordination and Knowledge Partitioning in the Auto Industry, *European Management Review*, 6: 250–64.

Zollo, M. and Sing, H. (2004) Deliberate Learning in Corporate Acquisitions: Post-Acquisition Strategies and Integration Capability in U.S. Bank Mergers, *Strategic Management Journal*, 25(13): 1233–56.

Zollo, M. and Winter, S. G. (2002) Deliberate Learning and the Evolution of Dynamic Capabilities, *Organization Science*, 13(3): 339–51.

Zucker, L. G., Darby, M. R., and Armstrong, J. S. (2002) Commercializing Knowledge: University Science, Knowledge Capture, and Firm Performance in Biotechnology, *Management Science*, 48(1): 138–53.

Zucker, L. G., Darby, M. R., and Brewer, M. (1998) Internal Human Capital and the Birth of U.S. Biotechnology Enterprises, *American Economic Review*, 88(1): 290–306.

Zuckerman, E. W. (1999) The Categorical Imperative, *American Journal of Sociology*, 104: 1398–498.

Index

abductive analysis 176–7
absorptive capacity 7, 57–9, 70–1, 252
  boundary-bridging assimilation 33–4
  boundary implications 58–62
  boundary spanning and innovation 241,
    248–9, 251, 253
  emerging economy firms 143, 151
  knowledge transformation 251
  knowledge translation 248–9
  open innovation 94, 100–1
  path-dependence and dynamic
    capabilities 63–6
  prior knowledge, role of 59–61
  reflective agency in path-dependent
    processes 66–70
  sticky information 141
academia
  novelty, pursuit of 155, 156
  as social system 155
  see also universities
accumulation, boundary-bridging 35–6, 37
acquisition, boundary-bridging 32–3, 37
actor network theory 174–5
agency theory 70
agile projects 206, 219–26
  boundary dilemmas 215–19
  individual project competence and new
    logics of project organizing 207–8
  literature review 208–14
  research methodology 214–15
Almeida, P. 192
ambiguous knowledge 3–4, 247–8
analogies, boundary-bridging search 31–2, 37
Anand, V. 232
Ancori, B. 30
Anderson, E. G. 229
Andersson, H. 195–6
Arçelik 144–9, 151–2, 153–4
architectural drawings, as boundary
    objects 172, 176–7, 188–9
  communication through 177–81, 182,
    185–6, 187, 190
  knowledge integration 185–8
  power relations 175, 181–5, 186–8, 189
architectural innovation 37
Argote, L. 238
Arthur, B. 63
articulability of knowledge 28–30
articulated knowledge 29–30, 37

assimilation, boundary-bridging 33–5, 37
Austin, J. R. 232
automotive industry in emerging
    economies 144, 153
  Fiat Tofaş case study 149–51, 152–3

Bain and Company 147
Banc One 34–5
Barrett, M. 174
Bartley, W. W. 77, 78, 83
base-of-the-pyramid innovations 145
Bechky, B. A. 74, 78–9, 156
Beckman, C. M. 126
Belderbos, R. 99
Berggren, C. 59, 100, 195–6
biotechnology industry 191–205
Birnoltz, J. P. 35
bisociation 36–7
black box principle 49–52, 56
Blomkvist, K. 26
BMW Sauber 129
Bogers, M. 87–8, 90
Boland Jr, R. J. 174
Borg, E. 210
Boschma, R. 22, 26
Bosch-Siemens 147
Bøtker Mortensen, T. 95
boundaries
  collaboration across social
    boundaries 155–70
  emergency through knowledge
    specialization 1, 19
  importance 140
  innovation 141
  in open innovation 90–3
  organizations as boundary maintaining
    systems 140
  temporal 228
  types 39
  see also disciplinary boundaries;
    geographical boundaries; glitches;
    knowledge boundaries; organizational
    boundaries; pragmatic boundaries;
    semantic boundaries; syntactic
    boundaries; team boundaries,
    knowledge retrieval across
boundary-bridging 30
  accumulation 35–6, 37
  acquisition 32–3, 37

boundary-bridging (*cont.*)
  assimilation 33–5, 37
  search 30–2, 37
  transformation 36–7
boundary configuration, new 67, 68
boundary crossing 67–8
  open innovation 94–6, 97–9, 100, 102
  performance effects 94–6, 97–9, 100, 102
boundary dilemmas 208, 214, 215–24
boundary objects
  boundary spanning and
    innovation 241–54
  communication 177–81
  and knowledge integration 172–3, 185–8
  sociopolitical dynamics of 171–2, 173–6,
    188–90
  power relations 181–5
  research methodology 176–7
boundary organizations
  collaboration across diverse
    communities 155–7
    research context, data, and
      methods 157–60
    research findings 160–70
  see also organizational boundaries
boundary reproduction 67
boundary-spanning individuals 9
  agile projects 206–26
  bridging scientists and informal R&D
    collaborations 191–205
  innovation 241–54
Bredin, K. 209–10, 212
bricolage 145
  boundary-bridging transformation 36, 37
bridging scientists and informal R&D
  collaborations 191–3, 204–5
  data and methods 200–1
  prior research and hypotheses 193–200
  results 202–4
Brusoni, S.
  knowledge-based theories of the firm 123
  knowledge boundaries 24, 28, 108
  lean management 80
  open innovation 90, 92
  technological specialization and
    interorganizational knowledge
    integration 193
  uncertainty 124, 137

Camuffo, A. 24
Carlile, P. R.
  communication barriers 246, 250
  innovation 141, 243
  knowledge boundaries 151
  knowledge transfer 247
  knowledge transformation 251

Carnabuci, G. 124
Carnegie School of organizational analysis 24, 30
catch-up approaches, emerging economy
  firms 142–4, 154
CEOs *see* chief executive officers
Chen, W. 143
Chesbrough, H. 87–8, 90
chief executive officers (CEOs)
  'managerial recipe' 66
  Structural Genomics Consortium 158, 163,
    165, 166
  temporal knowledge boundaries 28
China, innovation in 144, 149
Clark, K. B. 37
classical economic analysis 2
Coase, R. 107
codification
  of constraints 45
  of knowledge 30
Cohen, W. M. 33, 59–60, 61, 64
collaboration
  boundary objects 182, 187, 189
  across diverse communities 155–7
    research context, data, and
      methods 157–60
    research findings 160–70
collective design process management
  39–40, 56
  formal model of inter-specialist problem-
    solving 47–9, 56
    black box principle 49–52
    powerboat–sailboat rule 53–4
    sequential ordering of tasks 55
    sticky information principle 52–3
  glitches and disciplinary boundaries 40–4
  knowledge integration 44–5
  knowledge specialization 46–7
collective knowledge 6–7, 38
  boundary objects, sociopolitical dynamics
    of 171–90
  collaboration across diverse
    communities 155–70
  knowledge creation 72–84
Collins, H.
  communication 249
  interactional vs contributory expertise 211,
    222, 223
  specialist expertise 46n5, 50
combination
  boundary-bridging transformation 37
  knowledge creation (SECI) model 75, 80,
    81, 83
communicative practices embodied within
  boundary objects 171–2, 173–5, 189
  architectural drawings 177–81, 182, 185–6,
    187, 190

communities of practice
  boundary-bridging assimilation 34
  boundary objects 173
  path-dependent processes 69–70
  tacit knowledge 75
complexity theory 31
concept formation 34, 37
concurrent sourcing 115–16, 118–21
confidentiality, Structural Genomics
    Consortium 163, 164
conflict, boundary objects 182
constraints, codification of 45
contributory expertise 5–6
  agile projects 211, 222–4, 225–6
conversion-based bridging 74–6, 83
Coombs, R. 63–4
cooperation failures 42, 44n4
co-opetition 92–3
coordination failures 44n4
  and glitches, distinction between 42–3, 247
co-patenting 91–2, 99
copyright *see* intellectual property rights
core capabilities/competencies
  outsourcing 112, 116–17, 118–22
  uncertainty 137
corporate social responsibility 167
Cox, J. 54n8
creation of knowledge 72–4, 82–4
  conversion-based bridging 74–6
  interaction-based bridging 77–80
  remodelling 80–2
Cross, R. 74
Cyert, R. 3, 25, 62, 136

Dahlander, L. 95
Damasio, A. 29
decision-making processes
  agile projects 221
  architects 186–7
  Structural Genomics Consortium 159,
    161–2, 167–8
  transactive memory systems 235
departmentalization 3–4
depersonalization, boundary objects 182–5
design drawings *see* architectural drawings, as
    boundary objects
dialogue, boundary-bridging
    accumulation 35, 37
Dibaggio, L. 24, 193
differentiation of knowledge
  domain-specific knowledge boundaries 24
  increasing 2
  see also knowledge specialization
directories, organizational *see* transactive
    memory systems
disciplinary boundaries

collective design process
  management 40–4, 46–9, 51
  innovation 141
disciplinary knowledge
  agile projects 208, 213, 216–17, 218, 221–4,
    225–6
  individual project competence 207–8,
    210–11, 213, 221–4, 225–6
distribution of knowledge 2–3
  absorptive capacity 58–9
diverse communities, collaboration
    across 155–7
  research context, data, and
    methods 157–60
  research findings 160–70
domain-specific knowledge boundaries 23–4
Dougherty, D. 24
Drori, I. 193
Drury-Grogan, M. L. 212
Dunbar, K. 72–3
Durand, R. 65
Dyer, J. H. 252
dynamic capabilities
  absorptive capacity 63–7, 71
  boundary-bridging transformation 36
  path-dependence 64–7

Edelman, G. 29
Edison bridging scientists 192, 200, 201
education, and knowledge sharing 45
Edwards, A. 165
Einstein, A. 77–8
Eisenhardt, K. 32
Electrolux 145, 146, 149
elicitation, knowledge creation model
    81–2, 83
emergency medicine, boundary objects in 175
emerging economies 141–2, 144–5, 153–4
  Arçelik case study 145–9, 151–2
  catch-up approaches 142–4, 154
  Fiat Tofaş case study 149–51, 152–3
  innovation 139
Enberg, C. 24, 212
enrolment, boundary-bridging
    acquisition 32–3, 37
enterprise resource planning systems 107
epistemic communities 19, 20–2
epistemic uncertainty 43–4
Ericsson 79–80, 82
Eriksson, K. 63
European Union (EU)
  coolant substitutes 148
  Turkey's customs union 142, 145–7,
    149–50
Evans, R. 46n5, 50, 249
evolutionary economics 30–1

Ewenstein, B. 82, 83
exact replication, boundary-bridging
    assimilation 34–5, 37
excess knowledge 137
executive level agency 68–9
explicit knowledge 29
    SECI model 75–6, 81
externalization (SECI model) 75–6, 80, 81, 83

Faraj, S. 35
Fédération Internationale de l'Automobile
    (FIA) 128, 132
Ferrari 130
Fiat Tofaş 144–5, 146, 149–51, 152–3
financial crisis, global 41
Fixson, S. K. 122
flexibility competence 220, 221, 225
Foray, D. 30
Ford 149
Formula One racing constructors 125, 128–37
Franke, N. 31
Frenken, K. 26
frequency of transactions, and
    outsourcing 111–12, 116–17, 118–22

Galbraith, J. R. 35, 247–8
game theory 42, 43–4
Gann, D. M. 95
geographical boundaries
    international business literature 141, 153
    open innovation 88–9, 91, 93, 95–6
        empirical analysis 96–8, 99, 100, 102, 103
    transactive memory systems 228
George, G. 61, 101
Germany, patent transfer rates 33
Gerring, J. 34
Gibbons, M. 249
Giddens, A. 64, 67, 249
Gittelman, M. 192, 193, 201
GlaxoSmithKline (GSK) 157–8
glitches
    boundary objects 247
    collective design process
        management 40–4, 48, 49, 51, 56
global financial crisis 41
globalization
    emerging economies 143
    research and development 243
    spatial knowledge boundaries 26
global purchasing 100
global value chains
    open innovation 93
    spatial knowledge boundaries 26–7
Goldratt, E. 54n8
Gourlay, S. 73
Grand, S. 28

Grandori, A. 59
Granstrand, O. 99
Grant, R. M.
    boundary-bridging acquisition 32
    experts 224
    individual knowledge boundaries 22–3
    individual nature of knowledge creation 72
    knowledge integration 57, 59, 211
    methodological individualism 38
    rules 35
Griesbach, D. 28
Griesemer, J. R. 172
GSK (GlaxoSmithKline) 157–8
Gueldenberg, S. 73
Guttman, L. 246

Haas, P. M. 21
Hagedoorn, J. 94
Haier 149
Håkanson, L. 21
Hamel, G. 112
Hargadon, A. B. 74, 78–9, 195
Hayek, F. A. 3, 78, 83
Hedlund, G. 30
Hellgren, B. 66
Helting, H. 73
Henderson, K. 82
Henderson, R. 37
Hernes, T. 140
hierarchy, transactive memory systems 235,
    237, 239, 240
Hobday, M. 143
Holzner, B. 20–1
Honda 129
Hoopes, D. G. 24
Horng, C. 143
Hsiao, R. L. 174
Hsu, D. H. 195
Hull, R. 63–4
Human Genome Project 158
Huvila, I. 175
hypotheses, boundary-bridging search 32, 37
Hyundai 149, 151

Iansiti, M. 24, 211, 222
implicit knowledge 29
importance of managing knowledge
    integration across boundaries 1–4
incomplete knowledge 3–4
India, software industry 243
individual knowledge 38
individual knowledge boundaries 22–3
individual project competence 207–14, 224–6
    agile projects 213–15, 219–24, 225–6
individual-to-organization divide, bridging
    the 72–4, 82–4

conversion-based bridging 74–6
interaction-based bridging 77–80
remodelling knowledge creation 80–2
information technology
   outsourcing 107, 108–11, 120–2
      data analysis 115–20
      data collection 113–15
      empirical context 112–13
   Singapore 243
innovation 7–8
   absorptive capacity 59
   architectural 37
   base-of-the-pyramid 145
   boundaries 141
   boundary-bridging assimilation 33
   boundary-bridging transformation 36, 37
   boundary objects 173
   boundary spanning 241–54
   bridging scientists and informal R&D
      collaborations 191–205
   dynamic capabilities 64–5
   emerging economy firms 142, 144–5, 153, 154
      Arçelik 145–9, 151–2, 153–4
      Fiat Tofaş 149–51, 152–3
   knowledge boundaries and
      stickiness 140–2
   modular 37
   M-shaped skills 224
   Structural Genomics Consortium 157–8,
      161–7
   uncertainty and organizational
      boundaries 137
   see also open innovation
intellectual property rights (IPR) 254
   boundary-bridging acquisition 33, 37
   bridging scientists and informal R&D
      collaborations 196
   emerging economy firms
      Arçelik case study 148–9
      Fiat Tofaş case study 149, 151
   future research 254
   open innovation 91
   Structural Genomics Consortium 158,
      165, 166
   see also patents
interactional expertise 5–6, 211, 222–4, 225–6
   agile projects 206–26
   boundary spanning and innovation 248,
      249–50, 253
   formal model of inter-specialist problem-
      solving 47–56
   outsourcing 109, 111, 122
   transactive memory systems 227–40
interaction-based bridging 74, 77–80, 83
intermediation, impartial (Structural
   Genomics Consortium) 162–4, 168

internalization (SECI model) 75, 80, 81, 83
interpersonal competence 209, 221, 225
interpretive scheme 170
   Structural Genomics Consortium 164,
      167, 169
IPR *see* intellectual property rights
Istanbul Technical University (ITU) 145, 146

Jakubik, M. 73
Japan
   innovation 144
   patent transfer rates 33
Jensen, R. J. 140
joint ventures
   emerging economy firms 139, 143–4, 153
      Fiat Tofaş 144, 149–51, 152–3
   growing use of 252
   innovation 243
Joskow, P. 107

Kliesch-Eberl, M. 65
Knoben, J. 91
knowledge
   ambiguity 3–4, 247–8
   articulated 29–30, 37
   breadth vs depth 216–17, 223–4
   codified 30
   collectivity 212, 213, 221
   combination 21
   complementarity 194
   complexity 243–4, 246–7, 251, 253
   distribution 2–3, 58–9
   excess 137
   exchange 249
   implicit 29
   incompleteness 3–4
   individual 38
   matching 89, 93–4
      empirical analysis 96–100, 102,
         104, 105
   objective 77–9, 80, 81–2, 83
   overlap 194
   prior 59–61
   redundancy, transactive memory
      systems 235, 236, 239
   sharing 32, 45
   stickiness *see* sticky information
   subjective 77, 79
   transformation 246–7, 250–1
   translation 246–7, 248–50
   uncertainty 3–4
   unfathomable 74, 77–8, 80, 82
   see also collective knowledge; creation of
      knowledge; differentiation of
      knowledge; disciplinary knowledge;
      explicit knowledge; knowledge-based

theories of the firm; knowledge
boundaries; knowledge specialization;
supportive knowledge; tacit
knowledge; transfer of knowledge
knowledge-based theories of the firm
  central problem 123
  individual knowledge boundaries 22–3
  key concepts 57, 62
  knowledge integration 58, 108
knowledge boundaries 108–9
  absorptive capacity 58–62
  black box principle 51
  bridging, in learning activities 30–7
  bridging scientists and informal R&D
    collaborations 194–5
  challenge for knowledge integration 19–20
  collective design process
    management 40–5, 51
  dependence 243–4, 246
  difference 243, 246
  domain-specific 23–4
  emerging economy firms 139–54
  and epistemic communities 20–2
  individual 22–3
  in innovation and international business
    literature 140–2
  managing integration across 28–38
  open innovation 87, 88–9, 90–1, 92–5,
    95–6
    empirical analysis 96–100, 102,
      103, 104
  procedural 25
  reflective agency in path-dependent
    processes 67
  spatial 25–7
  structuration theory 67
  task-oriented 24–5
  temporal 27–8
  typology 22–8
  understanding 244, 246
knowledge specialization
  absorptive capacity 58–9, 62
  bridging scientists and informal R&D
    collaborations 194, 205
  collective design process management 40,
    42, 44, 46–7, 51
  efficiency and learning properties 20
  and emergence of boundaries 1, 19
  epistemic communities 20, 22
  increasing 2
  managing integration across knowledge
    boundaries 28
  social aspect of 20
  spatial knowledge boundaries 26
Koç Holding 144–5, 146, 147, 149, 153
Koestler, A. 36

Kogut, B. 36, 192, 198, 201
Korea
  Hyundai 151
  innovation 144

Lainer-Vos, D. 173, 189
Lane, P. J. 60, 94
Laursen, K. 90, 91, 95, 99
Lavie, D. 193
Lawrence, P. R. 1–2, 108
Lazzarotti, V. 90
lean management 80
Lee, K. 143
Leonard, D. 224
Leonard-Barton, D. 223–4
Levina, N. 174
Levinthal, D. A. 33, 59–60, 61, 64
Lewis, K. 229
LG 42
licensing agreements 195
  emerging economies 139, 143
    Arçelik 144, 147, 151–2
Liebeskind, J. P. 192
Lim, C. 143
Lim, K. 195
liminality competence 210, 220, 225
Lindkvist, L. 32, 79, 213, 221
linguistic socialization 211, 223
liquidity crisis 41
long-term vs short-term perspectives, agile
    projects 217–19, 220
Lopez-Vega, H. 32
Lorsch, J. W. 1–2, 108
Lubatkin, M. 60, 94

McKinsey 147
McLaren 131n1
Mahmood, I. P. 143
Majchrzak, A. 24, 35, 37
managerial competence 221, 225
March, J. G.
  absorptive capacity 62
  boundary-bridging search 31
  knowledge distribution 3
  rules 36
  task-oriented knowledge boundaries 24, 25
  uncertainty 136
Mars Climate Observer 40
matching knowledge 89, 93–4
  empirical analysis 96–8, 100–1, 102,
    104, 105
Mathews, J. A. 142, 143
Matsushita 75
Melero, E. 210
Melin, L. 66
Mell, J. N. 239

memory
  external 227–8
  internal 227
  see also transactive memory systems
Mercedes 130
Merck 158
metaphors, and knowledge creation 76, 81
Meyer, J. 25
Meyer, M. 195
Miele 148
Mitchell, V. L. 109, 121
MNEs/MNCs *see* multinational enterprises/
    corporations
modular innovation 37
modularity of products 110–11, 116–17,
    118–22
Montreal Protocol 148, 149, 152
Moreland, R. L. 238
M-shaped skills 223–4, 225–6
Muduli, A. 213, 221
multinational enterprises/corporations
    (MNEs/MNCs)
  and emerging economy firms 139, 143, 153
    Arçelik case study 147
    Fiat Tofaş case study 149–51, 152–3
    knowledge integration 140
    spatial knowledge boundaries 26

Nelson, R. R. 25
neo-institutional theory 70
Nerkar, A. 90
Nerur, S. 213, 222
Nesta, L. 24
new boundary configuration 67, 68
Nisbet, R. A. 76
Nonaka, I.
  articulated knowledge 30
  concept formation 34
  knowledge creation 73
  pragmatic boundaries 250
  SECI model 73, 74, 75–6, 80–1,
    82–3, 244
  semantic boundaries 248
  socialization 34
non-executive level agency 69
Nooteboom, B. 63
Novartis 158

objectification, knowledge creation
    model 81–2, 83
objective knowledge 77–9, 80, 81–2, 83
objects
  boundary *see* boundary objects
  boundary-bridging acquisition 33, 37
Oborn, E. 174
Oerlemans, L. A. G. 91

offshoring
  boundary objects 174
  open innovation 88, 96
  research and development 88
Okhuysen, G. 32
O'Mahony, S. 156
open innovation 87–90, 101–2, 243
  boundaries in 90–3
  empirical analysis 96–101, 103–5
  growing use of 252
  managing knowledge integration across
    boundaries 93–4
  performance effects of boundary crossing
    and knowledge integration 94–6
open science
  bridging scientists and informal R&D
    collaborations 195, 198, 199, 200
  Structural Genomics Consortium 158, 166,
    167, 169
Operti, E. 124
ordering of tasks, sequential 55
organizational boundaries 107–8
  agile projects 220
  bridging scientists and informal R&D
    collaborations 195
  international business literature 141, 153
  open innovation 87–9, 90–1, 93, 95–6
    empirical analysis 96–100, 101,
    102, 103
  outsourcing 116, 122
  project teams 220
  and uncertainty 123–38
  see also boundary organizations
organizational design 8–9
  emerging economy firms
    Arçelik case study 147–8, 151–2
    Fiat Tofaş case study 150–1, 152–3
  formal model of inter-specialist problem-
    solving 47–56
  importance 253
  mechanisms of knowledge
    integration 28–37
  open innovation 89, 93–4, 100–1
  outsourcing 106–7, 109, 112–13, 115–16,
    120–2
  uncertainty and organizational
    boundaries 123–4, 136–7
    Formula One racing constructors 126–7,
    130, 132–5, 138
organizational directories *see* transactive
    memory systems
organizational field 70
organizational resilience 240
organizational restructuring 228–40
organizational transactive memory systems
    see transactive memory systems

organization theory
  boundary objects, sociopolitical dynamics
    of 171, 173
  organizations as boundary maintaining
    systems 140
  practice turn 173
  uncertainty 125
original equipment manufacturing (OEM)
    contracts 143
  Arçelik 147
Østerlund, C. 172, 175, 179, 188
outsourcing 106–7, 121–2
  concurrent sourcing 115–16, 118–21
  core capabilities 110, 112, 116–17, 118–22
  'faraway' strategy 109, 111, 120
  frequency of transactions 110, 111–12,
    116–17, 118–22
  hypotheses development 109–12
  information technology 107, 108–11,
    120–2
    data analysis 115–20
    data collection 113–15
    empirical context 112–13
  modularity of products 110–11, 116–17,
    118–22
  open innovation 89, 95
  'so close' strategy 109, 112, 120–1
  standardization of processes 110, 111,
    116–17, 118–22
  supplier relationships 115, 116, 117–21
  uncertainty and organizational
    boundaries 124
    Formula One racing constructors 129
Özaltin Group 146

Palomeras, N. 210
Park, J. K. 122
Parmigiani, A. 115
Pasteur bridging scientists 192–3, 199–200,
    201, 202–5
patching, transactive memory systems
    235, 239
patents
  boundary-bridging acquisition 33
  bridging scientists and informal R&D
    collaborations 192–3, 194, 196,
    198–204
  co-patenting 91–2, 99
  open innovation 91–2, 99
  pharmaceutical industry 165, 166
  spatial knowledge boundaries 26
  Turkish firms 145
    Arçelik case study 148–9
    Fiat Tofaş case study 150–1
  see also intellectual property rights
path creation 67, 68

path-dependence
  absorptive capacity 61, 62, 63–6, 71
  change constraints, accumulation of 63–4
  dynamic capabilities 64–6
  reflective agency 66–70
path extension 67–8
Peltokorpi, V. 232, 239
Perkmann, M. 251
Perrow, C. 24
pharmaceutical industry
  knowledge complexity 244
  Structural Genomics Consortium 157–70
planning competence 209, 220, 221, 225
Podolny, J. M. 126
Polanyi, M.
  articulated knowledge 29–30
  knowledge creation 77, 81
  tacit knowledge 29, 73, 74, 76
Popper, K. R. 27, 74, 77–8, 80
Postrel, S. 24, 46, 47, 49, 51
powerboat–sailboat rule 53–4, 55, 56
power relations, and boundary objects 175,
    181–5, 186–8, 189
Praest Knudsen, M. 95
pragmatic boundaries
  boundary objects for communicating
    across 246, 250
  innovation 141, 151
    Arçelik case study 152
    Fiat Tofaş case study 152–3
Prahalad, C. K. 112
Prencipe, A. 28
prior knowledge 59–61
problem-solving
  boundary objects 174
  collective design process
    management 39–40, 47–9
  formal model 47–9, 56
    black box principle 49–52
    powerboat–sailboat rule 53–4
    sequential ordering of tasks 55
    stick information principle 52–3
  organizational restructuring 228–9, 238
procedural knowledge boundaries 25
process standardization 110, 111, 116–17, 118–22
product complexity 254
product modularity 110–11, 116–17, 118–22
project management 89, 93–4
  empirical analysis 96–8, 100–1, 102, 104, 105
prototypes 79–80
public–private partnerships 157
Puranam, P. 43–4
purchasing, global 99

R&D *see* research and development
Rafols, I. 195

Rank Xerox 35
Red Bull 130
Reebok 78–9, 82
reflective agency in path-dependent
    processes 66–70, 71
relational (interpersonal) competence 209,
    221, 225
Renault 130, 149
replication, exact, boundary-bridging
    assimilation 34–5, 37
research and development (R&D)
    absorptive capacity 60
    agile projects 217
    boundary-bridging assimilation 33–4
    bridging scientiss and informal R&D
        collaborations 191–205
    dynamic capabilities and path-
        dependence 65, 66
    emerging economy firms
        Arçelik 145, 147–8, 152, 154
        Fiat Tofaş 150
        Koç Holding 145
    globalization 243
    individual project competence 209
    offshoring 88
    social boundaries 155
    spatial knowledge boundaries 26–7
    Structural Genomics Consortium 157–8,
        161–7
    temporary organizations 206
    transnational firms 143
research institutes 92
resilience, organizational 240
resource-based theories
    competitive advantage 143
    outsourcing 106, 110
resource-dependence theory 70
Rittiner, F. 80
Ritzén, S. 208–9
Riusala, K. 140
Roettgers, J. 42n2
Rosenkopf, L. 90
routines
    boundary-bridging accumulation 35, 37
    dynamic capabilities and path-
        dependence 65
Rowan, B. 25
rules 35–6, 37

Salmon, F. 41n1
Salter, A. 90, 91, 95, 99
Saviotti, P.-P. 24
Schiele, H. 99
Schmiele, A. 99
Schreyögg, G. 65
Schumpeter, J. A. 3, 36, 92, 99

search processes 30–2, 37
    knowledge distribution 3
Searle, J. 29
SECI (Socialization, Externalization,
    Combination, Internalization)
    model 73–4, 75–6, 80–3, 244
semantic boundaries
    boundary objects for communicating
        across 246, 248
    innovation 141, 151
        Arçelik case study 152
        Fiat Tofaş case study 152
Sensiper, S. 224
sequential ordering of tasks 55
Shakir, M. 144
sharing knowledge
    boundary-bridging acquisition 32
    collective design process management 45
short-term vs long-term perspectives, agile
    projects 217–19, 220
Sieg, J. H. 35
Simon, H. A. 24, 25, 72
simultaneity 42
Singapore, information technology
    industry 243
Singh, H. 252
size of firms
    bridging scientists and informal R&D
        collaborations 205
    open innovation 101
    outsourcing 117, 118–19
skills, and boundary-bridging
    accumulation 35, 37
Smale, A. 140
Smith, A. 2
social aspect of knowledge specialization 20
social boundaries, collaboration
    across 155–70
socialization
    boundary-bridging assimilation 34, 37
    knowledge creation (SECI model) 75, 76,
        80, 81
    linguistic 211, 223
    swift socialization competence 220
social networks, transactive memory
    systems 235, 236, 239
social network theory 70
sociopolitical dynamics of boundary
    objects 171–2, 173–6, 188–90
    communication 177–81
    power relations 181–5
    research methodology 176–7
sociopolitical legacy, Structural Genomics
    Consortium 166–7
Söderlund, J. 28, 208, 209–10
Sofka, W. 99

software industry 243
South Korea
    Hyundai 151
    innovation 144
spatial knowledge boundaries 25–7
specialist capability, collective design process
    management 47–8, 49–51, 53–6
specialized knowledge *see* knowledge
    specialization
Sproull, L. 74
stakeholder theory 70
standardization of processes 110, 111,
    116–17, 118–22
Stanford University 36
Star, S. L. 172, 173
Steinle, C. 99
Steinmueller, W. E. 30
sticky information
    collective design process management 43,
        48, 52–3, 55, 56
    emerging economy firms 144, 153
        Fiat Tofaş case study 149–51
    in innovation and international business
        literature 140–2
strategic management theory 57, 66
Structural Genomics Consortium
    (SGC) 157–70, 250, 251
structuration theory 67, 249
subjective knowledge 77, 79
Subramanian, A. M. 200, 201
successful organizations, uncertainty and
    organizational boundaries 124,
    127–8, 137
    Formula One racing constructors 131,
        133–5
supplier relationships 115, 116, 117–21
supportive knowledge
    agile projects 208, 209, 213, 219–21, 225
    individual project competence 207–8,
        209–10, 213, 219–21, 224–5
sustainability transition 70
Sutcliffe, K. M. 126
Sutton, R. I. 195
swift socialization competence 220
syntactic boundaries
    boundary objects for communicating
        across 246, 247
    innovation 141, 151
        Arçelik case study 151–2
        Fiat Tofaş case study 152
Szulanski, G. 140, 141

tacit knowledge 28–9
    boundary-bridging mechanisms 37
    complexity 244
    innovation 242–3

knowledge creation 73, 74–5
    SECI model 75–6, 81
    socialization 34
Takeishi, A. 24
Takeuchi, H. 34, 73, 75–6, 248, 250
task-oriented knowledge boundaries 24–5
tasks, sequential ordering of 55
task specialization 46
team boundaries, knowledge retrieval
        across 227–30
    from efficient to reliable transactive
        memory systems 237–40
    organizational restructuring 231–7
    research approach 230–1
technological complementarity 94
Teece, D. J. 64, 65
Tell, F.
    boundary-bridging acquisition 32
    individual project competence 208
    knowledge integration 45, 59, 194
temporal boundaries 228
    knowledge boundaries 27–8
Tenkasi, R. V. 174
Thompson, J. D. 25, 126
Thomson Reuters 145
Tiwana, A. 110
Tofaş 144–5, 146, 149–51, 152–3
Toyota 34, 129, 149
trademarks *see* intellectual property rights
transaction cost economics 107–8
    outsourcing 106, 110, 111, 120
transactions, frequency of, and
        outsourcing 111–12, 116–17,
        118–22
transactive memory systems 227–30
    from efficiency to reliability 237–40
    incomplete/unreliable 234–7
    organizational restructuring 231–7
    processes 233–4
    research approach 230–1
    structure 232
transfer of knowledge 246–8
    boundary-bridging acquisition 32
    boundary-bridging assimilation 34
    by multinational corporations 140
    sticky information 141
transformation, boundary-bridging 36–7
trans-specialist understanding 47, 48,
    49–56
T-shaped skills 210, 222–3, 224, 225–6
Tsoukas, H. 74, 76
Tubitak 145, 146
Tuncay-Celikel, A. 150
Turkey 142, 144
    Arçelik 145–9, 151–2, 153–4
    Fiat Tofaş 149–51, 152–3

uncertainty
  epistemic 43–4
  field-level 124, 125, 126–7, 136–7
    Formula One racing constructors 129, 130–1, 133–5
  firm-specific 124, 125, 126–7, 136
    Formula One racing constructors 129, 130, 131, 133–5
  Formula One racing constructors 125, 128–35
  knowledge 3–4
  and organizational boundaries 123–38
UNCTAD 26
unfathomable knowledge 74, 77–8, 80, 82
United Kingdom, patent transfer rates 33
United Nations 148
United States of America
  coolant substitutes 148
  patent transfer rates 33
  Patient Protection and Affordable Care Act 41
universities
  bridging scientists and informal R&D collaborations 191–2, 193, 195, 198–9, 204
    research data and methods 201
    research results 202–4
  and emerging economy firms 148, 152, 154
  open innovation 92
  Structural Genomics Consortium 158, 161–7, 169
  see also academia

Vaast, E. 174
value chains, global

open innovation 93
spatial knowledge boundaries 26–7
van Krogh, G. 75
Vasudeva, G. 252–3
Vergne, J.-P. 65
Vestel 145
von Hippel, E. 53, 141

Wagenstetter, N. 32
Walker, G. 125
Ward, T. 73
Weber, D. 125
WebOS 42
Wellcome Trust 158
Whirlpool 148
white goods industry, Turkey 144, 145–9, 151–2, 153–4
Whyte, J. 82, 83
Williams 131n1
Winter, S. G. 25
World Bank 148

Xiao, Y. 35

Yakura, E. K. 32

Zaheer, A. 126
Zahra, S. A. 61, 101
Zander, U. 36
Zheng, W. 143
Zika-Viktorsson, A. 208–9
Zirpoli, F. 24
Zucker, L. G. 198
Zuckerman, E. W. 124